MW01141368

The Sporting News

FOOTBALL

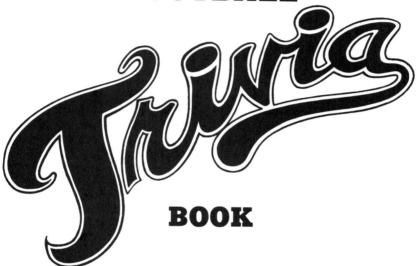

BOOK

Editor/Writer/Researcher
JOE HOPPEL

President-Chief Executive Officer
RICHARD WATERS

Editor
DICK KAEGEL

Director of Books and Periodicals
RON SMITH

Published in the United States by THE SPORTING NEWS Publishing Co., 1212 North Lindbergh Boulevard, St. Louis, Missouri 63132.

ISBN: 0-89204-201-X
10 9 8 7 6 5 4 3 2 1

First Edition

TABLE OF CONTENTS

Chapter illustrations by Staff Artist Bill Wilson.

INTRODUCTION

Trivia is a byproduct of a commitment to documentation—and of long and painstaking research.

In sports, baseball clearly has been the leader in record-keeping and chronicling of events. The National League, for example, has carefully documented its goings-on since the day in 1876 when the first big-league pitch was thrown.

Football hasn't been so meticulous. College football waited until 1937— 68 years after playing its first game—before keeping official national individual records. The National Football League, born in 1920, didn't compile official individual statistics until 1932.

But as football's popularity as a spectator sport has skyrocketed, so has the scope of its documentation. Every year, it seems, another statistic is being kept. And statistics breed trivia. More important, dogged football historians are continually providing new insight into the game's early years.

Additionally, football's showcase events and awards appear to take on more significance each year. As the Super Bowl's Roman numerals increase, so, too, do the anticipation and excitement surrounding the game. Interest in the draft of college talent seems higher every spring, speculation over Heisman Trophy contenders appears greater each autumn and the controversy over polls seems to intensify every season. And that's just for starters.

The result? Football has arrived as a trivia phenomenon.

The Sporting News Football Trivia Book combines the detail of a reference book with the brevity of typical trivia items, providing a complete review of football's famous, unusual and heretofore little-known events. After a chronological look at memorable games and memorable performances (flashbacks that divide pro and college football and trace the evolution of each), The Sporting News Football Trivia Book focuses on the pros and the colleges together in an alphabetical format. The book zeroes in on the draft, the Heisman Trophy, All-Americas, pro title games, bowl games, polls, league and team histories, tragic events, "firsts," "lasts," oddities, innovations, numbers and football-playing celebrities.

A few explanations: College-football entries emphasize events in what is now classified as NCAA Division I-A, which carries a "major college" designation within these pages. All-America recognition is limited to consensus choices, and references to the American Football League reflect activities in the AFL of the 1960s (unless otherwise indicated). If a wire-service designation does not accompany a team's ranking, it means only one polling system was in effect at the time or that the team was rated in the same position by the Associated Press and United Press International. And entries cover on-the-field action through January 1985.

Preliminaries aside, it's now time for the First Quarter—what else?— of The Sporting News Football Trivia Book.

Gus Dorais, former coach for the University of Detroit and the Detroit Lions of the National Football League, helped popularize the forward pass during his days as Notre Dame quarterback.

MEMORABLE GAMES IN COLLEGE HISTORY

IRISH PASS INTO 'BIG TIME'

Legend has it that Notre Dame quarterback Gus Dorais introduced the pass to football in his team's November 1, 1913, game against Army at West Point, N.Y. Not true. Passing actually had been legalized in the collegiate game seven years earlier. But there is little doubt that Dorais' aerial display that day popularized the pass and helped to make it an integral part of the game. At a time when teams threw as a last-ditch attempt to move the ball if their ground games were stymied, Coach Jesse Harper's Fighting Irish, hungry for national attention, made the passing game a key part of their game plan and stunned Army, 35-13, in the first notable intersectional game in Notre Dame football history. Since 1906, it had not been unusual for teams

9

employing the aerial game to do so on a spot-pass basis—that is, the quarterback would fire the ball into a predetermined area, and it was the intended receiver's job to get to that spot at the proper time. Notre Dame brought sophistication to the passing attack, though, with Dorais hitting his targets in full stride and proving how devastating a balanced pass/run offense could be. Dorais completed 13 of 17 passes against Army for 243 yards, and he also thwarted a Cadet drive with a third-quarter interception at the Irish goal line.

Supporting Cast:

● **Ray Eichenlaub.** Irish fullback who ran for two fourth-quarter touchdowns in this contest, the inaugural game of the Notre Dame-Army series.

● **Paul Hodgson.** Army player whose TD run in the first period cut Notre Dame's lead to 7-6.

● **Joe Pliska.** Notre Dame halfback whose second-period touchdown scamper tied the game at 13-13. Dorais' second of five extra-point kicks boosted the Irish into a 14-13 edge, an advantage they enjoyed at halftime. Pliska, Dorais' primary passing target on short routes, ran for a second TD in the fourth period.

● **Vernon Prichard.** Army took a 13-7 lead in the second quarter on Prichard's scoring run and Benny Hoge's conversion kick.

● **Knute Rockne.** Having worked with Dorais over the previous summer on aerial technique, Rockne was the No. 1 deep-threat receiver for Notre Dame. Feigning a limp at the outset of the game, the Irish end proved he was healthy later in the first quarter when he got behind the Army defense and hauled in a 25-yard pass from Dorais for the game's first score.

GEORGIA TECH 222, CUMBERLAND 0

Score by Quarters:

Cumberland	0	0	0	0 — 0
Georgia Tech	63	63	54	42 —222

"We were sort of getting to 'em in that last quarter," cracked Charlie Warwick, long after he had toiled for Cumberland College in this October 7, 1916, game in Atlanta.

Cumberland had fielded an excellent baseball team in the spring of 1916 and the school president wanted his athletic teams to move on to bigger and better things—like a date against a major-college football team. While Cumberland had been a small-college football force at the turn of the century—it had even taken on the Ramblin' Wreck in 1904 and 1905, losing by 18-0 and 15-0 scores—the Lebanon, Tenn., school was playing football on an informal basis by 1916. Georgia Tech agreed to play Cumberland, though, provided the challenger deposit a $3,000 check as forfeit money just in case it did not field a team on October 7. Cumberland rounded up 15 players for the trip to Atlanta and did indeed show up—but the squad didn't bother to practice for the big game. Practice might not have made perfect, but it may have helped. Coach John Heisman's Georgia Tech team had 32 possessions against Cumberland—and scored touchdowns on all of them. The Ramblin' Wreck didn't attempt a pass; there was no need. Tech scored on 19 of its 29 rushes, netting 501 yards on the ground (an average of 17.3 yards per carry).

Furthermore, Tech tallied TDs on five of six interception returns, five of nine punt runbacks, two of three fumble-recovery returns and one of five kickoff returns. Everett (Strup) Strupper scored 49 points, making eight touchdowns and booting one extra point. Strupper rushed eight times for 165 yards and six touchdowns (one a 60-yard sprint), and he scored on both of his punt returns (going 55 and 45 yards).

Supporting cast (and other details):

● **Jim Preas.** He ran the ball twice for Tech and scored TDs both times. Besides his 15- and five-yard scoring runs, Preas returned a fumble 10 yards for a touchdown and was successful on all 18 of his conversion kicks. Preas' fumble-recovery TD came on a Cumberland kickoff return—on which Preas had done the kicking off.

● **Tommy Spence.** He toted the ball three times for Tech and notched TDs all three times (two of his scoring runs were 35-yard dashes). Spence also scored on his only kickoff return of the day (90 yards) and collected a TD on his lone interception return (20 yards). Additionally, he made five of seven extra-point attempts (his two misses were Tech's only failures in 32 conversion tries).

● **Stan Fellers.** He returned two Cumberland punts, taking both for touchdowns, and intercepted two passes, returning both for TDs. Fellers had one carry from scrimmage, scoring on a 15-yard run.

● **Jim Senter.** Tech player who scored twice on runs and once on a 30-yard interception return.

● **George Griffin.** He ran for two Ramblin' Wreck touchdowns.

● **Marshall Guill.** He scored on interception and fumble-recovery returns.

● **Six Carpenter, Bob Glover, Canty Alexander, Buzz Shaver and Bill Fincher.** They rounded out the Tech scoring with six points each. Carpenter, Glover and Alexander scored on runs, Shaver on a punt return and Fincher on six conversions.

● **Morris Gouger.** Cumberland's top rusher of the day, Gouger ran for minus two yards on five carries and managed a five-yard gain (which equalled his club's longest run from scrimmage). Overall, Cumberland had minus 42 yards rushing on 34 carries.

● **Leon McDonald.** He had 14 aerial yards for Cumberland, completing two of 11 passes (with four interceptions, three of which were returned for touchdowns).

● **Cumberland,** which trailed 63-0 at the end of the first quarter, 126-0 at halftime and 180-0 after the third period, finished with zero first downs and a minus 28 yards in total offense. It lost the ball on fumbles nine times.

● **When the score** mounted to 28-0 in the opening minutes of the game, Cumberland resorted to kicking off on occasion rather than receiving following Tech touchdowns. Considering the bumbling nature of the visitors' offense, the theory was to keep Tech as far from the Cumberland goal line as possible. On Cumberland's first such kick-rather-than-receive attempt, Tech's Shaver returned the kickoff 70 yards to the Tennesseeans' 10-yard line. Later in the first period, Tech's Spence went 90 yards for a touchdown to further thwart the strategy.

● **While the game** was shortened (the third and fourth quarters were reduced by a total of 15 minutes), Tech still amassed a total of 1,179 yards, which included punt, kickoff, fumble-recovery and interception returns.

How did Warwick fare against Georgia Tech? He had one reception, good for four yards, and returned a kickoff five yards.

"We celebrated as best we could going back on the train," Warwick once said. "There were no serious injuries. And back in Lebanon, we remained heroes of a sort for a long time, having saved the school that $3,000."

THE CENTRE OF ATTENTION

Eastern football reigned supreme in the early years of the collegiate sport, and the East remained a power base into the 1920s. So, it was with some trepidation and a bit of boldness that the football team from little Centre College of Danville, Ky., ventured to Cambridge, Mass., for its October 29, 1921, game against Harvard. Centre, despite its small enrollment, was emerging as a football power in its own right (beating up, primarily, on Southern opposition). The Praying Colonels had gone undefeated in 1919 and then battled Harvard to a 14-14 halftime standoff in Cambridge in 1920 before bowing, 31-14. Still, the host Crimson appeared to be in another class, as evidenced by the caliber of its competition and the 25-game unbeaten streak (which included a 1920 Rose Bowl victory) that Harvard took into its 1921 clash against Centre. The Harvard-Centre game developed into a rugged defensive struggle, with the teams deadlocked 0-0 at halftime. Then, early in the third quarter, Centre quarterback Bo McMillin reversed his field and broke loose on a 32-yard touchdown run. The points held up (Tom Bartlett missed the conversion kick) as Centre prevailed, 6-0, in one of the most stunning upsets in collegiate football history. The outcome made a prophet of McMillin. Offered the game ball by Harvard captain Arnold Horween in 1920 after Centre's creditable-but-losing performance in Cambridge, McMillin begged off and said he "would be back next year to win the pigskin." Back he was, and win he did.

Supporting Cast:

● **Charley Moran.** Centre coach who introduced pregame prayer sessions to his team, leading to the Kentucky school's nickname. Moran, a longtime college football coach, umpired in baseball's National League from 1918 through 1939 and also played big-league baseball.

● **Red Roberts.** Centre player who provided the key interference on McMillin's TD gallop and who, according to the New York Times account of the game, "was all over the football lot" against Harvard.

FOUR HORSEMEN SIT TALL IN SADDLE

"Outlined against a blue-gray October sky, the Four Horsemen rode again. In dramatic lore, they are known as Famine, Pestilence, Destruction and Death. These are only aliases. Their real names are Stuhldreher, Miller, Crowley and Layden. They formed the crest of the South Bend cyclone before which another fighting Army football team was swept over the precipice at the Polo Grounds yesterday afternoon as 55,000 spectators

The legendary Four Horsemen of Notre Dame were in reality talented football players with the names of (left to right) Don Miller, Elmer Layden, Jim Crowley and Harry Stuhldreher.

peered down on the bewildering panorama spread on the green plain below."

New York Herald Tribune sportswriter Grantland Rice was moved to write such a beginning to his game story after watching Notre Dame's four backfield stars perform their magic against Army on October 18, 1924, at the Polo Grounds in New York. With fullback Elmer Layden running one yard for a second-quarter touchdown and left halfback Jim Crowley sprinting 20 yards for a third-period score, Notre Dame prevailed, 13-7, in the clash of national powers. Right halfback Don Miller rushed 19 times for 148 yards that day and Crowley carried the ball 17 times for 102 yards. Layden gained 60 yards on 21 attempts. Harry Stuhldreher, a 5-foot-7, 151-pound quarterback, completed two of three passes for 39 yards against Army and hit on 75.8 percent of his passes overall (25 of 33) in 1924. Miller, a 5-11, 160-pounder, and Crowley, 5-11 and 162, ran for 763 and 739 yards, respectively, in '24, and Layden, 6-0 and 162, rushed for 423 yards that season.

Supporting Cast:

● **Ed Garbisch.** He converted after Army's lone touchdown. (Crowley was one for two on Notre Dame's extra-point attempts.)

● **Chick Harding.** Army player who, with the Cadets behind, 13-0, in the fourth period, ran 12 yards for a touchdown.

● **Adam Walsh.** Fighting Irish lineman and captain who began the game with one broken hand and then fractured the other during the contest—but played all the way. Despite the two fractures, Walsh intercepted an Army pass in the fourth quarter.

On the same afternoon that the Four Horsemen earned their nickname, Illinois' Red Grange went on his touchdown rampage (four TDs in the first 12 minutes and five overall) against Michigan.

FOUR HORSEMEN RIDE INTO SUNSET

Stanford's Ernie Nevers, coming off a year in which he suffered two ankle fractures, put on a courageous performance against Notre Dame in the January 1, 1925, Rose Bowl. Despite playing on heavily taped ankles, Nevers rushed for 114 yards as Stanford dominated Notre Dame statistically in a game that many observers considered a battle for the national championship of the 1924 season. However, Stanford lost, 27-10, in a game that marked the Far West debut and first bowl appearance of the Fighting Irish—as well as the final collegiate performance of Notre Dame's Four Horsemen. Fullback Elmer Layden paced Coach Knute Rockne's opportunistic Irish in this meeting of unbeatens (Notre Dame was 9-0, Stanford 7-0-1), running three yards for a second-quarter touchdown and returning two interceptions for TDs. Layden's first interception runback was a 78-yarder in the second period that—coupled with Jim Crowley's conversion kick—boosted Notre Dame into a 13-3 edge, which held up as the Irish's halftime bulge. Then, with 30 seconds remaining in the game and Rockne's charges ahead, 20-10, Layden picked off another pass (both interceptions were against Nevers) and returned it 70 yards for a score. Crowley again converted.

Supporting Cast:

● **Murray Cuddeback.** His 27-yard field goal gave Coach Pop Warner's Stanford team a 3-0 first-quarter lead. Cuddeback also kicked the extra point after Stanford's lone touchdown of the game.

● **Ed Hunsinger.** When Stanford misplayed Layden's third-quarter punt, Hunsinger gathered up the fumbled ball and went 20 yards for a Notre Dame touchdown. Crowley added his second of three successful PAT kicks.

● **Ted Shipkey.** With Notre Dame ahead, 20-3, Stanford's Shipkey caught a seven-yard touchdown pass from Ed Walker late in the third period.

WINNING ONE FOR THE GIPPER

"When the breaks are beating the boys, tell them to go in there and win just one for the Gipper."

—Halfback George Gipp, speaking from his deathbed in 1920, about three weeks after helping Notre Dame to its second straight perfect season.

Notre Dame Coach Knute Rockne, the man to whom Gipp directed his legendary plea, waited almost eight years before encountering the situation he deemed worthy of the Gipp request. The moment came on November 10, 1928, at Yankee Stadium as the Fighting Irish gathered in the locker room

14

George Gipp

Good luck
rom
Gipp

The legendary George Gipp, an excellent runner, passer and punter for Notre Dame, died of pneumonia in 1920, about three weeks after leading the Irish to a second straight perfect season.

15

during halftime of their 0-0 game against Army, with Rockne telling his squad that "this is the day and you are the team." Notre Dame, which had compiled a 4-2 record at that point of the '28 season compared with Army's 6-0 mark, played inspired football in the second half and won, 12-6, getting the winning touchdown on a 35-yard pass from John Niemiec to Johnny O'Brien in the fourth quarter. O'Brien made the TD catch on his lone appearance of the game. The classic contest ended with Army perched on the Notre Dame 1-yard line.

Supporting Cast:

• **Chris Cagle.** Following O'Brien's scoring reception, Cagle returned the ensuing kickoff 55 yards to propel Army into threatening position. However, time ran out as the Cadets neared the goal line.

• **Jack Chevigny.** His one-yard TD run for Notre Dame tied the score at 6-6 in the third period.

• **Johnny Murrell.** Army player whose one-yard touchdown thrust gave the Cadets a 6-0 lead in the third quarter.

Notre Dame's ecstasy was short-lived in 1928. The Irish fell to Carnegie Tech, 27-7, in the week following the Army game for their first home-field defeat since 1905. And the Irish went on to finish with a 5-4 record, easily accounting for Rockne's worst season at Notre Dame.

Gipp, who was an excellent runner, passer and punter, was a consensus All-America in 1920 and he held Notre Dame's career rushing record (2,341 yards) for nearly 60 years. Following Notre Dame's next-to-last game of the season at Northwestern on November 20, 1920, Gipp remained in the Chicago area, where he contracted a strep throat. The 25-year-old Gipp died of pneumonia on December 14, 1920.

CATCHING UP WITH RIEGELS

California defender Roy Riegels did what came naturally during the second quarter of the January 1, 1929, Rose Bowl after finding himself in the right place at the right time and latching on to a Georgia Tech fumble. He took off for the end zone. "I was running toward the sidelines when I picked up the ball," Riegels said. "I started to turn toward my left, toward Tech's goal. Somebody shoved me and I bounded right off into a tackler. In pivoting to get away from him, I completely lost my bearings. . . ." That he did. Riegels, having snared the ball at Georgia Tech's 35-yard line, raced toward his own goal before being turned around by a teammate at the California 1. Georgia Tech players slammed Riegels to the turf, though, and Cal—while gaining possession—had the ball in precarious field position. Immediately trying to punt out of trouble in the 0-0 game, Cal became the victim of a safety when the Golden Bears' kick attempt was blocked, with the ball rolling out of the end zone. The two points proved decisive for Georgia Tech, which emerged with an 8-7 triumph to complete a perfect season (10-0).

Supporting Cast:

• **Benny Lom.** California player who caught up with Riegels on his 64-yard wrong-way run and got him re-oriented.

This sequence shows Roy Riegels' wrong-way path to immortality.

● **Vance Maree.** Georgia Tech lineman who blocked Cal's punt following Riegels' misplay, netting the Southerners a 2-0 lead.

● **Warner Mizell.** Georgia Tech player who had a third-quarter punt blocked by a rejuvenated Riegels (who brooded heavily at halftime), setting up California on Tech's 26. Cal, down by eight points, failed to capitalize.

● **Irv Phillips.** California player who, with his team trailing, 8-0, caught a 10-yard touchdown pass from Lom in the final minute-and-a-half of the game. Stan Barr kicked the conversion point.

● **Stumpy Thomason.** It was his fumble that Riegels took the wrong direction. And it was Thomason who expanded upon Georgia Tech's 2-0 halftime edge with a 15-yard scoring run in the third period.

UNBEATEN, UNSCORED UPON UNTIL. . .

The Duke Blue Devils scored seven or fewer points in five of their regular-season games in 1938. No matter, the Blue Devils still managed to go undefeated. And untied. The key? They also were unscored upon. That's right, the Blue Devils allowed nary a point in nine games. They opened the season with an 18-0 victory over Virginia Tech and proceeded to beat Davidson, 27-0; Colgate, 7-0; Georgia Tech, 6-0; Wake Forest, 7-0; North Carolina, 14-0; Syracuse, 21-0; North Carolina State, 7-0, and Pittsburgh, 7-0. Then came a date in the January 2, 1939, Rose Bowl against Southern California. And it was more of the same for the opposition. Goose eggs. But Duke's offense, which had averaged 12.7 points in the regular season, wasn't having much success, either. The Blue Devils held a 3-0 lead, though, with 2 minutes, 20 seconds left in the game. At that point, a Southern Cal assistant freshman coach made a bold move. The immediate result: Fourth-string quarterback Doyle Nave entered the game with the Trojans positioned at the Duke 34 (a penalty moved USC back to the 39). The ultimate result: Forty-one seconds away from a perfect, unscored-upon season, Duke saw it all disintegrate when Nave fired a touchdown pass to a second-string receiver. Southern Cal 7, Duke 3.

Supporting Cast:

● **Phil Gaspar.** He converted after Nave's scoring pass.

● **Al Krueger.** The end with whom Nave combined on his game-winning pass, a 19-yard completion on which Krueger got behind Duke defender Eric Tipton. Nave, in the game for four plays, completed four passes to Krueger (the first three covering 13, nine and minus-two yards).

● **Tony Ruffa.** On the second play of the fourth quarter, Ruffa sent Duke into a 3-0 lead with a 33-yard field goal.

● **Joe Wilensky.** The USC aide who, after the Trojans' front-line assistants had left their press-box perch late in the game, acted on his own by advising Trojans Coach Howard Jones to send in Nave for starting quarterback Grenny Lansdell (who had driven USC from its 39 to Duke's 34). Jones, thinking he was getting a consensus view of his assistants rather than one man's opinion, did just as Wilensky suggested. Wilensky, impressed by the practice habits and quick-strike potential of the Nave-Krueger duo, also asked that Krueger be the target of Nave's passes.

Al Krueger, a second-string Southern Cal receiver, catches the last-minute 1939 Rose Bowl touchdown pass that ruined Duke's unbeaten and unscored upon season.

Duke, which had held opponents scoreless for 599 minutes, 19 seconds of its 600-minute season only to suffer a stunning setback at the hands of USC, had company a year later. Tennessee shut out all of its regular-season opponents in 1939 (the Volunteers are the last major-college team to do so), but the Trojans popped the Vols' balloon in the January 1, 1940, Rose Bowl. Collecting second- and fourth-quarter touchdowns, USC recorded a 14-0 triumph over Tennessee (which had outscored its 10 regular-season opponents, 212-0).

GREAT EXPECTATIONS ALL FOR NOTHING

The outcome could hardly match the anticipation. And it didn't. The scenario was this: Top-ranked and unbeaten Army, national champion in 1944 and 1945 and winner of 25 consecutive games, vs. storied Notre Dame, also undefeated and rated No. 2, at Yankee Stadium on November 9, 1946. Frank Leahy was back as Notre Dame's coach after missing the '44 and '45 seasons because of service in the U.S. Navy. While Leahy was away, Coach Earl (Red) Blaik's Army teams had embarrassed the proud Fighting Irish by 59-0 and 48-0 scores. Notre Dame, 5-0 in the '46 season entering the clash against Army, had punished its opponents, 177-18. Army, 7-0, had outscored its opposition, 208-55. With skill-position standouts dotting both lineups, a wild shootout was expected in this meeting of titans. Final score . . . Army 0, Notre Dame 0. As an indication of the crunching defensive play that unfolded in a game not devoid of drama, Notre Dame held Army's Doc Blanchard (Mr. Inside) to 50 yards rushing on 18 carries and Glenn Davis (Mr. Outside)

19

to 30 yards on 17 attempts. The Irish finished with 225 yards in total offense, compared with the Cadets' 195.

Supporting Cast:

• **Terry Brennan.** Fighting Irish player who thwarted a third-quarter Army drive by intercepting a Davis pass at Notre Dame's 5-yard line. Immediately after the interception, Brennan reeled off Notre Dame's longest run from scrimmage that day by darting 22 yards. He finished with a game-high 69 yards rushing on 14 carries.

• **Hank Foldberg.** Army end whose fourth-and-two stop of Notre Dame's Bill Gompers after a one-yard gain ended the Fighting Irish's major threat of the game, an 85-yard march in the second quarter that reached the Cadets' 3. Gerry Cowhig's 20-yard run had gotten the ball to the 12, from where the Irish made eight yards on their ensuing first three downs (a two-yard pass from Johnny Lujack to Cowhig, a five-yard run by Gompers and a one-yard sneak by Lujack).

• **Johnny Lujack.** Notre Dame quarterback who completed only six of 17 passes for 52 yards (three interceptions) and gained just nine yards rushing on eight carries. However, in a crucial third-period play, Lujack made an open-field tackle on Blanchard at Notre Dame's 36 after the Army star had broken into the clear for a 21-yard gain. The Cadets' drive eventually was halted by Brennan's pass theft.

• **Arnold Tucker.** Army quarterback who got off the day's longest run from scrimmage, a 30-yard dash, on the last play of the first half before being felled by Lujack, Notre Dame's Johnny-on-the-spot. Tucker also showed his defensive prowess by making three interceptions (the second of which he returned 32 yards, setting up the Cadets' drive that was snuffed out by Brennan).

Army remained atop the Associated Press' poll (the lone wire-service listing at that time) in the week after the scoreless tie, but Notre Dame, which finished at 8-0-1, supplanted Army by season's end. The Cadets, 9-0-1, dropped to No. 2 in the final balloting after slipping past a weak Navy team, 21-18, in their season finale.

NO DAVIS, NO BLANCHARD . . . NO STREAK

Army no longer had Glenn Davis, Doc Blanchard and Arnold Tucker in its backfield, but the 1947 Cadets still enjoyed a 3-0-1 record—and had out-scored their opponents, 100-0—entering an October 25 game against Columbia on the Lions' home field in New York. Furthermore, Army had a 32-game unbeaten streak dating to 1944. Columbia was 2-2, having lost to Pennsylvania, 34-14, in its last outing, and the Lions seemingly posed no threat to Coach Earl (Red) Blaik's team. Sure enough, Army breezed to a touchdown on its first possession and built a 20-7 halftime lead. But thanks in large part to the pass-catching wizardry of Bill Swiacki, Columbia came to life for two fourth-quarter touchdowns and pulled off a 21-20 upset of the Cadets.

Supporting Cast:

• **Arnie Galiffa.** Ending a 55-yard drive, Army's quarterback scored on a one-yard run with fewer than 5 minutes played in the game. Jack Mackmull kicked the extra point.

● **Lou Kusserow.** He scored two touchdowns for Columbia. With Army in front, 14-0, in the second period, Kusserow went six yards for a touchdown and Ventan Yablonski made the conversion placement. Then, midway through the last quarter, with Army ahead, 20-14, Kusserow burst one yard to tie the score. Yablonski again delivered on the PAT, and Columbia slipped ahead with what proved to be the game's final point. Kusserow inflicted the final blow to the Cadets, halting an ensuing Army drive by intercepting a Galiffa pass.

● **Gene Rossides.** Columbia quarterback who was a key man in all three of the Lions' scoring drives. His three straight second-quarter completions moved the ball 53 yards, setting up Kusserow's first TD run. Early in the fourth quarter, with his team facing a 13-point deficit, Rossides hooked up with Bill Olson on completions covering 16 and 11 yards before gaining five yards on a run and then hitting Swiacki on a 28-yard scoring pass (a play on which Army protested that a diving, sliding Swiacki never had possession of the ball). Yablonski's PAT following Swiacki's grab made it a 20-14 game. Then, on a drive that began with $8\frac{1}{2}$ minutes left in the clash at Baker Field, Rossides marched Columbia 66 yards to its game-winning points. The key plays preceding Kusserow's second touchdown of the day were Rossides' 22-yard run and the quarterback's 26-yard strike to Swiacki (who made another lunging catch) that carried to the Army 3-yard line. Rossides finished with 18 completions in 27 pass attempts for 239 yards; Swiacki caught nine passes for 148 yards.

● **Elwyn (Rip) Rowan.** Capping a 61-yard Army march that featured Bill Gustafson's 28-yard gallop to the Columbia 1, Rowan went the final yard for a second-period Cadets touchdown. Mackmull's extra point made it 14-0. Rowan then zoomed 84 yards to a TD later in the quarter, but Mackmull missed the PAT (which enabled Columbia to record its shocker).

'SNOW BOWL' IN COLUMBUS

Underdog Michigan, hoping to knock off Big Ten Conference leader Ohio State and slip into the Rose Bowl (provided it received a major assist from Northwestern), didn't make a first down in its November 25, 1950, game against the Buckeyes in Columbus, Ohio. The Wolverines, who entered the game with a 4-3-1 overall record, didn't complete a pass, either, and they rushed for only 27 yards. But by the end of a game played under horrendous conditions—a driving snowstorm, strong winds and temperatures hovering around 10 degrees—the Wolverines had parlayed two blocked punts into a 9-3 triumph over Ohio State. Coupled with Northwestern's 14-7 upending of conference title contender Illinois on the same day, the victory earned Michigan the league championship and a New Year's Day date in Pasadena, Calif. Michigan's Tony Momsen, whose brother Bob played for the Buckeyes in 1950, made the game-winning touchdown in the so-called "Snow Bowl," scoring in the second quarter at Ohio Stadium. Snow fell so heavily during the game that it was difficult to see the players from the press box, and the elements reduced the game to a kicking duel—the teams combined for 45 punts—with no second-half scoring. Whenever first-down measurements were needed, which was rarely, brooms were used to clear snow

Ohio State (white helmets) and Michigan players chase across the snow-covered field for a loose ball during the 1950 game in Columbus, O. The Buckeyes came up with the first-quarter blocked punt to set up Ohio State's only score of the day—a 27-yard field goal.

from the yard-markers. And while 82,000-plus tickets were sold for the clash of archrivals, more than 30,000 ticket-holders failed to make it to the stadium (the blizzard had shut down public transportation, virtually paralyzing Columbus). The defeat was particularly bitter for defending Rose Bowl champion Ohio State, which was coming off an upset loss to Illinois and had boasted of a No. 1 national ranking prior to its game with the Fighting Illini.

Supporting Cast:

● **Chuck Gandee.** The Buckeyes' leading rusher with 15 yards on 11 carries. Ohio State, which managed only three first downs, had 41 yards in total offense (compared with Michigan's 27). Coach Wes Fesler's Buckeyes netted 16 yards on the ground and 25 yards in the air (completing three of 18 passes).

● **Vic Janowicz.** Somehow able to get adequate footing on the frozen field, Ohio State's versatile back booted a 27-yard field goal early in the first quarter to boost the Buckeyes into a 3-0 lead. The field goal came after a Michigan quick-kick attempt was blocked by Ohio State's Joe Campanella and recovered by the Buckeyes' Bob Momsen. Janowicz, closing out what would be a Heisman Trophy-winning season, punted 21 times for 672 yards, a 32-yard average. The second of two critical blocks against Janowicz (four of his punts were blocked overall) proved decisive. With 47 seconds remaining until halftime and the Buckeyes ahead, 3-2, Janowicz tried to punt on third-and-six from his end zone. The Wolverines' Tony Momsen blocked the kick and recovered the ball for a touchdown. Harry Allis kicked the extra point, giving Michigan a 9-3 advantage.

● **Chuck Ortmann.** Michigan tailback who 11 times punted out of bounds inside the Ohio State 15. Overall, Ortmann punted 24 times for 723 yards, a 30.1 average. Trying to pass on this frigid day, he went zero for nine.

● **Ralph Straffon.** Pacing Michigan's ballcarriers, Straffon rushed 12 times for 14 yards on the treacherous snow-covered turf.

● **Allen Wahl.** Michigan captain who, with Ohio State on top, 3-0, blocked a Janowicz punt in the first period. The ball rolled out of the end zone and into a snowbank for a safety, slicing the Buckeyes' lead to 3-2.

The "Snow Bowl" marked Fesler's last game as Ohio State coach. He was succeeded in 1951 by W.W. (Woody) Hayes.

'TOO FULL OF ALABAMA'

"I kept telling myself I didn't do it. I didn't do it. But I knew I had." Speaking was Tommy Lewis, Alabama football player. A couple hours earlier, as Rice's Dicky Moegle streaked down the right sideline toward an apparent touchdown in the January 1, 1954, Cotton Bowl in Dallas, fullback Lewis had leaped off the Crimson Tide bench in mid-play and, stunningly, smashed Moegle to the turf at the Alabama 40-yard line. "I guess I'm too full of Alabama," an emotional Lewis said after the game. Referee Cliff Shaw awarded a touchdown to Moegle, whose second-period run from scrimmage had begun at the Owls' 5. Lewis' impulsive play overshadowed the game-long exploits of Moegle, who turned in one of the top bowl efforts of all time by rushing for 265 yards on 11 carries (an average of 24.1 yards per attempt). Moegle, who at the outset of the second quarter had bolted 79 yards for a touchdown, was credited with a 95-yard TD run on Lewis' 12th-man play and he blasted 34 yards for another touchdown in the third quarter. Rice wound up winning, 28-6, after falling behind, 6-0, in the first period when Alabama scored, ironically, on a one-yard run by Lewis, who had reeled off 16- and 13-yard gains on the Tide's 49-yard touchdown march.

Supporting Cast:

● **Leroy Fenstemaker.** He kicked extra points after Moegle's three TDs.

● **Buddy Grantham.** Getting into the end zone on a seven-yard bootleg play in the fourth quarter, Grantham notched Rice's last TD of the game. Sammy Burk's conversion kick completed the game's scoring.

● **Bart Starr.** With Rice ahead, 7-6, nearing the middle of the second period, Alabama was driving—thanks largely to Bill Oliver's 54-yard run—when quarterback Starr fumbled away the ball at the Owls' 10 after scrambling for 10 yards. After a backfield-in-motion penalty cost the Owls five yards, Moegle set off on his fateful dash. Starr had given Alabama possession for its first-quarter scoring march by intercepting a Fenstemaker pass.

Lewis, described prior to the 1953 season by Alabama's Harold (Red) Drew as the best fullback he had coached in 16 years as a collegiate head coach, had run for two touchdowns (covering four and 30 yards) in the 1953 Orange Bowl as Alabama crushed Syracuse, 61-6.

The scene is set (right) as Rice's Dicky Moegle avoids Alabama defenders and streaks down the sideline toward an apparent touchdown in the 1954 Cotton Bowl in Dallas. Moegle did get his touchdown, but not in the conventional way. Alabama's Tommy Lewis, in an emotional outburst, jumped helmetless off the sideline and tackled Moegle (below). The referee awarded the TD to Rice.

LEWIS (A) MOEGLE (R) DeLAURENTIS (A) OLIVER (A) CHAPMAN (R)

ROSE BOWL'S 'WHODUNIT'

Kicking a game-winning field goal in the final 7 seconds of the Rose Bowl should enable a player to make a name for himself. For the star of the 1956 Rose Bowl, though, fame was late in coming—if only by 15 minutes or so. With Michigan State and UCLA deadlocked at 14-14 in the closing moments of the '56 classic, the Spartans were lined up at the Bruins' 24-yard line. It was field-goal time, and Gerry Planutis, who had made two extra-point kicks but missed two field-goal attempts earlier in the game, appeared to be Michigan State's man of the hour. The ball was placed down and the kick sailed true. Radio sent out the word nationwide: Planutis had kicked the decisive field goal, with his 41-yard boot giving Michigan State a 17-14 triumph. Inside the stadium, the public-address speaker, the press-box announcer and the official play-by-play account of the game delivered the same Planutis-oriented message. So? The Spartans had won, all right. And, yes, the score was 17-14. But Michigan State's hero that day was not Gerry Planutis.

Supporting Cast:

● **Bob Davenport.** He put UCLA on top with a two-yard scoring run in the first period of the January 2, 1956, game.

● **Jim Decker.** On the game's first play from scrimmage, UCLA's Decker intercepted an Earl Morrall pass, which led to Davenport's touchdown. Decker also converted after both of the Bruins' TDs.

● **Dave Kaiser.** It was Michigan State end Kaiser, not Planutis, who kicked the game-deciding field goal. Those covering the game had a poor view of the kick (and the kicker), with the boot coming from an angle on the opposite side of the field from the press box. The Spartans, aided by a penalty, had taken possession at UCLA's 19 with less than a minute to play but couldn't advance. Coach Duffy Daugherty then had his team take a delay-of-game penalty, enabling the Spartans to stop the clock and thus get the kicking tee onto the field. While most onlookers assumed that Planutis again was handling the Michigan State kicking chores, Daugherty had opted for his "long-range kicker," Kaiser, a sophomore who had missed on the only two field-goal attempts of his collegiate career during the regular season. It was not until reporters got into the Michigan State locker room after the game that the case of mistaken identity was fully straightened out.

● **Ronnie Knox.** With 1 minute, 34 seconds left in the game and the score tied, tailback Knox had his UCLA team in the huddle when the Bruins were assessed a 15-yard penalty—back to their 5—for unsportsmanlike conduct (a UCLA assistant was gesturing for a pass, breaking the no-coaching-from-the-sidelines rule). Knox then threw incomplete, but the Bruins drew another flag—this one for having an illegal receiver downfield. With the ball now on the 1, Knox punted and UCLA was called for yet another infraction —interfering with a fair-catch attempt (at the Bruins' 34).

● **John Lewis.** Michigan State end who caught a 67-yard touchdown pass, breaking a 7-7 tie early in the fourth quarter.

● **Clarence Peaks.** With Michigan State trailing, 7-0, after the first period, Peaks caught a 13-yard TD pass from Morrall in the second quarter. Then, on a halfback option, Peaks fired the scoring pass to Lewis in the final period. Peaks also was the Spartan who wasn't given a full opportunity to make a fair catch on UCLA's late-game punt.

● **Doug Peters.** Culminating a fourth-quarter drive on which Knox and Decker had combined on a 47-yard pass play, Peters scored for UCLA on a one-yard run. The PAT made it a 14-14 game.

IRISH CONQUEST AT NORMAN

Notre Dame, coming off consecutive losses to Navy and Michigan State, was an 18-point underdog as it ventured to Norman, Okla., for a November 16, 1957, game against the Oklahoma Sooners, whose record major-college winning streak had reached 47 games. Coach Terry Brennan's Fighting Irish, who had suffered through a 2-8 season in 1956, rebounded in 1957 by winning their first four games of the season before running into the Midshipmen and Spartans. Oklahoma was, well, typically Oklahoma. The Sooners were 7-0 at that point of the '57 season, with their latest triumph being an impressive 39-14 victory over Coach Frank Broyles' Missouri team in Columbia, Mo. Notre Dame, a 40-0 loser to Oklahoma in 1956 at Notre Dame Stadium, rose up this time and cut down the Sooners, 7-0, collecting the game-winning touchdown on halfback Dick Lynch's three-yard run in the fourth quarter. Not only did the Irish win, they did so with authority. Notre Dame topped Oklahoma in first downs, 17 to nine; rushing yards, 169 to 98, and passing yards, 79 to 47.

Supporting Cast:

● **Dick Royer.** Irish end whose 10-yard reception, carrying to the Sooners' 19-yard line, was a key play on Notre Dame's victorious fourth-quarter march (which covered 80 yards).

● **Nick Pietrosante.** Notre Dame workhorse ballcarrier who followed Royer's catch with a seven-yard blast to the 12.

● **Bob Williams.** After taking a four-yard loss back to the 16 on a broken play, Notre Dame's quarterback gave the ball to Lynch on a draw play that netted eight yards and a first down at the Oklahoma 8. Pietrosante then churned for four yards. Lynch was stopped for no gain, however, and Williams' sneak made only one yard, setting up a fourth-and-goal play at the Sooners' 3. With the Oklahoma defense bunched up on the line in anticipation of a Pietrosante rush, Williams faked to the fullback, rolled right and pitched out to Lynch, who scored standing up with 3 minutes, 50 seconds left in the game.

● **Monty Stickles.** He made the extra-point kick after Lynch's touchdown.

● **Bennett Watts.** Oklahoma quarterback who drove the Sooners to Notre Dame's 24 in the final minute-and-a-half of the game, hitting halfback John Pellow on a 40-yard pass to highlight the march.

● **Dale Sherrod.** Oklahoma player whose pass into the Irish end zone was intercepted by Williams with 22 seconds remaining in the game, sealing the Sooners' fate.

Oklahoma not only had its 47-game winning streak come to an end, Coach Bud Wilkinson's Sooners saw a 48-game unbeaten string snapped. Oklahoma had preceded its victory streak with a 7-7 tie against Pittsburgh in the second game of the 1953 season.

Notre Dame's Dick Lynch (No. 25 above) runs toward the end zone with the only touchdown in Notre Dame's 1957 upset of Oklahoma. Irish Coach Terry Brennan gets a victory ride (left) as the scoreboard tells the final tale of Oklahoma's streak-breaking loss.

Billy Cannon, LSU's Mr. Clutch, breaks through the Mississippi defense on his game-winning 89-yard punt return in a key 1959 game at Baton Rouge, La.

CANNON LEVELS OLE MISS

Louisiana State tackle Bo Strange perhaps summed up teammate Billy Cannon's ability best. "When you need it, that animal is there," Strange said of the Bayou Tigers' All-America halfback. "Cannon won't get 100 touchdowns against Podunk. But he'll get that big one against someone like Ole Miss." Johnny Vaught's Mississippi Rebels could attest to that, having just seen Cannon deliver in the clutch in one of the biggest collegiate games in the rich history of Southern football. This contest, played on the night of October 31, 1959, in Baton Rouge, La., was more than a regional battle, though, and it went beyond a titanic struggle between two bitter rivals. Conceivably, the national championship was at stake. LSU, the defending national champion, was ranked No. 1 in both wire-service polls entering the Mississippi game and hadn't allowed a touchdown all season in compiling a 6-0 record (the opposition had managed just two field goals). Ole Miss, also 6-0, was rated No. 3 in the polls and had yielded only seven points at that juncture of the '59 season. As might be expected, the game turned into a fierce defensive battle. Mississippi led, 3-0, with 10 minutes left in the game when the Rebels punted from their 42-yard line. "I didn't plan to take it," said Cannon, remembering that LSU Coach Paul Dietzel didn't want his players fielding kicks inside the 15. "But the ball took a high bounce and fell right into my arms (at the Tigers' 11). I took two steps forward and just started running." Absorbing repeated hits at the start of his runback, Cannon nevertheless blasted 89 yards to the end zone. Mississippi, despite a furious last-ditch march, could not recover and the Tigers won their 19th consecutive game. Final score: LSU 7, Ole Miss 3.

Supporting Cast:

● **Doug Elmore.** After Cannon's punt return, Mississippi drove 68 yards to the LSU 2 where, in the final half-minute of the game, Elmore tried to run for a touchdown on a fourth-down play. The Tigers stopped him at the 1.

● **Jake Gibbs.** Mississippi quarterback whose 47-yard punt on a third-and-17 play was returned for the TD by Cannon. Gibbs, a 37.7 punter overall in 1959, averaged 51.5 yards on six kicks against LSU.

● **Wendell Harris.** He kicked the conversion point for LSU after Cannon's score.

● **Ed Khayat.** Repulsed in its bid for a first-quarter touchdown after gaining possession on Cannon's fumble at the LSU 21, Mississippi turned to Khayat, who provided the Rebels with their only points of the night with a 22-yard field goal.

The No. 2-ranked team in both polls in the week preceding and the week following the Mississippi-Louisiana State game was Northwestern. The Wildcats lost their last three games of the season, however, and plunged out of the top 10.

The week after its dramatic victory over Mississippi, Louisiana State was upset by Tennessee, 14-13. In the final polls of the season, Ole Miss, 9-1, was ranked No. 2 and LSU, 9-1, was rated No. 3 (Syracuse, 10-0, headed the rankings). Then, in a rare rematch, Mississippi avenged its Halloween horror by dealing LSU a 21-0 defeat in the January 1, 1960, Sugar Bowl.

WISCONSIN WAKES UP

It was a classic matchup of No. 1 vs. No. 2. But it wasn't a classic football game—not until the final 12 minutes, that is. The combatants were top-ranked Southern California and No. 2-rated Wisconsin; the setting was the Rose Bowl in Pasadena, Calif., and the date was January 1, 1963. Southern Cal, sparked by Pete Beathard's four touchdown passes, was coasting, 42-14, in the fourth quarter when Wisconsin made a furious run at the Trojans.

The rally's principal figures:

● **Lou Holland.** With 11 minutes, 41 seconds left in the game and the Badgers staring at a 28-point deficit, Wisconsin's Holland scored on a 13-yard run. Gary Kroner than kicked the extra point, his third of the day, and it was Southern Cal 42, Wisconsin 21.

● **Ron VanderKelen.** Senior quarterback who fueled Wisconsin's surge by completing 18 of 22 final-period passes. After the Trojans' Ben Wilson had fumbled at his 29-yard line in the fourth quarter, the Badgers moved in for the score with 8:32 to play as VanderKelen hit Kroner with a four-yard pass. Kroner's PAT made it Southern Cal 42, Wisconsin 28.

● **Ernie Jones.** USC punter who was forced to down an errant center snap in the Trojans' end zone with 2:40 left, giving the Badgers a safety and cutting Southern Cal's lead to 42-30.

● **Pat Richter.** Wisconsin receiver who took a 19-yard TD pass from Van-

Ron VanderKelen, the quarterback who fueled Wisconsin's dramatic comeback bid in the 1963 Rose Bowl, throws a pass over Southern Cal defenders.

derKelen with 1:19 remaining. The catch was Richter's 11th and last of the game and brought his day's receiving production to 163 yards. Kroner's fifth and final PAT of the afternoon narrowed USC's edge to five points.

Having gotten back into the game with startling rapidity, the Badgers then tried an onside kick in an effort to complete the comeback. However, Southern Cal recovered the ball, ran three plays and then punted. As VanderKelen and his teammates attempted to set up at the line of scrimmage for one last fling, the final gun went off. The Trojans had fought off the Badgers, 42-37.

ARA, IRISH COME SO CLOSE

Notre Dame, leading Southern California, 17-0, at halftime of its final game of the 1964 season, was 30 minutes away from wrapping up a storybook year. The Fighting Irish, who had posted a 2-7 record in 1963, were unbeaten through nine games of Ara Parseghian's first year as Notre Dame coach and boasted the No. 1 ranking in both wire-service polls. Furthermore, senior quarterback John Huarte, who had thrown only one touchdown pass in his first two varsity seasons while attempting just 50 passes, had been voted the Heisman Trophy winner four days before the November 28 game at the Los Angeles Memorial Coliseum. The Trojans, three-time losers already in '64 and 12-point underdogs, didn't provide much early resistance as Notre Dame sought to nail down its first national championship since 1949 and its first undefeated, untied season since '49. The Irish, after recovering a fumble at the Trojans' 46-yard line, went on to notch a first-quarter field goal and then reeled off 73- and 72-yard scoring drives in the second period.

30

Confident that an upset of the Irish would thrust them into the Rose Bowl, the Trojans had plenty of motivation themselves and they marched 66 yards to a touchdown following the second-half kickoff. Slowly but surely, Notre Dame's grip on national honors was loosened. When the final gun sounded, the national title and perfect season had gotten away. Southern California 20, Notre Dame 17.

Supporting Cast:

● **Ken Ivan.** He booted Notre Dame's field goal, a 25-yarder, and converted after both of his team's touchdowns.

● **Jack Snow.** Notre Dame receiver who caught Huarte's 16th touchdown pass of the season, a 21-yard pitch, in the second quarter. Snow finished the day with 10 catches for 158 yards; Huarte completed 18 of 29 passes for 272 yards.

● **Bill Wolski.** Irish running back who, with Notre Dame ahead, 10-0, ran five yards for a second-period TD.

● **Mike Garrett.** His one-yard scoring run and Dick Brownell's conversion kick cut Notre Dame's lead to 17-7 in the third quarter.

● **Fred Hill.** After a third-period fumble at the USC 9 and a fourth-quarter holding penalty on an apparent Irish TD (a one-yard run by Joe Kantor) foiled Notre Dame scoring opportunities, the Trojans struck on a 10-play, 88-yard drive that ended with Hill taking a 23-yard pass from Craig Fertig with 5 minutes, 9 seconds left in the final quarter. The conversion attempt failed, leaving the Irish in front, 17-13.

● **Rod Sherman.** Having taken possession at the Notre Dame 40 with 2:10 remaining in the game following a punt return (an Irish punt to the Trojan 23 had been nullified by another holding penalty), Southern Cal drove in for the game-winning TD—and Sherman got it on a 15-yard pass from Fertig. Brownell added the PAT. Facing a fourth-and-eight play, Fertig hit Sherman at the 3 and the sophomore receiver slipped away from Irish defender Tony Carey for the TD with 1:33 to play. The moment was not without its symbolism. As Sherman shook free from Carey, who was wearing uniform number 1, the quest to clinch the No. 1 national ranking eluded Notre Dame.

Notre Dame Athletic Director Edward (Moose) Krause was gracious in defeat. "This is one of the greatest victories of all time," Krause told USC Coach John McKay. "Even better than your (USC's) 1931 victory." Krause was referring to the November 21, 1931, game at South Bend, Ind., in which Southern Cal stopped Notre Dame's 26-game unbeaten streak by jolting the Irish, 16-14, on Johnny Baker's field goal in the final minute of play. USC had trailed Notre Dame (Krause was a member of that Irish team), 14-0, entering the fourth quarter.

As great a triumph as the '64 upset of Notre Dame was, Southern Cal was in for disappointment. Two hours after the game, the Trojans were informed that Oregon State—with whom USC had shared the Athletic Association of Western Universities championship—had received the conference's bid to the Rose Bowl.

The final Associated Press and United Press International polls of 1964, released the week after the Irish-Trojans game, listed Alabama—led by quarterback Joe Namath—as No. 1. Notre Dame was rated third in both polls, behind Arkansas.

WINNING ISN'T EVERYTHING

"It's all over, and we're still Number 1," Notre Dame's Ara Parseghian said in the Spartan Stadium locker room after his Fighting Irish had run out the clock against No. 2-ranked Michigan State on November 19, 1966, to preserve a 10-10 tie in one of the most ballyhooed games in collegiate football history. Parseghian was heavily criticized, however, for his willingness to settle for a deadlock in a game of such magnitude (his top-ranked Irish were 8-0 entering the game and the runner-up Spartans had a 9-0 record). The Irish coach stuck to his guns, though, and obviously thought his strategy enhanced Notre Dame's national-championship aspirations. After all, an entrenched No. 1-ranked club usually yields its lofty status only in defeat. "We were No. 1 (in both wire-service polls) when we came, we fell behind, had some tough things happen, but you overcame them," Parseghian told his players. Parseghian was proved wrong on at least one of his post-game statements. His Irish no longer were No. 1—at least not in United Press International's rankings. While the Associated Press kept the Irish No. 1 in its poll that came out the week after the Notre Dame-Michigan State clash, UPI dropped Parseghian's team to No. 2 and elevated Coach Duffy Daugherty's Spartans to the top spot. Salvaging a tie against Daugherty's squad was not easy for the Irish. It was not until the first play of the fourth quarter that Notre Dame, trailing since early in the second period, drew even at 10-10 on Joe Azzaro's 28-yard field goal. With 4 minutes, 41 seconds to play, Azzaro had an opportunity to put the Irish ahead, but he was wide on a 41-yard attempt.

Supporting Cast:

● **Regis Cavender.** Breaking a scoreless tie, Michigan State's Cavender ran four yards for a touchdown 1:40 into the second quarter.

● **Nick Eddy.** Standout Notre Dame running back who missed the game after slipping on the train steps upon his team's arrival in East Lansing, Mich., and injuring his shoulder.

● **Bob Gladieux.** With Michigan State ahead, 10-0, in the second quarter, Gladieux caught a 34-yard touchdown pass for Notre Dame.

● **Terry Hanratty.** Notre Dame quarterback sensation who was forced out of the game in the first quarter with a shoulder separation when he was hit by Spartan defenders George Webster and Bubba Smith.

● **Dick Kenney.** Michigan State placekicker who converted after Cavender's TD and then booted a 47-yard field goal later in the second period.

● **Coley O'Brien.** Hanratty's replacement, O'Brien drove the Irish to their lone touchdown and fired the scoring pass to Gladieux. O'Brien was at center stage on Notre Dame's controversial final possession, with the Irish having a first-and-10 on their 30 with 1:24 to play and the score tied at 10-10. While many fans at Spartan Stadium and others watching the game on national television expected the Irish to mount a serious—although admittedly low-risk—bid to score, Notre Dame opted for three running plays that moved the ball to the Irish 39. On fourth-and-one, Parseghian took a chance on turning the ball over on downs—in shaky field position, no less—but O'Brien sneaked two yards. Apparently wanting to throw on the next play, O'Brien was nailed instead for a seven-yard loss. Then, with 6 seconds showing on the clock, he ran to the Notre Dame 39. The gun went off. Notre Dame 10, Michigan State 10.

While UPI demoted Notre Dame after its close-to-the-vest tie with Michigan State, the Fighting Irish finished the season as No. 1 in both wire-service polls. Michigan State had completed its season with the showdown against the Irish, but Notre Dame had one game left—against archrival Southern California in Los Angeles. The Irish pounded the Trojans, 51-0, and found their way back into the good graces of the UPI selectors.

SIMPSON UPENDS UCLA

With a Rose Bowl berth and a chance at the 1967 national title on the line and his once-beaten Southern California team trailing No. 1-ranked UCLA, 20-14, O.J. Simpson swept 64 yards to a fourth-quarter touchdown to spark the Trojans to a 21-20 victory over the Bruins in Southern Cal's regular-season finale. After faking to the right, Simpson swung around left end, cut back over the middle and, with Earl McCullouch screening off would-be tacklers, sped past the UCLA secondary on a play that Trojans Coach John McKay called "the damnedest run" he had ever seen. Simpson, who rushed 30 times for 177 yards, ran 13 yards for a second-period TD on a tackle-breaking carry as Southern Cal broke a 7-7 deadlock in the November 18, 1967, game played at the Los Angeles Memorial Coliseum. The Trojans, ranked third in the United Press International poll and fourth in the Associated Press listings entering the game, supplanted UCLA at the top of both polls the following week and stayed there.

Supporting Cast:

● **Rikki Aldridge.** He made the game-winning conversion kick after Simpson's long run, which came with 10 minutes, 38 seconds left in the game, and also booted the extra point following Simpson's first TD.

● **Gary Beban.** Quarterback who completed 16 of 24 passes for 301 yards and two touchdowns for UCLA, which went into the game with a 7-0-1 record.

● **Pat Cashman.** USC defender whose 55-yard interception return of a Beban pass at the end of the first quarter, coupled with Aldridge's first extra point of the day, enabled Southern Cal to tie UCLA, 7-7.

● **George Farmer.** With the Trojans ahead, 14-7, in the third quarter, Farmer teamed with Beban on a 53-yard scoring pass. Zenon Andrusyshyn's extra point made it a 14-14 game.

● **Greg Jones.** His 12-yard run and Andrusyshyn's PAT in the first quarter gave UCLA a 7-0 edge over USC, which was coming off a 3-0 loss at Oregon State, a defeat that had toppled the Trojans from the No. 1 ranking.

● **Dave Nuttall.** He took a 20-yard TD pass from Beban with 11:41 to play in the fourth quarter, snapping a 14-14 tie. Andrusyshyn's conversion attempt, nicked by USC's 6-foot-8 Bill Hayhoe, sailed wide but the Bruins had a 20-14 lead. However, Simpson then struck with his run from the Trojans' 36 to stagger the Bruins (who lost to Syracuse the next week).

HARVARD'S BELIEVE IT OR NOT

Regardless of the teams' records or their relative strengths, the matchup is referred to as The Game. And what occurred in that storied contest on November 23, 1968, staggers The Imagination. Archrivals Yale and Harvard had entered their 85th meeting in dramatic fashion—both sported perfect records. To the winner would go an undefeated and untied season, the outright Ivy League championship and the glory of having won The Game. The '68 clash could hardly live up to the hype surrounding it. Or so it seemed. But what unfolded on that Saturday afternoon at Harvard Stadium outdid the buildup—and how. With quarterback Brian Dowling running for two touchdowns and passing to Calvin Hill and Del Marting for two others, Yale enjoyed a 29-13 lead with less than a minute left in the final quarter. Then . . .

Supporting Cast:

● **Frank Champi.** With his team down by 16 points and poised at the Yale 15-yard line with 42 seconds remaining in the game, Harvard's reserve quarterback scrambled around in his search for an open receiver. Frantically eluding the Yale pursuit, Champi finally threw to Bruce Freeman at the Yale 3 and Freeman dashed into the end zone. Yale 29, Harvard 19. The TD pass, which capped an 86-yard march that began with 3 minutes, 31 seconds left in the game, had been preceded by a bizarre play in which Crimson tackle Fritz Reed ran 17 yards after picking up a Champi fumble.

● **Gus Crim.** Given a second chance because of a Yale penalty, Harvard collected two points on the conversion when fullback Crim bulled into the end zone. Yale 29, Harvard 21.

● **Bill Kelly.** Harvard player who recovered the Crimson's ensuing onside kick at the Yale 49. Champi's 14-yard scamper and a face-mask penalty took the ball to the Elis' 20 with 20 seconds to play, and Crim (who had scored a third-quarter touchdown for Harvard) gained 14 yards on a draw play. Champi then was thrown for a two-yard loss, leaving Harvard at the Yale 8.

● **Vic Gatto.** With 4 seconds left when the ball was put into play, Champi again led the Yale defense on a merry chase before he found Harvard captain Gatto alone in the end zone for an eight-yard scoring pass. Yale 29, Harvard 27. Time had expired on the stadium clock.

● **Pete Varney.** With Harvard fans in a frenzy and Yale followers in a state of shock and helplessness (their team's offensive unit never ran a play in the game's final 3½ minutes), the Crimson lined up for a two-point conversion attempt and Varney took a perfect toss from Champi. Yale 29, Harvard 29. Bedlam.

Champi, who had seen little action for the Crimson in '68, replaced starting Harvard quarterback George Lalich late in the first half against Yale. With the visitors in front, 22-0, Champi connected with Freeman on a TD pass with 44 seconds left in the second quarter and Harvard went into intermission facing a 22-6 deficit.

While ties often leave an empty feeling among players on both sides, this deadlock—considering the scope of the comeback and the time in which it was accomplished—clearly didn't. The Harvard Crimson newspaper perhaps expressed the home-school euphoria best with its game-story headline: "Harvard Beats Yale, 29-29." The record book shows, of course, that both teams posted undefeated (but not perfect) seasons in 1968, finishing 8-0-1, and that they shared the Ivy crown.

HOUSTON 100, TULSA 6

It was early in the third quarter of the November 23, 1968, game at the Astrodome between Houston and Tulsa, and the visiting Golden Hurricane had just scored on a 14-yard pass from Joe Fitzgerald to Mike Burkett. Tulsa still trailed by 18 points at this juncture, but plenty of time remained in the 24-6 game. Too much time, as it turned out, for the overmatched Hurricane. Houston broke loose for four touchdowns in the remainder of the third period, then leveled Tulsa with a seven-TD explosion in the final quarter. Successful on 10 of 11 extra-point kicks in the third and fourth quarters, Houston ran up 76 second-half points and annihilated the Hurricane, 100-6. Reserve quarterback Rusty Clark ran 11 yards for one Cougar touchdown and passed for three other scores, with all four TD plays coming in the fourth quarter. Houston's Paul Gipson, who rushed for 282 yards overall, ran 35 yards for the game's first score in the opening period and then went 17 and 14 yards for third-quarter touchdowns. And the Cougars' Elmo Wright scored on a 60-yard reception in the first period and on a 66-yard end-around play in the third quarter. Eleven players accounted for Houston's 14 touchdowns, with eight of the TDs coming on rushing plays, four on passes, one on an interception return and one on a punt return. The Cougars finished with 762 yards in total offense.

Supporting Cast:

● **Ken Bailey.** Houston quarterback who fired the TD pass to Wright and also made a one-yard touchdown run (in the second quarter) as the Cougars built a 24-0 halftime lead.

● **Carlos Bell.** Cougar halfback whose 21-yard scoring run in the third quarter marked the start of Houston's second-half touchdown spree. By the end of the third period, the Cougars led, 51-6.

● **Ted Heiskell.** His two-yard run netted Houston its first fourth-quarter touchdown.

● **Terry Leiweke.** His 13th extra-point kick of the night (in 14 attempts) gave Houston its 100th point. Leiweke also kicked a 36-yard field goal in the second quarter.

● **Johnny Peacock.** Houston defender who went 34 yards to a touchdown on a fourth-quarter interception return.

● **Mike Simpson.** With 22 seconds remaining in the game, Simpson scored on a 58-yard punt return to bring the Cougars' point total to 99.

● **Otis Stewart.** He caught the first of Clark's TD passes, a 19-yarder. Jim Strong and Larry Gatlin accounted for the other two with 28- and 26-yard scoring receptions, respectively.

In the 1967 meeting between Houston and Tulsa, the Golden Hurricane had scored a 22-13 victory.

A week before its 100-point outburst in 1968, Houston had rung up 793 yards in total offense and overwhelmed Idaho, 77-3.

KANSAS HAS ONE TOO MANY

With 1 minute, 16 seconds remaining in the January 1, 1969, Orange Bowl and unbeaten Penn State trailing Kansas, 14-7, Nittany Lions quarterback Chuck Burkhart hooked up with halfback Bob Campbell on a 47-yard pass that put the ball on the Jayhawks' 3-yard line. Kansas then altered its defense—and how—with one less player leaving the game than entering the contest. Fullback Tom Cherry took two cracks at the Kansas defense, but was repulsed for no gain on both plays. Burkhart prepared to hand off again, but he saw an opening and burst three yards into the end zone with 15 seconds left in the game. Burkhart then attempted to pass to Campbell for a two-point conversion, but the Jayhawks' defense—not lacking for manpower at this point—bottled up the intended receiver. Kansas fans breathed a sigh of relief; their team had held on, 14-13. Hold it. A flag had been thrown. Illegal procedure, Kansas. Too many men on the field. Given a reprieve, and with the ball now moved half the distance to the goal line, Penn State collected the game-winning conversion points as Campbell cracked 1½ yards over the left side. Penn State 15, Kansas 14.

Supporting Cast:

● **Rick Abernethy.** Kansas' 12th man (apparently)—and for three plays, no one noticed. "Nobody 'tapped' me out," said Abernethy, referring to the routine by which an incoming player notifies an on-field player of his removal from the game. "Everything was mass confusion at that point. Penn State was running a hurry-up offense . . . it was total pandemonium." Finally, on Kansas' fourth play in a 12-man defensive alignment, the officials spotted the transgression. While Abernethy time and again has been cited as the 12th man—a designation he heretofore never has disputed—a recent re-studying of the game films raises at least some doubt. Considering the tumult on the Jayhawks' sideline after Penn State hit on the long pass and the subsequent mix of Kansas players on the field (as revealed by the films), it now seems possible that Abernethy may not have acted alone in the defensive foul-up and that he might not have erred at all, depending upon the defensive formation that was called. But since no one involved in the play—coaches or players—can say definitively which defensive alignment was called, Abernethy continues to live with his 12th-man status (perhaps unjustly, perhaps not).

● **Charlie Pittman.** His 13-yard touchdown run and Bob Garthwaite's extra-point kick earned Penn State a 7-7 tie in the second quarter. Pittman's number also was called for the play on which Burkhart netted a TD with his improvised run.

● **Mike Reeves.** Kansas player who ran two yards for a touchdown in the first period. Bill Bell added the conversion kick. The Jayhawks had gained possession on a Pat Hutchens interception.

The picture's a little fuzzy, but it clearly shows that Kansas (white jerseys) did indeed have 12 players on the field during the closing moments of the 1969 Orange Bowl.

● **Mike Reid.** Penn State defensive tackle whose two sacks of quarterback Bobby Douglass forced a Kansas punting situation (which proved crucial) at the Jayhawks' 25 late in the game.

● **John Riggins.** After Donnie Shanklin's 40-yard punt return had thrust Kansas into scoring position, fullback Riggins went one yard for a TD with 12:38 left in the fourth quarter. Bell's conversion made it Jayhawks 14, Nittany Lions 7. Five minutes later, with Kansas maintaining its seven-point lead, Riggins was stopped short on a fourth-and-one play at the Penn State 5 as Kansas Coach Pepper Rodgers eschewed a field-goal attempt.

● **Neal Smith.** On Kansas' fourth-and-three play from the Jayhawks' 25 with the game clock inside the 2-minute mark, Penn State's Smith partially blocked a Bell punt and the ball rolled dead at midfield. Burkhart then unloaded his bomb to Campbell.

The triumph in Miami was the first bowl victory for Penn State Coach Joe Paterno, who was completing his third season as the Nittany Lions' coach.

SHOWDOWN IN FAYETTEVILLE

Unbeaten Texas, riding an 18-game winning streak, was ranked No. 1 in both wire-service polls entering its December 6, 1969, showdown against Arkansas at Fayetteville, Ark. The Razorbacks, also undefeated and enjoying a 15-game victory string, were rated No. 2 in the Associated Press poll and No. 3 (behind Penn State) in the United Press International rankings. Texas, facing a 14-0 deficit entering the fourth quarter, fought back for a 15-14 triumph over Arkansas as Longhorns Coach Darrell Royal contributed two key calls in the dramatic regular-season finale.

Supporting Cast:

• **Bill Burnett.** Less than 2 minutes into the game, which was attended by President Nixon, Arkansas' Burnett scored on a one-yard run and Bill McClard added the extra point. The touchdown was set up when run-oriented Texas fumbled on its 22-yard line on the second play of the game.

• **Bill Montgomery.** His 29-yard scoring pass to Chuck Dicus and McClard's conversion kick boosted Arkansas' lead to 14-0 in the third period. The Razorbacks, shutting down Texas' wishbone offense (the Longhorns had averaged 44 points per game), had gained possession on a Longhorn fumble at the Arkansas 47.

• **James Street.** Texas quarterback who got the Longhorns back into the game on the first play of the fourth quarter, shaking free for a 42-yard touchdown dash. Street then ran for two points. "We felt that was the time for the two-point conversion," said Royal, who had called for extra-point kicks after every other Longhorn TD of the '69 season. "If we had missed it, we could have still gone for two again and gotten a tie. But if we had kicked after the first touchdown and gone for two after the second, then the pressure is really on us."

• **Danny Lester.** Texas defender whose interception killed an Arkansas drive after the Razorbacks, their lead whittled to 14-8, had driven to the Longhorns' 8.

• **Randy Peschel.** On a fourth-and-three play at Texas' 43 with 4 minutes, 47 seconds left in the game, Street stunned the Arkansas defense by throwing deep and hitting Peschel on a 44-yard completion that carried to the Razorbacks' 13. "Every now and then you have to . . . pick a number," Royal said of his second critical call. "You don't use logic and reason. You just play a hunch. I never considered punting."

• **Jim Bertelsen.** After Texas' Ted Koy followed Peschel's clutch reception with an 11-yard run, Bertelsen went two yards for the game-tying touchdown. Happy Feller kicked the extra point, pushing the Longhorns ahead by one point with 3:58 remaining in the battle for the Southwest Conference championship and a shot at the national title.

• **Tom Campbell.** Longhorn player who foiled Arkansas' last-gasp hopes. Montgomery marched the Razorbacks from their 20 to the Texas 39 in the closing minutes and then tried to hit Dicus on a second-down pass. But Campbell slipped in front of the Arkansas receiver and intercepted the ball with 1:22 showing on the clock.

Texas nailed down the 1969 national championship by defeating Notre Dame, 21-17, in the January 1, 1970, Cotton Bowl and stretching its record to 11-0. Arkansas dipped to 9-2 after suffering a 27-22 loss to Mississippi in the Sugar Bowl.

Freddie Steinmark, Texas defensive back who intercepted two passes during the 1969 season, complained of leg soreness during the year and, with the pain increasing, went to the team doctor after playing in the Longhorns-Razorbacks game. Steinmark was sent to a hospital in Houston, where doctors discovered cancer. Steinmark's left leg was amputated six days after the game in Fayetteville.

Freddie Steinmark, the Texas player who had his leg amputated late in the 1969 season, toured the Astrodome 11 days after the operation was performed in Houston. The Astrodome message board saluted the honored guest.

Texas quarterback James Street talks strategy with Longhorn Coach Darrell Royal as the scoreboard reflects their late-game plight in the 1970 Cotton Bowl.

COTTON'S CLASSIC

Coming up with the key play of the game, Texas' Cotton Speyrer made a tumbling fourth-down catch of a James Street pass late in the fourth quarter of the 1970 Cotton Bowl as the No. 1-ranked Longhorns overcame Notre Dame, 21-17. The Fighting Irish, playing their first bowl game in 45 years and sky-high after Joe Theismann's 54-yard touchdown strike to Tom Gatewood, led 10-0 in the second period and seized a 17-14 edge in the final quarter. Texas, though, went on a 76-yard drive highlighted by a fourth-and-two play at the Notre Dame 10-yard line. On that play, Street underthrew Speyrer, but the Longhorns' receiver made a desperate grass-level catch at the 2. Billy Dale got the game-winning touchdown, going in from a yard out with 1 minute, 8 seconds remaining, and Happy Feller kicked the extra point.

Supporting Cast:

● **Jim Bertelsen, Ted Koy.** Bertelsen's one-yard scoring run and Feller's conversion kick brought the Longhorns within 10-7 at halftime, while Koy's three-yard touchdown burst and a Feller PAT put Texas ahead, 14-10, in the fourth quarter.

● **Tom Campbell.** Texas defender who snuffed out Notre Dame's last opportunity by intercepting a Theismann pass at the Longhorns' 14 in the final half-minute of the game.

● **Freddie Steinmark.** Cheering on the Longhorns from the sidelines, Texas' ailing defensive back was the recipient of the game ball. Steinmark had undergone amputation of his cancerous left leg three weeks earlier. (Steinmark died on June 6, 1971.)

● **Jim Yoder.** His touchdown reception (24 yards from Theismann) and Scott Hempel's extra-point kick enabled the Irish to take a three-point edge in the fourth quarter. Hempel also converted after Gatewood's second-period touchdown and booted a 26-yard field goal in the opening quarter.

NEBRASKA VS. OKLAHOMA, 1971

It was called the "Game of the Century." And this was before the phrase began popping up on sports pages every two or three years. The November 25, 1971, game in Norman, Okla., matched No. 1-ranked Nebraska, averaging 38.9 points per game that season and riding a 29-game unbeaten streak overall, against high-powered Oklahoma, whose No. 2 national rating was built largely by a scoring machine that had ground out 45 points per contest. If a key difference existed between the clubs, it was on defense. Entering the Thanksgiving Day game, Oklahoma's bend-but-won't-break Sooners had yielded 16.2 points per game in '71 while rolling to a 9-0 record. On the other hand, Nebraska's virtually impregnable Cornhuskers, 10-0, had permitted only 6.4 points per game. Coach Bob Devaney's Husker defense was dented in this game, however, as the Sooners racked up 467 yards in total offense, scored in every period and managed leads of 17-14 (halftime) and 31-28 (midway through the fourth quarter). But the Cornhuskers withstood the assault. Running back Jeff Kinney, who finished the day with four touchdowns and 174 yards rushing (on 30 carries), crashed into the end zone from two yards out with 1 minute, 38 seconds left in the game to cap a 74-yard drive. The extra-point kick made it Nebraska 35, Oklahoma 31. While the Sooners got the ball back—that fact seemed to bode well for Coach Chuck Fairbanks' team, considering the scoring-fest nature of the game—Oklahoma failed to move the ball in its final possession.

Supporting Cast:

● **John Carroll.** Oklahoma placekicker whose 30-yard field goal cut Nebraska's lead to 7-3 in the first quarter. Carroll was four for four on conversion kicks.

● **Rich Glover.** Nebraska middle guard who batted down a pass on Oklahoma's last offensive play of the game, a fourth-and-14 situation from the Sooners' 15-yard line. With 1:10 left in the game, Nebraska took over and proceeded to run out the clock.

● **Jon Harrison.** Oklahoma wide receiver who provided the Sooners with their two leads of the game. With Nebraska ahead, 14-10, in the final seconds of the first half, Harrison caught a 24-yard touchdown pass. Then, with the Cornhuskers in front, 28-24, Harrison latched on to a 16-yard scoring pass with 7:10 to play in the fourth quarter.

● **Jack Mildren.** Sooner quarterback who threw both of the touchdown passes to Harrison and ran for two scores. After Kinney's one-yard TD smash and a conversion kick had lifted Nebraska to a 14-3 lead in the second quarter, Mildren scampered two yards for a touchdown later in the period. And after Kinney had scored on runs of three yards and one yard in the third period as Nebraska seized a 28-17 lead, Mildren ran three yards for a Sooner TD in the final half-minute of the quarter. Despite Mildren's big day, Oklahoma's hopes died when a Mildren pass was knocked away by Glover in the game's last 70 seconds.

● **Greg Pruitt.** Oklahoma All-America running back who averaged 9.4 yards per carry overall in 1971 but was limited to 53 yards rushing on 10 attempts by the Husker defense.

● **Johnny Rodgers.** Nebraska standout who scored the first points of the game on an electrifying note, bolting 72 yards on a first-quarter punt return. Rodgers also turned in a key play on the Huskers' game-winning drive, making a diving, fingertip grab of a Jerry Tagge pass on a third-and-eight play from the Sooners' 46. The completion, good for 11 yards, came with 4:37 left in the fourth quarter and Nebraska trailing by three points. Kinney then covered 28 of the remaining 35 yards on five carries, with Rodgers netting the other seven yards on a reverse.

● **Rich Sanger.** He went five for five on Nebraska PAT attempts as the Huskers won their 21st consecutive game.

TIMELY CATCH FOR IRISH

Robin Weber had caught only one pass for Notre Dame in the 1973 regular season. But Weber's number was called in the waning moments of the December 31, 1973, Sugar Bowl as Notre Dame, ranked third in the Associated Press' pre-bowl ratings, tried to protect a 24-23 lead over top-ranked Alabama. On a third-and-eight play from his 3-yard line, Notre Dame quarterback Tom Clements—knowing that Coach Paul (Bear) Bryant's Crimson Tide would get the ball in good field position if the Fighting Irish were forced to punt—retreated into his end zone and hit Weber with a pass at the Notre Dame 38. The Irish then ran out the clock. Coach Ara Parseghian's unbeaten and untied Notre Dame team, which achieved the victory on Bob Thomas' 19-yard field goal with 4 minutes, 26 seconds remaining in the game, rode the triumph to the No. 1 ranking in AP's final poll.

Supporting Cast:

● **Randy Billingsley.** His six-yard touchdown run and Bill Davis' extra-point kick put Alabama ahead, 7-6, in the second quarter after the Irish had scored in the first period on Wayne Bullock's six-yard blast.

● **Greg Gantt.** Crimson Tide player whose 69-yard punt backed Notre Dame to its 1 in the game's closing minutes.

● **Al Hunter.** His 93-yard kickoff return for a touchdown and a Clements-to-Pete Demmerle conversion pass thrust the Irish into a 14-7 second-period lead.

● **Wilbur Jackson.** After closing within 14-10 in the second quarter on Davis' 39-yard field goal, Alabama went in front in the third period on Jackson's five-yard run. Davis converted.

● **Mike Stock.** Trailing 21-17 after Notre Dame had struck on Eric Penick's 12-yard TD run in the third period (Thomas added the conversion), Alabama slipped ahead, 23-21, in the final quarter when halfback Stock took the ball from quarterback Richard Todd and then threw to Todd on a 25-yard scoring play. The extra-point kick was wide. The Irish rebounded, though, with a 79-yard drive that led to Thomas' game-winning field goal.

TROJANS' BLITZ BURIES IRISH

With less than 1 minute remaining in the first half of the November 30, 1974, game at the Los Angeles Memorial Coliseum between Notre Dame and Southern California, the Irish enjoyed a 24-0 lead over the Trojans. Southern Cal then struck with devastating, if not unprecedented, force. The Trojans proceeded to score 55 consecutive points in only 17 minutes of game action —John McKay's team outscored Ara Parseghian's Notre Dame team, 49-0, in the second half—as USC battered an Irish squad that had ranked No. 1 nationally in total defense and allowed only nine TDs in 10 previous games. Tailback Anthony Davis started the Trojans on the way to their 55-24 triumph, scoring on a seven-yard pass from Pat Haden in the closing seconds of the first half.

Supporting Cast:

● **Wayne Bullock.** He scored the first points of the game, running two yards for a Notre Dame touchdown in the first quarter.

● **Pete Demmerle.** With the first period not quite half over, Demmerle caught a 29-yard scoring pass from Irish quarterback Tom Clements.

● **Dave Reeve.** Irish placekicker who booted a 20-yard field goal early in he second quarter, giving Notre Dame a 17-0 advantage, and converted after all three Notre Dame touchdowns.

● **Mark McLane.** His nine-yard run in the second period proved to be Notre Dame's last TD of the game.

● **Anthony Davis.** After his TD reception left USC trailing, 24-6, at halftime, Davis returned the second-half kickoff 100 yards for a touchdown to draw USC within 24-12. He then scored on a six-yard burst and, with Chris Limahelu's placement netting USC its first conversion point of the day, USC crept to a 24-19 deficit. Davis notched his fourth TD of the game later in the third period (after the Irish had lost the ball on a fumble at their 31), scoring on a four-yard sprint that shot the Trojans ahead, 25-24. Davis then darted in for a two-point conversion run.

● **Johnny (J.K.) McKay.** Son of the USC coach, McKay collected the Trojans' fourth and fifth TDs of the third period—No. 4 was set up by Marvin Cobb's 56-yard punt return—when he took 18- and 45-yard passes from Haden. Limahelu converted after both scores as Southern Cal boosted its lead to 41-24.

● **Shelton Diggs.** After Notre Dame fumbled away the ball at the outset of the fourth quarter, Diggs caught Haden's fourth touchdown pass of the day (a 16-yard strike).

● **Charles Phillips.** USC defensive back who accounted for the last TD of the game, going 58 yards on an interception return early in the fourth period. Limahelu's extra-point kick, his fifth of the game, completed the scoring onslaught.

SOONERS 82, BUFFALOES 42

With approximately 3½ minutes remaining in the first quarter of Oklahoma's October 4, 1980, game against Colorado, the Sooners held a 7-0 lead over the Buffaloes in a seemingly ordinary college football game. But what transpired in an ensuing 8-minute, 25-second span—and during the rest of the game—was not typical at all. Oklahoma and Colorado erupted for five touchdowns in a surge that started with Sooner halfback Buster Rhymes' 15-yard scoring run with 3:17 to play in the first quarter and ended with Rhymes' 17-yard TD sprint with 9:52 left in the second period. The offensive fireworks set the tone for the day as Oklahoma went on to outscore Colorado, 82-42, in Boulder, Colo., with the 124 points making the contest the highest-scoring game in major-college history. The Sooners set a national mark with 758 yards rushing (on 73 attempts) and rolled to 875 yards in total offense (also a record, but since broken by Nebraska). Coach Barry Switzer's team posted quarter leads of 21-7, 34-21 and 61-28.

Supporting Cast:

● **Willie Beebe.** After Rhymes bolted 18 yards for a touchdown on the final play of the first quarter, Colorado's Beebe ran two yards for a TD to start the second-period scoring. Tom Field then kicked the second of his six consecutive extra points for the Buffaloes.

● **Charlie Davis.** Colorado quarterback who fired touchdown passes to Reggie Harden (10 yards, second quarter) and Steve Jones (17 yards, fourth period).

● **Randy Essington.** He passed for a Colorado touchdown in the third period and ran one yard for a TD in the final quarter. Rhymes' fourth TD run of the day, a four-yarder with 35 seconds left in the third period, was sandwiched between Essington's scoring plays.

● **Jerome Ledbetter.** He scored the 18th and last touchdown of the game, going 99 yards for Oklahoma on a fourth-quarter kickoff return. Michael Keeling followed with his 10th conversion kick.

● **David Overstreet.** Sooner halfback who rushed for 258 yards on 18 carries but scored his only TD of the game on a 37-yard pass from J.C. Watts in the third period.

● **Rod Pegues.** He ran 43 yards for an Oklahoma touchdown in the fourth quarter. Overall, the Sooners made nine of their 12 TDs on the ground.

● **Darrell Shepard.** Sooner quarterback who reeled off a 64-yard scoring run in the third period and broke loose on an 89-yard TD jaunt in the fourth quarter.

● **Walter Stanley.** The Buffaloes' big-play man, Stanley returned a first-quarter kickoff 100 yards for a touchdown and was on the receiving end of Essington's scoring bomb (a 58-yarder).

● **Forrest Valora.** Sooner tight end who scored the first points of the third quarter, recovering teammate Watts' fumble in the end zone.

● **Chet Winters.** He began the scoring explosion with a two-yard TD run for Oklahoma with 10:29 left in the first quarter. Winters also ran eight yards for a second-period touchdown.

TIPTOEING THROUGH THE TUBAS

Four seconds remained in the tradition-laden Big Game when Stanford, which had just seized a 20-19 lead, kicked off to California in their November 20, 1982, clash at Memorial Stadium in Berkeley, Calif. Nothing short of a

California's Kevin Moen dances into the end zone with the winning touchdown as startled Stanford band members reflect the state of confusion that reigned at the close of the wild 1982 clash in Berkeley, Calif.

touchdown on the kickoff return could save the Golden Bears on this day. Nurturing a pipe dream but hardly expecting a miracle, Coach Joe Kapp's California squad watched as the squib kick sailed downfield toward . . .

● **Kevin Moen.** California player who took the final-play kickoff at the Golden Bears' 43-yard line. After an advance of about 10 yards and a brush with the Stanford pursuit, Moen threw an overhand lateral near the left sideline.

● **Richard Rodgers.** Cal player who caught Moen's lateral at the Cardinal 48. After a short run, Rodgers also lateraled the ball in an effort to keep the Golden Bears' faint hopes alive.

● **Dwight Garner.** Cal player who latched on to Rodgers' lateral at the Stanford 44. While falling to the ground—Cardinal fans claimed he should have been ruled down on the play—Garner flipped the ball back to the Stanford 48, where Rodgers just happened to be.

● **Rodgers (again).** With the ball in his grasp, Rodgers cut toward the middle of the field and then let fly with another lateral.

● **Mariet Ford.** Cal player who tucked in Rodgers' second lateral at the Stanford 46. Ford raced downfield but encountered Cardinal defenders at the 25. What to do? Ford lateraled, of course, but did so in a highly irregular fashion. Running at full speed, he tossed the ball blindly over his right shoulder, hoping against hope that someone in a blue Golden Bear jersey just might be there.

● **Moen (again).** Ford's hopes were realized, as Moen was in position to take the ball. Football in hand, Moen set off for the end zone.

• **Stanford band.** Prematurely on the field, the helmeted music-makers—much to their chagrin—provided a corridor of sorts for Moen by screening off potential tacklers. Moen burst through the band, knocking a trombone player to the ground, and scored. Five laterals. A touchdown. Miracles do happen. Final score: California 25, Stanford 20. (The play-by-play account of the game, a usually dry, nothing-but-the-facts recounting of the day's events, chronicled the feasibility of—and the need for—the extra-point attempt this way: "Are you kidding?")

Supporting Cast:

• **Joe Cooper.** California placekicker who made a 30-yard field goal in the second period and tacked on the extra point after Gale Gilbert's 29-yard touchdown pass to Ford later in that quarter as Cal built a 10-0 halftime bulge. Then, with Stanford on top at 14-10, Cooper delivered a 35-yard field goal early in the fourth period.

• **Vincent White.** Stanford player who caught touchdown passes of two and 43 yards in the third period as the Cardinal overcame California's halftime edge.

• **Wes Howell.** His catch of a 32-yard Gilbert TD pass lifted California into a 19-14 lead with 11 minutes, 24 seconds left in the final quarter.

• **John Elway.** Stanford quarterback who passed for 330 yards and two touchdowns in the Big Game. With California ahead, 19-17, late in the fourth quarter, he rifled a 29-yard pass to Emile Harry on a fourth-and-17 play from his 13 and proceeded to drive the Cardinal to the Cal 18 with 8 seconds to play in the game. At that point, Elway asked for a timeout.

• **Mark Harmon.** Stanford placekicker whose 22-yard field goal with 5:32 remaining in the fourth quarter reduced California's lead to 19-17. After Elway called time in the closing seconds of the game, Harmon went in and booted a 35-yarder that put Stanford in front, 20-19, with 4 seconds left and apparently wrapped up the game for the visitors. Stanford players poured on the field to congratulate Harmon and, as a result, Coach Paul Wiggin's team was assessed a penalty on the ensuing kickoff for unsportsmanlike conduct (delay of game). Because of the infraction, Harmon (who also had two conversion kicks in the game) was forced to kick off from his 25.

• **Gary Tyrrell.** The trombone player who was run over by Moen. Also felled was Scott DeBarger, a tenor-saxophone player.

The game's stunning final play was allowed to stand—despite both sides' cries of irregularities (some of which were substantiated but overlooked because of the confusion)—and went into the books as a 57-yard kickoff return by Moen, with a little help from his friends. The Big Play in the Big Game was the final play in the collegiate football careers for two of the four Cal players who handled the ball on the return—Moen, a senior defensive back, and Ford, a senior wide receiver.

MIAMI SOARS TO NO. 1

The 1983 Miami Hurricanes had accomplished plenty before their January 2, 1984, Orange Bowl game against No. 1-ranked Nebraska. A 25-point loser to Florida in its '83 opener, Miami went on to compile a 10-game winning streak preceding the bowl game and rose to a No. 4 ranking in United Press International's poll and a No. 5 rating on the Associated Press' list. Coach Howard Schnellenberger's Miami team wasn't about to rest on its laurels, though; the Hurricanes were thinking No. 1. While a matchup with the Cornhuskers, 12-0 in '83 and riding a 22-game winning streak overall, obviously would give Miami a shot at the top spot, the Hurricanes also needed some help on January 2. And they received it. Georgia upset previously unbeaten and second-ranked Texas in the Cotton Bowl, and UCLA pummeled Illinois in the Rose Bowl (the Illini were rated fourth on the AP chart, just ahead of Miami). That night, as the Hurricanes challenged Nebraska before a tumultuous crowd in Miami's home stadium, No. 3 Auburn took on Michigan in the Sugar Bowl. Auburn won, but the Tigers didn't overwhelm anyone with an offense that produced only three field goals. Miami, meanwhile, was clinging to a 31-24 lead in the Orange Bowl when Nebraska's Jeff Smith, on a fourth-and-eight play, bolted 24 yards to a touchdown with 48 seconds left in the game. Huskers Coach Tom Osborne then opted for a two-point conversion attempt—although a tie surely would have clinched the national title for the Big Eight Conference champions—and quarterback Turner Gill aimed a pass toward Smith. Defensive back Ken Calhoun, making the biggest play in Hurricane football history, moved in and knocked the ball out of Smith's hands. The Orange Bowl rocked. Miami 31, Nebraska 30.

Supporting Cast:

● **Bernie Kosar.** Miami's freshman quarterback who passed two and 22 yards to Glenn Dennison for first-period touchdowns and threw for 300 yards overall. Jeff Davis sandwiched a 45-yard field goal between the scoring passes as Miami, an 11-point underdog, jolted Nebraska by seizing a 17-0 first-quarter lead.

● **Ed Brown.** Hurricane receiver who caught six passes that night for 115 yards.

● **Dean Steinkuhler.** Nebraska's Outland Trophy-winning guard who got the Huskers on the scoreboard in the second period via a piece of Osborne gimmickry. Gill pretended to tuck in the snap from center on Miami's 19-yard line, but let the ball fall to the ground as he faked a rollout to the right. Steinkuhler picked up the "fumble" and lumbered into the end zone.

● **Scott Livingston.** After making the extra-point kick that followed a one-yard touchdown run by Gill in the second period, Livingston drew Nebraska even at 17-17 with a 34-yard field goal early in the third quarter. He was three for three on PAT attempts overall.

● **Alonzo Highsmith.** His one-yard burst—which capped a 10-play, 75-yard Hurricane march—and Davis' PAT produced a 24-17 Miami lead in the third period.

● **Albert Bentley.** Miami player whose seven-yard run culminated a six-play, 73-yard drive in the third quarter. After Davis drilled his fourth extra point of the night, Miami was ahead, 31-17, with 4 minutes, 44 seconds remaining in the period.

● **Mike Rozier.** The 1983 Heisman Trophy winner, Rozier gained 147 yards on 25 rushes before leaving the game late in the third quarter because of an ankle injury. His replacement, Smith, ran for 99 yards and two TDs, with both scores coming in the final quarter as Nebraska sliced Miami's advantage from 14 points to one. Smith went one yard to end a 76-yard march and his 24-yard jaunt completed a 74-yard Husker drive.

The day after the January 2, 1984, bowl games, both wire-service polls voted Miami No. 1 for the 1983 season. Nebraska was rated second and Auburn third.

FLUTIE VS. KOSAR

"You put the ball in the end zone," explained Doug Flutie, Boston College's quarterback and miracle worker. "We've got a couple guys down there, they've got a couple guys down there, (and) you see who comes up with it." On the last play of Boston College's November 23, 1984, game against Miami (Florida), the Eagles' Gerard Phelan was the player who came up with it—and the 48-yard touchdown pass lifted Flutie and company to a 47-45 victory over the stunned Hurricanes on a rainy, windy Friday afternoon at the Orange Bowl. Flutie and Miami quarterback Bernie Kosar brightened a dreary day—to say the least. In remarkable performances, Flutie completed 34 of 46 passes for 472 yards and three touchdowns and Kosar hit on 25 of 38 attempts for 447 yards and two TDs (the Hurricanes' standout yielded two interceptions, while Flutie suffered none). There was some impressive running, too, as exemplified by Miami's Melvin Bratton, who rushed for 134 yards and four touchdowns on the soggy turf. Bratton seemingly had won the game for the Hurricanes when, with Boston College ahead, 41-38, he ran one yard for a TD with 28 seconds to play. But Flutie proceeded to whisk his team 80 yards downfield, with his scrambling "prayer" pass to Phelan actually covering 64 yards in the air.

Supporting Cast:

● **Kelvin Martin.** Boston College receiver who scored the first points of the game, catching a 33-yard touchdown pass from Flutie in the first quarter. Ken Bell also collected an opening-period TD (on five-yard run) for the Eagles, who took a 14-7 edge into the second quarter.

● **Willie Smith, Warren Williams.** Miami players who scored second-period touchdowns on 10- and eight-yard passes from Kosar. However, the 5-foot-9¾ Flutie sandwiched a nine-yard touchdown scamper between Kosar's TD throws and then fired a 10-yard scoring strike to Phelan as Boston College built a 28-21 halftime lead. (Phelan finished the day with 11 catches for 226 yards and two TDs.)

● **Greg Cox, Kevin Snow.** After Bratton's two-yard run and a conversion kick had enabled Miami to tie the score in the third quarter, the Hurricanes' Cox and the Eagles' Snow traded field goals later in the period and the teams entered the final quarter in a 31-31 deadlock.

● **Steve Strachan.** With Boston College having fallen behind, 38-34, in the fourth quarter (Bratton went sideline to sideline on a 52-yard touchdown run as Miami seized the lead following a Snow field goal), Strachan sent the Eagles back in front with a one-yard scoring burst.

Eight days after the drama in Miami, Flutie was awarded the Heisman Trophy in New York.

FIRST QUARTER—PRO

MEMORABLE GAMES IN PRO HISTORY

COMING IN OUT OF THE COLD

Since Super Bowl XII was played at New Orleans' Superdome in 1978, an indoors battle for the National Football League crown has not been a highly unusual occurrence. However, that '78 meeting between the Dallas Cowboys and the Denver Broncos was not the first indoor NFL championship game. Not by a long shot. The initial NFL title game played inside was contested in 1932 when snow and extreme cold forced the Chicago Bears to move their championship-deciding game against the Portsmouth Spartans from Wrigley Field to Chicago Stadium. Actually, it wasn't until the 1933 season that the NFL split into divisions and had a pre-planned title game between divisional champions. In '32, though, the Bears, 6-1-6, and Spartans, 6-1-4, dead-

49

The first indoor NFL championship game (between the Chicago Bears and Portsmouth Spartans) was played in Chicago Stadium in 1932 because of snow and extreme cold. Because of the tight quarters, the teams competed on an 80-yard-long field with goal posts positioned on the goal line.

locked for the regular-season crown (ties were thrown out) and squared off on December 18 to settle the issue. Dirt was already down on the Chicago Stadium playing surface, as a circus had just been staged at the arena. The tight quarters permitted only an 80-yard-long field (some observers questioned whether it was that long), with the goal posts being moved from the end line to the goal line, and the playing conditions necessitated the drawing up of special rules, including one that moved the ball laterally toward midfield when plays ended close to the sidelines (thus decreasing the threat of player contact with the nearby walls). As 11,198 fans watched—the crowd might not have been half that large if the game had been played outdoors—the teams fought through three scoreless periods. Coach Ralph Jones' Bears finally broke through on a Bronko Nagurski touchdown pass and wound up winning, 9-0.

Supporting Cast:

●**Dutch Clark.** Portsmouth's star player who missed the game because he was tending to his job as Colorado College basketball coach.

●**Tiny Engebretsen.** He made Chicago's extra point after Nagurski's scoring pass.

●**Red Grange.** On a hotly disputed fourth-quarter play, Grange shook free in the end zone and caught Nagurski's TD pass as the Bears made good on a fourth-and-goal situation. Nagurski, who had run six yards on a first-and-goal play from Portsmouth's 7-yard line and then was stopped for no gain on the next two plays, started forward on fourth down in another apparent attempt to rush for a touchdown. However, Nagurski suddenly put on the brakes, dropped back a few steps and lofted the ball over the line and into Grange's hands in the end zone. At the time, NFL rules stipulated that passes had to come from at least five yards behind the line of scrimmage. Portsmouth Coach Potsy Clark protested that Nagurski hadn't retreated to the specified distance, but the officials upheld the play.

● **Dick Nesbitt.** Bears defender who set up Chicago's touchdown by intercepting an Ace Gutowsky pass and returning it to the Spartans' 7.

● **Mule Wilson.** Portsmouth player who fumbled center Clare Randolph's pass out of the end zone late in the final period, with the safety accounting for the Bears' last two points.

The Chicago Stadium game obviously had a major impact on the NFL rules-makers. In 1933, the league adopted the hashmark innovation of the Chicago-Portsmouth contest ("the ball will be moved in 10 yards to the hashmarks or inbounds lines whenever it is in play within five yards of the sidelines") and also decided to position the goal posts at the goal line. And in 1934, league rules were changed to permit pass attempts from any spot beyond the line of scrimmage.

THE 'SNEAKERS GAME'

The Chicago Bears, who had compiled a 13-0 regular-season record, enjoyed a 10-3 halftime lead over the New York Giants in the 1934 National Football League championship game played in bitterly cold weather at the Polo Grounds. Having defeated the Giants twice during the regular season, the Bears seemingly were on their way to a third straight NFL title. The playing conditions were frightful, though, with a frozen field making maneuverability extremely difficult and thus lessening—at least to some degree—Chicago's acknowledged superiority over New York. Both teams were slipping and sliding on the icy turf, but the talent-rich Bears still had the upper hand. New York, which had struggled to an 8-5 record in the regular season, knew when the day dawned that it would have to come up with a game-breaker to have a chance against the Bears. And the Giants came up with just such a man—their part-time clubhouse attendant. Final score: Giants 30, Bears 13.

Supporting Cast:

● **Bronko Nagurski.** With New York ahead, 3-0, after one quarter, Nagurski's one-yard touchdown run in the second period sent Chicago into the lead.

● **Jack Manders.** He converted after Nagurski's TD, kicked a 17-yard field goal later in the second quarter and then booted a 22-yarder in the third period as the Bears built a 13-3 edge heading into the fourth quarter.

● **Ray Flaherty.** Giants captain who, on the morning of the December 9 game, suggested to Coach Steve Owen that the New York team wear basketball shoes against the Bears for better traction. Flaherty said his college team, Gonzaga, had used sneakers successfully under similar conditions.

● **Abe Cohen.** After Flaherty, Owen, trainer Gus Mauch and other Giants personnel had discussed the sneakers idea, Cohen, the 5-foot clubhouse assistant, was dispatched to Manhattan College to gather the shoes. He made it back to the Polo Grounds by halftime, during which most of the Giants' regulars made the switch to the basketball footwear.

● **Ike Frankian.** While the sneakers-clad Giants failed to get untracked in the third period, their improved footing took hold in the fourth quarter as Frankian got into position to snare a 28-yard scoring pass. The conversion kick cut the Bears' lead to 13-10.

● **Ken Strong.** Being able to traverse the icy field significantly better now, Strong followed Frankian's touchdown catch with TD runs of 42 and 11 yards as New York vaulted into a 23-13 advantage. Strong, who made two extra points in the game, also kicked a 38-yard field goal for New York in the first period.

● **Ed Danowski.** He ran nine yards for the Giants' final TD, with Bo Molenda capping New York's 27-0 fourth-period blitz by tacking on the conversion kick. Danowski also fired the TD strike to Frankian.

● **Beattie Feathers, Harry Newman, Morris (Red) Badgro.** Key players who missed the game because of injuries. The Bears' Feathers was the NFL's leading rusher in 1934; Newman was New York's No. 1 passer, and Badgro was the Giants' top receiver.

BEARS 73, REDSKINS 0

Having lost to the Redskins, 7-3, three weeks earlier in a regular-season game and then called "crybabies" in Washington because of their complaints over the officiating in that contest, the Bears were in a testy mood when they took the field at Washington's Griffith Stadium for their December 8, 1940, NFL title game against the Redskins. And it didn't take the Monsters of the Midway long to vent their hostilities. On the game's second play from scrimmage, Chicago's Bill Osmanski broke loose on a 68-yard scoring run. Quarterback Sid Luckman and fullback Joe Maniaci also scored first-quarter touchdowns for the Bears, Luckman going one yard and Maniaci traveling 42 yards as Chicago rolled to a 21-0 lead. Luckman then hit Ken Kavanaugh on a 30-yard scoring strike in the second period as the Bears, running the T-formation with a precision that would prompt other NFL clubs to adopt the attack, built a 28-0 halftime bulge en route to the most lopsided victory—championship, playoff or regular season—in NFL history.

Supporting Cast:

● **Bob Snyder.** Coach George Halas' Bears were successful on seven of their 11 extra-point attempts, with Snyder accounting for two of the conversions with kicks. Jack Manders, Phil Martinovich, Dick Plasman and Joe Stydahar also kicked extra points for Chicago, while Maniaci scored the seventh conversion on a pass from Solly Sherman. (Because of the number of footballs lost to the crowd on earlier PAT tries, the Bears were forced to pass on their last two conversion attempts to ensure the availability of a ball and the completion of the game.)

● **Hampton Pool, George McAfee, Bulldog Turner.** Chicago defenders who returned pass interceptions for touchdowns in the third quarter as the Bears erupted for four TDs in that period (halfback Ray Nolting also scored, on a. 23-yard run from scrimmage) and seized a 54-0 lead. Pool ran back his interception 15 yards, McAfee went 34 yards and Turner covered 21 yards.

Chicago Bears Owner-Coach George Halas (right) and quarterback Sid Luckman had plenty of reason to smile on December 8, 1940. The Bears were well on their way to a 73-0 thrashing of the Washington Redskins in that season's NFL championship game.

Overall, the Bears intercepted eight passes that day.

● **Harry Clark.** The Bears struck for three fourth-quarter touchdowns, with Clark scoring on 44- and one-yard runs and Gary Famiglietti sandwiching a two-yard TD burst between Clark's scores. Chicago's first 10 TDs of the afternoon were scored by different players before Clark became the lone repeater by notching the Bears' 11th and last touchdown of the game.

CLOUD OVER TITLE GAME

When Giants standout Frank Filchock first appeared on the field at the Polo Grounds for New York's December 15, 1946, National Football League championship game against the Chicago Bears, he was the target of boos from the hometown fans. In a stunning development, it had been disclosed earlier in the day that Filchock and teammate Merle Hapes were under investigation in connection with alleged bribery attempts. A gambler reportedly offered both players $2,500 if they would ensure that the Giants lost the title game by more than the 10 points by which Chicago was favored. Additionally, the players would benefit from the winnings of a $1,000 bet placed against the Giants and they also would gain lucrative off-season employment. Hapes admitted receiving the offer, but Filchock—New York's passing and rushing leader in '46—indicated to authorities that he had not been approached. Since Hapes acknowledged being contacted by the gambler but failed to report the incident to the league, NFL Commissioner Bert Bell barred the fullback from the '46 championship game; Filchock, whose involvement appeared peripheral at most, was permitted to play. And play he did. Despite not leaving an inquiry until the early-morning hours of game day and then suffering a broken nose in the first period, Filchock rallied the Giants from a two-touchdown deficit with first- and third-period scoring passes. Bloodied but unbowed, and victimized by six interceptions, Filchock battled throughout. But the Bears struck for 10 fourth-period points and won, 24-14.

Supporting Cast:

● **Steve Filipowicz.** After a scoreless second period, New York tied the score at 14-14 early in the third quarter when Filipowicz caught a five-yard touchdown pass from Filchock and Ken Strong added the conversion.

● **Ken Kavanaugh.** Bears receiver whose 21-yard scoring reception coupled with Frank Maznicki's extra-point kick gave Chicago a 7-0 lead in the first quarter.

● **Frank Liebel.** After Dante Magnani's 19-yard interception return and Maznicki's PAT had boosted Chicago to a 14-0 advantage, New York's Liebel caught a 38-yard touchdown pass from Filchock in the final 2 minutes of the first period and Strong kicked the conversion.

● **Sid Luckman.** Besides passing to Kavanaugh for Chicago's first TD, Luckman broke a 14-14 tie early in the fourth quarter by running 19 yards against the flow for a touchdown on a play in which he faked a handoff and hid the ball on his hip. Maznicki followed with a conversion kick and then booted a 26-yard field goal with about 5 minutes left in the game.

Bell suspended Filchock (who subsequently acknowledged that he, too, had received a bribe offer) and Hapes indefinitely for their impropriety in fail-

New York's Frank Filchock (40), playing under the cloud of a gambling investigation, is tackled by Chicago's Bulldog Turner (66) during the 1946 NFL championship game.

ing to report the offers. However, there was no evidence that either player had taken a bribe or in any way affected play on the field. In all, four gamblers were implicated in the case.

The NFL lifted Filchock's suspension in 1950 and ended Hapes' ban in 1954. Filchock, a standout in Canadian professional football during his banishment, attempted only three more passes in the NFL (with the '50 Baltimore Colts) once he was reinstated; Hapes never played again in the NFL.

HELLO, NATIONAL FOOTBALL LEAGUE

The Cleveland Browns had rung up a 47-4-3 regular-season record and captured four league titles in the four years of the All-America Football Conference's existence, but plenty of skeptics still remained in the pro football world. The AAFC, those non-believers said, was hardly of big-league caliber; the Browns surely were beating up on inferior competition. So, it was with considerable delight that National Football League backers took note of the 1950 NFL schedule. The first game of that schedule matched the Philadelphia Eagles, 1948 and 1949 NFL champions, against one of three AAFC teams absorbed by the NFL—the Cleveland Browns. Now, the truth would be known. "The Eagles may chase us off the gridiron, but we'll be on hand for the game with no alibis," Cleveland Coach Paul Brown said. It was on the night of September 16, 1950, in Philadelphia that the Browns showed up

55

Jubilant members of the Cleveland Browns celebrate their 1950 NFL championship game victory over the Rams. The Browns were coached by Paul Brown (foreground, white scarf) and quarterbacked by Otto Graham (standing, center, in white sweatshirt).

. . . and the upstart Cleveland team shot down the Eagles, 35-10. Quarterback Otto Graham baffled the Philadelphia defense, completing 21 of 38 passes for 346 yards and three touchdowns, and converted many fans in the throng of 71,237 into believers. The Eagles played without the injured Steve Van Buren, who had led the NFL in rushing in four of the five previous seasons.

Supporting Cast:

● **Rex Baumgardner.** Cleveland player who scored the game's final touchdown on a two-yard run in the fourth quarter. Chubby Grigg added the conversion kick, his fifth of the evening.

● **Dub Jones.** After Cliff Patton's 15-yard field goal had given Philadelphia a 3-0 lead, the Browns' Jones teamed with Graham on a 59-yard scoring pass in the first period.

● **Dante Lavelli.** Browns receiver who, with Cleveland ahead, 7-3, in the second quarter, caught a 26-yard touchdown pass from Graham.

● **Pete Pihos.** With Cleveland on top, 21-3, in the fourth quarter, Pihos scored the Eagles' lone TD of the game by hauling in a 17-yard pass from Bill Mackrides. Patton tacked on the extra point. The Browns rebounded, though, as Graham scored on a one-yard sneak and Baumgardner added his touchdown.

● **Mac Speedie.** In front at halftime, 14-3, Cleveland struck again in the third period when Graham connected with Speedie on a 13-yard scoring strike.

The Browns went on to compile a 10-2 regular-season record in their first

NFL season, beat the New York Giants in a playoff game and won the league championship by defeating the Los Angeles Rams. Cleveland, in fact, played in the NFL title game in its first six seasons in the league, adding '54 and '55 crowns to the one it collected in 1950.

VICTORY FOR COLTS, PRO FOOTBALL

When Baltimore's Alan Ameche burst into the end zone against the New York Giants after 8 minutes, 15 seconds had expired in the sudden-death period of the 1958 National Football League championship game, the touchdown ended a contest that ranks as perhaps the most important in pro football history. In fact, many observers categorize the game—won by the Colts, 23-17—as the greatest ever played. It was in this game, played December 28, 1958, that pro football's quest for nationwide acceptance was realized among a baseball-oriented public. And no wonder. The Colts and Giants engaged in a classic struggle that evolved into the first overtime game in NFL history (regular season or postseason). It was high drama acted out by some of the best players the game has ever known, with the stirring events at Yankee Stadium captivating a national television audience and proving a landmark for pro football's TV marketability. After the Giants were forced to punt on the first possession of the overtime period, the Colts drove 80 yards for the victory. Ameche's one-yard run, capping the 13-play march, broke a 17-17 tie that had been forged on a Baltimore field goal in the dying seconds of regulation play. Ameche also accounted for his team's first touchdown, scoring on a two-yard run in the second quarter.

Supporting Cast:

● **Pat Summerall.** His 36-yard field goal for New York in the opening period produced the first points of the game.

● **Raymond Berry.** Colts receiver who made a 15-yard scoring reception in the second quarter as Baltimore rolled to a 14-3 halftime lead. Berry finished the game with 12 catches for 178 yards.

● **Mel Triplett.** Giants runner whose one-yard touchdown run, coupled with Summerall's conversion kick, drew New York within 14-10 in the third quarter. New York had moved into scoring position on a pass play originating from its 13-yard line, with Kyle Rote hauling in a bomb from quarterback Charley Conerly. Rote fumbled on the play at Baltimore's 25, but teammate Alex Webster grabbed the ball and advanced to the Colts' 1.

● **Frank Gifford.** New York standout who put the Giants ahead early in the fourth quarter, latching on to a 15-yard TD pass from Conerly as Coach Jim Lee Howell's team took a 17-14 edge. The scoring play (Summerall added the extra point) helped to atone for Gifford's two second-quarter fumbles deep in Giants territory that led to Baltimore's first two touchdowns.

● **Gino Marchetti.** With a little more than 2 minutes left in regulation play and his team down by three points, Baltimore's Marchetti, assisted by Gene (Big Daddy) Lipscomb, put the clamps on Gifford on a third-and-four running play from the Giants' 40. The hit on Gifford stopped the Giants' player inches short of a first down—New York protested that he had made the necessary yardage—and forced a Don Chandler punt that gave Baltimore one more opportunity. The Colts paid for the big play, though, as Marchetti came out of the pileup with a broken ankle and was carried to the sidelines. Meanwhile, the Giants insisted that the concern over Marchetti had led to an incorrect spotting of the ball and robbed New York of a first down.

● **Johnny Unitas.** After the Colts took possession on their 14 following Chandler's punt, quarterback Unitas drove Baltimore goalward in a march that began with 1:56 remaining in regulation play. Three straight Unitas-to-Berry passes, netting 62 yards, highlighted the drive. (Overall, Unitas completed 26 of 40 passes for 349 yards and one touchdown.)

● **Steve Myhra.** With the clock running after Unitas' third successive strike to Berry (a 22-yard gain) put the ball on New York's 13, Colts placekicker Myhra rushed onto the field. With the ball spotted at the 20, Myhra delivered a game-tying and overtime-forcing field goal with 7 seconds left.

THE COIN-FLIP CAPER

Given the choice of taking the wind or the football as the Dallas Texans prepared to enter sudden-death overtime against the Houston Oilers in the 1962 American Football League championship game, Texans captain Abner Haynes ended up with neither. In a classic case of "all's well that ends well," Haynes gave a jumbled—and patently wrong—answer upon winning the coin flip . . . but the Texans overcame the blunder and went on to defeat the Oilers, 20-17, on a field goal that came 2 minutes, 54 seconds into the second overtime period. Dallas Coach Hank Stram, confident in his defense and at the same time fearful that a tricky wind and the Texans' poor punting game might quickly get his team into trouble in the overtime, wanted the wind in the extra session and indicated his willingness to give Houston first crack at the ball to get it. Zeroing in on the Oilers' options, Stram told Haynes: "If they win the toss and elect to receive, we'll kick to the clock." Any precise phraseology covering the possibility of Dallas winning the flip apparently was lost in the hubbub—or the wording was taken for granted—because Haynes called the coin toss correctly, yet went full-bore ahead with the "we'll kick to the clock" line. The official, taken aback by the response, pondered what Haynes had uttered and arrived at one conclusion: Whatever the Texans really wanted, they had to leave Houston one choice in the matter. Pressed on his decision, Haynes blurted, "We'll kick." The Oilers, of course, shot back: "We'll take the wind." Despite having the ball in their hands and the wind at their backs as the overtime began at Jeppesen Stadium in Houston, the Oilers could not take advantage of Haynes' gaffe in a game that became the longest in pro football history to that point in time. Forgotten amid the coin-flip uproar was that Haynes, one of the AFL's first great players, had made both of Dallas' touchdowns that day, scoring in the second quarter on a 28-yard reception and a two-yard run as the Texans built a 17-0 halftime bulge.

Supporting Cast:

● **George Blanda.** Houston quarterback whose 15-yard scoring pass to Willard Dewveall and ensuing extra-point kick in the third period reduced Dallas' lead to 17-7. Blanda then drew the Oilers closer with a 31-yard field goal about 4 minutes into the fourth quarter.

● **Harold (Red) Bourne.** Referee who had to sort out what Haynes did or didn't want on the coin toss preceding overtime play.

Alan Ameche's overtime burst into the end zone (above) gave Baltimore a victory over the New York Giants in the 1958 NFL championship game and capped what many observers consider the greatest game in pro football history. Colts defensive stalwart Gino Marchetti (left) was forced to watch the extra period from the sideline after breaking his ankle near the end of regulation play.

- **Tommy Brooker.** Placekicker who made the game-winning field goal, a 25-yarder, ending the 77-minute, 54-second battle. Brooker also booted a 16-yard field goal in the first period and converted after both of Haynes' TDs in the December 23 game.

- **Bill Hull.** Texans defensive lineman who, with Houston driving late in the fifth period, picked off a Blanda pass at the Dallas 27 and returned it 23 yards. The interception, which came on a second-and-11 play that originated at the Texans' 36 and set up the game's decisive march, was Dallas' fifth of the day against Blanda (who finished with 23 completions in 46 pass attempts for 261 yards and one touchdown).

- **Jack Spikes.** Dallas fullback who sparked the drive that led to Brooker's title-deciding kick in the sixth period, catching a 10-yard pass from Len Dawson (9 for 14 passing overall, for 88 yards and one TD) and breaking loose on a 19-yard run.

- **Charlie Tolar.** His one-yard scoring burst and Blanda's PAT with 5:38 left in regulation play earned the Oilers a 17-17 tie.

Stram's 1962 AFL champions never played another game as the Dallas Texans. The Texans franchise, a charter member of the AFL in 1960, was moved to Kansas City in 1963 and the team was renamed the Chiefs.

72 ENOUGH FOR REDSKINS

With 7 seconds left in the November 27, 1966, National Football League game between Washington and the New York Giants, the Redskins' Charlie Gogolak trotted onto the field to attempt a 29-yard field goal. The crowd was abuzz. Gogolak stepped forward and, in his soccer-style delivery, booted the ball goalward? The kick was . . . good! A dramatic one-point victory, perhaps? Not quite. Final score: Redskins 72, Giants 41. The game did prove a landmark contest, however, with the teams combining for an NFL-record 113 points and the Redskins establishing an NFL regular-season mark for one team with their 72-point spree. As for Gogolak's late field goal in a blowout game, a play which stunned virtually everyone, Washington Coach Otto Graham explained it this way: "He (Gogolak) hadn't had a (field-goal) chance all day and he missed two against Cleveland last Sunday. I'm not one to run up a score on anybody."

Supporting Cast:

- **Rickie Harris.** With the Redskins ahead, 48-28, entering the fourth quarter, Washington's Harris began the final-period scoring with a 52-yard punt return.

- **Allen Jacobs.** With New York down, 20-0, in the second quarter, the Giants' Jacobs scored on a six-yard run (it was the only TD in his three-year NFL career). Also scoring New York touchdowns that day were: Gary Wood, on a one-yard run in the second period; Joe Morrison, on a 41-yard pass from Wood in the third quarter; Homer Jones, on a 50-yard pass from Wood, also in the third period; Aaron Thomas, on an 18-yard pass from Tom Kennedy in the fourth quarter; and Danny Lewis, on a one-yard run in the final period. Pete Gogolak, Charlie's brother, converted after five of New York's TDs.

- **Joe Don Looney.** He scored Washington's final touchdown of the first half on a nine-yard run. The Redskins led at intermission, 34-14, in the game played in Washington.
- **Bobby Mitchell.** He ran 45 yards in the fourth quarter for the Redskins' 10th and last TD, after which Charlie Gogolak converted for the ninth straight time.
- **Brig Owens.** Washington defensive back who made three interceptions, returning one 60 yards for a touchdown in the fourth period. Owens also had a 62-yard fumble-recovery return for a TD in the second quarter.
- **Charley Taylor.** He caught 32- and 74-yard TD passes from Redskins quarterback Sonny Jurgensen, both coming in the third period.
- **A.D. Whitfield.** He scored on a five-yard pass from Jurgensen and on a 63-yard run as the Redskins seized a 13-0 first-quarter lead. Whitfield collected his third touchdown of the day in the second period on a one-yard thrust.

SUPER BOWL I

"In my opinion, the Chiefs don't rate with the top names in the NFL. They are a good football team with fine speed, but I'd have to say NFL football is better. Dallas is a better team and so are several others. That's what you wanted me to say, wasn't it?"

—Green Bay Coach Vince Lombardi, addressing the media after his NFL champion Packers had defeated Kansas City, the American Football League titlist, in the first Super Bowl, played January 15, 1967, in Los Angeles.

Lombardi, Green Bay and the National Football League had reason to gloat. Sure, the AFL had made major gains—on and off the field—in its seven seasons of competition. And, yes, the junior circuit had even effected a merger with the senior league in June of 1966, with the agreement aimed at ending the escalating bidding war for player talent and curbing pro football strife overall. But the NFL would concede nothing when it came to the issue of superiority on the playing field. So, when the terms of the merger (full implementation of which would be realized in the fall of 1970) included a "world championship" clash between the league titlists, the NFL—specifically, Green Bay—was ready to assert itself. As well prepared as the Packers were, though, they weren't expecting the upstart Chiefs to play them nearly head-to-head into the third period. Kansas City was trailing only 14-10 as it faced a third-and-five situation at its 49-yard line after advancing the ball 20 yards following the second-half kickoff. Quarterback Len Dawson, under a heavy pass rush, unloaded a wobbly pass. Green Bay's Willie Wood intercepted the ball and returned it 50 yards to the Chiefs' 5. Green Bay scored on the next play, and the Chiefs never recovered. The Packers, who had won their fourth NFL crown in six years in 1966, ended up 35-10 winners in a game that stirred NFL and AFL partisans alike but failed to capture the fancy of the paying customers. With a crowd of 61,946 on hand, Super Bowl I played to more than 30,000 empty seats at the Los Angeles Memorial Coliseum.

Supporting Cast:

• **Don Chandler.** Green Bay placekicker who was five for five on his extra-point attempts against Kansas City.

• **Curtis McClinton.** He scored Kansas City's lone touchdown of the game, catching a seven-yard pass from Dawson in the second quarter. The Chiefs' conversion kick made it a 7-7 game.

• **Max McGee.** Veteran Green Bay receiver who caught only four passes in the entire regular season preceding the first Super Bowl but had seven receptions—two for TDs—against the Chiefs. Filling in for Boyd Dowler, who was injured early in the game, McGee scored the game's first points in the opening period when he latched on to an underthrown pass with one hand—he balanced the ball on his hip—and jogged into the end zone on a 37-yard scoring play. McGee, who had 138 yards in receptions for the day, caught a 13-yard touchdown pass in the third quarter that, coupled with a conversion kick, increased Green Bay's lead to 28-10.

• **Mike Mercer.** He converted after McClinton's TD and then inched Kansas City within 14-10 with a 31-yard field goal in the second quarter.

• **Elijah Pitts.** After Wood's third-period interception, it was Pitts who ran for the Green Bay touchdown from the Kansas City 5. Chandler's PAT made it 21-10, Packers. Pitts also scored Green Bay's final TD on a one-yard burst in the fourth quarter.

• **Bart Starr.** Packers quarterback who put on a dazzling performance, completing 16 of 23 passes for 250 yards and two touchdowns. Under his direction, Green Bay converted 10 of 13 third-down situations.

• **Jim Taylor.** The leading rusher in Super Bowl I with 53 yards, Green Bay's Taylor broke a 7-7 tie in the second period with a 14-yard scoring run.

• **Fred (The Hammer) Williamson.** Chiefs defensive back who, in pregame hype, vowed to punish the Packers with his physical style of play, only to be knocked cold himself late in the game.

THE ICE BOWL

Seeking their third straight National Football League championship and fifth league crown in seven seasons, the Green Bay Packers faced a third-and-goal situation against Dallas with 16 seconds left in the 1967 title game. The Packers were about two feet away from scoring, with Dallas clinging to a 17-14 lead. Quarterback Bart Starr called a timeout, Green Bay's last of the game, and jogged over to meet with Coach Vince Lombardi. On a day fit for neither man nor beast nor football—the temperature at game time was minus 13 degrees and there was a stiff wind—Starr, the strategy decided, made his way back to the huddle on the frozen turf at Green Bay's Lambeau Field. Spectators pondered the Packers' options: A pass attempt could not be ruled out, with a completion surely meaning victory and an incompletion stopping the clock and setting up a chance at a game-tying field goal or another rushing attempt. Of course, there was the threat of an interception,

Green Bay receiver Max McGee, a forgotten man during the 1966 NFL regular season, catches a 13-yard touchdown pass from Bart Starr, his second TD reception of the game, in the Packers' Super Bowl I victory over Kansas City.

Green Bay quarterback Bart Starr (15) scores the winning touchdown in the closing seconds of the Packers-Cowboys 1967 'Ice Bowl' championship game.

too. A run clearly had its pluses, considering the Packers' crushing ground attack and the short yardage needed. But on the negative side, a rushing play would run out the clock; if the Packers came up short, there would be no time for a fourth-down play. And the numbing weather increased the risk of a fumble. Starr took the snap from center Ken Bowman and . . . followed guard Jerry Kramer goalward. Kramer, with help from Bowman, moved Dallas tackle Jethro Pugh outside and Starr dived in for the score with 13 seconds left. Touchdown (and NFL title), Green Bay. "We gambled, we won—it was as simple as that," Lombardi said after the 21-17 triumph.

Supporting Cast:

● **Donny Anderson.** After Green Bay encountered a second-and-19 play from its 49 on the game-winning drive (12 plays, 68 yards), Anderson hauled in 12- and nine-yard passes from Starr to net the Pack a first down at the Dallas 30. With 54 seconds remaining in the game, Anderson ran two yards on a play that gave Green Bay a first down at the Dallas 1. Then he gained only about a foot on two carries before Starr made his decisive plunge.

● **George Andrie.** With the Packers ahead, 14-0, in the second quarter, the Dallas defensive end rumbled seven yards for a TD on a fumble recovery. Willie Townes' jarring hit on Starr had knocked the ball loose.

● **Boyd Dowler.** Packers receiver who caught an eight-yard touchdown pass from Starr in the first quarter and a 43-yard scoring pass from the veteran quarterback in the second period. Don Chandler converted after both TDs (and also added the extra point following Starr's touchdown) in the December 31 clash.

● **Chuck Mercein.** With the ball at the Dallas 30 on Green Bay's victorious march (which began with 4 minutes, 50 seconds to play in the game), Mercein got the ball to the 3 with a 19-yard reception of a Starr pass and an eight-yard run.

● **Don Meredith.** Dallas quarterback who had a frustrating afternoon in the frigid conditions, completing 10 of 25 passes for only 59 yards (compared with Starr's 14-of-24 day for 191 yards and two TDs). "A frozen field penalizes the team with the diversified offense," Meredith said. "It took away a lot of things we normally do—quick-starting plays, cuts and—aw, so much I can't list it."

● **Dan Reeves.** Dallas halfback who, with Green Bay in front, 14-10, jolted the Packers on the first play of the fourth quarter by taking a handoff from Meredith and throwing a 50-yard touchdown pass to Lance Rentzel.

● **Danny Villanueva.** He booted a 21-yard field goal for Dallas in the second quarter (the Packers led, 14-10, at halftime) and converted after both Cowboy touchdowns.

RAIDERS, JETS AND HEIDI

The 1968 season was in its stretch run, and the New York Jets and the Oakland Raiders were fighting for American Football League divisional titles. Jim Turner had just kicked a 26-yard field goal for the Jets, sending his team into a 32-29 lead over the Raiders late in a nationally televised game played in Oakland on November 17. The game was particularly attractive for television, pitting the defending AFL champion Raiders against glamour quarterback Joe Namath and the fast-rising Jets. With TV viewers throughout the country caught up in the late-game excitement, the Raiders returned the ensuing kickoff to their 22-yard line as the scoreboard clock ticked down. One minute, 1 second remained in the contest. Could the Raiders bounce back behind their "Mad Bomber," Daryle Lamonica? Would the Jets come up with the big plays defensively? Stay tuned, folks. Stay tuned? Gladly. However, instead of watching the likes of New York's Gerry Philbin, Johnny Sample and Ralph Baker and Oakland's Fred Biletnikoff, Hewritt Dixon and Warren Wells fight it out to the finish, most of the nation's viewers focused on . . .

Supporting Cast:

● **Heidi.** That's right, Heidi. With 61 seconds to play in the tight and crucial AFL game, the visage of the Swiss miss flashed upon TV screens. Heidi was the subject of a two-hour special, a program for which NBC cut away from the Jets-Raiders clash promptly at 7 p.m., New York time, so the network could telecast the production in its entirety. (Because of network time-zone programming policies, West Coast viewers not affected by the existing blackout rule saw the football game to its conclusion.)

● **Charlie Smith.** As the Heidi show beamed across the nation and fuming football fans wondered what was happening in Oakland, the Raiders moved quickly downfield. The payoff came when Smith, whose kickoff return and screen-pass reception had netted 42 yards (a Jets penalty advanced the ball 15 more yards), hauled in a 43-yard touchdown pass from Lamonica with 42 seconds left. After George Blanda added the extra point, a message flashed across the bottom of TV screens: Raiders 36, Jets 32.

● **Preston Ridlehuber.** When the Jets' Earl Christy mishandled the kickoff that followed Oakland's go-ahead score, the Raiders' Ridlehuber pounced on the fumble at the New York 2 and fell into the end zone. Touchdown, Oakland. Blanda again converted. Final score: Raiders 43, Jets 32.

Fans, irate over missing the climactic moments of the game on TV, besieged NBC with complaints and the callers grew more vocal when they learned of the game's whirlwind ending (NBC's overloaded switchboard eventually blew a fuse). Stung by the reaction, NBC promised to avoid such plug-pulling in the future.

Oakland's Lamonica threw four touchdown passes in the game, also hooking up with Wells, Biletnikoff and Billy Cannon. Additionally, Smith scored on a run for the Raiders. Namath ran for one Jets touchdown and passed for another (connecting with Don Maynard, who had 10 receptions for 228 yards), Bill Mathis rushed for a New York TD and Turner contributed four field goals in all.

The Jets and Raiders went on to capture their divisional crowns, with New York winning comfortably in the East and Oakland posting a playoff victory over Kansas City to break a tie in the West. Six weeks after the "Heidi Game," the Jets and Raiders staged a rematch in the AFL championship game—and New York prevailed, 27-23, to advance to Super Bowl III.

'WELCOME TO THE AFL'

With Green Bay having won the first two Super Bowls by margins of 25 and 19 points, there was little doubt that Super Bowl III—scheduled January 12, 1969, in Miami's Orange Bowl—would be another ho-hum triumph for the National Football League. While the Green Bay teams of 1966 and 1967 were powerhouses, the 1968 Baltimore Colts seemed a cut above (some observers even called them one of the NFL's all-time great teams). Baltimore had dominated the NFL in 1968, steamrolling to a 13-1 regular-season record and crushing Cleveland, 34-0, in the league's championship game. The Colts' opposition in the Super Bowl would be the New York Jets, the American Football League's third different entrant in three years in pro football's climactic game. Brash Joe Namath, the Jets' quarterback, provided some pre-Super Bowl controversy by "guaranteeing" a Jets victory. Fat chance. Depending on the oddsmaker, Coach Weeb Ewbank's New Yorkers were underdogs from 17 to 23 points. How much of a mismatch did the game turn out to be? Well, the score was closer than in Super Bowls I and II; still, the victor thoroughly outplayed the vanquished. There was, however, one noteworthy variation in the theme: The AFL representative was the convincing winner this time. Solid in every phase of the game and sparked by Namath's passing (17 completions in 28 attempts for 206 yards) and leadership, the Jets rocked the football world by upending the error-prone and luckless Colts, 16-7.

Supporting Cast:

● **Randy Beverly.** Having recovered a fumble at the Jets' 12-yard line late in

New York Jets quarterback Joe Namath wears a well-deserved smile as he watches his team put the finishing touches on its 1969 Super Bowl III victory over Baltimore.

the first quarter, Baltimore failed to convert on the opportunity when New York defensive back Beverly—on a third-and-four play—made a lunging interception of a deflected pass in the end zone. The theft came on the second play of the second period. Beverly picked off another Colts pass in the fourth quarter.

● **Jerry Hill.** His one-yard TD run in the fourth quarter and Lou Michaels' conversion kick accounted for Baltimore's points.

● **Earl Morrall.** Obtained from the New York Giants as quarterback insurance in August and then thrust into the starting lineup because of the Colts' injury situation, Morrall emerged as The Sporting News' 1968 Player of the Year in the NFL as he threw for 26 touchdowns. Morrall had a nightmarish Super Bowl, though, completing only six of 17 passes for 71 yards and yielding three interceptions.

● **Jimmy Orr.** Baltimore receiver who was a key figure in perhaps the most crucial play of the game. With 25 seconds remaining in the first half and Coach Don Shula's Colts trailing, 7-0, Orr was wide open at the Jets' 10 on Baltimore's flea-flicker play and waved frantically for attention as he headed goalward. After handing off to Tom Matte at New York's 42 and then getting the ball back from the Colts' No. 1 rusher, Morrall unloaded a pass. Unable to see Orr down the left sideline, Morrall aimed the ball toward Hill at the Jets' 12—and New York's Jim Hudson intercepted the down-the-middle throw. "I had to turn to the right in order to take the pass from Matte," Morrall explained later, "and when I looked up, Jimmy wasn't in my line of vision. Hill was, so I went to him." Instead of scoring a "cinch" touchdown, tying the game and perhaps benefiting from a change in momentum, Baltimore had turned the ball over.

● **Johnny Sample.** A member of the Colts' 1958 and 1959 NFL champions (coached by Ewbank), the Jets' Sample intercepted a Morrall pass in the second period after Baltimore—thanks to a 58-yard run by Matte—had reached New York's 16.

● **George Sauer Jr.** Namath's primary receiver, he caught eight passes for 133 yards.

● **Matt Snell.** Following Beverly's interception early in the second period, the Jets drove 80 yards in 12 plays for New York's lone touchdown. Snell, who finished with 121 yards rushing against Baltimore, got the TD on a four-yard run.

● **Jim Turner.** After Matte fumbled on the first play from scrimmage in the second half, the Jets went on to collect a 32-yard field goal by Turner (who had converted after Snell's touchdown). Turner kicked a 30-yard field goal later in the third quarter and then booted a nine-yarder early in the fourth period as the Jets' lead climbed to 16-0.

● **Johnny Unitas.** Relegated to a second-line role in 1968 because of an elbow injury, the Colts' longtime quarterback star was called upon late in the third quarter with his club facing a 13-0 deficit. Unitas completed 11 of 24 passes (he had one intercepted) for 110 yards during his stint, directing the Colts to their only touchdown. After Hill scored with 3 minutes, 19 seconds remaining in the game, Baltimore recovered an onside kick and Unitas drove the Colts to New York's 19. But Unitas could get the Colts no closer, and one of the greatest upsets in sports history was assured.

"It'll take the NFL 20 years to catch up," Sample cracked after the game.

"Hello, world, welcome to the American Football League," Turner said.

The impact of the January 1969 goings-on in Miami—the Jets' breakthrough triumph for the AFL and the Namath-inspired ballyhoo surrounding the game—surely established the Super Bowl as one of America's premier athletic events.

THE NFL'S LONGEST DAY

It ranks as the longest National Football League game ever played, lasting 82 minutes and 40 seconds. It was the last game that the Kansas City Chiefs played at Municipal Stadium, their home field for their first nine seasons. And, in a startling turnaround for a Kansas City team that had played in two of the first four Super Bowls, the contest stands as the Chiefs' last appearance in the playoffs (entering the 1985 season). The final score in this American Conference divisional playoff game, played on Christmas Day, 1971, was Miami 27, Kansas City 24. After finishing regulation play tied at 24-24, the Dolphins of Coach Don Shula and the Chiefs of Coach Hank Stram battled through a scoreless fifth period before Miami prevailed on Garo Yepremian's 37-yard field goal (which came 7:40 into the second overtime period).

Supporting Cast:

● **Larry Csonka.** His 29-yard run in the sixth period moved Miami from its 35-yard line to the Chiefs' 36. After the Dolphins gained six yards on three running plays, Yepremian delivered his game-winning field goal (Karl Noonan was the holder). Csonka had scored Miami's first points of the game in the second quarter, running one yard for a touchdown after the Chiefs had seized a 10-0 lead in the first quarter.

● **Marv Fleming.** With 1:36 remaining in regulation play and Kansas City leading, 24-17, Miami's Fleming caught a five-yard TD pass from Bob Griese. Yepremian's conversion kick tied the score.

● **Jim Kiick.** After Kansas City's Jim Otis had snapped a 10-10 tie with a one-yard TD burst in the third quarter, Miami's Kiick went one yard for a touchdown later in the period and the teams entered the final quarter deadlocked, 17-17.

● **Ed Podolak.** In one of the top postseason performances of all time, Kansas City's Podolak netted 350 total yards. He rushed 17 times for 85 yards, caught eight passes for 110 yards, returned three kickoffs for 153 yards and ran back two punts for two yards. Podolak, who hauled in a seven-yard TD pass from Len Dawson in the first quarter and then broke a 17-17 tie with a three-yard run in the final period, seemingly maneuvered the Chiefs into position to win in regulation play by going 78 yards on a kickoff return immediately after Miami had fought back for the 24-24 tie.

● **Jan Stenerud.** After the Chiefs had run three plays following Podolak's kickoff return to the Miami 22, Stenerud attempted a 31-yard field goal with 35 seconds left in regulation time and the score tied. The kick sailed wide to the right, and sudden-death overtime drew near. Stenerud, who kicked a 24-yard field goal in the first quarter and made three extra points overall, had a 42-yard field-goal try blocked in the first overtime period.

Yepremian, who converted after all three Dolphin touchdowns, had booted a 14-yard field goal in the second quarter that tied the score at 10-10. He missed a 52-yard field-goal attempt in the fifth period.

Nine years earlier, the Stram-coached Dallas Texans (who moved to Kansas City in 1963 and became the Chiefs) beat the Houston Oilers, 20-17, for the American Football League championship in a game also decided in the sixth period.

THE 'IMMACULATE RECEPTION'

"He was hustling," Steelers Coach Chuck Noll said of his rookie running back, Franco Harris. "And good things happen to people who hustle." Miraculous things, even. With 22 seconds left in the 1972 American Conference divisional playoff game between Pittsburgh and Oakland, Harris and his Steeler teammates trailed, 7-6, and faced a fourth-and-10 situation at their 40-yard line. Pittsburgh quarterback Terry Bradshaw, trying to move the ball into field-goal range, had thrown incompletions on three successive pass attempts but took to the air for one more try. Under heavy pressure from the Oakland rush and with his primary receiver bottled up, Bradshaw let fly with a pass aimed at Steeler running back Frenchy Fuqua (who was streaking downfield). The pass never made connections with Fuqua . . . but, incredibly, the ball found its way to Harris. Touchdown, Steelers. Final score: Pittsburgh 13, Oakland 7.

Supporting Cast:

• **Barry Pearson.** Rookie wide receiver who, seeking his first National Football League reception, was Bradshaw's intended target on Pittsburgh's fourth-down play in the game's final seconds. Pearson, on the Steelers' active roster for the first time after spending the regular season on the taxi squad, was unable to get open and Bradshaw went to Fuqua instead.

• **Jack Tatum.** Raiders defender who reached Fuqua at the same time the ball did. Tatum put his fist into the ball, knocking it backward. Just before the ball hit the turf at Three Rivers Stadium, the in-flight Harris snatched it up at Oakland's 42 and proceeded downfield.

• **Jimmy Warren.** As Tatum received congratulations from a couple of teammates for apparently foiling Pittsburgh's last-gasp play, Raiders defensive back Warren stood as Harris' lone obstacle to the end zone. Warren angled Harris toward the sideline, but Harris fought off Warren's shove and went across the goal line standing up with 5 seconds left in the game.

• **Fred Swearingen.** Referee who rejected Oakland's argument that the Bradshaw pass had ricocheted off Fuqua's shoulder pads (and not off Tatum's fist) to Harris. If the Raiders' contention had been correct, the play should not have been allowed because existing rules stipulated that a pass could not be ruled complete if the ball bounced off one offensive player directly to another. Swearingen left the field after the play and went to a baseball dugout, where he conferred by telephone with Art McNally, an NFL supervisor of officials and pressbox observer. After explaining the situation to McNally, Swearingen returned to the field and signaled a touchdown.

• **Roy Gerela.** His 18-yard field goal in the third period and 29-yard boot in

One of the more extraordinary plays in pro football history occurred on December 23, 1972, when Pittsburgh running back Franco Harris (left) stunned the Oakland Raiders by picking off a deflected pass in the closing moments of an AFC playoff game and running for the game-winning touchdown. Confusion reigned (below) until the referees declared the catch legal.

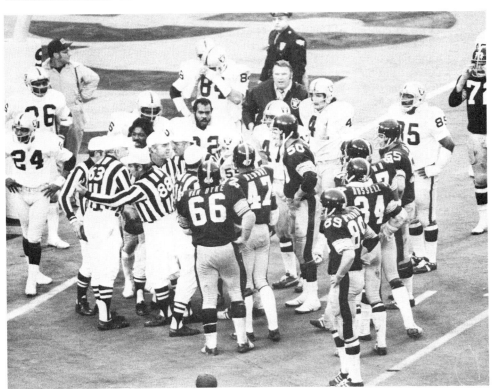

the fourth quarter gave Pittsburgh a 6-0 lead in the December 23 game. Gerela also converted after Harris' TD.

●**Ken Stabler.** A fourth-quarter replacement for quarterback Daryle Lamonica (who had been ineffective all afternoon against the Steelers' harassing defense), Stabler drove Oakland 80 yards in 12 plays in the game's final minutes and capped the scoring march himself with a 30-yard run that tied the contest at 6-6 with 1 minute, 13 seconds remaining. George Blanda's conversion kick sent the Raiders ahead, 7-6.

●**Jerry DePoyster.** Following Oakland's go-ahead drive, DePoyster kicked off for the Raiders and his boot hit the Steelers' goal post. Starting at its 20, Pittsburgh moved to its 40 on Bradshaw's nine-yard pass to Harris and his 11-yard strike to Fuqua. And then came the stunning play that went into the record books as a 60-yard touchdown pass, Bradshaw to Harris.

Eight days after its stirring victory, Pittsburgh lost to Miami, 21-17, in the AFC championship game. The triumph was the 16th straight (including postseason play) for the Dolphins, who went on to win the Super Bowl over Washington and finish 17-0.

MIAMI'S PERFECT; GARO'S NOT

Super Bowl VII will be remembered as the game in which the Miami Dolphins completed their record-setting 17-0 National Football League season. It also will live on because of Miami placekicker Garo Yepremian's not-ready-for-prime-time impression of Dolphins passer Bob Griese. With Miami in control of the game, 14-0, and 2 minutes, 7 seconds left to play in the January 14, 1973, contest at the Los Angeles Memorial Coliseum, the Dolphins tried to tack on an insurance field goal from 42 yards out. Yepremian hit the ball squarely—but right into the path of an onrushing Redskins player. Instead of falling on the ball, Yepremian picked it up and attempted to pass. As Miami coaches, players and fans shuddered, the ball slipped out of Garo's hand and was plucked out of the air by. . .

Supporting Cast:

●**Mike Bass.** Washington's Bass proceeded to return Yepremian's bobble 49 yards for a touchdown, with the play ruled a fumble recovery and not a pass interception (Yepremian's arm was not in a forward motion when he lost the ball). Curt Knight made the extra-point kick, bringing the Redskins within seven points. Washington's final possession, which began at the Redskins' 30-yard line with 1:14 remaining in the game, was a disaster as the 'Skins lost 13 yards on four plays against the Dolphins' No-Name Defense. Final score: Dolphins 14, Redskins 7. A perfect season for Coach Don Shula's team.

●**Bill Brundige.** Washington lineman who blocked Yepremian's fourth-period field-goal attempt.

●**Larry Csonka.** Miami fullback who rushed for 112 yards against Washington on only 15 carries.

●**Jim Kiick.** After the Dolphins' Nick Buoniconti had intercepted a Bill Kilmer pass in the second quarter and returned the ball 32 yards to the Redskins' 27, Miami went on to score a touchdown on Kiick's one-yard run

One of the classic plays in Super Bowl history occurred in 1973 when Dolphins kicker Garo Yepremian, his field goal attempt blocked (above), grabbed the deflection and tried to throw the infamous pass that resulted in a 49-yard Washington fumble return for a touchdown.

with 18 seconds left in the first half. Yepremian's PAT gave Miami a 14-0 halftime bulge.

● **Earl Morrall.** The Sporting News' 1972 Player of the Year in the American Conference (substituting for the injured Griese, he started in 11 consecutive Miami victories and deftly directed the Dolphins' attack), the 38-year-old Morrall returned Miami's No. 1 quarterback job to Griese for Super Bowl VII. "I explained to Earl that I thought the team would be stronger if we started a healthy Griese," Shula said of his decision to go with his regular—and now physically fit—quarterback. Griese, sidelined in week five of the season because of an ankle fracture, had relieved Morrall in the December 31 AFC title game and ignited the Dolphins past Pittsburgh. Against Washington, Griese completed eight of 11 passes for 88 yards and one touchdown.

● **Jake Scott.** His end-zone interception of a Kilmer pass stopped a fourth-quarter Washington drive that had reached the Miami 10—and Scott's 55-yard runback on the play set into motion the Miami march that led to Yepremian's ill-fated flirtation with the passing game. Scott also picked off a Kilmer pass in the second period.

● **Howard Twilley.** On the next-to-last play of the first quarter, Miami's Twilley caught a 28-yard touchdown pass from Griese to cap a six-play, 63-yard drive. Yepremian kicked the extra point as the Dolphins, in only the seventh season of their existence, went ahead, 7-0.

NO TROPHY THIS TIME

The Miami Dolphins, with Super Bowl VII and VIII championship trophies tucked away, seemed a step closer to a berth in Super Bowl IX when they seized a 26-21 lead over the Oakland Raiders late in the fourth quarter of their December 21, 1974, American Conference divisional playoff game in Oakland. Benny Malone's 23-yard touchdown run and Garo Yepremian's conversion kick had turned the trick, bringing Miami back from a 21-19 deficit. Now the Dolphins had to hold on for 2 minutes, 8 seconds to earn a spot in the AFC title game against the winner of the next day's playoff game between Pittsburgh and Buffalo. Such a time span proved more than enough, however, for quarterback Ken Stabler and his Raider teammates to work their magic. Completing five straight passes, Stabler drove Oakland to the Miami 14-yard line. Clarence Davis then scooted six yards to the Dolphins' 8, and the game clock was nearing the half-minute mark. Stabler went back to pass and Miami's Vern Den Herder took aim on him. Grasped at the ankles by Den Herder and about to tumble to the turf, Stabler floated a pass toward Davis in the end zone. Incredibly, Davis outfought a crowd of Miami defenders for the ball as the clock ticked down to 26 seconds. Touchdown, Raiders. George Blanda's fourth extra point of the day made it 28-26, Oakland. Miami's bid for a fourth straight Super Bowl appearance—the Dolphins had lost to Dallas in Super Bowl VI before beating Washington and Minnesota in the next two National Football League title games—would fail.

Supporting Cast:

● **Fred Biletnikoff.** Oakland overcame Miami's 10-7 halftime lead when Biletnikoff scored on a 13-yard pass from Stabler in the third quarter. Biletnikoff had eight receptions overall for 122 yards; Stabler finished with 20 completions in 30 pass attempts for 293 yards and four touchdowns.

● **Cliff Branch.** Having fallen behind, 19-14, in the fourth period, the resilient Raiders rebounded again when Stabler and Branch teamed on a 72-yard touchdown play. Stabler's heave from the Oakland 28 was caught by Branch at the Dolphins' 27 and Branch, after falling down untouched and then springing up, ran in for the score. The PAT gave Oakland a 21-19 edge with 4:37 to play.

● **Larry Csonka.** The day's top rusher, he gained 114 yards on 24 carries.

● **Nat Moore.** Dolphins player who got the game off to a rousing start by returning the opening kickoff 89 yards for a touchdown. Yepremian booted the PAT.

● **Charlie Smith.** He caught a 31-yard TD pass from Stabler in the second period and Blanda followed with the extra point, tying the score at 7-7. Yepremian countered with a 33-yard field goal later in the quarter, regaining the lead for Miami.

● **Paul Warfield.** Dolphins receiver who grabbed a 16-yard scoring pass from Bob Griese in the third period, boosting Miami into a 16-14 lead (the conversion attempt failed). The Dolphins added to their advantage approximately 3 minutes into the fourth quarter when Yepremian boomed a 46-yard field goal.

● **Phil Villapiano.** Raiders linebacker who killed Miami's hopes by intercepting a Griese pass with 21 seconds to play in the game.

THE 'HAIL MARY' PASS

Only 32 seconds remained in the 1975 National Conference divisional playoff game at Metropolitan Stadium in Bloomington, Minn., as the Dallas Cowboys, trailing the Minnesota Vikings, 14-10, prepared for a second-and-10 play at the 50-yard line. Needing a touchdown to win, the Cowboys seemingly didn't have a prayer. "Our only hope was to throw and hope for a miracle," Dallas Coach Tom Landry said. Throw is exactly what Cowboys quarterback Roger Staubach did, only he underthrew a pass intended for Drew Pearson. However, Pearson came back for the ball and snatched it away from Viking defenders Nate Wright and Terry Brown and rolled into the end zone with 24 seconds showing on the clock. "I reached back and got it on my hip (with one hand)," Pearson said. "Our chances were slim and none." Coach Bud Grant and his Vikings screamed for a call of offensive pass interference on the play, claiming that Pearson had pushed Wright to get at the ball. The officials would have none of that argument, and Dallas emerged as a 17-14 victor. "I guess it's a 'Hail Mary' pass," Staubach offered. "You throw it up and pray he catches it." Earlier on the 85-yard drive, the Cowboys had reached the 50 via a 25-yard completion—Staubach to Pearson—on a fourth-and-16 play from the Dallas 25.

Supporting Cast:

● **Doug Dennison.** Trailing at halftime, 7-0, Dallas rebounded for a 7-7 tie in the third quarter, with Dennison notching the touchdown on a four-yard run.

● **Chuck Foreman.** He snapped a scoreless tie in the second period, going one yard for a Minnesota touchdown. The Vikings had taken possession at the Dallas 4 when Cowboys lineman Pat Donovan, incorrectly thinking that teammate Cliff Harris had touched a Minnesota punt, tried to gather in the ball but lost it to the Vikings' Fred McNeill (the play was ruled a muffed punt).

● **Toni Fritsch.** Dallas placekicker whose fourth-quarter field goal from 24 yards out nudged the Cowboys into a 10-7 lead. Fritsch also converted after both of Dallas' TDs.

● **Brent McClanahan.** Capping a 70-yard Minnesota march, he scored from a yard out with 5 minutes, 24 seconds left in the game to push Minnesota in front, 13-10. Fred Cox then added his second extra-point kick of the game.

● **Armen Terzian.** Field judge who was knocked unconscious (but was not seriously injured) when struck by a whiskey bottle thrown by an irate fan soon after Pearson's controversial catch in the December 28 game.

OPPORTUNE FUMBLE FOR RAIDERS

The San Diego Chargers led the Oakland Raiders, 20-14, with 10 seconds remaining in their September 10, 1978, National Football League game in San Diego and the Raiders poised at the Chargers' 14-yard line. Oakland's hopes appeared doomed, however, when quarterback Ken Stabler fumbled as he was hit by Chargers defensive end Fred Dean. With the clock running out and the Raiders still a significant distance from the goal line, not even a "normal" fumble recovery could save the Raiders this time. But Oakland had never relied on "normal" events in pulling off numerous miracle finishes over the years, and the Raiders weren't about to start now. Final score: Raiders 21, Chargers 20.

Supporting Cast:

● **Pete Banaszak.** After Stabler fumbled the ball—"I was trying to throw the ball about the time I got hit . . . I fumbled it on purpose," the veteran quarterback said—Banaszak guided the ball toward the goal line. "Sure, I batted it," the Oakland running back said. "I could see a San Diego guy right alongside me. If I picked it up, he would have tackled me and the game would have been over."

● **Dave Casper.** Raiders tight end who, after giving the ball a kick following Banaszak's batting act, pounced on the ball in the end zone with no time on the clock, making the score 20-20. "I got lucky," Casper said. "Sure, I helped the ball along into the end zone. I saw the fumble come out of the pile."

● **Errol Mann.** Oakland placekicker who converted after Casper's fumble-recovery touchdown, giving the Raiders their one-point victory. Mann also made extra points after Stabler's touchdown passes to Morris Bradshaw (44 yards, fourth quarter) and Casper (six yards, second period).

● **Hank Bauer.** He ran one yard for a San Diego touchdown in the second quarter and went two yards for a fourth-period TD that, coupled with Rolf Benirschke's second conversion kick of the day in three attempts, boosted the Chargers to a 20-7 advantage with 8 minutes, 26 seconds to play. The Chargers also scored on a Dan Fouts-to-Pat Curran pass play of 14 yards in the second quarter.

DRAMA IN MIAMI

"There has never been a game like this," Chargers Coach Don Coryell said. "It was probably the most exciting game in pro football history." Dolphins Coach Don Shula, whose team blundered its way through the opening period, might not have seen things quite the same way. Shula, after all, was on the losing end of the 1981 American Conference divisional playoff game, while Coryell was on the triumphant side of the 41-38 overtime shootout contested in Miami's Orange Bowl on January 2, 1982. The game ran the gamut of emotions, thanks to big plays, misplays, unusual plays and a stirring Miami comeback that saw the Dolphins overcome a 24-0 deficit and

San Diego receiver Kellen Winslow pulls away from a Miami tackler after catching a pass in the Chargers-Dolphins 1981 AFC playoff game.

take a 38-31 lead. When the drama had been played out, it was San Diego placekicker Rolf Benirschke who was in the starring role. Benirschke booted a game-winning 29-yard field goal 13 minutes, 52 seconds into the extra session.

Supporting Cast:

● **Wes Chandler.** After Benirschke had kicked a 32-yard field goal, Chandler returned a Miami punt 56 yards for a first-quarter touchdown and Benirschke added the extra point. San Diego 10, Miami 0. Then, seven plays after Miami misplayed the ensuing kickoff, Chuck Muncie ran one yard for a Chargers touchdown and Benirschke again converted, making the score 17-0.

● **Dan Fouts.** Chargers quarterback who threw for 433 yards and three TDs. Fouts' eight-yard scoring strike to James Brooks and Benirschke's third conversion kick of the day increased San Diego's lead to 24-0 in the first quarter. After Miami roared back to tie the game at 24-24, Fouts teamed with Kellen Winslow on a 25-yard touchdown pass in the third quarter. The resilient Dolphins then struck for consecutive TDs—one in the third quarter, the other in the fourth—and seized a 38-31 edge, but Fouts hit Brooks with a nine-yard scoring pass with 58 seconds left in the game and Benirschke's PAT tied the score at 38-38.

● **Andra Franklin.** Miami rookie running back whose fumble gave San Diego possession for its game-tying 82-yard march late in the fourth quarter.

● **Tony Nathan.** His 12-yard run for Miami at the outset of the final period broke a 31-31 deadlock. Uwe von Schamann kicked the extra point for the Dolphins, who had taken possession on a Lyle Blackwood interception.

• **Don Strock.** Dolphins quarterback who relieved starter David Woodley in the second quarter and passed for four TDs and 403 yards. After von Schamann made a 34-yard field goal in the second period to give Miami its first points of the game (Chargers 24, Dolphins 3), Strock rifled three touchdown passes that—combined with von Schamann's conversion kicks after each score—evened the game at 24-24. Strock hit Joe Rose on a one-yarder in the second quarter to get Miami rolling. Then, on a flea-flicker play, he passed 15 yards to Duriel Harris, who lateraled to Nathan at the Chargers' 25 and Nathan scored with time running out in the first half. The score at intermission: San Diego 24, Miami 17. The Dolphins pulled even in the third period, the touchdown coming on a Strock-to-Rose pass covering 15 yards. Following the Fouts-to-Winslow TD strike, Strock found Bruce Hardy on a 50-yard scoring aerial later in the third quarter and von Schamann's extra point tied the contest at 31-31.

With time expiring in regulation play, San Diego's Winslow (who finished with 13 receptions for 166 yards) tipped von Schamann's 43-yard field-goal attempt. Von Schamann also failed on a 34-yard try in overtime (the kick was blocked by Leroy Jones). Benirschke was off target on a 27-yarder in the extra period before coming through with his game-winner.

A GIANT LEAP FOR 49ERS

"I thought it was too high," said San Francisco's 6-foot-4 Dwight Clark, discussing the third-and-three pass thrown in his direction in the end zone during the final minute of the 49ers' 1981 National Conference championship game against Dallas. The 49ers, trailing, 27-21, at Candlestick Park, were at the Cowboys' 6-yard line when the play started. ". . . I don't jump that well," Clark continued. "And I was real tired. I had the flu last week and I had trouble getting my breath on the last drive. I don't know how I caught the ball. . . ." But catch it a leaping Clark did, capping an 89-yard drive that consumed 4 minutes, 3 seconds and tied the game at 27-27. Ray Wersching kicked the extra point, as he did after all four 49er touchdowns, and San Francisco held on for 51 more seconds to secure a 28-27 victory and a spot in Super Bowl XVI.

Supporting Cast:

• **Doug Cosbie.** With San Francisco in front, 21-20, in the final quarter, Cosbie caught a 21-yard touchdown pass from Danny White.

• **Johnny Davis.** His two-yard TD run and Wersching's third extra point of the day moved San Francisco into a 21-17 third-quarter lead in the game played on January 10, 1982.

• **Tony Dorsett.** Cowboys running back whose five-yard scoring run in the second period overcame a 14-10 San Francisco edge in the seesaw game. Dallas was on top, 17-14, at halftime.

• **Lenvil Elliott.** He rushed for key yardage on the 49ers' winning march, including a seven-yard gain that advanced the ball from Dallas' 13 to the 6 and set up Clark's heroics.

• **Tony Hill.** The 49ers were ahead, 7-3, in the first quarter when Dallas' Hill and White teamed on a 26-yard scoring pass.

San Francisco's Dwight Clark goes high to haul in a touchdown pass from quarterback Joe Montana during the closing seconds of the 49ers' 1981 NFC championship game victory over Dallas. Clark's TD and Ray Wersching's extra-point kick resulted in a 28-27 final score.

● **Joe Montana.** San Francisco quarterback who fired three touchdown passes, hitting Freddie Solomon on an eight-yard scoring play in the first period and finding Clark on a 20-yarder in the second quarter and again on the six-yarder in the fourth period. On the game-winner to Clark, Montana rolled right as three Cowboys pressured him and, approaching the sideline, let fly with a pass that seemed hopelessly overthrown. Montana threw for 286 yards overall, with Clark accounting for 120 of the total on eight catches.

● **Lawrence Pillers.** With the clock winding down after Clark's leaping grab, Dallas saw its Super Bowl hopes die when Pillers' sack of White caused a fumble. Jim Stuckey recovered for the 49ers, whose victory was accomplished despite six turnovers (three interceptions, three fumbles).

● **Rafael Septien.** Dallas placekicker who had a 44-yard field goal in the first quarter and a 22-yarder in the fourth period, the first cutting San Francisco's lead to 7-3 and the last reducing the 49ers' edge to 21-20. Septien also kicked three extra points.

93 MINUTES, 33 SECONDS

When Los Angeles' Mel Gray broke loose on a 24-yard touchdown jaunt against Michigan on June 30, 1984, in a United States Football League play-off game, the run not only gave the Express a 27-21 victory over the Panthers, it ended the longest game in professional football history (the contest continued to hold that distinction entering 1985). Gray, a running back from Purdue who suffered a season-ending broken arm on the play, crossed the goal line 3 minutes, 33 seconds into the third overtime, meaning the two USFL clubs toiled 93 minutes, 33 seconds at the Los Angeles Memorial Coliseum before reaching a decision.

Supporting Cast:

● **Novo Bojovic.** Michigan placekicker who missed a 37-yard field-goal attempt in the first overtime and failed on a 36-yarder in the second overtime. Bojovic, whose miss from the 36 came with 36 seconds remaining in the sixth period, made three conversion kicks.

● **Bobby Hebert.** Panthers quarterback who tossed two TD passes, the first a 22-yarder to Ken Lacy in the second period and the second a two-yarder to Mike Cobb in the fourth quarter. The scoring passes, coupled with Bojovic's extra points, thrust Michigan into 14-10 and 21-13 advantages.

● **Cleo Miller.** After Los Angeles took a 10-0 lead, Miller got Michigan on the scoreboard with a three-yard touchdown run in the second period.

● **Kevin Nelson.** His one-yard TD burst with 52 seconds left in regulation and quarterback Steve Young's ensuing two-point conversion run rallied the Express to a 21-21 tie and forced the game into sudden-death overtime. Nelson had scored on a five-yard run in the first period.

● **Jojo Townsell.** After the Express and the Panthers struggled through two scoreless overtimes, Townsell got Los Angeles winging on its game-winning drive in the seventh period by catching 19- and 28-yard passes from Young.

● **Tony Zendejas.** He booted a 32-yard field goal for the Express in the second quarter and kicked a 34-yarder in the third period. Zendejas also converted after Nelson's first touchdown.

MEMORABLE PERFORMANCES (Individual & Team)

GRANGE GOES GALLOPING

Michigan was boasting a 20-game unbeaten streak as it prepared for its October 18, 1924, game at Illinois. The Illini had won 10 straight games. Dedication ceremonies for Illinois' Memorial Stadium, which had opened almost a year earlier, would be part of the day's festivities. But no speeches or marching bands could match the manner in which Illinois' Red Grange put his stamp on the Champaign, Ill., facility. In the first 12 minutes of the game, Grange streaked to four touchdowns on plays averaging 65.5 yards. The Galloping Ghost, a junior, returned the opening kickoff 95 yards for a TD, then reeled off scoring runs of 67, 56 and 44 yards as the Illini raced to a

27-0 first-quarter lead. Grange added a 13-yard touchdown sprint in the third period and then threw a 20-yard TD pass in the fourth quarter. When the dust cleared, Illinois owned a 39-14 victory over the Wolverines with Grange accounting for 402 yards (212 yards on 15 rushes, 126 on three kickoff returns and 64 on six pass completions in eight attempts). Grange also intercepted a pass that day.

Supporting Cast:

• **Earl Britton.** He was successful on three extra-point attempts for Illinois.

• **Marion Leonard.** He caught Grange's TD pass.

• **Tod Rockwell.** His one-yard burst in the final quarter gave the Wolverines their second touchdown.

• **Herb Steger.** Michigan player who ran 15 yards for a TD in the second quarter.

SHOWBOATING IN STARKVILLE

Mississippi's A.L. (Showboat) Boykin showed off his scoring talents on December 1, 1951, setting a major-college record by making seven touchdowns in one game as the Rebels walloped Mississippi State, 49-7, in Starkville, Miss. Boykin scored on runs covering 85, 21, 14, 12, 14, 1 and 5 yards and rushed for 187 yards overall on 14 carries (a 13.4 average per attempt).

Supporting Cast:

• **Jimmy Lear.** Ole Miss quarterback who accounted for the rest of the Rebels' points, hitting on all seven conversion-kick tries.

BROWN'S 43-POINT FINALE

Playing the final regular-season game of his collegiate career, fullback Jim Brown gave Syracuse fans an unforgettable performance on November 17, 1956, against Colgate. Brown scored six touchdowns and made seven conversion kicks, setting a major-college scoring mark of 43 points in one game. Brown, who ran 1, 15 and 50 yards for first-quarter touchdowns and rumbled eight yards for a second-period TD, tallied all 27 of the Orangemen's first-half points as Syracuse seized a 20-point lead. Brown went 19 yards for a third-period touchdown and rammed in from the 1 for a fourth-quarter score as the Orange coasted to a 61-7 triumph over the Red Raiders. Overall, Brown gained 197 yards on 22 carries in a game played at Syracuse's Archbold Stadium.

Supporting Cast:

• **Dan Ciervo.** His two-yard burst in the fourth quarter gave Syracuse its ninth and last touchdown of the day.

• **Ferd Kuczala.** Reserve quarterback who ran one yard for a Syracuse touchdown in the third quarter. The TD was the Orangemen's third of the period.

• **Chuck Zimmerman.** His third-period quarterback sneak for a TD opened the second-half scoring and marked Syracuse's first points of the game not scored by Brown.

In the January 1, 1957, Cotton Bowl in Dallas, Brown rushed for three touch-

**Illinois' incomparable Red Grange heads upfield en route to a 95-yard open-
ing-kickoff return in the Illini's 1924 victory over Michigan.**

Syracuse fullback Jim Brown plows through the line for a short gain during the 1957 Cotton Bowl against Texas Christian. Brown accounted for 21 Syracuse points in a 28-27 loss to TCU.

downs and made three of four extra-point attempts against Texas Christian. However, TCU edged Syracuse, 28-27, with the Horned Frogs' Chico Mendoza providing the winning margin by blocking Brown's third conversion-kick try of the day.

SOONERS WIN 47 STRAIGHT

Oklahoma owns major-college football's longest winning streak, having rolled to 47 consecutive triumphs from 1953 to 1957. Not only did the Sooners win with unprecedented regularity, they prevailed decisively (winning 25 of the 47 games by 25 or more points). Oklahoma's streak began on October 10, 1953, in Dallas, when the Sooners edged Texas, 19-14. Victory No. 47 came on November 9, 1957, in Columbia, Mo., as Bud Wilkinson's team thumped Missouri, 39-14. Headlining the victory parade were the Sooners' national-championship teams of 1955 and 1956, which went 21-0 overall (including an Orange Bowl triumph over Maryland on January 2, 1956). The 1954 Sooners also went undefeated. Oklahoma won 20 of the 47 games on its home field in Norman, Okla., racked up 20 victories in opponents' stadiums, beat Texas five times at the "neutral site" of Dallas and scored two Orange Bowl triumphs in Miami.

The Sooners built their record streak against 14 teams, going 5-0 vs. Kansas, Kansas State, Colorado, Missouri, Iowa State and Texas; 4-0 against Nebraska and Oklahoma A&M (which became Oklahoma State in 1957, the year its admission into league play turned the Big Seven Conference into the Big

Oklahoma Coach Bud Wilkinson and his Sooners enjoy a triumphant moment during the 1955 season. The Sooners had plenty such moments during the 1950s, compiling 47 straight wins from 1953 to 1957.

Eight); 2-0 vs. Maryland, North Carolina and Pittsburgh, and 1-0 against Notre Dame, California and Texas Christian. During its string, Oklahoma punished most of its opponents. Among the cumulative scores were: 235-18 vs. Kansas; 174-7 vs. Kansas State; 223-14 vs. Iowa State; 119-28 vs. Texas; 180-20 vs. Nebraska, and 162-7 vs. Oklahoma A&M. The Sooners averaged 34.5 points per game over the 47 contests; opposing teams scored at a 5.9 clip.

Notre Dame, which had been the last team to beat the Sooners before the streak began (the Irish won, 28-21, in Norman in the 1953 season opener), ended Oklahoma's winning streak on November 16, 1957, upsetting the Big Eight juggernaut, 7-0, in Norman.

Oklahoma's record streak, with home opponents capitalized:

1953

21	NOTRE DAME	28
7	Pittsburgh	7
19	Texas (D)	14
45	KANSAS	0
27	COLORADO	20
34	Kansas State	0
14	Missouri	7
47	IOWA STATE	0
30	Nebraska	7
42	OKLAHOMA A&M	7

ORANGE BOWL

7	Maryland	0

1954

27	California	13
21	TEXAS CHRISTIAN	16
14	Texas (D)	7
65	Kansas	0
21	KANSAS STATE	0
13	Colorado	6
40	Iowa State	0
34	MISSOURI	13
55	NEBRASKA	7
14	Oklahoma A&M	0

1955

13	North Carolina	6
26	PITTSBURGH	14
20	Texas (D)	0
44	KANSAS	6
56	COLORADO	21
40	Kansas State	7
20	Missouri	0
52	IOWA STATE	0
41	Nebraska	0
53	OKLAHOMA A&M	0

ORANGE BOWL

20	Maryland	6

1956

36	NORTH CAROLINA	0
66	KANSAS STATE	0
45	Texas (D)	0
34	Kansas	12
40	Notre Dame	0
27	Colorado	19
44	Iowa State	0
67	MISSOURI	14
54	NEBRASKA	6
53	Oklahoma A&M	0

1957

26	Pittsburgh	0
40	IOWA STATE	14
21	Texas (D)	7
47	KANSAS	0
14	COLORADO	13
13	Kansas State	0
39	Missouri	14
0	NOTRE DAME	7
32	Nebraska	7
53	OKLAHOMA STATE	6

ORANGE BOWL

48	Duke	21

D: Game played in Dallas.

Washington holds the major-college record for the longest unbeaten streak, playing 63 games without a defeat from 1907 to 1917. Included within the Huskies' undefeated string of 59 victories and four ties were 39 straight triumphs (1908-1914), a winning streak that ranks second to Oklahoma's national mark. Michigan went undefeated for 56 games from 1901 to 1905, compiling 29- and 26-game winning streaks around a 6-6 tie against Minnesota in 1903.

CHRISTY 29, SOUTH CAROLINA 26

Halfback Dick Christy completed his North Carolina State career in storybook fashion on November 23, 1957, scoring all of his team's points in a 29-26 triumph over South Carolina that wrapped up the Atlantic Coast Conference championship for the Wolfpack. The ending to the game, played in Columbia, S.C., proved particularly dramatic as Christy, with time having expired and the score tied, attempted his first varsity field goal on his last play as a collegian. The result? Christy was on target with a 36-yard boot. Christy had scored earlier on a two-yard run and on three one-yard bursts and had made conversion kicks after two of the touchdowns.

Supporting Cast:

● **Alex Hawkins.** With North Carolina State ahead, 26-19, in the fourth quarter, South Carolina's Hawkins fired a 16-yard scoring pass (off a double reverse) to Julius Derrick with 1 minute, 9 seconds remaining and then kicked the game-tying extra point.

● **Tom Katich.** Time was about to expire in the deadlocked game when the Wolfpack's Katich threw a long pass that was intercepted by Hawkins and

86

returned to the North Carolina State 20-yard line. However, the Gamecocks' defense was penalized for pass interference on the play and, with the clock having run out, the Wolfpack had another chance. Christy then came through with his field goal.

A LINEMAN'S DREAM

Playing defensive tackle for Ohio State in 1958, Jim Marshall had a dream game for a lineman. The future Minnesota Vikings standout scored both of Ohio State's touchdowns as the Buckeyes and Purdue played to a 14-14 tie on November 8 in Columbus, O. In the first 2 minutes of the game, Marshall returned a blocked punt 22 yards for a TD. He then intercepted a deflected Boilermaker pass in the second quarter and ran it back 25 yards for a score.

Supporting Cast:

● **Richard Brooks.** With 2 minutes, 2 seconds left in the game and Ohio State leading, 14-6, Brooks caught a seven-yard touchdown pass from Ross Fichtner and then hauled in a game-tying two-point conversion pass from Purdue halfback Clyde Washington.

● **Jim Houston.** He blocked the Purdue punt and deflected the Boilermaker pass on Marshall's scoring plays.

● **Bob Jarus.** His three-yard TD run in the fourth quarter gave Purdue its first points of the game. A pass attempt for a two-point conversion failed.

● **David Kilgore.** Ohio State kicker who coverted after both of Marshall's touchdowns.

Sixteen years earlier, on October 10, 1942, Illinois lineman Alex Agase scored two TDs—including the game-winner—as the Illini downed Minnesota, 20-13, in Champaign, Ill. Agase ran 35 yards for a touchdown in the second quarter after stealing the ball from the hands of Minnesota star Bill Daley. Then, with 3 minutes left in the game and the score tied 13-13, Agase pounced on an errant Gopher snap from center that had sailed into the Minnesota end zone.

SIX COMPLETIONS, SIX TOUCHDOWNS

Texas-El Paso quarterback Brooks Dawson turned in a one-for-the-book performance on October 27, 1967, passing for touchdowns against New Mexico on his first six completions of the game. Dawson, who entered the game on the Miners' third offensive play, threw incompletions on his first three attempts. Besides the six TD passes, Dawson completed only three other passes in the game and finished with nine completions in 20 attempts for 376 yards. Averaging 41.8 yards per completion and running nine yards for a fourth-quarter touchdown, Dawson powered UTEP to a 75-12 triumph over the Lobos in Albuquerque.

Supporting Cast:

● **Bob Wallace.** UTEP player who teamed with Dawson on a 25-yard scoring pass early in the first quarter.

● **Larry McHenry.** His first-quarter touchdown catch was Dawson's second TD pass of the game and the quarterback's shortest scoring strike—10 yards.

- **Volley Murphy.** Murphy caught TD passes of 74, 86 and 52 yards in the first, second and third quarters, respectively. They accounted for Dawson's third, fifth and sixth scoring passes. Murphy had four receptions overall (one with Billy Stevens at quarterback) for 234 yards.
- **Paul White.** Dawson's fourth straight completion, resulting in his fourth touchdown, went to White. The 83-yard scoring play came in the second quarter.

During the 1968 season, Dawson threw 65 passes in a game against California-Santa Barbara without an interception and later in the season passed for 304 yards in the fourth quarter to rally UTEP past Brigham Young.

REAVES' DAZZLING DEBUT

John Reaves' collegiate debut was auspicious—to say the least. In his first varsity appearance on September 20, 1969, Florida's Reaves fired five touchdown passes—four in the first half as the Gators amassed a 38-6 lead—and sparked his team to a 59-34 victory over the Houston Cougars in Gainesville, Fla. Reaves, a sophomore quarterback, completed 18 of 30 passes for 342 yards.

Supporting Cast:

- **Carlos Alvarez.** On the third play of the game, the Gators' Alvarez, also a sophomore, made his first collegiate reception—and it went for a touchdown. Reaves was on the throwing end of the 70-yard pass play. The Reaves-Alvarez combination also clicked on a 21-yard TD pass in the second quarter, accounting for Reaves' third touchdown aerial of the afternoon.
- **Ken Bailey.** Houston senior quarterback who threw for all five of the Cougars' touchdowns, hitting Elmo Wright three times on scoring passes and Mike Parrott twice. Four of Bailey's TD passes were in the second half.
- **Tommy Durrance.** Florida running back who caught Reaves' fourth and fifth scoring passes of the day, a 46-yarder in the second quarter and a three-yarder in the third period.
- **Garry Walker.** Fullback who scored on Reaves' second touchdown pass, a two-yard pitch in the first quarter.

SHAW THROWS FOR NINE SCORES

San Diego State, riding a record passing performance by Dennis Shaw, overwhelmed New Mexico State, 70-21, on November 15, 1969, in San Diego. Shaw hurled nine touchdown passes—unprecedented in major-college history—for Coach Don Coryell's Aztecs, who bolted to a 49-14 halftime lead over the Aggies. Shaw, completing 26 of 42 passes overall for 441 yards and combining with only two receivers during his TD onslaught, tossed seven of his scoring passes in the first half. After a scoreless third quarter in which he yielded interceptions on three straight possessions, Shaw came back to pitch two more TD passes in the final quarter.

Supporting Cast:

- **Phil Corley.** New Mexico State player whose four-yard scoring reception with 32 seconds left in the game capped a touchdown binge in which all 13 of the game's TDs were scored on pass plays.

● **Tim Delaney.** He caught six of Shaw's touchdown passes, establishing a major-college record for scoring receptions in one game. Delaney hauled in TD passes of two and 22 yards in the first quarter, 34 and 31 yards in the second quarter and 30 and nine yards in the fourth quarter. Delaney totaled 275 yards in receptions.

● **Rhett Putman.** New Mexico State quarterback who threw for three touchdowns.

● **Tom Reynolds.** Aztecs receiver who had only four catches in the game but scored on three of them. Reynolds and Shaw combined for the game's first touchdown on a 14-yard play in the first quarter and then accounted for the final two TDs of the first half on 33- and seven-yard pass plays in the second quarter.

● **Brian Sipe.** Reserve San Diego State quarterback who teamed with Eugene Carter on a 28-yard scoring pass in the fourth quarter. Sipe's TD pass was sandwiched between Shaw's eighth and ninth touchdown passes.

DAVIS DESTROYS IRISH

Southern California's Anthony Davis put on one of college football's most stirring offensive displays on December 2, 1972, scoring six touchdowns as the Trojans drubbed Notre Dame, 45-23, at the Los Angeles Memorial Coliseum. The sophomore tailback collected his first and fifth TDs in dramatic fashion. Davis took the game's opening kickoff and sprinted 97 yards for a score; then, after Southern Cal's lead had been reduced to 25-23, he went 96 yards on a kickoff return late in the third period. Davis, whose 22 rushes against the Fighting Irish netted 99 yards, also scored on one- and five-yard runs in the first quarter, a four-yard thrust in the third period and an eight-yard dash in the final quarter.

Supporting Cast:

● **Tom Clements.** Quarterback who rallied the Irish within two points of the Trojans after Notre Dame had fallen behind by 19-3 and 25-10 scores. He hit Willie Townsend on a five-yard scoring pass in the second quarter, found Gary Diminick on an 11-yard touchdown pitch in the third period and, with USC ahead, 25-17, teamed with Mike Creaney on a 10-yard TD pass with 1 minute, 19 seconds left in the third quarter. Bob Thomas accounted for Notre Dame's other points with a 45-yard field goal in the first quarter and two conversion kicks.

● **Sam Cunningham.** Trojan fullback who threw key blocks for Davis on his TD runs from scrimmage and tallied the last points of the game on a one-yard TD burst in the fourth period.

In the 1974 Southern Cal-Notre Dame game in Los Angeles, senior tailback Davis scored four touchdowns—one on a kickoff return—as the Trojans roared from behind to batter the Irish, 55-24.

FOUR 1,000-YARD SEASONS

Only two players in major-college history have rushed for 1,000 or more yards in all four of their varsity seasons. Pittsburgh's Tony Dorsett was the first to turn in such a performance, surpassing the 1,000-yard mark from

1973 through 1976. In the first year after Dorsett's departure from the collegiate ranks, North Carolina's Amos Lawrence began a 1,000-yards-a-season streak that ran through 1980. The year-by-year rushing figures for Dorsett, who averaged 5.7 yards per carry in his Panther career, and Lawrence, who averaged five yards per attempt for the Tar Heels:

DORSETT			LAWRENCE		
Year	Attempts	Yards	Year	Attempts	Yards
1973	288	1586	1977	193	1211
1974	220	1004	1978	234	1043
1975	228	1544	1979	225	1019
1976	338	1948	1980	229	1118
	1074	6082		881	4391

CATCH 22

Playing against New Mexico on November 3, 1973, Brigham Young's Jay Miller caught 22 passes, a major-college record. Miller's exploits, which included three touchdown receptions, helped BYU to a 56-21 triumph over the Lobos in Provo, Utah.

Supporting Cast:

• **Wayne Bower.** He caught three passes for the Cougars that day—and all went for touchdowns.

• **Randy Litchfield.** Reserve BYU quarterback who teamed with Miller for the receiver's final two receptions of the day, four-yard plays in the fourth quarter.

• **Gary Sheide.** Sheide threw for six touchdowns against New Mexico, hitting Miller on 33-, 17- and six-yard scoring plays and finding Bower on 13-, two- and seven-yard TD completions. Miller had the following reception/yardage totals while combining with Sheide: Three catches, 61 yards (one touchdown), first quarter; six, 74 yards (one TD), second quarter; four, 54 yards, third quarter; seven, 66 yards (one TD), fourth quarter. Miller had 263 yards in receptions overall; Sheide totaled 408 yards passing, completing 32 of 50 attempts (one interception).

CROMWELL ADAPTS IN A HURRY

A former safety making his first collegiate start at quarterback, Nolan Cromwell quickly found the knack of running Kansas' newly installed wishbone offense in a September 27, 1975, game against Oregon State in Lawrence, Kan. Cromwell carried the ball 28 times for 294 yards, setting a major-college rushing record for a quarterback and breaking Kansas' overall rushing mark of 283 yards established by Gale Sayers in 1962. Cromwell, a defensive back under Coach Don Fambrough in his first two seasons as a Jayhawk, was moved into the starting quarterback job in the third week of the '75 season (Bud Moore's first year as Kansas coach). With Cromwell, a junior, running 79 yards for a second-quarter touchdown and averaging 10.5 yards per carry overall, the Jayhawks downed the Beavers, 20-0.

Supporting Cast:

• **Dennis Kerbel.** Kansas placekicker who booted 23- and 37-yard field

Nolan Cromwell, a defensive back during his first two years at Kansas and a Pro Bowl safety for the NFL's Los Angeles Rams after his collegiate playing days were over, took over at quarterback in the third week of the 1975 season. Running the Jayhawks' wishbone in a game against Oregon State, Cromwell set a major-college rushing record for a quarterback with 294 yards.

goals in the first period, a 41-yarder in the second quarter and a 20-yarder in the final period. The Jayhawks also scored on a fourth-quarter safety.

FRANKLIN TOES THE MARK

Through the 1975 season, no major-college placekicker had booted two field goals of 60 or more yards in one season, and only Air Force's Dave Lawson had connected on two such attempts in a career (a 60-yarder in 1974 and a 62-yarder in 1975). Furthermore, no one had made one beyond 63 yards. However, on October 16, 1976, in College Station, Tex., Texas A&M's Tony Franklin boomed 64- and 65-yard field goals in one game, sparking the Aggies to a 24-0 triumph over the Baylor Bears. Franklin, who had kicked a 24-yard field goal in the first quarter, made his 64-yarder in the second period and hit on his 65-yarder in the third quarter.

Supporting Cast:

● **Curtis Dickey.** With Texas A&M ahead, 17-0, in the third quarter, Dickey darted 35 yards for a touchdown. Franklin's conversion kick completed the game's scoring.

● **David Walker.** He threw a 15-yard TD pass to Gary Haack in the second period, then ran for a two-point conversion.

On the same day that Franklin made his prodigious kicks, Ove Johansson of Abilene Christian set a collegiate record (all classifications) with a 69-yard field goal against East Texas State.

Russell Erxleben (Texas, 1977), Steve Little (Arkansas, 1977) and Joe Williams (Wichita State, 1978) now share the major-college record for the longest field goal, 67 yards. (Two weeks after Erxleben kicked his 67-yarder for Texas against Rice, the Longhorns were victims of Little's 67-yard boot.) While Erxleben also made 64- and 60-yard field goals during the '77 season, Franklin remains the lone player in major-college history to have kicked two 60-yarders in one game.

CARSON'S FIRST SIX CATCHES

Wide receiver Carlos Carson's first six receptions as a college player couldn't have produced better results—Carson scored on each catch. As a Louisiana State sophomore in 1977, Carson caught his initial college pass in the opening quarter of a September 24 game in Baton Rouge, La., against Rice and turned it into a 22-yard scoring play. Before the first half was over, Carson had caught three more passes—all for touchdowns—as LSU built a 28-0 lead on the way to a 77-0 triumph. Carson added a fifth TD reception in the second half and finished the game with five catches for 201 yards and five touchdowns. The following week, Carson had one catch against Florida —and it went for 15 yards and a touchdown.

Supporting Cast:

● **Steve Ensminger.** LSU quarterback who threw four first-half touchdown passes to Carson in the Rice game, the last three covering 29, 63 and 20 yards. Ensminger had only one other completion in the game.

● **David Woodley.** LSU quarterback who combined with Carson on a 67-yard scoring pass in the third quarter of the Rice contest. Woodley then completed one pass in the Florida game—the TD strike to Carson—as the Bayou Tigers breezed to a 36-14 victory in Baton Rouge.

WILSON PASSES FOR 621 YARDS

Quarterback Dave Wilson of Illinois established an NCAA single-game record of 621 yards passing on November 8, 1980, but Wilson's spree was in vain as Ohio State scored a 49-42 victory at Columbus, O. Wilson, who completed 43 of 69 passes and was intercepted three times, threw six touchdown passes against the Buckeyes, with five coming in the second half after the Illini fell behind, 35-7.

Supporting Cast:

● **Lee Boeke.** Illinois player who caught the first of Wilson's second-half scoring passes, a 38-yard completion. He had five catches overall for 110 yards.

● **Joe Curtis.** The Illini's leader in receptions with 10, which netted 96 yards.

● **Greg Dentino.** He scored Illinois' first and third touchdowns on 24- and eight-yard passes from Wilson and had six catches for 105 yards.

● **Greg Foster.** He caught two passes for a total of only three yards—but scored twice. Foster was on the receiving end of Wilson's fifth and sixth scoring passes, making two- and one-yard catches in the fourth quarter (the latter coming with 11 seconds left in the game).

● **Mike Martin.** Collecting a game-high 147 yards in receptions, Martin hauled in a 13-yard pass in the third quarter for Wilson's fourth TD throw of the day. Martin's touchdown and Mike Bass' conversion kick cut Ohio State's lead to 35-28, but the Buckeyes prevailed on fourth-quarter scoring runs by Calvin Murray and Tim Spencer.

● **Art Schlichter.** Ohio State quarterback who also enjoyed a big day, passing for four touchdowns.

BRYANT'S SCORING BINGE

All North Carolina had to do at the outset of the 1981 college football season was point Kelvin Bryant toward the end zone and the tailback would do the rest. Bryant scored 15 touchdowns in the first three games of '81 as the Tar Heels outscored East Carolina, Miami (O.) and Boston College by a cumulative 161-21 score. Bryant rushed for 520 yards on 70 attempts in the three games, an average of 7.4 yards per carry. He rushed for 211 yards and six touchdowns against East Carolina, scoring on runs of 1, 45, 4, 7, 32 and 4 yards as the Tar Heels prevailed, 56-0. Bryant ran for 136 yards against Miami, making touchdown runs of 8, 2, 1 and 4 yards and also scoring on a 15-yard pass from Rod Elkins in a 49-7 rout. In North Carolina's 56-14 trouncing of Boston College, Bryant had scoring runs of 2, 2, 39 and 4 yards and gained 173 yards rushing overall. Bryant, though, suffered a knee injury in the opening quarter of North Carolina's next game, against Georgia Tech, and scored only three touchdowns the rest of the season and finished the year with 1,015 yards rushing. Arthroscopic surgery forced Bryant to miss four full games.

Supporting Cast:

● **Victor Harrison.** Of the eight Tar Heel touchdowns (out of 23) not scored by Bryant in the first three games of the '81 season, Harrison notched two of them on eight- and 10-yard TD passes from Elkins (against Boston College).

● **Bobby Ratliff.** He also scored two touchdowns in the three games, running two yards for a score in the East Carolina game and going one yard for a TD against Boston College.

North Carolina's other non-Bryant TDs in the three-game stretch: Alan Burrus' one-yard run against East Carolina, Greg Poole's 28-yard interception return against Miami, Larry Griffin's 16-yard catch of a Scott Stankavage pass against Miami and Mark Smith's 63-yard reception of an Elkins pass against Boston College.

ALLEN'S 2,342 YARDS

Marcus Allen holds the major-college record for most yards rushing in one season, gaining 2,342 for Southern California in 1981. Allen picked up 200 or more yards in a record five consecutive games and finished the year with eight 200-plus performances (another mark). And the Trojan standout averaged 5.8 yards per carry and 212.9 yards rushing per game. The 1981 regular-season rushing statistics for Allen (who scored 22 touchdowns on the ground and one on a reception), with home opponents capitalized:

		Attempts	Yards
September 12	TENNESSEE	22	210
September 19	Indiana	40	274
September 26	OKLAHOMA	39	208
October 3	Oregon State	35	233
October 10	ARIZONA	26	211
October 17	STANFORD	40	153
October 24	Notre Dame	33	147
October 31	WASHINGTON STATE	44	289
November 7	California	46	243
November 14	Washington	38	155
November 21	UCLA	40	219
		403	2342

OLE MISS QB ON TARGET

"Pinpoint accuracy" surely applied to the passing performance put on by Mississippi quarterback Kent Austin on November 6, 1982, in Jackson, Miss. Picking Tulane's pass defense clean, Austin set a major-college record for completion percentage in one game (minimum 15 attempts) by hitting on 18 of 19 passes as the Rebels trounced the Green Wave, 45-14. Austin threw for 269 yards and two touchdowns while completing 94.7 percent of his passes.

Supporting Cast:

● **James Harbour.** He teamed with Austin on a 55-yard pass play that netted Ole Miss a second-quarter touchdown.

● **Buford McGee.** McGee caught a 57-yard TD pass from Austin in the fourth quarter.

● **Andre Thomas.** While Austin had the Rebels' passing game in gear, Thomas kept Ole Miss rolling on the ground. He rushed for 106 yards and three touchdowns.

Southern Cal running back Marcus Allen picks up five of his single-season record 2,342 yards during a 1981 game against Arizona.

RUEBEN MAYES' 357 ...

Offense was the name of the game when Washington State and Oregon collided on October 27, 1984, at Eugene, Ore. The visiting Cougars compiled 663 yards in total offense, and the Ducks gained 478 yards overall. The Pacific-10 Conference teams combined for 91 points. Of the total of 58 passes attempted in the game, only one was intercepted. And Washington State made eight yards per offensive play, Oregon 6.2. Cries of "Defense, Defense" were few and far between at Autzen Stadium. It was in this setting that one of major-college football's most prized records—the individual rushing-yardage mark—fell. Washington State's Rueben Mayes, who the week before had made five touchdowns against Stanford, went on a 357-yard rushing rampage against Oregon and thus surpassed—by one yard—the single-game mark established six years earlier by Eddie Lee Ivery of Georgia Tech. Mayes carried the ball nine times in the first quarter, netting 41 yards, and then emerged as a threat to Ivery's mark with an 11-carry, 156-yard second period. The Cougars' standout carried the ball only seven times in the third quarter but gained 73 yards, giving him 270 yards entering the final period. Mayes rushed 12 times in the fourth quarter for 87 yards, breaking Ivery's record on his last carry (a four-yard gain that came about a minute from the finish). Mayes, who toted the ball 39 times overall, averaged 9.2 yards per attempt in the game (won by Washington State, 50-41).

Supporting Cast:

● **Rick Chase.** Washington State player who carried the ball once against Oregon, on a fake-punt play—and ran 77 yards for a touchdown. The Cougars collected all six of their touchdowns on the ground, with Mayes making scoring runs of two, 69 and 12 yards, Mark Rypien sneaking one yard for a score and Richard Calvin going eight yards for a TD.

● **Tony Cherry, Chris Miller.** Oregon's big guns offensively, with Cherry rushing for 83 yards and two touchdowns and Miller passing for 238 yards and one TD.

Mayes' explosive day against Oregon also enabled him to set a major-college record for rushing yardage in two straight games. Having gained 216 yards against Stanford on October 20, Mayes recorded a consecutive-game total of 573 yards.

... AND EDDIE LEE IVERY'S 356

November 11, 1978, was a wintry day at the Air Force Academy's Falcon Stadium. It was 22 degrees at kickoff, with a 16-mile-per-hour wind blowing and snow falling. It was hardly the kind of an afternoon on which to expect a scintillating performance. Georgia Tech's Eddie Lee Ivery was undeterred, however, despite gaining only 11 yards on his first four carries that day against Air Force. After the slow start, Ivery shredded the Falcons' defense by gaining 345 yards on his final 22 carries. Included in Ivery's dash to a then-record 356 yards rushing were touchdown sprints of 73, 80 and 57 yards. Ironically, Ivery (who averaged 13.7 yards per carry against the Falcons) fumbled away the ball on his record-setting play, a 21-yard gain. Georgia Tech walloped Air Force, 42-21.

SECOND QUARTER—PRO

MEMORABLE PERFORMANCES (Individual & Team)

MORE THAN SLINGIN' FOR BAUGH

While Sid Luckman of the Chicago Bears was giving the National Football League a lesson in passing artistry (seven touchdown passes) on the same day in New York, the Redskins' Sammy Baugh was conducting a clinic on versatility in Washington. Throwing for four touchdowns and becoming the first NFL player to intercept four passes in one game, Baugh led the Redskins to a 42-20 pounding of the Detroit Lions on November 14, 1943. Additionally, Baugh's quick kicks repeatedly bottled up the Detroit offense.

Supporting Cast:

● **Bob Masterson.** Redskins player who caught two of Baugh's touchdown passes. Bob Seymour and Joe Aguirre were on the receiving end of the others.

● **Frank Sinkwich.** Although he was the victim of all four of Baugh's interceptions, Sinkwich had his moments, too. He tossed two touchdown passes for the Lions, intercepted a Baugh pass and returned it for a TD and got off a 79-yard, non-scoring run from scrimmage.

303 YARDS FOR RECEIVER BENTON

Jim Benton owns the National Football League record for most reception yardage in one game, catching 10 passes for 303 yards in a November 22, 1945, contest in Detroit and helping the Cleveland Rams to a 28-21 victory over the Lions.

Supporting Cast:

● **Bob Waterfield.** Rams passer who teamed with Benton on the receiver's lone touchdown reception of the game, which came on a 70-yard play.

Five years after Benton's big game, Detroit's Cloyce Box threatened the NFL reception-yardage mark for one game. Playing against the Colts on December 3, 1950, in Baltimore, Box hauled in 12 passes that netted 302 yards and four touchdowns. Box combined with Bobby Layne on three of the TD pass plays and hooked up with Fred Enke on the other as the Lions roared to a 45-21 triumph.

HARDY: RIDICULOUS TO SUBLIME

It has to rank as one of the sports world's greatest individual turnabouts. On September 24, 1950, quarterback Jim Hardy of the Chicago Cardinals set a National Football League record for passing futility by throwing eight interceptions against the Philadelphia Eagles in the Cards' season opener at Comiskey Park. In the Cardinals' next game, against the Baltimore Colts at Comiskey Park, Hardy rebounded to toss six touchdown passes (one shy of the NFL mark).

Supporting Cast:

● **Russ Craft.** He intercepted four of Hardy's passes as Philadelphia breezed to a 45-7 victory.

● **Joe Sutton.** Eagles defender who picked off three passes against the erring Hardy, who also lost the ball on fumbles three times. Hardy, who completed only 12 of 39 passes against Philadelphia, saw three of his interceptions set up Eagle touchdowns and watched as his fumbles led to two Eagle TDs and a field goal.

● **Bob Shaw.** He caught five of Hardy's six touchdown passes against the Colts on October 2, 1950, with the TD-reception total being unprecedented in NFL history. Chicago, trailing 13-7 at halftime, stormed back and flattened Baltimore, 55-13, in a Monday night game.

FEARS' 18 RECEPTIONS

Tom Fears holds the National Football League record for most receptions in one game, catching 18 passes for the Los Angeles Rams in a December 3,

1950, game against Green Bay in Los Angeles. Fears totaled 189 yards on his catches (10 of which came in the fourth quarter) and scored two touchdowns as the Rams overwhelmed the Packers, 51-14.

Supporting Cast:

● **Glenn Davis.** He notched Los Angeles' first two touchdowns of the game, scoring on a four-yard run and on a nine-yard pass reception in the second quarter. The Rams also scored on a safety in the second period on their way to a 16-7 halftime lead.

● **Norm Van Brocklin.** Rams passer who threw for 212 yards and three TDs against Green Bay. He connected with Davis in the second quarter, then teamed with Elroy Hirsch (37 yards) and Fears (11 yards) in the third period.

● **Bob Waterfield.** Los Angeles quarterback who passed for 139 yards and two touchdowns. He hit Vitamin Smith with a three-yard scoring pass in the third quarter and found Fears on a four-yard TD pass play in the final quarter.

● **Tank Younger.** His three-yard burst in the fourth period was the Rams' seventh and last TD of the game.

VAN BROCKLIN'S 554-YARD GAME

Norm Van Brocklin got the 1951 National Football League season off to a rousing start for Los Angeles, passing for a league-record 554 yards as the Rams walloped the New York Yanks, 54-14, on September 28 at the Los Angeles Memorial Coliseum. Van Brocklin completed 27 of 41 passes in the Friday night game, with five of his completions going for touchdowns. He also scored a TD on a one-yard run.

Supporting Cast:

● **Elroy (Crazy Legs) Hirsch.** Rams receiver who teamed with Van Brocklin on 46-, 47-, 26- and one-yard touchdown passes.

● **Vitamin Smith.** Smith and Van Brocklin combined on a 67-yard pass play, good for another Los Angeles touchdown.

Ram passers rank 1-2 on the NFL single-game yardage chart. Vince Ferragamo claimed the No. 2 spot on December 26, 1982, throwing for 509 yards in the Rams' 34-26 loss to the Chicago Bears. Ferragamo, who completed 30 of 46 attempts, tossed three touchdown passes in the game played at Anaheim Stadium.

TWO PUNT RETURNS FOR TDs—TWICE

Only four players in National Football League history have returned two punts for touchdowns in one game and one of those four, Detroit's Jack Christiansen, accomplished the feat twice—within $5\frac{1}{2}$ weeks. As a Lions rookie in 1951, Christiansen returned Los Angeles punts 69 and 48 yards for scores (in the second and fourth quarters, respectively), but the Rams prevailed in the October 14 game, 27-21. On November 22, Christiansen raced 72 and 89 yards to touchdowns on third-period punt returns against Green Bay as the Lions romped to a 52-35 victory. Both games were played in Detroit.

Supporting Cast:

● **Bobby Layne.** He paced the Lions' offense against Green Bay, hurling four TD passes (two to Leon Hart, one to Bob Hoernschemeyer and one to Doak Walker). Hoernschemeyer also made an 85-yard run for a touchdown.

● **Bob Waterfield.** His two touchdown passes (to Elroy Hirsch and Norb Hecker), two field goals and three conversion kicks helped the Rams overcome Christiansen's heroics. Los Angeles also scored on a Norm Van Brocklin-to-Tom Fears pass.

Dick Christy scored on 70- and 64-yard punt returns in New York on September 24, 1961, pacing the Titans to a 35-28 triumph over the Denver Broncos. On September 26, 1976, in Denver, the Broncos' Rick Upchurch sped 73 and 36 yards for punt-return TDs as Denver defeated the Cleveland Browns, 44-13. And on October 11, 1981, in Atlanta, LeRoy Irvin of the Rams ran back punts 75 and 84 yards to help Los Angeles past the Falcons, 37-35.

UNITAS' TD-PASS STREAK: 47 GAMES

Baltimore quarterback Johnny Unitas had one touchdown pass in each of the Colts' final three regular-season games of 1956, but such a performance was hardly an attention-getter. Unitas, though, began to attract the spotlight in 1957 when he continued to ring up TD passes, game by game. The touchdown-pass streak extended into 1958 . . . and 1959 . . . and 1960. Through game 10 of the 1960 season, Unitas had thrown touchdown passes in a record 47 consecutive regular-season National Football League games. In game 11 of the '60 campaign, though, the string ended where it had begun—at the Los Angeles Memorial Coliseum. Unitas and the Colts failed to score a touchdown in their December 11 meeting with Los Angeles—Johnny completed 17 of 38 pass attempts for 182 yards and was intercepted once—as Baltimore lost to the Rams, 10-3. During his 47-game string, Unitas completed 697 of 1,298 passes (he was intercepted 61 times) for 10,645 yards and 102 touchdowns as he led the Colts to a 31-16 record. Unitas, who missed two games because of injury in 1958, passed for four TDs in one game seven times during the stretch.

Supporting Cast:

● **Raymond Berry.** Colts receiver who accounted for more than one-third of Unitas' TD passes during the streak, hauling in 38 scoring receptions. When Unitas threw for four touchdowns against both Dallas (October 30) and Green Bay (November 6) in successive games in 1960, Berry was on the receiving end of six of the scoring passes.

● **Lenny Moore.** He and Unitas teamed on an 80-yard scoring pass against Detroit on December 4, 1960, in Baltimore, extending to 47 the number of consecutive games in which Unitas had tossed at least one TD pass. Later in the game against the Lions, Moore scored on a 38-yard pass from Unitas. Moore caught 27 TD passes from Unitas during the streak.

● **Jim Mutscheller.** He got the streak going on December 9, 1956, in Los Angeles, taking a three-yard scoring pass from Unitas. Mutscheller had 25 touchdown passes from Unitas in the 47 games. (Rounding out the list of Colts who scored on touchdown passes from Unitas during the streak: Alan

Ameche, four TD catches; L.G. Dupre and Alex Hawkins, three each, and Jerry Richardson, two.)

Unitas' record streak is nearly double that of his nearest challenger in the NFL record book. Daryle Lamonica, the No. 2 man, passed for TDs in 25 straight games for the Oakland Raiders from 1968 to 1970.

Unitas threw for one touchdown in the 1958 NFL championship game against the New York Giants and passed for two scores in the Colts' 1959 title meeting with the Giants, meaning his streak actually reached 49 games. However, postseason statistics are not included in NFL records.

TITTLE: SEVEN TDs, 505 YARDS

New York quarterback Y.A. Tittle equalled a National Football League record on October 28, 1962, when he tossed seven touchdown passes, leading the Giants past the Washington Redskins, 49-34, at Yankee Stadium. Tittle, who completed 12 straight passes in one stretch, hit on 27 of 39 passes overall and was not intercepted. Besides matching the touchdown-pass mark achieved earlier by Sid Luckman, Adrian Burk and George Blanda and tied seven years later by Joe Kapp, Tittle also threw for 505 yards (which now ranks third on the all-time NFL list).

Supporting Cast:

● **Frank Gifford.** He caught Tittle's sixth and longest touchdown pass of the day, a 63-yard completion in the third quarter.

● **Joe Morrison.** Giants player who scored on Tittle's first and third TD passes, first-half plays covering 22 and two yards.

● **Del Shofner.** While he caught only one of Tittle's scoring passes, a 32-yarder in the third quarter, Shofner was the veteran quarterback's favorite target. He made 11 receptions for 269 yards.

● **Norm Snead.** Quarterback who paced the Redskins' offense with four scoring passes, including 44- and 80-yard completions to Bobby Mitchell, and a one-yard touchdown run.

● **Joe Walton.** He caught Tittle's second, fifth and seventh TD passes, scoring on plays of four, 26 and six yards. The catches came in the second, third and fourth quarters.

Luckman, playing for the Chicago Bears, was the first NFL player to throw seven TD passes in one game, accomplishing the feat against the New York Giants on November 14, 1943. Luckman, who passed for 433 yards as the Bears romped, 56-7, at the Polo Grounds, threw two touchdown passes to both Jim Benton and Hampton Pool and one each to Connie Berry, George Wilson and Harry Clark (who ran for Chicago's other touchdown).

Burk's seven touchdown passes came against the Redskins on October 17, 1954, in Washington as the Philadelphia Eagles rolled to a 49-21 victory. Burk, who totaled only 242 yards passing, connected three times on scoring aerials with both Pete Pihos and Bobby Walston and once with Toy Ledbetter. Burk's seventh TD pass, to Pihos, came with 10 seconds left in the game. (Six weeks later, Burk fired five more scoring passes against the Redskins as the Eagles won, 41-33, in Philadelphia.)

Like Burk, Houston's Blanda teamed with only three receivers to enter the record book. Accounting for all of his team's points in the Oilers' 49-13 rout of the New York Titans on November 19, 1961, in Houston, Blanda tossed three touchdown passes to both Billy Cannon and Bill Groman and hurled one to Charley Hennigan. He threw for 418 yards. Additionally, Blanda kicked all seven extra points for the Oilers.

Kapp's seven TD passes went to six Minnesota players as the Vikings overwhelmed the Baltimore Colts, 52-14, on September 28, 1969, in Bloomington, Minn. Gene Washington caught two of Kapp's touchdown throws, while Dave Osborn, Bob Grim, Kent Kramer, John Beasley and Jim Lindsey accounted for the others. Kapp amassed 449 yards passing.

MARSHALL RUNS WRONG WAY

Minnesota Vikings defensive end Jim Marshall picked up a San Francisco fumble in the fourth quarter of an October 25, 1964, game at Kezar Stadium and lumbered 60 yards to the goal line—his own goal line, that is. "I thought they were cheering me on," Marshall said of the frantic Viking coaches and players who were screaming at him from the sidelines. "About the 5-yard line, I looked around and things just didn't seem right. Fran (Tarkenton, Minnesota quarterback) was yelling at me from the sidelines and pointing in the opposite direction. I couldn't think of anything else to do, so I threw him the ball." Marshall's pitch came inside the end zone, with the ball rolling out of play for a safety (had the ball stayed within the end zone, the 49ers would have had a chance to recover it for a touchdown). Despite the blunder, the Vikings, ahead by 10 points preceding the play, held on for a 27-22 National Football League victory.

Supporting Cast:

● **Bruce Bosley.** San Francisco center who, with hand extended, "congratulated" Marshall on his misplay immediately after it occurred. The two-point play cut Minnesota's lead to 27-19.

● **Tommy Davis.** Placekicker who booted a 48-yard field goal for the 49ers on San Francisco's ensuing possession after the safety, bringing the 49ers within five points.

● **Carl Eller.** Minnesota defensive lineman whose 45-yard, right-way run with a fumble recovery, combined with Fred Cox's conversion kick, boosted the Vikings to a 27-17 edge in the fourth quarter.

● **Bill Kilmer.** 49er who advanced a couple steps after making a fourth-period catch of a George Mira pass, then fumbled. Marshall, obviously disoriented, picked up the loose ball and headed in the same direction that Kilmer was going.

● **Fran Tarkenton.** With San Francisco ahead, 17-13, entering the last quarter, Tarkenton sent the Vikings in front with an eight-yard TD run. Cox added the extra point.

● **Roy Winston.** Minnesota linebacker whose interception of a Mira pass on the 49ers' 11 set up Tarkenton's scoring run. Winston had three interceptions in the game.

Baltimore receiver Lenny Moore takes off after hauling in a pass from Johnny Unitas during a 1964 game against Los Angeles. Moore scored touchdowns in an NFL-record 18 straight games from 1963 to 1965.

MOORE'S TOUCHDOWN STREAK

Lenny Moore scored touchdowns for the Baltimore Colts in 18 consecutive National Football League regular-season games from 1963 to 1965, establishing an NFL record. Moore made touchdowns in the Colts' seventh, eighth and ninth games of the 1963 season, sat out the last five games of '63 because of an injury, collected TDs in all 14 of Baltimore's games in 1964 and ran for a score in the first game of the '65 season.

Supporting Cast:

● **Johnny Unitas.** Colts quarterback who teamed with Moore on a 13-yard touchdown pass in an October 27, 1963, game against Green Bay, marking the beginning of Moore's streak. Unitas and Moore teamed for three other scoring passes in the 18 games (in both game one and game 13 of the streak, a pass from Unitas accounted for Moore's only TD of the day).

● **Raymond Berry.** On December 6, 1964, Unitas completed a pass to Jimmy Orr at the Detroit 35 and Orr rambled to the 5, where he fumbled. Teammate Berry knocked the loose ball into the end zone, and Moore recovered it for a touchdown. The freak play enabled Moore to extend his TD-scoring streak to 16 games.

Moore scored 24 touchdowns in the 18 games, with 19 coming on runs, four on receptions and one on a fumble recovery. The streak ended on September 26, 1965, when Moore was shut out in a game against Green Bay in Milwaukee.

Moore's touchdown plays during the 18-game streak, with dates, sites (H: home, A: away) and opponents listed:

October 27, 1963	H	Green Bay	13-yard pass from Unitas
November 3, 1963	H	Chicago	25-yard run
November 10, 1963	H	Detroit	4 run
September 13, 1964	A	Minnesota	2 run, 70 pass-Unitas
September 20, 1964	A	Green Bay	52 pass-Unitas, 4 run
September 27, 1964	H	Chicago	3 run
October 4, 1964	H	Los Angeles	12 run, 32 run
October 12, 1964	H	St. Louis	5 run
October 18, 1964	H	Green Bay	21 run, 5 run
October 25, 1964	A	Detroit	11 run
November 1, 1964	H	San Francisco	2 run, 5 run
November 8, 1964	A	Chicago	2 run
November 15, 1964	H	Minnesota	74 pass-Unitas
November 22, 1964	A	Los Angeles	18 run
November 29, 1964	A	San Francisco	2 run
December 6, 1964	H	Detroit	fumble recovery in end zone
December 13, 1964	H	Washington	3 run, 1 run
September 19, 1965	H	Minnesota	1 run

SAYERS GOES ON TD TEAR

Gale Sayers, playing the next-to-last game of his scintillating rookie season for the Chicago Bears, tied a National Football League record on December 12, 1965, scoring six touchdowns as the Bears crushed the San Francisco 49ers, 61-20, at Wrigley Field. Sayers scored on an 80-yard pass play in the first quarter, 21- and seven-yard runs in the second period, 50- and one-yard runs in the third period and on an 85-yard punt return in the final quarter. Sayers, who finished with 22 touchdowns in his first pro season, rushed nine times against the 49ers for 113 yards.

Chicago running back Gale Sayers (left) exploded for six touchdowns in one of the great performances in NFL history. While the Bears were crushing San Francisco on that December 12, 1965, afternoon, Green Bay's Paul Hornung (No. 5, below, in action against the New York Giants) was scoring five TDs in the Packers' 42-27 victory over Baltimore.

Supporting Cast:

● **Jon Arnett.** He scored the Bears' ninth and last touchdown, running two yards in the fourth quarter.

● **Rudy Bukich.** Besides teaming with Sayers on the long scoring pass, quarterback Bukich combined with Mike Ditka (29 yards, first quarter) and Jimmy Jones (eight yards, final period) for the Bear TD passes.

On the same afternoon that produced Sayers' exploits, Green Bay's Paul Hornung scored five touchdowns as the Packers defeated the Colts, 42-27, at Baltimore's Memorial Stadium. Hornung scored on runs of two, nine and three yards and on 50- and 65-yard passes from Bart Starr.

The first NFL player to make six TDs in a game was Ernie Nevers of the Chicago Cardinals, who scored all of his team's points on November 28, 1929, in a 40-6 triumph over the Chicago Bears. Nevers' TDs, which all came on the ground, covered 20, 4, 6, 1, 1 and 10 yards. Contributing four conversion placements as well, Nevers established a single-game NFL individual scoring record of 40 points that still stands. The Bears' touchdown was scored by Grange—Garland (Gardie) Grange, Red's brother. Young Grange and Walt Holmer teamed on a 60-yard pass play.

The only other player in NFL history to tally six TDs in a game was Cleveland's Dub Jones (father of future NFL quarterback Bert Jones). Jones scored on runs of 2, 11, 27 and 43 yards and on 34- and 43-yard passes from Otto Graham as the Browns routed the Chicago Bears, 42-21, on November 25, 1951, in Cleveland.

TDs ON TWO KICKOFF RETURNS

Only twice in National Football League history have players returned two kickoffs for touchdowns in one game. Interestingly, though, those feats were accomplished in successive seasons. On November 6, 1966, Philadelphia's Timmy Brown ran back first- and second-quarter kickoffs 93 and 90 yards to fuel the Eagles to a 24-23 triumph over the Dallas Cowboys. On November 12, 1967, Travis Williams raced 87 yards with the opening kickoff and traveled 85 yards later in the first quarter as the Green Bay Packers built a 35-7 opening-period lead on their way to a 55-7 manhandling of the Cleveland Browns.

Supporting Cast:

● **Donny Anderson.** Besides Williams, running back Anderson was a big gun for Green Bay in its '67 rout of Cleveland in Milwaukee. Anderson scored four touchdowns, running two, nine and three yards for scores and catching a 27-yard TD pass from Bart Starr.

● **Aaron Martin.** He gave the Eagles a third kick-return touchdown in their 1966 rematch against Dallas in Philadelphia, going 67 yards with a Cowboy punt in the second quarter. The Eagles' triumph avenged a 56-7 pasting that the Cowboys had handed Philadelphia earlier in the year.

BAKKEN GETS HIS KICKS

St. Louis' Jim Bakken kicked a National Football League-record seven field goals on September 24, 1967, lifting the Cardinals to a 28-14 victory over the Steelers in Pittsburgh. None of the kicks was a long-range shot—the field goals coming from 18, 24, 33, 29, 24, 32 and 23 yards out—but Bakken's 22-point day proved more than a match for the Pittsburgh offense. Bakken kicked four field goals in the first half—two in each quarter—as the Cardinals built a 19-7 lead, then booted three in the fourth period after the Steelers had closed within five points. He attempted nine field goals overall.

Supporting Cast:

● **Chet Anderson.** After the Cardinals had taken a 16-0 edge, Pittsburgh's Anderson hauled in a five-yard touchdown pass from Bill Nelsen in the second quarter.

● **Willie Asbury.** His one-yard TD run in the third quarter, coupled with Mike Clark's second extra-point kick of the game, narrowed Pittsburgh's deficit to 19-14.

● **Jim Hart.** St. Louis quarterback who scored the Cards' only touchdown on a 23-yard run in the first period. Bakken converted after Hart's score.

LATOURETTE PROPELS CARDINALS

Chuck Latourette ran his way into the record books on September 29, 1968, and at the same time ignited the St. Louis Cardinals to a 21-20 National Football League victory over the New Orleans Saints at Tulane Stadium. Latourette, who set a one-game NFL mark for punt-return average (minimum three attempts) with a 47.7 mark, dashed 86 yards for a touchdown on a fourth-quarter punt runback to lift the Cardinals from the gloom of a 17-0 deficit. He had two other punt returns against the Saints, a 45-yarder and a 12-yarder.

Supporting Cast:

● **Dan Abramowicz.** Saints receiver who hooked up with Bill Kilmer on a 29-yard scoring pass in the second quarter and a 10-yard TD pass in the third period. Charlie Durkee, who kicked a 21-yard field goal in the first quarter and a 36-yarder in the fourth period, converted after both touchdowns.

● **Willis Crenshaw.** With New Orleans ahead, 20-14, in the fourth quarter, Crenshaw ran one yard for a Cardinal touchdown to tie the game. Jim Bakken's extra point, his third of the day, provided the margin of victory.

● **Jamie Rivers.** St. Louis linebacker who preserved the Cards' triumph by blocking a Durkee field-goal attempt—the Saints had driven to St. Louis' 27-yard line—on the last play of the game.

● **Dave Williams.** After Latourette's return had put the Cards on the scoreboard, Williams scored on a nine-yard pass from St. Louis quarterback Charley Johnson later in the fourth quarter.

Latourette's big day was just a shade better than that enjoyed two years earlier by another Cardinal, Johnny Roland. Latourette's record average came on three attempts that netted 143 yards. Roland, playing at Philadelphia on October 2, 1966, ran back three punts for 142 yards (a 47.3 average) and, like Latourette, had an 86-yard return for a TD. The Cards beat the Eagles, 41-10.

BLANDA TO THE RESCUE

For five consecutive Sundays during the 1970 National Football League season, George Blanda was the magic man for the Oakland Raiders. And, incredibly, Blanda was 43 years old at the time and playing in his 21st pro season. Not only did Blanda's sterling, clutch performances propel Oakland toward the American Conference West title, they helped earn the veteran kicker/quarterback selection as The Sporting News' AFC Player of the Year. With Blanda demonstrating his kicking and passing wizardry, the Raiders went 4-0-1 in the five-game stretch after beginning the season with a 2-2-1 record.

The game-by-game breakdown:

● **October 25,** at Oakland. Taking over for the injured Daryle Lamonica, Blanda fired two touchdown passes to Raymond Chester and one to Warren Wells as the Raiders thumped the Pittsburgh Steelers, 31-14. Lamonica, sidelined by a first-period back injury, had connected with Chester on another Oakland TD pass before departing.

● **November 1,** at Kansas City. Blanda kicked a 48-yard field goal with 3 seconds left in the game, enabling the Raiders to tie the Chiefs, 17-17.

● **November 8,** at Oakland. Again working in relief of an ailing Lamonica, who suffered a shoulder injury in the fourth quarter, Blanda hit on a 14-yard scoring pass to Wells late in the last period and added the game-tying conversion kick against Cleveland. Then, with 3 seconds to play, Blanda made a 52-yard field goal to give the Raiders a 23-20 triumph over the Browns.

● **November 15,** at Denver. With Oakland trailing the Broncos, 19-17, with fewer than 4 minutes to play, Blanda was called on at quarterback. This time, Lamonica was healthy but the Raiders sought a late-game spark. Blanda delivered, completing four of six passes and driving his team 80 yards (all on his passing) to a touchdown. Capping the drive was Blanda's 20-yard TD pitch to Fred Biletnikoff with 2:28 to go. Final score: Oakland 24, Denver 19.

● **November 22,** at Oakland. The Raiders fought off the San Diego Chargers, 20-17, with the winning points coming on a 16-yard Blanda field goal with 4 seconds remaining. (Despite managing only a split of its last four regular-season games, Oakland captured the AFC West crown with an 8-4-2 record.)

DEMPSEY'S MIRACLE

When Errol Mann's 18-yard field goal pulled the Detroit Lions in front of New Orleans, 17-16, on November 8, 1970, the afternoon appeared a lost cause for the Saints. After all, only 11 seconds remained in the National Football League game, which was played at Tulane Stadium. But then....

The Cast:

● **Al Dodd.** On the Saints' first play from scrimmage after Mann's field goal, Dodd caught a 17-yard pass from Bill Kilmer. The completion moved the ball to New Orleans' 45-yard line.

● **Joe Scarpati.** With 2 seconds showing on the clock following Dodd's reception, Scarpati went in to hold for a desperation field-goal attempt.

Tom Dempsey, the former NFL kicker who was born with half a right foot, lifted New Orleans to a dramatic victory over Detroit with a record-setting 63-yard field goal in 1970.

● **Tom Dempsey.** Having kicked three field goals (29, 27 and eight yards) earlier in the game, Dempsey took aim on the ball as Scarpati placed it on the turf at New Orleans' 37. If successful on his kick, Dempsey would shatter—by seven yards—the National Football League record for the longest field goal. (Bert Rechichar had booted a 56-yarder for Baltimore in 1953.)

"I knew I could kick the ball that far, but whether or not I could kick it straight that far kept running through my mind," said Dempsey, who was born with half of a right foot and wore a special kicking shoe approved by the league. Dempsey whipped his right leg into the football and the ball set sail downfield. Dempsey said he couldn't see whether his 63-yard try had cleared the crossbar. Soon, he had a clue. "I saw the referee's hands go up and heard everybody start yelling and I knew it was good," Dempsey said at the time. "It's quite a thrill. I'm still shook up."

New Orleans 19, Detroit 17.

NELSON STANDS ALONE—AGAIN

Philadelphia's Al Nelson became the first player in National Football League history to return a missed field goal 100 yards, achieving the feat in the Eagles' 33-21 triumph over the Cleveland Browns on December 11, 1966. Jerry Williams of the Los Angeles Rams (1951), Carl Taseff of the Baltimore Colts (1959) and Timmy Brown of the Eagles (1962) had shared the previous record with 99-yard returns of field-goal misses. Nelson was forced to share his spot in the record book, though, on September 19, 1971, when Green Bay's Ken Ellis went 100 yards against the New York Giants for the first points of a 42-40 game won by the Giants. Apparently not wishing to share his record, Nelson regained undisputed possession of the NFL field-goal-return mark the very next week by taking a Dallas Cowboy miss 101 yards for a touchdown.

Supporting Cast:

● **Mike Clark.** Dallas placekicker who, with the Cowboys leading 42-0, attempted a 48-yard field goal against the Eagles with 1 minute, 33 seconds left in a September 26, 1971, game in Philadelphia. Nelson fielded the miss a yard deep in the end zone and raced the distance. Dallas won, 42-7.

● **Pete Gogolak.** Giants placekicker whose missed field goal was returned the length of the field by the Packers' Ellis in '71. Ellis' runback came in the first quarter of the game played in Green Bay.

● **Lou Groza.** Cleveland placekicker whose miss in a '66 Browns-Eagles game in Philadelphia led to Nelson's 100-yard TD sprint, which occurred in the second quarter.

TATUM'S RUMBLE WITH A FUMBLE

Oakland Raiders defensive back Jack Tatum did something on September 24, 1972, that few men in National Football League history were able to do—he made George Halas take a back seat. On November 4, 1923, Halas had scampered a record 98 yards with a fumble recovery for the Chicago Bears, establishing an NFL mark that would stand for nearly half a century. Halas' run came at Marion, O., against the Oorang Indians. In the Raiders' second game of the '72 season in Green Bay, Tatum scooped up a fumble in Oakland's end zone and dashed 104 yards for a first-quarter touchdown that—coupled with the extra point—boosted Oakland to a 10-7 lead on its way to a 20-14 triumph.

Supporting Cast:

• **George Blanda.** He kicked a 43-yard field goal in the first period for the game's first score, added a 14-yard field goal in the third quarter and contributed two conversion kicks for the Raiders.

• **John Brockington.** Brockington scored the Packers' two touchdowns on one-yard runs in the first and second quarters.

• **MacArthur Lane.** Green Bay running back whose fumble was returned by Tatum for the record distance. Packers Coach Dan Devine thought Lane's misplay should have been called a muffed lateral—such a miscue cannot be advanced by the defending team—but the officials ruled that Lane had possession of the ball long enough for it to be called a fumble.

• **Charlie Smith.** Raiders running back whose one-yard scoring run in the third period enabled Oakland to overcome a 14-13 deficit.

DOLPHINS GO 17-0, BROWNS 15-0

The 1972 Miami Dolphins are the only National Football League team to sweep through an entire season (including postseason play) undefeated and untied, fashioning a 17-0 overall record. The Cleveland Browns went 15-0 overall in 1948, however, while winning the All-America Football Conference championship. Before the NFL adopted divisional play (and thus postseason playoffs) in 1933, the Canton Bulldogs (twice) and the Green Bay Packers (once) had gone undefeated—but ties marred their seasons. Canton was 10-0-2 in 1922 and 11-0-1 in 1923, and Green Bay finished 12-0-1 in 1929. The Chicago Bears posted perfect regular-season marks in 1934 and 1942, going 13-0 and 11-0, but the Bears lost to the New York Giants in the 1934 NFL title game and fell to the Washington Redskins in the 1942 championship contest. Game-by-game results for the '72 Dolphins and the '48 Browns, with home opponents capitalized:

1972 DOLPHINS, 17-0

20	Kansas City	10
34	HOUSTON	13
16	Minnesota	14
27	New York Jets	17
24	SAN DIEGO	10
24	BUFFALO	23
23	Baltimore	0
30	Buffalo	16
52	NEW ENGLAND	0
28	NEW YORK JETS	24
31	ST. LOUIS	10
37	New England	21
23	New York Giants	13
16	BALTIMORE	0

DIVISONAL PLAYOFF

20	CLEVELAND	14

AFC CHAMPIONSHIP

21	Pittsburgh	17

SUPER BOWL

14	Washington	7

1948 BROWNS, 15-0

19	LOS ANGELES	14
42	Buffalo	13
28	Chicago	7
21	CHICAGO	10
14	Baltimore	10
30	BROOKLYN	17
31	BUFFALO	14
35	NEW YORK	7
28	BALTIMORE	7
14	SAN FRANCISCO	7
34	New York	21
31	Los Angeles	14
31	San Francisco	28
31	Brooklyn	21

AAFC CHAMPIONSHIP

49	BUFFALO	7

Miami Dolphins Coach Don Shula got a well-deserved victory ride after his team had capped its perfect 1972 season with a win over Washington in Super Bowl VII.

Miami won its 1973 regular-season opener against San Francisco, stretching its winning streak (including postseason play) to an NFL record-tying 18 consecutive games. (The Oakland Raiders defeated Miami in week two of the '73 season in a game played at Berkeley, Calif.) The 1933-34 and 1941-42 Bears also won 18 straight games. The Bears prevailed in their last four games of the 1933 regular season, won the NFL title game against the Giants and then went 13-0 in the regular season of '34. Chicago won its last five games of the 1941 regular season, beat Green Bay in a Western Division playoff game, won the NFL championship game against the Giants and finished 11-0 in the '42 regular season.

In 1922 and 1923, Canton established the NFL mark for the most consecutive games without a defeat, 24. The Bulldogs compiled a 21-0-3 record in those pre-playoff years. The Chicago Bears also put together a 24-game unbeaten streak in regular-season play, going on a 23-0-1 tear that began in 1941 and ended in 1943. Cleveland went 29 games (including postseason action) without a loss during a 1947-1949 stretch against AAFC competition, winning 27 times and tying twice. The Browns' undefeated string included 18 straight victories.

2,003 . . . A RUSHING ODYSSEY

When O.J. Simpson of the Buffalo Bills rushed for 250 yards and broke loose for 80- and 22-yard touchdown runs in the opening game of the 1973 National Football League season, it seemed to signal that the "Juice" was going to have a banner year. The signals were clear. By the halfway point of the 14-game regular season, Simpson had compiled 1,025 yards on the ground (an average of 146.4 per game) and was well on course to shatter Jim Brown's one-season NFL rushing record of 1,863 yards (set with the Cleveland Browns in 1963). Needing "only" 839 yards in the final seven games of the season (a 119.9 per-game mark) to surpass Brown's total, Simpson stumbled in the first two of those contests by gaining 79 yards at New Orleans and 99 at home against Cincinnati. Simpson rebounded for 381 yards in his next three games, increasing his season total to 1,584 with two games left. To eclipse Brown's mark, O.J. needed a total of 280 yards against New England (December 9 in Buffalo) and the New York Jets (December 16 in New York). Simpson obviously sensed his rendezvous with history—and it showed against the Patriots. Playing on a snow-covered field at Rich Stadium, he ripped the New England defense for 219 yards on 22 carries and boosted his season figure to 1,803 yards (60 yards short of tying Brown). Now, Brown's record appeared easily within O.J.'s grasp and the almost magical figure of 2,000 yards was even a possibility (although admittedly a remote one). On Simpson's eighth carry of the day in the Bills-Jets regular-season finale at snowy Shea Stadium, Brown's record passed into history when O.J. racked up a six-yard gain in the first quarter. And with nearly 6 minutes remaining in the game, Simpson scaled the 2,000-yard peak with a seven-yard gallop. Simpson's day: 34 attempts, 200 yards. Simpson's season: 332 attempts, 2,003 yards.

Simpson's 2,003-yard season, game by game, 1973, with home opponents capitalized:

		Attempts	Yards
September 16	New England	29	250
September 23	San Diego	22	103
September 30	N.Y. JETS	24	123
October 7	PHILADELPHIA	27	171
October 14	BALTIMORE	22	166
October 21	Miami	14	55
October 29	KANSAS CITY	39	157
November 4	New Orleans	20	79
November 11	CINCINNATI	20	99
November 18	MIAMI	20	120
November 25	Baltimore	15	124
December 2	Atlanta	24	137
December 9	NEW ENGLAND	22	219
December 16	New York Jets	34	200
		332	2003

Supporting Cast (the members of the Bills' offensive line, called the Electric Company):

- **Left tackle,** Dave Foley.
- **Left guard,** Reggie McKenzie.
- **Center,** Bruce Jarvis (who played in eight games before being sidelined by a knee injury), Mike Montler.
- **Right guard,** Joe DeLamielleure.
- **Right tackle,** Donnie Green.
- **Tight end,** Paul Seymour.

DICKERSON RUSHES IN

After 14 games of the 1984 season, second-year pro Eric Dickerson of the Los Angeles Rams had gained 1,792 yards on 326 carries. It wasn't a Simpson-esque performance, but it was a glittering effort. Dickerson, though, had two more games in which to set a single-season National Football League rushing record—the NFL schedule had been expanded to 16 games six years earlier—and Houston and San Francisco remained on the Rams' schedule. On December 9, 1984, against the Oilers at Anaheim Stadium, Dickerson's 27th and last carry of the day—a nine-yard run in the fourth quarter—boosted the Ram standout's game rushing total to 215 yards and his season output to an NFL-record 2,007 yards. Dickerson concluded regular-season play five nights later with a 98-yard rushing production against the 49ers in San Francisco, finishing with 2,105 yards.

Dickerson's 2,105-yard season, game by game, 1984, with home opponents capitalized:

		Attempts	Yards
September 3	DALLAS	21	138
September 9	CLEVELAND	27	102
September 16	Pittsburgh	23	49
September 23	Cincinnati	22	89
September 30	NEW YORK GIANTS	22	120
October 7	ATLANTA	19	107
October 14	New Orleans	20	175
October 22	Atlanta	24	145
October 28	SAN FRANCISCO	13	38
November 4	St. Louis	21	208
November 11	CHICAGO	28	149
November 18	Green Bay (Milwaukee)	25	132
November 25	Tampa Bay	28	191
December 2	NEW ORLEANS	33	149
December 9	HOUSTON	27	215
December 14	San Francisco	26	98
		379	2105

PAYTON RUSHES FOR 275 YARDS

Feeling weak before the game because of a persistent flu bug, Chicago Bears running back Walter Payton wasn't optimistic about turning in a top-level performance on November 20, 1977, against the Minnesota Vikings. Payton, though, clearly had bad vibes. The Bears' standout served notice that he was alive and well in the first half, rushing for 144 yards on 26 carries, scoring on a one-yard run as Chicago seized a 10-0 lead and apparently mounting a threat to O.J. Simpson's National Football League record of 273 yards rushing in one game. Simpson's mark seemed safe, though, when Payton's total stood at 210 with about 3 minutes to play. However, Payton streaked 58 yards on his next attempt (his 38th carry of the game) to

On a snowy day at New York's Shea Stadium, O.J. Simpson broke Jim Brown's one-season rushing record in a 1973 game between the Buffalo Bills and the Jets. The game was stopped momentarily (above) as Simpson was awarded the game ball and congratulated by friend and foe alike. In a 1984 game, Los Angeles' Eric Dickerson (left, No. 29) got a hug from teammate Norwood Vann after breaking Simpson's one-season rushing mark in a game against Houston.

reach the Minnesota 9-yard line. Needing six yards to break Simpson's mark, Payton gained seven yards on his final two carries of the day (although the Bears failed to score on the drive). The final statistics for Payton (who rushed 14 times in the second half for 131 yards): 40 carries, 275 yards and a 6.9 rushing average. Chicago won, 10-7, at Soldier Field.

Supporting Cast:

● **Bob Avellini.** Chicago quarterback who attempted only six passes (he completed four) as the Bears relied almost entirely on a rushing offense.

● **Matt Blair.** Vikings linebacker who accounted for his team's lone touchdown when he blocked a Bob Parsons punt in the third quarter, picked up the ball on the 10 and ran it in for the score.

● **Robin Earl.** With the Bears gaining 343 yards on the ground, Earl contributed 60 rushing yards in support of Payton.

● **Bob Thomas.** His 37-yard field goal with 43 seconds to play in the first half proved to be the margin of victory. Thomas also made the extra-point kick after Payton's touchdown run earlier in the second quarter.

Simpson's 273-yard game came on November 25, 1976, when Simpson and the Buffalo Bills lost to the Detroit Lions, 27-14, in Pontiac, Mich. Simpson, who scored on runs of 48 and 12 yards, carried the ball 29 times for Buffalo, which saw its losing streak extend to eight games.

Simpson's 250-yard spree against New England in the Bills' 1973 season opener rates third on the all-time NFL single-game rushing list. With Simpson toting the ball 29 times and making two touchdown sprints, Buffalo stung the Patriots, 31-13, on September 16 in Foxboro, Mass.

MARSHALL'S PLAYING STREAK

When defensive end Jim Marshall first appeared in the National Football League, the Minnesota Vikings did not exist, the league was playing a 12-game schedule and Vince Lombardi had yet to coach the Green Bay Packers to an NFL title. By the time Marshall retired, the Vikings had competed in four Super Bowls, the league was playing a 16-game schedule and Lombardi, who coached Green Bay to five NFL championships, had passed from the scene almost a decade earlier. But Marshall's story involves considerably more than longevity—it's also one of continuity and endurance. Marshall, in fact, never missed a game during his 20 years in the NFL, playing a record 282 consecutive regular-season games. Marshall, who spent his first pro season with the Saskatchewan Roughriders of the Canadian Football League in 1959, broke into the NFL with the Cleveland Browns in 1960. After seeing duty in all 12 of the Browns' games that season, Marshall was traded to Minnesota. He played 14 games yearly with the Vikings for the next 17 seasons (1961-1977), then appeared in all 16 games for Minnesota in both 1978 and 1979. When he played his final NFL game, Marshall was two weeks shy of his 42nd birthday.

Supporting Cast:

● **Tommy Kramer.** In Marshall's NFL finale, played December 16, 1979, in Foxboro, Mass., Kramer was a standout for the Vikings. He completed 35 of 61 passes for 308 yards and one touchdown, but Minnesota lost to New

England, 27-23. Fifteen of the completions went to running back Rickey Young, who caught a 13-yard TD pass from Kramer.

● **Bobby Mitchell.** When Marshall made his NFL debut, playing for Cleveland on September 25, 1960, in Philadelphia, Mitchell led the Browns to a 41-24 victory. He rushed 14 times for 156 yards, scored on runs of 51 and 30 yards and caught an 11-yard touchdown pass from Milt Plum. Jim Brown contributed 153 yards rushing for Cleveland and scored on a one-yard run.

TODD COMPLETES 42 PASSES

Entering the fourth quarter of his team's September 21, 1980, game against the San Francisco 49ers, New York Jets quarterback Richard Todd was a frustrated man. Todd had completed 24 of 35 passes for 272 yards, but the Jets had failed to score a touchdown and seemed hopelessly out of the game as the 49ers enjoyed a 30-6 lead. Todd didn't quit, though, and the stick-to-itiveness paid dividends for the signal-caller—and got the Jets within 10 points at the final gun. Todd hit on 18 more passes in the final quarter to set a National Football League single-game mark of 42 completions. Three of Todd's fourth-period completions went for touchdowns, but the 49ers held on for a 37-27 victory at Shea Stadium. Todd, who attempted 60 passes against San Francisco, finished with 447 aerial yards. He was intercepted once.

Supporting Cast:

● **Paul Darby.** He scored the only touchdown of his NFL career on a 13-yard pass from Todd. The scoring play was the final TD of the game and marked Darby's lone reception of the day.

● **Steve DeBerg.** The 49ers' first and last TDs came on passes by DeBerg.

● **Derrick Gaffney.** He caught Todd's first touchdown pass of the game, a 15-yarder in the fourth quarter. Gaffney had three receptions overall.

● **Clark Gaines.** Jets running back who caught 17 of Todd's passes—the NFL single-game reception record is 18—for 160 yards.

● **Bruce Harper.** Among his seven receptions for the Jets was a nine-yarder that gave Todd his second scoring pass.

● **Pat Leahy.** Jets placekicker who made a 49-yard field goal in the second period and a 35-yarder in the third quarter.

● **Joe Montana.** San Francisco quarterback who threw for two touchdowns and ran for another.

● **Mickey Shuler.** He caught seven passes for 63 yards—the same totals achieved by Jets teammate Harper.

Others contributing to Todd's record completion total were Bobby Jones, who had three catches, and Johnny (Lam) Jones, Jerome Barkum, Kevin Long and Wesley Walker, all of whom had one.

CONSECUTIVE 200-YARDERS

When Houston's Earl Campbell rushed for 200 or more yards in two straight National Football League games in 1980, he accomplished a feat performed by only one other player, O.J. Simpson, in league history. (Simpson had achieved consecutive 200-yard games twice in his career, in 1973 and 1976.) Campbell rushed 33 times for 203 yards on October 19 as the Oilers defeated the Tampa Bay Buccaneers, 20-14, then toted the ball 27 times for 202 yards on October 26 to spark Houston past the Cincinnati Bengals, 23-3. Both games were played in the Astrodome. Simpson compiled 273 yards on 29 carries for Buffalo in a November 25, 1976, game at the Pontiac Silverdome and netted 203 yards on 24 attempts in the Bills' next game, December 5 in Miami. Despite Simpson's heroics, Buffalo lost to the Detroit Lions, 27-14, and fell to the Dolphins, 45-27. Simpson was able to crack the 2,000-yard barrier in 1973 when he closed the regular season with 219- and 200-yard games against New England and the New York Jets. The Bills routed the Patriots, 37-13, in Buffalo, and decked the Jets, 34-14, in New York.

Supporting Cast:

● **Jim Braxton.** Simpson's running mate in the Bills' backfield, he supported O.J. with 70 ground yards against New England and 108 yards against the Jets in the final two weekends of the '73 season.

● **Cedric Brown.** Tampa Bay defender who capitalized on a rare Campbell error to put the Bucs back into their 1980 game with the Oilers. A fourth-quarter fumble by Campbell was picked up by Tampa Bay's Danny Reece, whose lateral to Brown resulted in an 80-yard scoring play. Garo Yepremian's conversion kick brought the Buccaneers within six points, but the Oilers held on.

● **Freddie Solomon.** Dolphins player who took the shine off Simpson's consecutive 200-yard games in 1976 when he dazzled the Bills with a 79-yard punt return for a touchdown, a 53-yard TD reception and a 59-yard scoring run.

CARMICHAEL'S STRING

When Philadelphia's Harold Carmichael caught one pass in the Eagles' 14-0 loss at Washington in 1972, it marked the beginning of the longest pass-catching streak in National Football League history. By the time the Eagles were preparing for the crucial 1980 regular-season finale against the Dallas Cowboys in Irving, Tex., Carmichael had caught passes in 127 straight games. Dallas, though, put the clamps on Carmichael, thanks in large part to a crunching defense.

Supporting Cast:

● **Ron Jaworski.** When Carmichael broke Dan Abramowicz's NFL mark of catching passes in 105 consecutive games (1967-1974), Jaworski was the Eagles' quarterback. Carmichael's streak reached 106 games on November 4, 1979, in Philadelphia during a contest against Cleveland in which the Eagles' receiver caught five passes from Jaworski for 95 yards and one touchdown. The Browns won, 24-19.

● **John Reaves.** Eagles quarterback who got Carmichael's string going with a 21-yard completion to the 6-foot-8 target on October 8, 1972, against the Redskins.

● **Dennis Thurman.** Dallas defender whose second-quarter hit on Carmichael on December 21, 1980, shook up the Eagles' star and limited the remainder of his playing time that day to one series in the second half. While Jaworski completed 18 passes in the game, none went to Carmichael. Dallas, needing to win by 25 points to edge Philadelphia for the National

Conference East title (based on a divisional net-points tiebreaker rule), seized a 35-10 lead in the fourth quarter, but the Eagles nailed down the divisional crown by drawing within 35-27 at the final gun.

Carmichael made 434 catches in the 127 games (capping his streak with two receptions against St. Louis on December 14, 1980) for 6,603 yards and 66 touchdowns. His record performance was challenged by Mel Gray of the St. Louis Cardinals (1973-82), but Gray's string ended at 121 games.

IRVIN'S MANY HAPPY RETURNS

LeRoy Irvin's 75-yard punt return for a touchdown in the first quarter of the Los Angeles Rams' October 11, 1981, game in Atlanta was just a preview of what was to come. Before the day was over, the Rams' Irvin had scored on another punt return—an 84-yarder in the fourth quarter—and established a National Football League record with 207 yards in punt returns in one game (he returned six punts overall against the Falcons). Irvin's second punt-run-back TD, which came with 8 minutes, 23 seconds left in the game and Los Angeles trailing, 35-27, thrust the Rams into position to win with a late-game field goal.

Supporting Cast:

● **William Andrews.** His 25- and two-yard runs, in the second and fourth quarters, respectively, accounted for Atlanta's first and last TDs of the day.

● **Steve Bartkowski.** Falcons quarterback who fired touchdown passes to Junior Miller (11 yards, second quarter), Alfred Jenkins (23 yards, second quarter) and Alfred Jackson (eight yards, third quarter).

● **Frank Corral.** His third field goal of the game, a 25-yarder with 24 seconds remaining, earned the Rams a 37-35 triumph.

● **Jeff Rutledge.** Taking over for Los Angeles quarterback Pat Haden, who suffered a deep leg bruise in the second quarter, Rutledge threw a one-yard scoring pass to Henry Childs in the second quarter and a 36-yard TD pass to Drew Hill in the third quarter.

Irvin became the fourth player in NFL history to record two punt-return touchdowns in one game. Jack Christiansen did it twice for the Detroit Lions in 1951, Dick Christy performed the feat for the New York Titans in 1961 and Rick Upchurch achieved it for the Denver Broncos in 1976.

WINSLOW'S FIVE TD CATCHES

The Oakland Raiders led the San Diego Chargers, 21-14, in the second quarter of their November 22, 1981, National Football League game in Oakland before Kellen Winslow and the Chargers went to work. Winslow scored the game's next four touchdowns on pass receptions—two in the second quarter and two more in the third—and later tacked on a fifth TD catch as the Chargers went on a 41-0 roll en route to a 55-21 triumph. Winslow finished with 13 catches for 144 yards.

Supporting Cast:

● **James Brooks.** When Winslow wasn't excelling, Brooks was. The rookie running back rushed for 97 yards, caught five passes for 38 yards and had punt and kickoff returns totaling 147 yards.

● **Dan Fouts.** Chargers quarterback who tossed 15- and 29-yard scoring passes to Winslow in the second quarter and four- and five-yard TD passes to the San Diego standout in the third quarter. Fouts completed 28 of 44 attempts for 296 yards and six touchdowns (also connecting with Brooks and Charlie Joiner for scores). He had one interception.

● **Chuck Muncie.** San Diego running back who connected with Winslow on a three-yard option pass in the fourth quarter, accounting for Winslow's NFL record-tying fifth touchdown reception of the game. Muncie also ran for a TD, his one-yard carry giving the Chargers their first score of the game in the opening period.

Bob Shaw is the only other player in NFL history to haul in five touchdown passes in one game, accomplishing the feat for the Chicago Cardinals on October 2, 1950.

DORSETT GOES 99 YARDS

"I was just thinking of getting out of the backfield," said Tony Dorsett, reflecting on a fourth-period play in the 1982 regular-season finale between the Dallas Cowboys and the Minnesota Vikings. "I saw a hole open up and went around my blocker to the right." Dorsett went around some other people, too. In fact, the Cowboys' star running back bolted 99 yards to set a National Football League record for the longest run from scrimmage. Dorsett carried the ball 16 times overall that night, gaining 153 yards. Minnesota, needing a victory to avoid a first-round rematch against the Cowboys (at Dallas) in the playoffs, overcame Dorsett's performance and beat the Cowboys, 31-27, on January 3, 1983, at the Metrodome.

Supporting Cast:

● **Timmy Newsome.** After Minnesota seized a 24-13 lead in the fourth quarter on John Turner's 33-yard interception return for a touchdown and Rick Danmeier's conversion kick, Dallas' Newsome fumbled the ensuing kickoff and the Cowboys were forced to take possession at their 1-yard line. On the first play from scrimmage, Dorsett sprinted down the right side of the field and tightroped the sidelines on his way to the end zone.

● **Ron Springs.** His two-yard TD run and Rafael Septien's extra point lifted Dallas into a 27-24 lead in the fourth quarter.

● **Rickey Young.** He teamed with Vikings quarterback Tommy Kramer on the game-winning play, a 14-yard scoring pass with 1 minute, 52 seconds left in the game. (The triumph sent the Vikes against Atlanta in the playoffs, and Minnesota beat the Falcons in Minneapolis before losing at Washington in the second round of postseason play.)

BRADLEY'S SIX INTERCEPTIONS

Four Tampa Bay players combined for 43 pass attempts in the Bandits' April 2, 1983, United States Football League game at Tampa Stadium. The leading pass catcher of the Bandit bombs was Luther Bradley—and therein lies a story. Bradley played for the Chicago Blitz. Bradley caught six Bandit passes—Tampa Bay's No. 1 receiver in the game had five receptions—and he returned the interceptions a total of 127 yards. Chicago won, 42-3, with Bradley contributing a 93-yard interception return for a touchdown in the third quarter.

Supporting Cast:

● **Jimmy Jordan.** Tampa Bay quarterback off whom Bradley intercepted two passes.

● **Greg Landry.** Landry threw two touchdown passes to Trumaine Johnson (who had seven catches for 146 yards) and ran for a third score, pacing the Chicago offense.

● **Sam Platt.** He was Tampa Bay's leading receiver—at least among those wearing Bandit uniforms. Running back Platt had five receptions.

● **John Reaves.** Bandits quarterback who had four of his passes picked off by Bradley in the game, which was played in the fifth week of the USFL's first season.

99-YARD PASS PLAYS IN NFL

With the Washington Redskins leading the Los Angeles Raiders, 10-0, in the second quarter of their October 2, 1983, game in Washington, the Raiders struck with devastating quickness as quarterback Jim Plunkett and wide receiver Cliff Branch combined on the fifth 99-yard pass play in National Football League history. The touchdown catch was Branch's lone reception of the day. Scoring 28 consecutive points at one stretch later in the game, the Raiders built a 15-point edge in the fourth quarter. The Redskins roared back, though, for a 37-35 triumph.

Supporting Cast:

● **Calvin Muhammad.** He caught two of the four touchdown passes thrown by Plunkett, scoring on 35- and 22-yard plays in the third quarter.

● **Greg Pruitt.** After Plunkett and Todd Christensen had teamed for a two-yard scoring pass earlier in the fourth quarter (coupled with Chris Bahr's extra point, Christensen's TD had given Los Angeles a 28-20 lead), Pruitt went 97 yards for a Raider touchdown on a punt return.

● **Joe Theismann.** With the Redskins trailing, 35-20, Theismann rallied Washington to 17 points in a 5-minute, 42-second span late in the game. He fired an 11-yard TD strike to Charlie Brown and, with 33 seconds left in the contest, completed a game-winning, six-yard scoring pass to Joe Washington. Mark Moseley sandwiched a 34-yard field goal between Theismann's fourth-period TD passes.

Being involved in a 99-yard pass play was nothing new to the Washington franchise. Of the five such completions in NFL history, four have come in Redskin games. Three times, the Redskins made the notable plays.

Washington's Frank Filchock was on the throwing end of the NFL's first 99-yard scoring pass, delivering the big play in an October 15, 1939, game in Washington against the Pittsburgh Pirates. With the Redskins at their 1-yard line in the third quarter after being assessed a clipping penalty, Filchock passed to Andy Farkas at the 4 and Farkas outran the Pirate defense to the end zone. Washington went on to pound Pittsburgh, 44-14.

It was 24 years until the NFL recorded its next 99-yard TD pass. Trailing 27-7 in the third quarter of a September 15, 1963, game in Cleveland, the Redskins were buoyed by a 99-yard connection, George Izo to Bobby Mitchell. The Browns prevailed in the season opener, however, 37-14, as Jim Brown scored three touchdowns, rushed for 162 yards and totaled 100 yards in receptions.

On October 16, 1966, Detroit was losing to the Colts, 38-7, in the fourth period of a game played at Baltimore's Memorial Stadium when Lions quarterback Karl Sweetan and Pat Studstill combined on a 99-yarder. Led by Johnny Unitas' four touchdown passes, the Colts blitzed the Lions, 45-14.

Five years to the day after Izo's bomb, Washington's Sonny Jurgensen burned the Chicago defense with a 99-yard strike to Gerry Allen in the second quarter. Jurgensen tossed four TD passes overall—the other three all went to Pat Richter—as the Redskins downed the Bears, 38-28, in their September 15, 1968, season opener in Chicago. (Allen caught only one other scoring pass in his NFL career, a 16-yarder from Jurgensen in a November 12, 1967, game against the San Francisco 49ers.)

MARINO THROWS FOR 48 TDs

Entering the 1984 season, the National Football League record for touchdown passes in a season was 36, with George Blanda and Y.A. Tittle sharing the mark. Miami quarterback Dan Marino, having thrown for 32 touchdowns through the 12th week of the '84 season, proceeded to fire four scoring passes in each of the Dolphins' final four games and left the record book in tatters. Besides the unprecedented 48 TD passes, second-year pro Marino set NFL season records with 362 completions, 5,084 yards passing and four 400-yard games. The game-by-game breakdown of Marino's 1984 season, with home opponents capitalized:

	Comp.-Att.-Int.	Yards	TDs
September 2 .... Washington	21-28-0	311	5
September 9 .... NEW ENGLAND	16-27-2	234	2
September 17 .... Buffalo	26-35-1	296	3
September 23 .... INDIANAPOLIS	14-29-0	257	2
September 30 .... St. Louis	24-36-0	429	3
October 7 .... Pittsburgh	16-24-1	226	2
October 14 .... HOUSTON	25-32-0	321	3
October 21 .... New England	24-39-1	316	4
October 28 .... BUFFALO	19-28-3	282	3
November 4 .... New York Jets	23-42-2	422	2
November 11 .... PHILADELPHIA	20-34-1	246	1
November 18 .... San Diego	28-41-1	338	2
November 26 .... NEW YORK JETS	19-31-0	192	4
December 2 .... LOS ANGELES RAIDERS	35-57-2	470	4
December 9 .... Indianapolis	29-41-1	404	4
December 17 .... DALLAS	23-40-2	340	4
	362-564-17	5084	48

HALFTIME

COLLEGE DRAFTS AND AWARD WINNERS

DAN ABRAMOWICZ

A 17th-round draft choice of New Orleans out of Xavier (Ohio) in 1967, Abramowicz went on to set a National Football League record by catching passes in 105 consecutive games (the mark has since been broken). Despite his lowly draft status, Abramowicz played in the NFL for eight-plus seasons with the Saints, San Francisco 49ers and Buffalo Bills and concluded his NFL career with 369 receptions for 5,686 yards and 39 touchdowns.

ALEX AGASE

Line standout who won consensus All-America honors while playing for the

123

Purdue Boilermakers in 1943 and received the same recognition while a member of Illinois' Fighting Illini in 1946.

HARRY AGGANIS, STEVE FILIPOWICZ, DON LUND

First-round National Football League draft picks who played major league baseball. Agganis, Boston University quarterback, was an opening-round selection of the Cleveland Browns in 1952. Fordham backfield standout Filipowicz was the No. 1 draft choice of the NFL's New York Giants in 1943, and he played with the NFL club in addition to his stint in baseball's big leagues. Michigan halfback Lund was the Chicago Bears' first draft pick in 1945.

BILLY ANDERSON

Junior-college back who was the Chicago Bears' first-round pick in the 1953 National Football League draft. Anderson, who starred at Compton Community College in California, was the sixth player selected overall in '53. He spent two seasons with the Bears.

SCOTT APPLETON, TOMMY NOBIS

Texas players who gave the Longhorns two Outland Trophy winners in a three-year span in the 1960s. Appleton captured the Outland in 1963 and Nobis won the interior-lineman honor in 1965. In 1977, Brad Shearer became the third Texas standout to receive the Outland.

ARMY, UCLA

Schools that have produced four of the six players who have won consensus All-America honors three times in the last half-century. Army backfield stars Glenn Davis and Felix (Doc) Blanchard were both consensus choices in 1944, 1945 and 1946. UCLA linebacker Jerry Robinson was a consensus All-America in 1976, 1977 and 1978, and Bruins defensive back Kenny Easley was honored in 1978, 1979 and 1980.

The only other three-time consensus All-Americas in the last 50 years have been Southern Methodist halfback Doak Walker in 1947, 1948 and 1949 and Georgia running back Herschel Walker in 1980, 1981 and 1982.

STEVE AUGUST, TOM LYNCH, TERRY BEESON

The players Seattle selected in the 1977 National Football League draft with choices obtained from Dallas in a trade that gave the Cowboys—and denied the Seahawks—the opportunity to draft Heisman Trophy winner Tony Dorsett of Pittsburgh. With Tampa Bay scheduled to draft from the No. 1 spot and having indicated it would take Southern California running back Ricky Bell, Dallas sought to move up from a 14th-slot position and accomplished that objective by swinging a trade with Seattle (which, like Tampa Bay, was coming off its first NFL season). In the deal, the manpower-hungry Seahawks—originally slated to draft from the second spot—swapped first-round draft position with the Cowboys and also acquired three second-round picks from Dallas. In the first round, Tampa Bay chose Bell, Dallas took Dorsett as the draft's No. 2 pick and the Seahawks picked Tulsa offensive lineman

August in Dallas' former No. 14 spot. In the second round, Seattle used former Dallas choices (No. 2 and No. 13) to select Boston College offensive lineman Lynch and Kansas linebacker Beeson. The No. 26 pick in round two also belonged to Seattle as a result of the Seahawks-Cowboys trade, but Seattle dealt that choice back to Dallas for wide receiver Duke Fergerson.

TERRY BAKER

Holds the distinction of winning the Heisman Trophy, being the No. 1 player selected in the entire National Football League draft, making a Holly-wood-script type of play in a bowl game and competing in NCAA basketball's Final Four—all in the same school year, 1962-63. Oregon State's Baker, the Heisman recipient for the 1962 season, was made the top pick in the 1963 NFL draft (actually held on December 3, 1962) by the Los Angeles Rams. Ten days after receiving the Heisman and 12 days following the draft, Baker scored the only points in the Liberty Bowl by running 99 yards for a touchdown as Oregon State defeated Villanova, 6-0, in Philadelphia. Three months later, the first Heisman winner from the Far West was a starting guard when the Oregon State basketball team took on Cincinnati in the semifinals of the NCAA Tournament. Baker failed to score against the Bearcats, missing all nine of his field-goal attempts, as Cincinnati coasted into the championship game. He then scored seven points when the Beavers lost to Duke in the third-place game.

STEVE BARTKOWSKI

California quarterback who was chosen No. 1 overall in the 1975 National Football League draft by the Atlanta Falcons.

BERT BELL

Philadelphia Eagles owner (and future National Football League commissioner) who founded the draft—and then failed to sign any of the nine picks that his club made in the first such player selection process (1936).

RICKY BELL, MARVIN POWELL, GARY JETER

Three Southern California players who were among the first five players chosen overall in the 1977 National Football League draft. The Tampa Bay Buccaneers used the No. 1 pick of the draft on Bell, the Trojans' standout running back. The New York Jets made offensive tackle Powell the fourth selection in the entire draft and the New York Giants, choosing fifth in the first round, opted for defensive tackle Jeter.

ANGELO BERTELLI

Notre Dame quarterback who finished second in the Heisman Trophy balloting as a sophomore in 1941. The only other sophomores to finish in the runner-up spot in the Heisman voting were Army's Glenn Davis in 1944 and Georgia's Herschel Walker in 1981. (Forty-three seniors and seven juniors have won the Downtown Athletic Club award.)

ANGELO BERTELLI

Despite playing only six games for Notre Dame in 1943, he was an easy winner in that season's Heisman Trophy voting. Before being ordered to report to the U.S. Marine base at Parris Island, S.C., Bertelli threw 10 touchdown passes as he led the Fighting Irish to a 6-0 record. Bertelli stole the show in his farewell appearance, passing for three TDs and running for another score as Notre Dame—on the way to a 9-1 season—pounded Navy, 33-6, on October 30 at Cleveland.

JAY BERWANGER

The first recipient (1935) of an honor that, a year later, became known as the Heisman Memorial Trophy. When Berwanger won the award in '35 for his exploits at the University of Chicago, the honor was called the Downtown Athletic Club Trophy and was intended for the best college football player east of the Mississippi River. After the death in 1936 of the DAC's first athletic director, John W. Heisman, the award was renamed the Heisman Memorial Trophy and voting for the honor was expanded. Beginning in '36, the Heisman would go to the outstanding college football player in the United States.

JAY BERWANGER

The first draft choice in National Football League history. When the NFL initiated the draft on February 8, 1936, the Philadelphia Eagles opened the proceedings by making the Downtown Athletic Club Trophy winner the No. 1 pick. The Eagles then traded the rights to the former University of Chicago star to the Chicago Bears, who failed to sign Berwanger.

FELIX (DOC) BLANCHARD

The first of seven players to win the Heisman Trophy as a junior. Blanchard, a standout runner for Army, captured the award in 1945. Other Heisman winners as juniors: Doak Walker, Southern Methodist, 1948; Vic Janowicz, Ohio State, 1950; Roger Staubach, Navy, 1963; Archie Griffin, Ohio State, 1974; Billy Sims, Oklahoma, 1978, and Herschel Walker, Georgia, 1982.

FELIX (DOC) BLANCHARD, GLENN DAVIS

Army superstars who were first-round choices in National Football League drafts despite their service obligations. Blanchard, in fact, also had one season of collegiate football eligibility remaining when he was made an opening-round pick of the Pittsburgh Steelers in 1946. Blanchard, the Cadets' Mr. Inside, never played professional football, though. Davis, a first-round selection of the Detroit Lions in the 1947 NFL draft, eventually played two pro seasons, 1950 and 1951, with the Los Angeles Rams (who obtained the rights to Mr. Outside from the Lions).

The Dallas Cowboys picked Navy quarterback Roger Staubach in the 10th round of the 1964 NFL draft.

Army stars Glenn Davis (left) and Doc Blanchard won Heisman honors in consecutive years and were both first-round NFL draft picks, despite their service obligations.

BLANCHARD, DAVIS, LUJACK, HART

Heisman Trophy winners (past, future) who were all in uniform at Yankee Stadium on November 9, 1946, when Army played Notre Dame. The Cadets' Felix (Doc) Blanchard was the 1945 Heisman recipient, Army's Glenn Davis was en route to the '46 Downtown Athletic Club award, Notre Dame's Johnny Lujack would cop the Heisman in 1947 and Leon Hart of the Fighting Irish would take the honors in 1949. Blanchard, Davis and Lujack were key players in the '46 Cadets-Irish clash, which ended in a 0-0 tie, while freshman Hart did not play.

PETE BROCK, STAN BROCK

Brothers who completed their collegiate eligibility at Colorado four years apart, these linemen were first-round draft picks by National Football League teams—and each was the 12th player taken in his draft. Pete was chosen by the New England Patriots in 1976, and Stan was selected by the New Orleans Saints in 1980.

JOHN BROCKINGTON

The first of four Ohio State players selected in the opening round of the 1971

National Football League draft. Running back Brockington was picked by the Green Bay Packers, who had the ninth choice overall in the draft. The Oakland Raiders, choosing from the 19th spot in round one, opted for Buckeyes defensive back Jack Tatum. The San Francisco 49ers used the 23rd pick of the first round on Ohio State defensive back Tim Anderson and the Minnesota Vikings, drafting 24th, went for Buckeyes running back Leo Hayden.

BILL BROOKS, LOYD PHILLIPS

Arkansas' Outland Trophy-winning players, with Brooks getting the interior-lineman honor in 1954 and Phillips receiving the award in 1966.

JIM BROWN

Syracuse's blockbuster back who, as a senior, was a fifth-place finisher in the Heisman Trophy voting and the sixth man taken in the National Football League draft. Finishing in front of Brown, who rushed for 986 yards in eight games for the 1956 Orangemen, in the Heisman balloting were winner Paul Hornung of Notre Dame, Johnny Majors of Tennessee and Tommy McDonald and Jerry Tubbs, both of Oklahoma. And taken ahead of Brown in the NFL draft were top choice Hornung (by Green Bay), Southern California's Jon Arnett (by the Los Angeles Rams), Stanford's John Brodie (by San Francisco), Michigan's Ron Kramer (by Green Bay) and Purdue's Len Dawson (by Pittsburgh). Brown was chosen by Cleveland.

ROOSEVELT BROWN

The New York Giants' 27th-round choice in the 1953 National Football League draft, Brown went on to establish himself as a pillar in the Giants' offensive line and won election to the Pro Football Hall of Fame. Brown played collegiately at Morgan State.

TOM BROWN, BOBBY BELL

Minnesota's recipients of the Outland Trophy, with Brown achieving the honor in 1960 and Bell winning the interior-lineman award in 1962.

ROSS BROWNER

Defensive end who became Notre Dame's third Outland Trophy winner and the school's first Outland recipient in 28 years (since guard Bill Fischer in 1948) when he won the interior-lineman award in 1976.

RICK BRYAN, SCOTT CASE, THOMAS BENSON

The Atlanta Falcons' first three picks in the 1984 National Football League draft—and all were defensive players from Oklahoma. Bryan was selected in the first round, while Case and Benson were second-round choices.

PAUL BRYANT

Alabama end—and the "Bear" of future college-coaching fame—who was among the 81 players chosen in the National Football League's first draft. The Brooklyn Dodgers chose Bryant in the fourth round of the 1936 draft.

DICK BUTKUS, GALE SAYERS, STEVE DeLONG

The Chicago Bears' first-round selections in the 1965 National Football League draft—and two of the picks, Butkus and Sayers, made the Pro Football Hall of Fame after starring for the Bears. Choosing from the third spot of the opening round with a pick acquired from Pittsburgh, the Bears selected linebacker Butkus of Illinois. Then, up again in the No. 4 slot with their own choice, the Bears went for Kansas halfback Sayers. And, from the sixth position in round one, Chicago used a selection obtained from Washington to choose Tennessee defensive lineman DeLong (who opted to play in the American Football League).

EARL CAMPBELL

Texas running back who was the first player picked in the entire 1978 National Football League draft. Campbell was drafted by the Houston Oilers.

CANTON, COOPERSTOWN, KINGS ISLAND

Cal Hubbard is the only man who is enshrined in both the Pro Football Hall of Fame in Canton, O., and baseball's Hall of Fame in Cooperstown, N.Y.— and he also is a member of the College Football Hall of Fame, whose headquarters at Kings Island, O., opened in 1978. Hubbard, a football star at both Geneva and Centenary, was an outstanding lineman for nine seasons (1927-1933, 1935-1936) in the National Football League, an American League umpire for 16 years (1936-1951) and then a supervisor of umpires.

THE CAROLINAS

The New Orleans Saints led off the 1981 National Football League draft by selecting South Carolina running back George Rogers and the New York Giants zeroed in on the same region of the country by making North Carolina linebacker Lawrence Taylor the second pick of the entire draft.

BILL CARPENTER

Army's last consensus All-America. The Cadets' receiver won the honor in 1959.

KEN CARPENTER

The first National Football League draft choice in Cleveland Browns history. A halfback from Oregon State, Carpenter was drafted in 1950.

GEORGE CONNOR

Notre Dame tackle who received the first Outland Trophy, awarded to the nation's outstanding interior lineman by the Football Writers Association of America. Connor won the honor in 1946.

CONSENSUS ALL-AMERICA TEAM

The NCAA-formulated select squad that is made up from five All-America teams—those chosen by the Associated Press, United Press International, Football Writers Association of America, American Football Coaches Association and the Walter Camp Foundation. A plurality of first-team All-America designations within this group is decisive. If, for example, Player A is on three of the five teams at a particular position and Player B is on the other two, Player A is the consensus All-America. Ties are possible.

TOM COUSINEAU, JOHN ELWAY

The first players chosen in the 1979 and 1983 National Football League drafts—but neither broke into the NFL with the club that drafted him. Ohio State linebacker Cousineau, picked No. 1 overall in the 1979 draft by the Buffalo Bills, began his pro career with the Montreal Alouettes of the Canadian Football League in '79 before entering the NFL in 1982 with the Cleveland Browns (who had obtained the rights to Cousineau via a trade). The Baltimore Colts made Stanford quarterback Elway the first choice in the entire 1983 draft but quickly dealt his rights to the Denver Broncos.

DICK CRAYNE

The "forgotten man" of the National Football League's first-ever opening-round draft picks. While the eight other first-round choices in the NFL's initial draft, 1936, continue to gain occasional mention since they were chosen by franchises still in existence (even if some have relocated), Crayne was selected by the now-defunct Brooklyn Dodgers team. A fullback out of Iowa, Crayne spent two years with the Dodgers.

JOHN DAVID CROW

The only Paul (Bear) Bryant-coached player to win the Heisman Trophy. Crow won the Heisman in 1957 while playing for Texas A&M, whose Aggies were in their fourth and last season under Bryant (who moved to Alabama in 1958).

CHARLES DALY

Four-time All-Americas were not unheard of at the turn of the century (with the collegiate game still limited geographically and dominated by an elite few), but quarterback Daly provided a twist to his laurels. Daly won consensus All-America honors in 1898, 1899 and 1900 at Harvard, then moved on to the U.S. Military Academy and won consensus recognition for Army in 1901.

CORBY DAVIS

Indiana fullback who was the first selection in the entire 1938 National Football League draft. Davis was chosen by the Cleveland Rams, a franchise that had made its NFL debut in 1937.

ERNIE DAVIS

The first black player to win the Heisman Trophy. Davis, Syracuse running star, won the award in 1961 when he averaged 5.5 yards per carry while rushing for 823 yards. Davis scored 15 touchdowns in '61 and completed his only pass attempt of the season—for 74 yards and a touchdown.

The runner-up in the '61 Heisman voting was another black player, Ohio State fullback Bob Ferguson.

GLENN DAVIS, DOC BLANCHARD, ARNOLD TUCKER

Players who gave Army three of the top five finishers in the 1946 voting for the Heisman Trophy. The Cadets' Davis won the award, while teammates Blanchard and Tucker were fourth and fifth in the balloting. Georgia's Charley Trippi was the runner-up, and Notre Dame's Johnny Lujack came in third.

GLENN DAVIS, CHARLIE JUSTICE

The only two-time runners-up in the history of the Heisman Trophy voting. And while Army's Davis could boast of winning the award, North Carolina's Justice couldn't. Davis finished second as a sophomore in 1944 and was No. 2 as a junior in 1945 before winning the Heisman in 1946. Justice's runner-up finishes came in his junior (1948) and senior (1949) seasons.

PETE DAWKINS

The last Army player to win the Heisman Trophy, having received the award in 1958. Previous Cadet winners were Felix (Doc) Blanchard in 1945 and Glenn Davis in 1946.

Five military-academy athletes overall have captured the Heisman, with Navy accounting for the other two honorees. Joe Bellino was awarded the Heisman in 1960, and Roger Staubach—the last service-academy player to receive the trophy—was presented the award in 1963.

GUS DORAIS

Notre Dame's first consensus All-America. The Fighting Irish quarterback earned the honor in 1913.

JOHNNY DRAKE

The first draft choice in Rams history, having been selected when the now California-based National Football League franchise was located in Cleveland. Drake, a rushing star at Purdue, was drafted in 1937.

BILL DUDLEY

The first overall No. 1 draft choice in National Football League history to be enshrined in the Pro Football Hall of Fame. Dudley, chosen from the leadoff position of the 1942 draft by the Pittsburgh Steelers, had been a consensus All-America at Virginia in 1941. He led the NFL in rushing, interceptions and punt returns in 1946 and stood out for three clubs—the Steelers, Detroit Lions and Washington Redskins—during his pro career. Dudley, who played his final NFL season in 1953, entered the Pro Football Hall of Fame in 1966.

RANDY DUNCAN

The top pick in the entire 1959 National Football League draft, quarterback Duncan ended up throwing exactly one touchdown pass in his American professional football career. Duncan was drafted No. 1 out of Iowa by the Green Bay Packers, but chose instead to play in the Canadian Football League (for the British Columbia Lions). In 1961, Duncan joined the Dallas Texans of the American Football League and, in his lone U.S. pro season, completed 25 of 67 passes as a backup to Cotton Davidson. Duncan's scoring pass was a 47-yard completion to Abner Haynes in a September 24, 1961, game against the Oakland Raiders (which Dallas won, 42-35).

EIGHT

The number of Heisman Trophy winners who never entered professional football. The last in the line of Heisman recipients not to play in the pro ranks was Ernie Davis, who never had the opportunity because of illness. Davis, who was awarded the Heisman in 1961, was hospitalized in Evanston, Ill., in the summer of 1962 during workouts for Chicago's College All-Star Game. The Syracuse All-America, looking ahead to his first pro season with the Cleveland Browns (who had obtained the rights to the National Football League's No. 1 draft choice from the Washington Redskins via trade), was found to have leukemia. He missed the 1962 NFL season and his health deteriorated after a period of remission. On May 18, 1963, Davis died at age 23. Other Heisman winners who didn't play professionally: Jay Berwanger (the 1935 honoree), Larry Kelley (1936), Clint Frank (1937), Nile Kinnick (1939), Felix (Doc) Blanchard (1945), Dick Kazmaier (1951) and Pete Dawkins (1958). Business interests, other non-football careers, additional schooling, low pro football salaries (at the time) and military obligations contributed to the Heisman winners' non-entry into pro football (Kelley reportedly signed with the Boston Shamrocks of the American Football League in 1937 but gave up the notion of competing in the pros before playing a down).

FRANK ELISCU, ED SMITH

The sculptor who created the Downtown Athletic Club Trophy (as the Heisman Trophy was called in 1935) and the New York University football player who posed for the artwork. Smith was a three-year letterman at NYU and helped the '35 Violets to a 7-1 record by passing for 558 yards. Eliscu's model then played for the National Football League's Boston Redskins in 1936 and for the Green Bay Packers in 1937.

JOHN ELWAY, DAN MARINO

The first and last of the six quarterbacks selected in the first round of the 1983 National Football League draft. Stanford's Elway was taken No. 1, by the Baltimore Colts, and Pittsburgh's Marino was chosen in the 27th slot of the opening round by the Miami Dolphins. Other quarterbacks drafted in the first round in '83: Todd Blackledge of Penn State, No. 7, by the Kansas City Chiefs; Jim Kelly of Miami (Florida), No. 14, by the Buffalo Bills; Tony Eason of Illinois, No. 15, by the New England Patriots; and Ken O'Brien of California-Davis, No. 24, by the New York Jets.

The following year, there were no quarterbacks drafted in round one. Maryland's Boomer Esiason was the first quarterback to be picked in the 1984 NFL draft—by Cincinnati, in the 10th position of round two.

47

Of the 50 Heisman Trophy winners through 1984, the number of recipients who were quarterbacks or running backs. Besides those who passed and ran the ball (for the most part), three Heisman awardees primarily were pass catchers—Yale end Larry Kelley (1936), Notre Dame end Leon Hart (1949) and Nebraska wingback Johnny Rodgers (1972).

SAM FRANCIS

The first of the National Football League's No. 1 draft choices (overall) to play in the NFL. Selected by the Philadelphia Eagles from the top position in the 1937 draft, Nebraska fullback Francis played for the Chicago Bears (who obtained him in a trade) in 1937 and 1938 before moving on to Pittsburgh and Brooklyn in an NFL career that ended after the 1940 season. The league's first-ever No. 1 pick, Jay Berwanger (1936), did not play pro ball.

IRVING FRYAR, DEAN STEINKUHLER

Nebraska players who were taken 1-2 in the first round of the 1984 National Football League draft. The New England Patriots led off the draft by choosing wide receiver Fryar, and the Houston Oilers then picked offensive lineman Steinkuhler.

JIM GRABOWSKI

When the Miami Dolphins participated in their first draft, the 1966 American Football League selection process, the club's No. 1 choice was Grabowski, a running back from Illinois (who opted to sign with the Green Bay Packers of the National Football League).

BOB GRIESE, LEROY KEYES, MIKE PHIPPS

The players who gave Purdue three Heisman Trophy runners-up in a four-year span. Griese finished second to Florida's Steve Spurrier in 1966, Keyes was No. 2 behind Southern California's O.J. Simpson in 1968 and Phipps was runner-up to Oklahoma's Steve Owens in 1969. The Boilermakers have never had a Heisman winner.

Besides Purdue (1968-1969), Army, North Carolina, Iowa and Tulsa have had Heisman runners-up in consecutive years. Army's Glenn Davis was No. 2 in 1944 and 1945; North Carolina's Charlie Justice was second in 1948 and 1949; Iowa's Alex Karras was runner-up in 1957 and the Hawkeyes' Randy Duncan was No. 2 in 1958, and Tulsa's Jerry Rhome was second in 1964 and the Golden Hurricane's Howard Twilley was runner-up in 1965.

ARCHIE GRIFFIN, DAVE RIMINGTON

Ohio State running star Griffin is the only two-time winner of the Heisman

Trophy, while Nebraska center Rimington is the lone player to have won the Outland Trophy twice. Griffin was the Heisman recipient in 1974 and 1975, and Rimington was awarded the Outland in 1981 and 1982.

TOM HARMON

Made the No. 1 pick overall in the 1941 National Football League draft by the Chicago Bears, Michigan halfback Harmon signed with the New York Americans of the American Football League and made his pro debut with that AFL club in '41. Harmon played only one game for the Americans, preferring to emphasize his broadcasting career. He was a member of the NFL's Los Angeles Rams in 1946 and 1947.

HARVARD

The record-holder for most consecutive years with at least one representative on the consensus All-America team, having placed a player (or players) on the select squad for 28 straight seasons (1889 through 1916).

JOHN HAVLICEK

Ohio State basketball star whose all-around athletic prowess prompted the Cleveland Browns to select him in the seventh round of the 1962 National Football League draft. The Browns drafted Havlicek as a receiver.

JOHN W. HEISMAN

A player at both Brown and Pennsylvania, Heisman went on to football fame as an innovator and longtime coach (Oberlin, Akron, Auburn, Clemson, Georgia Tech, Pennsylvania, Washington and Jefferson, Rice). He was athletic director of New York's Downtown Athletic Club when he died at age 66 on October 3, 1936.

KING HILL

The last of the National Football League's bonus draft picks. From 1947 through 1958, the NFL began its draft by giving the No. 1 choice overall to a team lucky enough to win a blind draw; thus, in this preliminary to the regular inverse-order-of-finish draft, the higher-rung teams had just as good a chance to land the No. 1 pick as the also-ran clubs. As soon as a team won the bonus pick, that club was excluded from future bonus-pick sweepstakes. The Chicago Cardinals were the last team to get the bonus selection (the process wasn't abandoned until all clubs had won the pick), and the Cards drafted Hill, Rice quarterback, in '58. The first 11 bonus choices:

1947   Chicago Bears—Bob Fenimore, Oklahoma A&M
1948   Washington Redskins—Harry Gilmer, Alabama
1949   Philadelphia Eagles—Chuck Bednarik, Pennsylvania
1950   Detroit Lions—Leon Hart, Notre Dame
1951   New York Giants—Kyle Rote, Southern Methodist
1952   Los Angeles Rams—Billy Wade, Vanderbilt
1953   San Francisco 49ers—Harry Babcock, Georgia
1954   Cleveland Browns—Bobby Garrett, Stanford

John Heisman, namesake for college football's most coveted award, was coaching the Quakers of Pennsylvania in 1922.

1955   Baltimore Colts—George Shaw, Oregon
1956   Pittsburgh Steelers—Gary Glick, Colorado A&M
1957   Green Bay Packers—Paul Hornung, Notre Dame

PAUL HORNUNG

The only player who was not a consensus All-America in the season in which he won the Heisman Trophy. Notre Dame quarterback Hornung, who received the Heisman in 1956, took a back seat to Stanford signal-caller John Brodie on the '56 consensus All-America squad.

Hornung *was* a consensus All-America for the Fighting Irish in 1955.

PAUL HORNUNG

The lone player to win the Heisman during a season in which his team posted a losing record. While Notre Dame struggled to a 2-8 mark in 1956, Fighting Irish standout Hornung edged Tennessee's Johnny Majors for the top spot in the Heisman balloting. Jay Berwanger is the only other player to be awarded the Heisman in a non-winning year, earning the trophy in 1935 when his Chicago team finished 4-4.

JOHN HUARTE

Notre Dame quarterback who was named winner of the Heisman Trophy before being presented with a collegiate varsity letter. Huarte played only briefly for the Fighting Irish in his sophomore season of 1962 (four pass completions in eight attempts) and little more in his junior year of 1963 (20

135

for 42), failing to earn a letter. As a senior in 1964, Huarte completed 114 of 205 passes for 2,062 yards and 16 touchdowns—and he won the Heisman, plus a letter, in the process. The Heisman announcement not only preceded Notre Dame's postseason awarding of letters, it came four days before the Irish concluded their season with a game at Southern California.

IT SOUNDS LIKE . . . OR DOES IT?

While Notre Dame's Joe Theismann once acknowledged that his name was actually pronounced "THEES-mann," a Heisman Trophy campaign slogan of "Theismann—as in Heisman" (with the name conveniently pronounced "THIGHS-mann") nevertheless developed in behalf of the Fighting Irish quarterback. As catchy (and fact-stretching) as the phrase might have been, Theismann finished as the runner-up for the Downtown Athletic Club award in his Heisman-contending season of 1970. Stanford's Jim Plunkett outpolled Theismann by more than 800 votes.

VIC JANOWICZ, PAUL GIEL

The only Heisman Trophy winner and the lone Heisman runner-up to play major league baseball—and when pitcher Giel made his big-league debut, Heisman recipient Janowicz was the third batter he faced. Giel, 1953 Heisman runner-up from Minnesota, made his first appearance in the majors on July 10, 1954, at New York's Polo Grounds, working the ninth inning for the Giants in a 10-7 loss to Pittsburgh. He struck out all three men he faced—Pirates pitcher George O'Donnell, shortstop Gair Allie and third baseman Janowicz (who began his major league career as a catcher). Janowicz, who won the Heisman in 1950 while a junior at Ohio State, played a total of 83 games for the Pirates in 1953 and 1954 and batted .214 overall with two home runs and 10 runs batted in. Giel pitched in 102 big-league games for the Giants, Pirates, Twins and A's.

Mississippi's Jake Gibbs, third in the 1960 Heisman voting, became a major league catcher and appeared in 538 games with the Yankees. California's Jackie Jensen, fourth in the 1948 Heisman balloting, played the outfield for the Yankees, Senators and Red Sox and three times was the American League leader or co-leader in RBIs.

DAVID JAYNES

Kansas quarterback who was the World Football League's first draft pick. When the fledgling 12-team league met to draft collegiate talent on January 22, 1974, only four clubs had coaches. But the WFL plunged ahead. The Memphis franchise, which was to become the Houston Texans before the league got off the ground, went first in the draft and opted for Jaynes. (The WFL franchise originally intended for Toronto wound up in Memphis.)

BOB JOHNSON

A center from Tennessee who became the first-ever draft pick of the current Cincinnati Bengals franchise in 1968.

ED (TOO TALL) JONES

The Dallas Cowboys have had the first selection in the entire draft only once since joining the National Football League in 1960, and the Cowboys used that pick on Tennessee State defensive lineman Jones in 1974.

K.C. JONES, PAT RILEY

Pro basketball coaches—their teams have met in National Basketball Association Championship Series play—who were National Football League draft selections because of their athletic skills. Jones, a basketball star at the University of San Francisco, was a 30th-round pick (as an end) of the Los Angeles Rams in 1955, while Kentucky basketball standout Riley was an 11th-round choice (also as a receiver) of the Dallas Cowboys in 1967.

LARRY KELLEY, CLINT FRANK

Yale's Heisman Trophy recipients and the second and third players to be presented the award. Kelley won the Heisman in 1936; Frank was the winner in 1937.

LES KELLEY

When New Orleans announced the first draft selection in the National Football League club's history in 1967, the Saints called the name of Kelley, a fullback from Alabama. Kelley went on to play linebacker for New Orleans.

NILE KINNICK, CALVIN JONES

Iowa's only Heisman Trophy winner and the Hawkeyes' first Outland Trophy recipient—and both fell victim to air tragedies soon after their award-winning seasons. Kinnick, who won the Heisman in 1939, was killed in June 1943 when his Navy plane crashed in the Gulf of Paria in the Caribbean Sea. Jones, the Outland honoree in 1955, died in December 1956 while aboard a Canadian airliner that crashed after departing Vancouver, British Columbia. Jones had been in Vancouver to play in Canadian pro football's all-star game.

Alex Karras became the third Hawkeye to win either of the top two trophies, receiving the Outland in 1957.

IZZY LANG

Recipient of the only touchdown pass that 1964 Heisman Trophy winner John Huarte threw during his career in the American Football League and National Football League. Active in six seasons overall in the AFL and NFL, Huarte attempted a total of only 48 passes (he completed 19 and yielded four interceptions) while playing for the Boston Patriots, Philadelphia Eagles, Kansas City Chiefs and Chicago Bears. Huarte, as a member of the Eagles, tossed his lone scoring pass on September 22, 1968, hitting Lang on a 23-yard strike in a 34-25 loss to the New York Giants.

Huarte fared better in the World Football League, firing 24 touchdown passes for Memphis in 1974 and four more for the Southmen in 1975.

JIM LAWRENCE

Texas Christian halfback who in 1936 became the first draft pick of the National Football League's Cardinals franchise, then based in Chicago and now headquartered in St. Louis.

FRANK LEAHY

The only man to have coached four Heisman Trophy winners. Heisman awardees Angelo Bartelli (1943), Johnny Lujack (1947), Leon Hart (1949) and Johnny Lattner (1953) all played for Leahy at Notre Dame.

RUSS LETLOW

Guard from the University of San Francisco who was the first draft selection in Green Bay history, having been selected by the Packers in 1936.

ART LEWIS

Ohio University lineman who in 1936 became the first draft choice in New York Giants history.

BOB LILLY

Defensive lineman from Texas Christian who was the first draft pick in Dallas Cowboys history. Dallas, having missed out on the National Football League draft that preceded its first NFL season (1960) because of the franchise's late entry into the league, made its first-ever selection in round one of the 1961 draft. The Cowboys had traded their own first-round pick of 1961 to Washington in a 1960 deal that sent quarterback Eddie LeBaron to Dallas, but on draft day they acquired the Cleveland Browns' first-round selection for their own top choice of 1962. And, picking in Cleveland's place, the Cowboys opted for Lilly.

JACK LOSCH, BART STARR

Green Bay's first-round pick in the 1956 National Football League draft and the Packers' 17th-round selection in that draft. Top choice Losch, a halfback from Miami (Florida), played one season for Green Bay, carrying the ball only 19 times and gaining just 43 yards; Starr, a quarterback from Alabama, spent 16 years with the Packers, passing for 24,718 yards and 152 touchdowns. Starr led Green Bay to five NFL championships and won a spot in the Pro Football Hall of Fame.

LOUISIANA TECH

While national powerhouses Michigan State (1967) and Southern California (1968 and 1969) had produced the No. 1 picks overall in the previous three drafts, the honor went to Louisiana Tech in 1970 when the Pittsburgh Steelers made Bulldogs quarterback Terry Bradshaw the first selection in the National Football League draft.

RICHIE LUCAS

One of the first-round picks in the 1960 American Football League draft, the AFL's first such player selection process (held, actually, on November 22, 1959). Lucas, a quarterback from Penn State, was chosen by Buffalo. Other first-round choices, announced as a group (with no order of selection indicated), were: Boston, halfback Ron Burton of Northwestern; Dallas, quarterback Don Meredith of Southern Methodist; Denver, center-placekicker Roger Leclerc of Trinity (Connecticut); Houston, halfback Billy Cannon of Louisiana State; Los Angeles, tight end Monty Stickles of Notre Dame; Minneapolis, quarterback-defensive back Dale Hackbart of Wisconsin; and New York, quarterback George Izo of Notre Dame. (At draft time, the AFL still had team nicknames to bestow and wasn't even firm in its geographic makeup. The clubs became known as the Buffalo Bills, Boston Patriots, Dallas Texans, Denver Broncos, Houston Oilers, Los Angeles Chargers, New York Titans and, in the case of the soon-in-transit Minneapolis franchise, the Oakland Raiders.)

DAN MARINO

The first draft choice in United States Football League history. When the USFL conducted its initial draft on January 4-5, 1983, the Los Angeles Express led off round one by choosing Marino, a quarterback from Pittsburgh.

TOMMY MASON

A backfield standout at Tulane, he gained the distinction of being the first player ever drafted by the Minnesota Vikings (1961).

RUEBEN MAYES

Until 1984, Washington State had never had a consensus All-America football player—but running back Mayes changed that, winning the select designation in '84 for the Cougars.

McALISTER, JOHNSON, BROWN

Highly coveted collegiate seniors who, on the eve of the 1974 National Football League draft, signed contracts with the Southern California Sun of the yet-to-play-a-game World Football League. The signings, considered a coup for the new league, gave the Sun two excellent running backs in James McAlister and Kermit Johnson (a consensus All-America), both of UCLA, and an outstanding offensive lineman in Southern Cal's Booker Brown (also a consensus All-America). McAlister, Johnson and Brown were the Sun's top three selections in the WFL's draft, which had been conducted the previous week.

EARL McCULLOUCH

The fifth and last Southern California Trojan taken in the first round of the 1968 National Football League-American Football League draft. Wide receiver McCullouch was drafted by the Detroit Lions, who picked 24th in the opening round. Trojans chosen earlier were offensive tackle Ron Yary, No. 1, by the Minnesota Vikings; offensive tackle Mike Taylor, No. 10, by the Pittsburgh Steelers; defensive end Tim Rossovich, No. 14, by the Philadelphia Eagles; and running back Mike Hull, No. 16, by the Chicago Bears.

DON MEREDITH, DON PERKINS

Having completed their collegiate careers in 1959, they became property of Dallas' new National Football League team in 1960 and evolved into mainstays for the club—but neither was drafted by the Cowboys franchise. The Cowboys, in fact, did not participate in the draft that preceded their first NFL season (1960) because Dallas had yet to gain admission into the league; still, the Cowboys wound up with two draftees around whom their offense eventually was built. Quarterback Meredith, who played at Southern Methodist and was a favorite of Dallas fans, was chosen by the Chicago Bears in the third round of the 1960 NFL draft and Perkins, a running back from New Mexico, was picked by the Baltimore Colts in the ninth round. Both players had signed personal-services contracts, however, with Clint Murchison Jr. (the man behind Dallas' NFL bid) and their rights were officially obtained by Dallas—via trades for third- and ninth-round draft choices in 1962—once Murchison won approval for an NFL expansion franchise. Touching off the draft maneuvering was Murchison's—and the NFL's—fear of losing Meredith to Dallas' American Football League team, another pro football newcomer. Meredith played for the Cowboys from 1960 through 1968, passing for 17,199 yards and 135 touchdowns. Perkins, whose NFL debut was delayed one season because of a foot injury, played for Dallas from 1961 through 1968 and rushed for 6,217 yards and 42 touchdowns (he scored 45 TDs overall). In July 1969, the two Cowboy greats retired.

MIAMI DOLPHINS

The National Football League team that drafted Joe Theismann, selecting the Notre Dame quarterback in the fourth round in 1971. Theismann, though, began his professional career in the Canadian Football League and spent three seasons with the Toronto Argonauts. The Washington Redskins acquired the NFL rights to Theismann from Miami in January 1974 (in exchange for a first-round draft choice in 1976), and signed him in March of '74.

MICHIGAN STATE

The school that accounted for four of the top eight choices in the opening round of the first combined National Football League-American Football League draft, held March 14-15, 1967. The Spartans chosen were: Bubba Smith, first, by Baltimore; Clint Jones, second, by Minnesota; George Webster, fifth, by Houston, and Gene Washington, eighth, by Minnesota.

DON MILLER

The lone member of Notre Dame's Four Horsemen who was not a consensus All-America. Quarterback Harry Stuhldreher, halfback Jim Crowley and fullback Elmer Layden were consensus All-America players for the Fighting Irish in 1924, and they were joined in the backfield by Illinois' Red Grange. Halfback Miller led the Irish in rushing in '24, gaining 763 yards, and averaged 6.8 yards per carry in his varsity career.

DICK MODZELEWSKI, RANDY WHITE

Two Maryland Terrapins have won the Outland Trophy—Modzelewski in 1952 and White in 1974.

BRICK MULLER

The first player from the Far West to gain consensus All-America recognition. California end Muller won the honor in 1921 and again in 1922.

JOE NAMATH, GALE SAYERS

Namath, from Alabama, and Sayers, out of Kansas, were the 11th- and 12th-place finishers in the Heisman Trophy balloting in 1964, the year that the award went to Notre Dame's John Huarte. All three players were seniors in '64.

NEBRASKA, OKLAHOMA

The schools that rank 1-2 in Outland Trophy winners. Nebraska is tops with five Outland recipients (Larry Jacobson in 1971, Rich Glover in 1972, Dave Rimington in 1981 and 1982 and Dean Steinkuhler in 1983), and Oklahoma is second with four (Jim Weatherall in 1951, J.D. Roberts in 1953, Lee Roy Selmon in 1975 and Greg Roberts in 1978).

STEVE NIEHAUS

The Seattle Seahawks made Notre Dame defensive lineman Niehaus the first selection in their draft history, choosing him in 1976.

1972, 1977, 1978, 1983

The only four seasons in which the Heisman Trophy winner and the Outland Trophy recipient came from the same school—and Nebraska accounted for two of the four "doubles." In 1972, the Cornhuskers' Johnny Rodgers won the Heisman and teammate Rich Glover was awarded the Outland; in 1983, Nebraska's Mike Rozier took the Heisman and the Huskers' Dean Steinkuhler copped the Outland. Texas was a double winner in 1977 with Earl Campbell (Heisman) and Brad Shearer (Outland), and Oklahoma turned the trick in 1978 with Billy Sims (Heisman) and Greg Roberts (Outland).

TOMMY NOBIS

Texas linebacker who was the first draft choice (1966) in Atlanta Falcons history.

LEO NOMELLINI

Lineman from Minnesota who was the first National Football League draft choice (1950) in the history of the San Francisco 49ers.

NOTRE DAME

The leader in producing the first pick in the entire National Football League draft. Fighting Irish players have been chosen No. 1 overall five times—in 1944 (Angelo Bertelli), 1946 (Frank Dancewicz), 1950 (Leon Hart), 1957 (Paul Hornung) and 1972 (Walt Patulski). Bertelli and Dancewicz were drafted by the Boston Yanks, Hart was selected by the Detroit Lions, Hornung was chosen by the Green Bay Packers and Patulski was picked by the Buffalo Bills.

NOTRE DAME

While the Fighting Irish rank third on the all-time (1889 through 1984) consensus All-America list behind early-day football powers Yale and Harvard, it's a different story—to put it mildly—when considering All-America selections from 1935 through '84, when the shift in the collegiate game's power base was complete. From 1889 through 1984, Yale had 100 consensus choices overall, Harvard totaled 89 and Notre Dame 79. But in the 50-year period from '35 through '84, the Fighting Irish had 62 consensus All-Americas, Yale just three and Harvard only one.

The team leaders in total consensus All-Americas, 1889-1984 (with consensus picks covering the 50 seasons from 1935 through 1984 in parentheses): Yale 100 (3), Harvard 89 (1), Notre Dame 79 (62), Princeton 65 (4), Michigan 55 (33), Southern California 51 (42), Ohio State 49 (38), Pennsylvania 46 (4), Oklahoma 43 (43), Pittsburgh 41 (21), Army 37 (16), Nebraska 34 (30), Texas 32 (32), Minnesota 29 (16), Alabama 28 (24), Tennessee 24 (22), Penn State 23 (18), Stanford 23 (15), Navy 22 (11) and UCLA 20 (20).

When the Ivy League was dropped from major-college football status in 1982, standout Ivy players were consigned to a lower-level—NCAA Division I-AA—All-America squad.

NOTRE DAME, OHIO STATE, SOUTHERN CAL

The leading producers of Heisman Trophy honorees, having accounted for 15 of the 50 winners. Notre Dame leads with six Heisman winners (Angelo Bertelli in 1943, Johnny Lujack in 1947, Leon Hart in 1949, Johnny Lattner in 1953, Paul Hornung in 1956 and John Huarte in 1964), while Ohio State is second with five (Les Horvath in 1944, Vic Janowicz in 1950, Howard Cassady in 1955 and Archie Griffin in 1974 and 1975). Southern California has fielded four Heisman recipients (Mike Garrett in 1965, O.J. Simpson in 1968, Charles White in 1979 and Marcus Allen in 1981).

DON NOTTINGHAM

Of the 442 players selected in the 1971 National Football League draft, Nottingham was the 441st taken. Baltimore, coming off a victory in Super Bowl V, chose the Kent State running back and—against all odds—he made the grade in the NFL. Nottingham, who gained the nickname "The Human Bowling Ball" because of his squat build, spent seven seasons in the league and scored 35 touchdowns overall—12 of them in 1975, a year in which he ground out 718 yards rushing for Miami. He divided his pro career between

Former Miami running back Don Nottingham, dubbed "The Human Bowling Ball" because of his compact build, was the 441st player selected in the 1971 NFL draft.

Baltimore (31 games) and Miami (67 games), and appeared in Super Bowl VIII with the Dolphins.

DAVEY O'BRIEN

The shortest Heisman Trophy winner of all time. The 5-foot-7 O'Brien, a star quarterback at Texas Christian, captured the Heisman in 1938.

DAVEY O'BRIEN

The first Heisman Trophy winner to play in the National Football League. O'Brien, who won the Heisman in 1938 after throwing 19 touchdown passes and leading Texas Christian to the national championship (as awarded by the Associated Press poll, the lone wire-service ranking system of the day), played for the Philadelphia Eagles in 1939 and 1940. A first-round draft choice of the Eagles, O'Brien proved he could play in the pros despite his lack of size. An effective passer for woefully weak Philadelphia teams, O'Brien gave up the game after two seasons to join the Federal Bureau of Investigation.

OKLAHOMA, SOUTHERN CALIFORNIA

Through the 1984 season, the Sooners had been represented on consensus All-America teams for 14 consecutive years and Trojan players had made the select squads for 13 straight seasons. Starting the Oklahoma streak in

The Olsen brothers, Merlin (left) and Phil, were 1971 teammates while playing for the Los Angeles Rams.

1971 were running back Greg Pruitt and center Tom Brahaney, while Southern Cal's string began in 1972 with tight end Charles Young.

MERLIN OLSEN, PHIL OLSEN

The only two consensus All-America football players in Utah State history—and the linemen are brothers. Merlin won the honor in 1961, while Phil was a consensus pick in 1969.

JIM PARKER

The first of three Ohio State players to win the Outland Trophy. Parker, a guard, was honored in 1956. Buckeyes middle guard Jim Stillwagon received the trophy in 1970 and Ohio State offensive tackle John Hicks was given the award in 1973.

PHILADELPHIA, CHICAGO CARDINALS, TAMPA BAY

The only National Football League teams to have had the No. 1 overall pick in two straight drafts. The Philadelphia Eagles led off the NFL's first two drafts, picking Chicago's Jay Berwanger in 1936 and Nebraska's Sam Francis in 1937. The Cardinals chose first in 1939 and 1940, selecting Ki Aldrich of Texas Christian and then George Cafego of Tennessee. And the Tampa Bay Buccaneers drafted from the top spot in 1976 and 1977, opting for Southern California's Ricky Bell and Oklahoma's Lee Roy Selmon.

TOMMY PROTHRO

The only man to have been head coach for Heisman Trophy winners at two schools. Prothro coached at Oregon State when the Beavers' Terry Baker claimed the award in 1962 and he was the head man at UCLA when the Bruins' Gary Beban won the honor in 1967.

KEN RICE

Auburn offensive lineman who was the American Football League's first formal No. 1 draft pick, being selected by the Buffalo Bills in 1961. The AFL and the National Football League went head-to-head in the drafting process —and in the bidding for talent—from 1960 through 1966 before beginning their common draft in 1967. In 1960, the AFL had no formal No. 1 choice, instead announcing its entire first round as a group; the first player taken in the '60 NFL draft was Louisiana State's Billy Cannon, by the Los Angeles Rams. While Rice was the first player drafted by the AFL in '61, Tulane's Tommy Mason—chosen by the Minnesota Vikings—was the first man picked by the NFL. Other No. 1 choices leaguewide during the period of separate drafts and signing wars: 1962—NFL, Ernie Davis of Syracuse, by Washington; AFL, Roman Gabriel of North Carolina State, by Oakland. 1963 —NFL, Terry Baker of Oregon State, by the Los Angeles Rams; AFL, Buck Buchanan of Grambling, by the Dallas Texans (Kansas City). 1964—NFL, Dave Parks of Texas Tech, by San Francisco; AFL, Jack Concannon of Boston College, by Boston. 1965—NFL, Tucker Frederickson of Auburn, by the New York Giants; AFL, Larry Elkins of Baylor, by Houston. 1966—NFL, Tommy Nobis of Texas, by Atlanta; AFL, Jim Grabowski of Illinois, by Miami.

JOHNNY RODGERS, MIKE ROZIER

Honored in 1972 and 1983, they are the Heisman Trophy recipients who played for Nebraska.

GEORGE ROGERS

The first consensus All-America football player (1980) in South Carolina history—and he made '80 a particularly notable year for the Gamecocks by also winning the Heisman Trophy that season.

CAL ROSSI

UCLA halfback who was a first-round draft selection of the Washington Redskins for two straight years, 1946 and 1947. In '46, there was one small oversight on the Redskins' part, a blunder that indicates that era's lack of sophisticated scouting procedures—Rossi was a year away from being eligible for the draft. Not about to admit defeat in their quest for Rossi, the Redskins drafted him No. 1 again in '47—and this time Rossi simply declined Washington's offer.

LEE ROY SELMON

Oklahoma defensive lineman who in 1976 became the first player to be drafted by the Tampa Bay Buccaneers franchise.

17

The number of entrants in the Pro Football Hall of Fame's first class of inductees. Elected in 1963 as charter members of the Canton, O., shrine were: Sammy Baugh, Bert Bell, Johnny Blood (McNally), Joe Carr, Dutch

Clark, Red Grange, George Halas, Mel Hein, Wilbur (Pete) Henry, Cal Hubbard, Don Hutson, Curly Lambeau, Tim Mara, George Preston Marshall, Bronko Nagurski, Ernie Nevers and Jim Thorpe.

17

The number of Texas Longhorns selected in the 12 rounds of the 1984 National Football League draft—the most players chosen from one team since 1946, when 18 former Notre Dame players (including some who had finished their collegiate careers elsewhere) were picked. The '46 draft went 30 rounds, however.

SIMS

The name of the No. 1 draft choice in the National Football League twice in a three-year span. In the 1980 NFL draft, the Detroit Lions chose Oklahoma running back Billy Sims from the leadoff spot; in 1982, the New England Patriots made Texas defensive lineman Kenneth Sims the top selection in the entire draft.

FRANK SINKWICH, HERSCHEL WALKER

Of schools with two or more Heisman Trophy winners, Georgia has gone the longest between honorees—with the Bulldogs' Sinkwich and Walker receiving the award 40 years apart. Sinkwich became Georgia's first Heisman winner in 1942, and Walker was awarded the trophy in 1982.

FRANK SINKWICH

The Detroit Lions, picking from the leadoff position for the first time in the eight-year history of the National Football League draft, made Georgia backfield sensation Sinkwich the No. 1 choice of the entire 1943 draft.

BRUCE SMITH

The No. 1 choice overall in the 1985 National Football League draft. Virginia Tech's defensive-line standout was chosen by the Buffalo Bills, marking the fourth straight year that an American Conference East team had the first pick in the draft.

BUBBA SMITH, TODY SMITH

Brothers who were first-round draft choices four years apart. Bubba, Michigan State defensive lineman, was taken by the Baltimore Colts as the No. 1 pick of the 1967 National Football League-American Football League draft. Tody, a defensive lineman from Southern California, was selected by the Dallas Cowboys from the 25th spot of the first round in the 1971 NFL draft.

ED SMITH

The New York University backfield star and Heisman Trophy model who was selected in the third round of the National Football League's first draft —held in 1936—by the Boston Redskins.

RILEY SMITH

The first National Football League draftee to play in the league. Smith, a quarterback from Alabama, was picked from the No. 2 slot overall in the 1936 NFL draft by the Boston Redskins and played three seasons (primarily as a kicker) with the 'Skins franchise (which moved to Washington in 1937). The players selected immediately ahead of and behind Smith in the first round of the '36 draft—No. 1 pick Jay Berwanger and No. 3 choice Bill Shakespeare—shunned pro football after starring for Chicago and Notre Dame as collegians. Philadelphia drafted Berwanger and Pittsburgh chose Shakespeare.

SOUTHERN CALIFORNIA

The only school to have had players taken No. 1 overall in successive National Football League drafts. The Minnesota Vikings made Southern Cal tackle Ron Yary the top choice in the 1968 NFL draft, and the Buffalo Bills picked Trojans running back O.J. Simpson from the leadoff spot in 1969.

SOUTHERN CALIFORNIA

Through 1985, the runaway leader in producing first-round choices since the first combined National Football League-American Football League draft was conducted (in 1967, as a result of the leagues' merger agreement). The Trojans accounted for 34 opening-round picks in the 19 drafts held from '67 through '85, with Southern Cal having three or more players taken in the first round in seven of those years.

Ohio State had 20 first-round selections from '67 through '85, Notre Dame boasted 19, Oklahoma had 15 and Alabama and Michigan each totaled 14.

The common draft carried an "NFL-AFL" label from 1967 through 1969, then became known as simply the NFL draft when the pro football merger was fully implemented in 1970 (and AFL teams came under the NFL umbrella as the major part of the American Conference).

TIM SPENCER

The second player chosen overall in the United States Football League's first draft (1983) and the first USFL draftee to sign with the new pro football league. Spencer, a running back from Ohio State, was selected and signed by the Chicago Blitz.

AMOS ALONZO STAGG

Yale end who was selected to the first All-America team in 1889.

STANFORD, MISSISSIPPI, SANTA CLARA

Schools whose quarterbacks went 1-2-3 in the first round of the 1971 National Football League draft. Stanford's Jim Plunkett was chosen first, by the Boston Patriots; Mississippi's Archie Manning went in the No. 2 spot, to the

New Orleans Saints, and Santa Clara's Dan Pastorini was selected from the third position, by the Houston Oilers.

ROGER STAUBACH, O.J. SIMPSON

The first Heisman Trophy winners to gain election to the Pro Football Hall of Fame, making the Canton, O., shrine as members of the 1985 induction class. Staubach won the Heisman Trophy in 1963 and later starred for the Dallas Cowboys, while Simpson captured the Heisman in 1968 and went on to pro stardom with the Buffalo Bills (he also played for the San Francisco 49ers).

JIM STILLWAGON

Ohio State middle guard who in 1970 became the first winner of the Vince Lombardi/Rotary Award, an honor bestowed upon the outstanding college lineman of the year by the Rotary Club of Houston.

Nebraska leads in Lombardi Award recipients, three, with the Cornhuskers' Rich Glover winning the award in 1972, Dave Rimington capturing the honor in 1982 and Dean Steinkuhler being singled out in 1983.

JOE STYDAHAR

The only first-round choice in the initial National Football League draft (1936) to earn a spot in the Pro Football Hall of Fame. Stydahar, a tackle from West Virginia, was taken in the sixth slot of the opening round by the Chicago Bears.

Three other players from the first NFL draft played their way into the Pro Football Hall of Fame: Tuffy Leemans, a second-round pick out of George Washington by the New York Giants; Notre Dame's Wayne Millner, an eighth-round selection of the Boston Redskins, and Colgate's Dan Fortmann, a ninth-round choice of the Bears.

PAT SULLIVAN

The only Heisman winner from a college once coached by the man for whom the trophy was named. Sullivan was awarded the Heisman in 1971, a season in which he threw 20 touchdown passes for Auburn. More than 70 years earlier (1895-1899), the Tigers were coached by John W. Heisman.

GEORGE TALIAFERRO

The first black player to be drafted by a National Football League team. The Chicago Bears picked Taliaferro, an Indiana backfield standout, in the 13th round of the 1949 draft. However, Taliaferro played for the Los Angeles Dons of the rival All-America Football Conference in '49 before making his NFL debut in 1950 with the New York Yanks.

TAMPA

Florida school that dropped football two seasons after producing the No. 1 pick in the entire National Football League draft. John Matuszak, Spartans defensive lineman, was chosen in the top spot of the 1973 NFL draft by the Houston Oilers. After fielding football teams in the fall of '73 and 1974, Tampa abandoned the sport.

TAMPA

University whose final football team, its 1974 squad, had a first-round National Football League draft choice. Tampa offensive tackle Darryl Carlton was picked by the Miami Dolphins from the 23rd position of the opening round of the 1975 draft.

13

The number of schools with one-time representation on the list of Outland Trophy winners. Those schools are: Army (Joe Steffy, 1947), Auburn (Zeke Smith, 1958), Duke (Mike McGee, 1959), Georgia (Bill Stanfill, 1968), Kentucky (Bob Gain, 1950), Michigan State (Ed Bagdon, 1949), North Carolina State (Jim Ritcher, 1979), Penn State (Mike Reid, 1969), Pittsburgh (Mark May, 1980), Southern California (Ron Yary, 1967), Tennessee (Steve DeLong, 1964), Utah State (Merlin Olsen, 1961) and Virginia Tech (Bruce Smith, 1984).

JIM THORPE

One of seven members of the Pro Football Hall of Fame who played major league baseball. The others are Morris (Red) Badgro, Paddy Driscoll, George Halas, Greasy Neale, Ernie Nevers and Clarence (Ace) Parker.

Y.A. TITTLE

Having already played three full professional seasons, including the 1950 campaign with the National Football League's Baltimore Colts, Tittle was the No. 1 selection of the San Francisco 49ers in the 1951 NFL draft. The strange set of circumstances revolved around the failure of the Colts franchise to survive. Tittle had played for Baltimore in 1948 and 1949 when the Colts were members of the All-America Football Conference and accompanied the team into the NFL when the club was absorbed by the senior league in 1950. When the Colts franchise folded after one season in the NFL, the Baltimore players were made available to the rest of the league as part of the 1951 collegiate draft—and the 49ers went for quarterback Tittle.

Another Colts franchise was born in Baltimore in 1953, and it remained in the Maryland city for 31 seasons before shifting to Indianapolis in 1984.

Tittle, as a collegiate senior out of Louisiana State, had been the Detroit Lions' first-round choice in the 1948 NFL draft.

WALLY TRIPLETT

The National Football League's first black draft choice to play in the NFL. Triplett, a halfback from Penn State, was selected by Detroit in the 19th round of the 1949 draft and emerged as the Lions' No. 3 rusher in '49.

CHARLEY TRIPPI

The second Georgia athlete in three years to be the first player taken overall in the National Football League draft, halfback Trippi was picked No. 1 by the Chicago Cardinals in 1945.

21

The number of schools that have produced Heisman Trophy winners on a one-time-only basis. Honored once with Heisman recipients: Auburn (Pat Sullivan, 1971), Boston College (Doug Flutie, 1984), Chicago (Jay Berwanger, 1935), Florida (Steve Spurrier, 1966), Iowa (Nile Kinnick, 1939), Louisiana State (Billy Cannon, 1959), Michigan (Tom Harmon, 1940), Minnesota (Bruce Smith, 1941), Oregon State (Terry Baker, 1962), Penn State (John Cappelletti, 1973), Pittsburgh (Tony Dorsett, 1976), Princeton (Dick Kazmaier, 1951), South Carolina (George Rogers, 1980), Southern Methodist (Doak Walker, 1948), Stanford (Jim Plunkett, 1970), Syracuse (Ernie Davis, 1961), Texas (Earl Campbell, 1977), Texas A&M (John David Crow, 1957), Texas Christian (Davey O'Brien, 1938), UCLA (Gary Beban, 1967) and Wisconsin (Alan Ameche, 1954).

JOHNNY UNITAS

University of Louisville quarterback who was a ninth-round choice of the Pittsburgh Steelers in the 1955 National Football League draft. Unitas, who passed for 2,912 yards and 27 touchdowns in his four-year career at Louisville, had an injury-plagued senior season in 1954 and completed only 44 of 110 passes for 527 yards and three TDs.

GENE UPSHAW, MARVIN UPSHAW

Brothers who were first-round choices in successive pro drafts. Gene, an offensive lineman out of Texas A&I, was selected by the Oakland Raiders in the 17th slot of the opening round of the 1967 National Football League-American Football League draft. The Cleveland Browns, drafting from the 21st position in the first round of the 1968 NFL-AFL selection process, picked Marvin, a defensive lineman from Trinity (Texas).

BILLY VESSELS, STEVE OWENS, BILLY SIMS

Oklahoma players who have been awarded the Heisman Trophy, with Vessels being honored in 1952, Owens in 1969 and Sims in 1978.

BILLY VESSELS

Oklahoma running star who was the first National Football League draft pick (1953) of the Colts franchise that is now based in Indianapolis. When Vessels was drafted, the Colts were headquartered in Baltimore.

SID WAGNER

Michigan State guard who was the first player ever drafted by the Detroit Lions (1936).

Josephine Wistert roots for her son Alvin while listening to a 1949 broadcast of a Michigan game. Pictures of her three sons, (left to right) Francis, Albert and Alvin, line the top of the radio. All three were consensus All-Americas at Michigan.

HERSCHEL WALKER

Georgia running back who was third in the Heisman Trophy voting as a freshman in 1980, second as a sophomore in 1981 and first as a junior in 1982. In February 1983, Walker signed with the New Jersey Generals of the United States Football League.

HERSCHEL WALKER, MIKE ROZIER, DOUG FLUTIE

Three straight Heisman Trophy winners (1982, 1983 and 1984) who chose to sign with United States Football League teams. Georgia's Walker became a member of the New Jersey Generals, Nebraska's Rozier began his pro career with the Pittsburgh Maulers and Boston College's Flutie opted for the USFL's Generals.

CASPAR WHITNEY, WALTER CAMP

Whitney is the man who came up with the idea of picking All-America football teams and Camp is the person who popularized the practice while choosing "dream teams" for Collier's magazine. Sports expert Whitney turned to Camp, his friend and Yale football legend, for advice on the selection of the 1889 and 1890 All-America teams that appeared in Whitney's magazine, The Week's Sport. Whitney chose All-America squads for Harper's Weekly from 1891 through 1896, and Camp selected the 1897 All-America team for Harper's before Whitney resumed the practice after returning from abroad. Beginning in 1898 and continuing until his death in March 1925 (with the exception of war-torn 1917), Camp picked All-America teams for Collier's. Succeeding Camp in the Collier's selection role was Grantland Rice.

DAVE WINFIELD

Versatile Minnesota Gopher athlete and major league baseball star-to-be who was a 17th-round pick—as a tight end—of the Minnesota Vikings in the 1973 National Football League draft. Winfield also was a pro basketball draftee, being chosen by the Atlanta Hawks in the fifth round of the 1973 National Basketball Association draft and picked by the Utah Stars in the sixth round of the '73 American Basketball Association senior draft.

In the NFL draft, Winfield was taken after the Buffalo Bills had selected Colorado defensive back John Stearns six spots earlier in the 17th and last round. Stearns also turned to baseball, becoming a big-league catcher.

FRANCIS, ALBERT AND ALVIN WISTERT

Brothers who all won consensus All-America status while playing tackle for Michigan—and Alvin finished his collegiate career at age 33. Francis (also known as "Whitey") was a consensus All-America for the Wolverines in 1933, Albert gained the distinction in 1942 and Alvin was honored in 1948 and 1949. Alvin, actually the middle brother, got a late start on his college education—family obligations and military service were among the contributing factors—and finally wound up at Michigan after a short stay at Boston University. All three Wisterts wore number 11 at Michigan.

WYOMING

A school that never was represented on a consensus All-America football team through the 1982 season but then had players named to the 1983 and 1984 squads. Punter Jack Weil was an '83 consensus All-America, and Cowboys tight end Jay Novacek was honored in '84.

YALE

The all-time leader in consensus All-Americas with 100. However, Yale's last consensus All-America came in 1944 when end Paul Walker was honored. Heisman Trophy winners Larry Kelley (1936) and Clint Frank (1937) were the 98th and 99th consensus All-America selections in Yale history.

YALE, ARMY, OHIO STATE

The only schools to have Heisman Trophy winners in successive years. Yale's Larry Kelley and Clint Frank won in 1936 and 1937, Army's Felix (Doc) Blanchard and Glenn Davis were victorious in 1945 and 1946 and Ohio State's Archie Griffin earned the trophy in 1974 and again in 1975.

THIRD QUARTER

POSTSEASON FUN

AIR FORCE ACADEMY

Fielding a team that featured members of the academy's first senior class, Air Force capped a remarkable 1958 season—the Falcons went 9-0-1 in the regular portion of the schedule—by tying Texas Christian, 0-0, in the Cotton Bowl on January 1, 1959. The only "blemish" on the Falcons' regular-season record was, in fact, a major accomplishment—an eye-opening 13-13 tie against Big Ten Conference power Iowa in Iowa City.

ALABAMA

Held to one first down in the 1942 Cotton Bowl game, the Crimson Tide parlayed seven interceptions and five recoveries of Texas A&M fumbles into a 29-21 triumph over the Aggies.

ALABAMA

The Crimson Tide owns the single-game scoring record in Big Four (Rose, Orange, Sugar and Cotton) bowl play, having set the mark on January 1, 1953, in a 61-6 Orange Bowl trouncing of Syracuse.

ALABAMA

The only school to have won all of the Big Four bowl games—the Rose, Orange, Sugar and Cotton—twice. Through the January 1, 1985, bowl games, the Crimson Tide had gone 4-1-1 in the Rose, 7-3 in the Sugar, 4-3 in the Orange and 2-4 in the Cotton.

Alabama, in fact, is the all-time leader in bowl appearances (37) and in trips to the Big Four bowls (29).

MARCUS ALLEN

Los Angeles Raiders running back who rushed for a Super Bowl-record 191 yards against Washington on January 22, 1984, leading his club to a 38-9 drubbing of the Redskins in Super Bowl XVIII.

LANCE ALWORTH, BUTCH WILSON

Key figures in the closing minutes of the 1962 Sugar Bowl game between Arkansas and No. 1-ranked Alabama. With Alabama clinging to a 10-3 lead and Arkansas poised at the Crimson Tide's 40-yard line, Razorbacks quarterback George McKinney unloaded a pass goalward and barely missed connections with the fleet and surehanded Alworth. After a second pass failed, McKinney went deep again and Alabama defender Wilson intercepted the ball inches from the goal line. The unbeaten Tide then ran out the clock, with quarterback Pat Trammell keeping—and firmly gripping—the ball on three rushing attempts.

AMERICAN FOOTBALL LEAGUE ALL-STAR GAME

Western Division All-Stars were pitted against their Eastern counterparts in eight of the nine AFL All-Star Games played from January 1962 through January 1970, and the West won six times. In the All-Star Game that followed the 1965 season, the AFL champion Buffalo Bills played the league's All-Stars (and the Bills lost, 30-19). No All-Star Game was played after the AFL's first season, 1960. Perhaps the most notable occurrence in AFL All-Star history was the January 1965 shifting of the game site—on five days' notice—from New Orleans' Tulane Stadium to Houston's Jeppesen Stadium. Protesting what they called widespread racial discrimination in New Orleans, black All-Stars took their complaints to the AFL Players' Association. The association upheld the claim, and AFL Commissioner Joe Foss moved the game to Houston.

Arkansas' Roland Sales (21), making up for the absence of Ben Cowins, the team's leading runner who was suspended before the 1978 Orange Bowl, breaks loose from Oklahoma defenders on a long-gainer en route to a 205-yard performance that helped the Razorbacks upset the No. 2-ranked Sooners.

ELMER ANGSMAN, CHARLEY TRIPPI

The big-play men whose heroics in the 1947 National Football League championship game against Philadelphia led the Chicago Cardinals to the NFL crown (which the Cardinals franchise hasn't won since). Angsman twice bolted 70 yards to touchdowns from the line of scrimmage, while Trippi scored on a 44-yard run and on a 75-yard punt return as the Cardinals downed the Eagles, 28-21, at Comiskey Park.

ARIZONA STATE

Winner of four of the first five games in the history of the Fiesta Bowl, a postseason game that is played on Arizona State's home field. In the first Fiesta Bowl, played December 27, 1971, at Sun Devil Stadium in Tempe, Ariz., Arizona State outlasted Florida State, 45-38. The Sun Devils then beat Missouri, 49-35, in the December 23, 1972, game and downed Pittsburgh, 28-7, on December 21, 1973. After Oklahoma State and Brigham Young met in the Tempe game that followed the 1974 season (the Cowboys won, 16-6), Arizona State edged Nebraska, 17-14, in the December 26, 1975, Fiesta Bowl.

155

ARIZONA STATE, FLORIDA

While the Associated Press and United Press International agreed on Oklahoma as the national collegiate champion in 1975 and both wire services opted for Brigham Young as No. 1 in final 1984 polls, The Sporting News chose Arizona State as the best in the land in '75 (with Oklahoma No. 2) and made Florida the top-ranked team in '84 (with Brigham Young in the fourth slot).

No school has won The Sporting News' national title more than once in the publication's 10 years of ratings. The Sporting News honored Pittsburgh in 1976, Notre Dame in 1977, Southern California in 1978, Alabama in 1979, Georgia in 1980, Clemson in 1981, Penn State in 1982 and Miami (Florida) in 1983, in addition to the Sun Devils in 1975 and the Gators in 1984.

ARKANSAS

Playing without injured All-America guard Leotis Harris and three other offensive standouts (including Ben Cowins, the club's leading runner) who were suspended from the team because of a dormitory incident, the Razorbacks got a 205-yard rushing performance from unheralded Roland Sales and upset the No. 2-ranked Oklahoma Sooners, 31-6, in the 1978 Orange Bowl.

ARKANSAS

The Razorbacks enjoyed variety in their bowl menu from 1977 through 1982, appearing in postseason games after each of those six seasons and competing in six different bowls. The Razorbacks made the following postseason stops: After the '77 season, the Orange Bowl; 1978, Fiesta Bowl; 1979, Sugar Bowl; 1980, Hall of Fame Classic; 1981, Gator Bowl, and 1982, Bluebonnet Bowl.

LEE ARTOE

Chicago lineman who returned a second-period Washington fumble 52 yards for a touchdown in the 1942 National Football League title game as the Bears, who went 11-0 in the regular season, tried to complete a perfect year. The Redskins, still smarting from the 73-0 defeat inflicted by the Bears two years earlier on the same Griffith Stadium turf, rebounded on Sammy Baugh's touchdown pass to Wilbur Moore and Andy Farkas' scoring run and prevailed, 14-6, to gain revenge—at least partially—for their humiliation in the 1940 championship game.

AP, UPI POLLS

Begun in mid-October 1936, the Associated Press' poll of sportswriters and broadcasters rated the nation's collegiate football teams on a weekly basis to the end of each regular season for 31 of its first 32 years of existence (through 1967), deviating from the format only in 1965 when—with AP's top three teams all 10-0 and its No. 1 through No. 6 teams scheduled to play on January 1, 1966—the final poll was delayed until after the New Year's Day bowl games. However, beginning in 1968 and continuing to the present, AP

Ohio State Coach Woody Hayes is restrained (left) after punching Clemson defender Charlie Bauman late in the 1978 Gator Bowl game. Hayes, who was fired the next day, arrives at his Columbus, O., home (below) in the company of a police escort.

has waited until the conclusion of the bowl games to release its final rankings. The United Press International poll, featuring balloting by a board of coaches, made its debut in 1950. From '50 through 1973, UPI presented its final rankings at the end of the regular season; in 1974, however, it adopted the policy of releasing its final ratings after the bowl games.

AUBURN, MICHIGAN STATE

They squared off in the first Orange Bowl game played in the Orange Bowl stadium (then known as Burdine Stadium, for a leading Miami businessman), a structure that replaced the wooden bleachers that had occupied the same site. On January 1, 1938, Auburn held Michigan State to two first downs and won, 6-0.

RALPH BAKER

New York Jets linebacker who covered an errant Oakland pitch in the final 2 minutes of play, enabling the Jets to hold on for a 27-23 victory in the 1968 American Football League championship game. New York had just seized the lead on Joe Namath's six-yard touchdown strike to Don Maynard, but the Raiders roared back and mounted a drive that reached the Jets' 24-yard line. Oakland quarterback Daryle Lamonica then attempted a swing pass to Charlie Smith, with the ball falling to the turf unattended. Johnny-on-the-spot Baker alertly pounced on the ball—the play was ruled a lateral and not an incomplete pass—and the Jets advanced to Super Bowl III.

BALTIMORE COLTS, DALLAS COWBOYS

Teams that played in the most error-filled game in Super Bowl history. Baltimore lost possession of the ball four times on fumbles and three times on interceptions in Super Bowl V, and Dallas lost one fumble and yielded three interceptions. Besides the 11 turnovers, the game—won by the Colts, 16-13—was marred by 14 penalties.

REGGIE BARNETT

His interception of a Richard Todd pass at Notre Dame's 34-yard line with 68 seconds left in the 1975 Orange Bowl ensured a 13-11 victory for the Fighting Irish over Alabama's Crimson Tide. The triumph over Alabama, rated No. 1 in the United Press International poll entering postseason play, came in Ara Parseghian's final game as Irish coach.

CHARLIE BAUMAN

Clemson defender who was punched by Ohio State Coach Woody Hayes late in the December 29, 1978, Gator Bowl game when he ran out of bounds in front of Hayes after killing the Buckeyes' hopes for victory—Clemson won, 17-15—by intercepting an Art Schlichter pass. Hayes, who was completing his 28th season as Ohio State coach, was fired the next day.

JOE BELLINO

Navy's Heisman Trophy winner who made a sensational, leaping catch of a

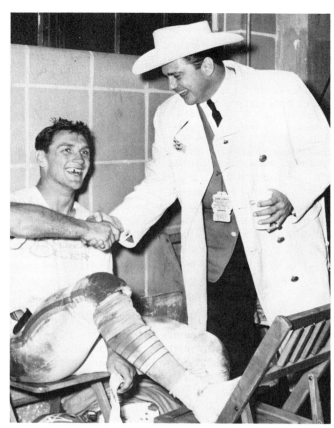

Houston Owner K. S. (Bud) Adams (right) congratulates Oilers halfback Billy Cannon after Cannon had teamed with quarterback George Blanda to give Houston a victory over the Los Angeles Chargers in the AFL's first championship game in 1960.

Hal Spooner pass in the end zone in the 1961 Orange Bowl, but otherwise had a tough day against Missouri's rock-ribbed defense. While contributing his 27-yard touchdown reception, Bellino could gain only four yards rushing on eight carries—overall, the Midshipmen had minus eight yards on the ground—as Missouri scored a 21-14 victory. The bowl triumph was a first for the Tigers, who had lost all seven of their previous postseason games (beginning with a setback at the hands of Southern California in the 1924 Los Angeles Christmas Festival).

BOB BERRY

He never played in a Super Bowl game despite being a member of three Super Bowl teams. Eligible for Super Bowls VIII, IX and XI as a reserve quarterback for the Minnesota Vikings, Berry was relegated to an observer's role behind Fran Tarkenton in the first two games (against Miami and Pittsburgh) and watched Tarkenton and Bob Lee direct the Vikings in the third game (against Oakland).

GEORGE BLANDA, BILLY CANNON

Clinging to a 17-16 lead over the Los Angeles Chargers in the fourth quarter of the American Football League's first title game, the Houston Oilers locked up the 1960 AFL championship when Cannon took a short pass from Blanda and turned it into an 88-yard touchdown play. Houston won, 24-16.

BLUE-GRAY GAME

Collegiate postseason all-star game between North and South teams, contested in Montgomery, Ala. When the senior standouts first met on January 2, 1939, the Blue scored a 7-0 victory.

ROBBIE BOSCO

Brigham Young quarterback who, despite being hobbled by leg and ankle injuries he incurred early in the game, passed for 343 yards in the December 21, 1984, Holiday Bowl in San Diego as the top-ranked Cougars overcame Michigan, 24-17. BYU, 12-0 in the regular season and trying to nail down the national title with an impressive victory, faced a 17-10 deficit in the fourth period but rebounded on Bosco's touchdown passes to Glen Kozlowski and Kelly Smith. While its triumph wasn't overwhelming, Brigham Young retained its No. 1 rating in both wire services' post-bowls polls.

TERRY BRADSHAW

Pittsburgh quarterback who threw a Super Bowl-record four touchdown passes on January 21, 1979, powering the Steelers past the Dallas Cowboys, 35-31, in Miami. Dallas, trailing 35-17 late in the game, rallied on Roger Staubach's scoring passes to Billy Joe DuPree and Butch Johnson, but Pittsburgh safely handled an onside kick in the final 17 seconds of the 13th Super Bowl and clinched the victory.

BRIGHAM YOUNG

A participant in all seven Holiday Bowls played through 1984. While a loser to Navy and Indiana in the first two Holiday Bowls (played after the 1978 and 1979 seasons) in San Diego, the perennial Western Athletic Conference champion collected four victories in the next five Holiday games.

AARON BROWN

Kansas City end whose crushing fourth-quarter hit on Minnesota's Joe Kapp drove the Vikings' quarterback from Super Bowl IV and seemed to typify the defensive vise that the American Football League's Chiefs applied in the January 11, 1970, game played in New Orleans. Kansas City intercepted three Minnesota passes that day, recovered two Viking fumbles and held the National Football League champions' vaunted rushing game to 67 yards overall as the Chiefs scored a 23-7 victory. Quarterback Len Dawson, put through an emotional wringer during Super Bowl week after his name was mentioned in connection with a U.S. Justice Department investigation of sports gambling (Dawson was never implicated), deftly guided the Chiefs' multi-faceted attack—the so-called Offense of the '70s—and broke the Vikings' backs when he teamed with wide receiver Otis Taylor on a 46-yard scoring pass in the third quarter. The Chiefs' triumph gave the AFL a 2-2 split in the four Super Bowls that matched the AFL's titlists against the NFL champions.

Kansas City's Dave Hill (right) congratulates teammate Otis Taylor after the wide receiver had broken Minnesota's back with a 46-yard TD reception in the Chiefs' Super Bowl IV victory.

JIM BROWN

Having run for a league-leading 1,527 yards in the 1958 National Football League regular season, Brown was a marked man when he and his Cleveland teammates took on the New York Giants in a '58 playoff game to break an Eastern Conference first-place tie. Led by linebacker Sam Huff, the Giants' defense—always a major test for Cleveland's great fullback—held Brown to eight yards on seven carries as New York scored a 10-0 victory. The triumph propelled the Giants into a date with destiny—an NFL title-game showdown against the Baltimore Colts at Yankee Stadium.

JOHN BROWN

Pittsburgh player who hauled in a 33-yard touchdown pass from Dan Marino in the final 35 seconds of the 1982 Sugar Bowl, enabling the Panthers to edge Georgia, 24-20.

JOHNNY MACK BROWN

With Alabama trailing Washington, 12-0, at halftime of the Crimson Tide's first Rose Bowl game, future film star Brown caught two touchdown passes in the Tide's 20-point third-quarter rally and helped his team to a 20-19 triumph over the Huskies in the 1926 classic. Alabama's spurt occurred—perhaps not coincidentally—when Washington star George Wilson was forced to the sidelines because of an injury. Alabama, the first Southern team to play in the Rose Bowl, made six appearances in the Pasadena, Calif., game from 1926 through 1946 and compiled a 4-1-1 record.

RAYMOND BROWN

The first of four Mississippi quarterbacks to win the Sugar Bowl's Outstanding Player Award in a six-year span. Brown was honored in 1958, Bobby Franklin in 1960, Jake Gibbs in 1961 and Glynn Griffing in 1963.

TOM BROWN

Green Bay defender whose fourth-down interception of a Don Meredith pass in the end zone ensured the Packers a 34-27 victory over Dallas in the 1966 National Football League title game and gave the Pack a berth in Super Bowl I. The Cowboys, who had trailed, 34-20, earlier in the fourth quarter, bounced back into contention on Meredith's 68-yard touchdown pass to Frank Clarke. Dallas then drove to a first down at the Green Bay 2-yard line in the closing moments before an offsides penalty and a stiff Packer defense—Brown's big play came with 28 seconds remaining in the game—stymied the Cowboys. Bart Starr tossed four touchdown passes for Green Bay.

WILLIE BROWN

Veteran defensive back who capped Oakland's scoring in Super Bowl XI—the game in which the Raiders won their first National Football League championship—by intercepting a Fran Tarkenton pass and returning it 75 yards for a touchdown in the Raiders' 32-14 romp over the Minnesota Vikings in Pasadena, Calif.

BOYD BRUMBAUGH, ERNIE HEFFERLE

Mississippi State was leading Duquesne, 12-7, in the final 3 minutes of the 1937 Orange Bowl when passer Brumbaugh and receiver Hefferle teamed up on a 72-yard touchdown strike that brought the Dukes a 13-12 victory.

BUCKNELL, MIAMI (FLORIDA)

Opponents in the first official Orange Bowl game, played January 1, 1935, at the current Orange Bowl stadium site in Miami. Bucknell romped, 26-0. The postseason game was an outgrowth of the 1933 and 1934 Palm Festival games—contested at Miami's Moore Park—that matched Miami against Manhattan and then the Hurricanes against Duquesne.

CALIFORNIA

The Golden Bears took unbeaten records (10-0, 10-0 and 9-0-1) into the 1949, 1950 and 1951 Rose Bowls and came out of the Pasadena, Calif., game a loser each time. California lost to Northwestern, 20-14, in the '49 Rose Bowl, fell to Ohio State, 17-14, in the '50 game and was beaten by Michigan, 14-6, on January 1, 1951.

Dallas quarterback Don Meredith (17) cuts loose the desperation pass that ended up in the hands of Green Bay's Tom Brown, ensuring the Packers' 34-27 victory over the Cowboys in the 1966 NFL championship game.

Bucknell (white uniforms) and Miami (Florida) squared off in the first Orange Bowl game, played January 1, 1935, at the current Orange Bowl site in Miami.

'CALTECH'

The team name that mysteriously appeared on the scoreboard in the fourth quarter of the 1984 Rose Bowl game and which, 23 years earlier, had mysteriously flashed from the University of Washington card section at the Pasadena, Calif., classic. California Institute of Technology students, never lacking for ingenuity, tapped into the Rose Bowl scoreboard computer system in '84 and made the board read, "Caltech 38, MIT 9" (when, in fact, UCLA was ahead of Illinois by that score en route to a 45-9 victory). At the '61 Rose Bowl game, Washington students assumed they were flashing the name of their school during a card trick—only to find that infiltrators had schemed to make "Caltech" show up instead.

HUGH CAMPBELL, BUD GRANT, FRANK (POP) IVY

Highly successful coaches in the Canadian Football League, as indicated by their postseason success. Campbell coached Edmonton to five straight Grey Cup titles (1978 through 1982), Grant guided Winnipeg to four CFL crowns (1958, 1959, 1961, 1962) in five seasons and Ivy directed Montreal to three consecutive Grey Cup championships (1954 through 1956).

DUKE CARLISLE, PHIL HARRIS

In a dream matchup sending No. 1-ranked Texas against No. 2-rated Navy in the 1964 Cotton Bowl, Texas' pass-catch duo of Carlisle and Harris stole the spotlight from Navy's Roger Staubach (the 1963 Heisman Trophy winner) and sparked the Longhorns to a surprisingly easy 28-6 victory over the Midshipmen. Carlisle threw touchdown passes of 58 and 63 yards to Harris, and the Texas quarterback ran for a third score.

DAVE CASPER

With 53 seconds having elapsed in the second overtime period of the 1977 American Conference divisional playoff game between Oakland and Baltimore, Casper caught a 10-yard touchdown pass from Ken Stabler and the Raiders emerged with a 37-31 victory over the Colts.

CATAWBA, MARYVILLE

North Carolina and Tennessee schools that met in the inaugural Tangerine Bowl, contested in Orlando, Fla., on January 1, 1947. Catawba won, 31-6. Having risen significantly in stature in the past decade, the Orlando clash became known as the Florida Citrus Bowl effective with its December 17, 1983 game (in which Tennessee downed Maryland, 30-23).

DON CHANDLER, TOM MATTE

Key figures in the 1965 Western Conference overtime playoff game in Green Bay, Wis., between the National Football League's Green Bay Packers and Baltimore Colts. Chandler kicked a game-tying—and much-disputed —22-yard field goal with 1 minute, 58 seconds left in regulation play and then booted the Packers to a 13-10 victory with a 25-yard kick that came 13:39 into overtime. Game films and photographs—and even comments from Green Bay fans who witnessed the kick from the end zone—lent credence to the Colts' claim that Chandler's 22-yarder had sailed wide of the goal post. Matte, normally a halfback, turned in his second straight workmanlike performance at quarterback for the Colts in the absence of the injured Johnny Unitas and Gary Cuozzo. Matte, who the week before had rushed for 99 yards as Baltimore's signal-caller in a key regular-season victory over Los Angeles, wore a wristband with basic plays written on it as he guided the Colts.

CHECK THAT SCORE

It sounded like a baseball result, but it was indeed the final score of a 1970 National Conference divisional playoff game: Dallas 5, Detroit 0. Mike Clark's 26-yard field goal, tenacious defensive play that featured George Andrie's end-zone sacking of Lions quarterback Greg Landry and Duane Thomas' 135 yards rushing powered the Cowboys.

CHICAGO COLLEGE ALL-STAR GAME

Played every summer except one from 1934 through 1976, this game matched pro champions from the previous season against a collegiate all-star squad. Thirty-nine of the 42 games in the series pitted the defending National Football League titlist against the College All-Stars and another game matched an NFL divisional champion against the All-Stars. The other two contests sent Super Bowl-winning American Football League champions against the collegians. The pro champs dominated the competition, compiling a 31-9-2 record. The 1974 game was canceled because of an NFL players-owners dispute.

STEVE CICHY, JOE GRAMKE, JOE MONTANA

Trailing Houston, 34-12, midway through the last quarter of the 1979 Cotton Bowl, Notre Dame put on a miracle finish and overtook the Cougars at the final gun, 35-34—with Cichy, Gramke and Montana leading the way. Cichy got things rolling by returning a blocked punt 33 yards for a touchdown and Montana hit Vagas Ferguson on a two-point conversion pass. Three minutes later, Montana ran two yards for a TD and teamed with Kris Haines for a two-point conversion. With the game winding down and its lead having dwindled to 34-28, Houston decided against a punt on a fourth-and-one play from its own 29-yard line and Notre Dame's Gramke stopped the Cougars' Emmett King short of first-down yardage in the final half-minute of play. Montana took the Irish in, tying the score on an eight-yard pass to Haines as time expired. Joe Unis then kicked the extra point. Notre Dame 35, Houston 34.

CLEMSON

The winner of the first Bluebonnet Bowl game, played December 19, 1959, in Houston. The Tigers downed Texas Christian, 23-7.

CLEMSON

With No. 3-ranked Alabama having lost in the afternoon to Texas in the Cotton Bowl and No. 2 Georgia involved in a wild game (which it would lose in the final 35 seconds) with Pittsburgh in the Sugar Bowl, No. 4 Nebraska took dead aim on the national championship in its showdown against No. 1 Clemson in the January 1, 1982, Orange Bowl. Clemson, whose place atop the polls was constantly being challenged (critics said the Tigers played a weak schedule), fell behind, 7-3, in the first quarter but then scored the game's next 19 points and went on to a 22-15 triumph that ensured the national title for the Atlantic Coast Conference champions. The key touchdown for Clemson came in the third period when the Tigers, clinging to a 12-7 lead, scored on Homer Jordan's 13-yard pass to Perry Tuttle.

GARY COLLINS, FRANK RYAN

After the Cleveland Browns and Baltimore Colts battled to a 0-0 halftime standoff in the 1964 National Football League title game, Cleveland receiver Collins hauled in touchdown passes of 18, 42 and 51 yards from Ryan in the second half and the Browns coasted to a 27-0 victory.

COLUMBIA . . . AND KF-79

Pulling off perhaps the greatest upset in Rose Bowl history, Columbia surprised Stanford, 7-0, in the waterlogged 1934 game—and the Lions' KF-79 play proved decisive. Columbia's lightweight reputation—in terms of both

Cleveland's Gary Collins reaches for and pulls in a 42-yard touchdown pass from quarterback Frank Ryan during the 1964 NFL championship game against Baltimore. Collins and Ryan also teamed on 18- and 51-yard TD passes as the Browns recorded a 27-0 victory.

its football prowess and the physical makeup of its squad—seemed to portend a mismatch. If, that is, there was to be any match at all. Violent rainstorms flooded the area in the days preceding the game and left eight inches of water on the floor of the Rose Bowl stadium. Constant pumping of the field made conditions playable (but still deplorable), and Columbia was ready—weather or not. The Lions scored the game's lone touchdown on their patented KF-79 play, which was a vital part of the spinner series in Coach Lou Little's single-wing offense. On a second-quarter play from Stanford's 17-yard line, KF-79—a deception-oriented play emphasizing deft faking and making any of three players potential ballcarriers—was called. Al Barabas was the man who got the ball this time, much to Stanford's befuddlement, and Barabas bolted to the end zone. At day's end, bigger and stronger Stanford had dominated the statistics but Columbia had won the game.

CONVENTION HALL, ATLANTIC CITY, N.J.

Site of the December 19, 1964, Liberty Bowl game between Utah and West Virginia. A financial flop overall and plagued by cold weather in its first five games in Philadelphia (1959 through 1963), the Liberty Bowl was moved indoors and to New Jersey in '64. However, only 6,059 fans—about half of the Convention Hall's capacity—turned out for the game, which Utah won handily, 32-6. In '65, the bowl game found a permanent home in Memphis, Tenn.

167

FRANK CORRAL

He scored all of the points in the 1979 National Conference championship game. Kicking field goals of 19, 21 and 23 yards, Corral booted the Los Angeles Rams to a 9-0 victory over the Tampa Bay Buccaneers.

COTTON BOWL

The only one of the Big Four bowls—Rose, Orange, Sugar and Cotton—to have had successive tie games and the leader among the Big Four with four deadlocked contests overall (neither the Orange Bowl nor the Sugar Bowl has had a tie game). Arkansas and Louisiana State battled to a 0-0 standoff in the 1947 Cotton Bowl, and Southern Methodist and Penn State played to a 13-13 tie in the '48 game in Dallas. Texas and the Randolph Field service team fought to a 7-7 stalemate in the 1944 Cotton classic, and Air Force and Texas Christian played to a 0-0 draw in '59. The Rose Bowl has had three tie games—Alabama-Stanford, 7-7, in 1927; Navy-Washington, 14-14, in 1924, and Washington and Jefferson-California, 0-0, in 1922.

ROGER CRAIG

San Francisco player who scored a Super Bowl-record three touchdowns on January 20, 1985, helping the 49ers to a 38-16 conquest of the Miami Dolphins at Stanford Stadium in Stanford, Calif. Craig caught scoring passes covering eight and 16 yards from Joe Montana and ran two yards for a TD in Super Bowl XIX.

SAM CUNNINGHAM

Southern California fullback who dived over the Ohio State defense for four short-yardage touchdowns in the 1973 Rose Bowl as the No. 1-ranked Trojans clobbered the Buckeyes, 42-17. Cunningham scored all of his TDs (a two-yard thrust and three one-yard carries) in the second half as Southern Cal went on a 35-point tear after a 7-7 halftime deadlock.

DALLAS COWBOYS, MIAMI DOLPHINS

National Football League teams that have made a record five trips to the Super Bowl. Each club has a 2-3 mark in Super Bowl competition.

MIKE DAVIS

Trailing 14-12 in the final minute of a 1980 American Conference divisional playoff game against Oakland but within chip-shot range of a game-winning field goal, the Cleveland Browns surprisingly tried a second-down pass from the Raiders' 9-yard line. And the Browns went down to defeat on a frigid, windy day in Cleveland when Oakland defensive back Davis intercepted Brian Sipe's throw.

TED DEAN, CHUCK BEDNARIK

With Philadelphia trailing Green Bay, 13-10, in the fourth quarter of the 1960 National Football League championship game, the Eagles' Dean traveled 58

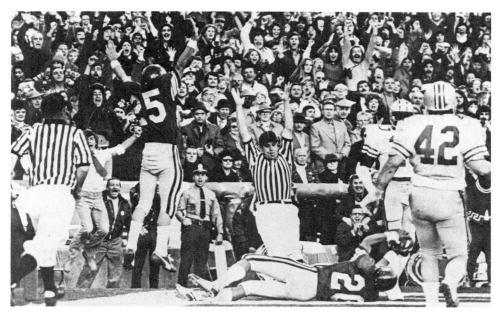

Sprawled on the ground in the end zone, Southern Cal's Shelton Diggs displays the ball after catching a two-point conversion pass from Trojans quarterback Pat Haden. The play came with about 2 minutes to play in the 1975 Rose Bowl and completed Southern Cal's 18-17 comeback victory over Ohio State.

yards on a kickoff return and later capped the possession with a five-yard scoring run as Philadelphia emerged with a 17-13 triumph. Bednarik turned in the NFL's last 60-minute performance, playing all the way at center on offense and at linebacker on defense, and he stopped the Packers' Jim Taylor at the Eagles' 9-yard line on the game's final play after the fullback had taken a 13-yard pass from Bart Starr.

DENVER BRONCOS

The most bumbling team in Super Bowl history. The Broncos turned over the ball eight times (four interceptions, four lost fumbles) in Super Bowl XII and bowed to the Dallas Cowboys, 27-10.

SHELTON DIGGS

Sprawled on the ground in the final 2 minutes of the 1975 Rose Bowl, Diggs pulled in a two-point conversion pass from quarterback Pat Haden that enabled Southern California to overcome Ohio State, 18-17. Trailing 17-10 seconds earlier, the Trojans closed within one point when Haden hit Johnny (J.K.) McKay with a 38-yard touchdown pass. The triumph helped boost USC, ranked No. 4 for the 1974 season by United Press International entering the game, to the top spot in UPI's first-ever post-bowls final poll.

CARL DODD

His 82-yard interception return for a touchdown capped top-ranked Oklahoma's 20-6 victory over Maryland in the 1956 Orange Bowl. The triumph was the 30th straight for the Sooners, whose whirlwind style of play (quick huddles, sprinting to positions, springing up after plays) eventually took its toll on the Terrapins. Maryland, which managed to lead, 6-0, at halftime, entered the game with 15 consecutive victories.

BILL DORAN, BOBBY LAYNE

With a little more than 2 minutes remaining in the 1953 National Football League championship game and Detroit trailing Cleveland, 16-10, Lions receiver Doran hauled in a 33-yard touchdown pass from quarterback Layne. Doak Walker then kicked the extra point as Detroit captured the NFL crown with a 17-16 triumph.

TONY DORSETT

His 202 yards rushing and Pittsburgh's suffocating defense led the top-ranked Panthers to a 27-3 rout of Georgia in the 1977 Sugar Bowl.

A.J. DUHE

Miami linebacker who intercepted three of Richard Todd's passes in the 1982 American Conference championship game, including an early-fourth-quarter toss that he returned 35 yards for a touchdown, as the Dolphins downed the New York Jets, 14-0.

DUKE

With Alabama leading the Blue Devils, 26-20, late in the 1945 Sugar Bowl game, Duke parlayed an intentional safety by the Crimson Tide and George Clark's 20-yard touchdown run into a 29-26 triumph.

DURHAM, N.C.

Site of the only Rose Bowl game—the January 1, 1942, classic—not played in Pasadena, Calif. With the United States at war (Pearl Harbor had been bombed only 3½ weeks before the scheduled Rose Bowl date), military conditions forbade the gathering of large crowds on the West Coast and that situation apparently meant the cancellation of the '42 Rose Bowl, which was to have pitted Oregon State against Duke. However, Wallace Wade, Duke coach and athletic director, offered his stadium for the game and the contest was moved to the Blue Devils' campus in Durham. The visiting Beavers went on to upset previously unbeaten and untied Duke, 20-16.

EAST-WEST SHRINE GAME

San Francisco-area collegiate all-star classic whose 60th game overall was played on January 5, 1985, at Stanford Stadium in Stanford, Calif., with the West defeating the East, 21-10. Game one in the postseason series to aid crippled children was played on December 26, 1925, at Ewing Field in San Francisco, and a touchdown reception by California's Brick Muller gave the West a 6-0 victory. Kezar Stadium was the most notable home of the East-West Game, having played host to the "Strong Legs Run, That Weak Legs Might Walk" contest 40 times (beginning with game two). One game—the

January 3, 1942, clash—was moved from the Bay Area to New Orleans because of wartime crowd restrictions on the West Coast.

EDMONTON ESKIMOS

Canadian professional football's Grey Cup champions for five consecutive years, 1978 through 1982.

WEEB EWBANK

The only man to coach both National Football League and American Football League teams to championships. Ewbank directed the 1958 and 1959 Baltimore Colts to NFL crowns and guided the 1968 New York Jets to the AFL title (and Super Bowl championship).

TOM FEARS, NORM VAN BROCKLIN

With the score tied, 17-17, midway through the fourth period of the 1951 National Football League title game between Los Angeles and Cleveland, quarterback Van Brocklin and receiver Fears teamed on a Rams pass play that went for 73 yards and a touchdown as Los Angeles notched a 24-17 victory.

59 DEGREES BELOW ZERO

The wind-chill factor at Cincinnati's Riverfront Stadium for the 1981 American Conference championship game (played on January 10, 1982) between the Bengals and the San Diego Chargers. Cincinnati prevailed, 27-7, with Ken Anderson tossing two touchdown passes.

GENE FILIPSKI

Twenty-two years after their "Sneakers Game" of 1934, the New York Giants and the Chicago Bears met again for the National Football League title on an icy field. While the scene in 1956 was Yankee Stadium and not the Polo Grounds, the outcome was the same—the Giants, aided by basketball footwear and brimming with confidence after Gene Filipski scooted 58 yards across the treacherous turf with the opening kickoff, won convincingly. Charley Conerly passed for two touchdowns and Alex Webster ran for two others as New York crushed Chicago, 47-7, on a frigid, windy day.

FLORIDA, NEBRASKA

Opponents in the 41st and last Sugar Bowl game played at Tulane Stadium. On December 31, 1974, Nebraska's Cornhuskers edged the Florida Gators, 13-10.

47, 26

The number of bowl games played after the 1948 and 1949 collegiate football seasons, with the cutback coming after the NCAA discouraged postseason games that lacked sound financial backing. Helping to cut the bowl lineup nearly in half was the stipulation that 80 percent of all bowl-game receipts must go to competing colleges. Among the games played during and after the postseason-game glut were the Rice Bowl, Salad Bowl, Pineapple Bowl, Cigar Bowl, Raisin Bowl, Prairie Bowl, Vulcan Bowl, Ice Bowl, Lily Bowl, Refrigerator Bowl, Glass Bowl, Fruit Bowl, Fish Bowl, Grape Bowl, Paper Bowl, Oleander Bowl, Spindletop Bowl, Corn Bowl, Pear Bowl, Smoky Mountain Bowl, Bean Bowl, Oriental Rice Bowl, Iodine Bowl and Bamboo Bowl. The postseason games involved major colleges, small colleges, junior colleges, all-star teams and service squads.

43:38

The minutes and seconds of playing time in what proved to be the final College All-Star Game. With the Pittsburgh Steelers leading the College All-Stars, 24-0, in the third quarter of the July 23, 1976, game, a violent thunderstorm flooded Chicago's Soldier Field. The combination of the downpour, severe lightning and strong winds was a risk to participants and spectators alike, and the game was called with 1 minute, 22 seconds remaining in the period,

ROD GARCIA

His field goal with 12 seconds left in the game gave Coach John Ralston's Stanford team its second straight upset triumph in the Rose Bowl, this one a 13-12 victory over Michigan in the January 1, 1972, classic. Stanford tied the score, 10-10, in the final period on a drive that featured a daring fake-punt play from its own 33-yard line, then fell behind on a controversial safety. With Michigan ahead, 10-3, and Stanford presumably ready to punt on fourth-and-10, Jackie Brown ran 31 yards to Michigan's 36 and he later scored from the 24. But the Wolverines regained the lead when Stanford's Jim Ferguson, after fielding a missed Wolverine field-goal attempt and getting out across the goal line, was driven back into the end zone by Ed Shuttlesworth (many observers thought Ferguson was down outside the end zone). Don Bunce's passing rallied Stanford, though, and Garcia delivered the game-winning field goal from 31 yards out. A year earlier, Stanford had cut down Ohio State, 27-17.

GREGG GARRITY

Penn State receiver whose key receptions helped the second-ranked Nittany Lions upend No. 1-rated Georgia, 27-23, in the 1983 Sugar Bowl, with the victory propelling Penn State to its first national championship. The Nittany Lions rolled to a 20-3 lead, but the Bulldogs cut the deficit to 20-17 entering the fourth quarter. On Penn State's fifth play of the final period, Todd Blackledge hit Garrity with a 48-yard touchdown pass. Then, with the Nittany Lions guarding a four-point lead in the final minutes of the game, Garrity caught a possession-preserving six-yard pass from Blackledge on a third-and-three play originating at Penn State's 32-yard line. Georgia's offensive unit never touched the ball again. In the game's rushing duel, Penn State's Curt Warner ran for 117 yards and two touchdowns and Georgia's Herschel Walker netted 103 yards and one TD.

Cleveland quarterback Otto Graham runs one yard for the final touchdown of his illustrious career during the Browns' victory over the Rams in the 1955 NFL championship game.

GEORGIA

Outgained in total net yards, 328 to 127, and able to complete only one of 13 passes, the No. 1-ranked Bulldogs nevertheless nailed down the 1980 national championship by taking advantage of Notre Dame mistakes and then holding off the Fighting Irish, 17-10, in the January 1, 1981, Sugar Bowl. An Irish misplay on a kickoff return and a Notre Dame fumble led to Georgia touchdown "drives" of one yard and 22 yards, and the Bulldogs collected a field goal after blocking a Notre Dame three-point attempt. Herschel Walker ran for both of Georgia's touchdowns.

GEORGIA, GEORGIA TECH, NOTRE DAME

Besides Alabama (which has won all of the Big Four bowl games at least twice), the only schools to have posted victories in the Rose, Sugar, Orange and Cotton bowls. Georgia has a 1-0 record in the Rose, a 2-1 mark in both the Cotton and Orange and a 2-4 ledger in the Sugar. Georgia Tech is 1-0 in the Rose, 4-0 in the Sugar, 3-2 in the Orange and 1-1 in the Cotton. Notre Dame is 1-0 in the Rose, 3-1 in the Cotton and 1-1 in both the Sugar and Orange.

GOTHAM BOWL, GARDEN STATE BOWL

Bowl games in the New York metropolitan area that failed to survive. The Gotham Bowl made its debut at the Polo Grounds on December 9, 1961

(Baylor defeated Utah State, 24-9), moved to Yankee Stadium in 1962 (Nebraska outlasted Miami of Florida, 36-34) and then died. The Garden State Bowl in East Rutherford, N.J., came upon the postseason scene on December 16, 1978, and had a four-year run before disbanding. Garden State winners were Arizona State (over Rutgers, 34-18), Temple (over California, 28-17), Houston (over Navy, 35-0) and Tennessee (over Wisconsin, 28-21).

OTTO GRAHAM

Playing his final professional game, Graham passed for two touchdowns and ran for two TDs as he led the Cleveland Browns to a 38-14 triumph over the Los Angeles Rams in the 1955 National Football League championship game. A year earlier, he had thrown for three TDs and rushed for three others as Cleveland battered Detroit, 56-10, in the NFL title clash. Graham led the Browns to league championships in all four years of the All-America Football Conference's existence and guided Cleveland to three NFL crowns and six divisional titles during his six years in that league—meaning that Graham played in league championship games in each of his 10 seasons as a pro.

OTTO GRAHAM

He coached the College All-Stars a record 10 times—no one else guided the collegiate squad more than three times—in Chicago's College All-Star Game. Graham was a winner in his first outing in 1958, coaching the All-Stars past the Detroit Lions, 35-19, but won just once after that (over the Green Bay Packers, 20-17, in 1963) and finished with a 2-8 record. Only Graham and Bo McMillin (2-0) won as many as two games as the collegians' coach.

BUD GRANT, DON SHULA

Coaches who have suffered the most defeats in Super Bowl competition—four. Grant's Minnesota Vikings lost in Super Bowls IV, VIII, IX and XI (to Kansas City, Miami, Pittsburgh and Oakland); Shula's Baltimore Colts fell in Super Bowl III (to the New York Jets) and his Miami Dolphins were beaten in Super Bowls VI, XVII and XIX (by Dallas, Washington and San Francisco). Shula, though, has two Super Bowl victories while Grant has been blanked. Next to Grant and Shula on the Super Bowl losers' list is Tom Landry (2-3).

GREEN BAY, CHICAGO BEARS

The most frequent winners in Chicago's College All-Star Game. The Packers compiled a 6-2 record in the summer attraction and the Bears posted a 5-1-1 mark against the All-Stars. The Baltimore Colts went 3-0 and the Cleveland Browns won three of four games, while the New York Giants and the Pittsburgh Steelers both were 2-0.

GREY CUP

The name of the trophy awarded to the Canadian Football League champion and also the commonly used name for the CFL title game itself.

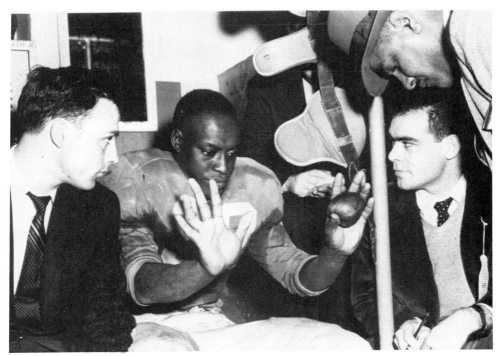

When the 1956 Sugar Bowl ended, members of the press gathered around Pittsburgh's Bobby Grier to discuss the controversial pass interference call that resulted in a 7-0 Georgia Tech victory.

BOBBY GRIER

The first black player in Sugar Bowl history, appearing in the 1956 contest, and he figured in the game's key play. With Georgia Tech positioned at the Pittsburgh 32-yard line in the first quarter, Tech quarterback Wade Mitchell sailed a pass toward Don Ellis. Pittsburgh defender Grier was cited for interference on the play—an official ruled that he shoved Ellis—and the ball was placed on the Panthers' 1. Mitchell then ran for what proved to be the game's only touchdown and he added the extra point. While Pittsburgh dominated the game statistically and Grier had his moments (he made a spectacular reception and got off a 26-yard run from scrimmage), Georgia Tech emerged a 7-0 victor.

LARRY GRIGG

Oklahoma halfback who scored the lone touchdown in the 1954 Orange Bowl as the Sooners upset No. 1-ranked Maryland, 7-0. Grigg also stood out defensively for the Sooners, who benefited from the fact that Terrapins quarterback standout Bernie Faloney played only briefly because of a knee injury.

LOU GROZA

His 16-yard field goal in the final half-minute of the 1950 National Football League championship game earned the Cleveland Browns, playing their first season in the league after dominating the All-America Football Conference, a 30-28 triumph over the Los Angeles Rams and the NFL crown. Groza, whose conversion-kick miss after the Browns' second touchdown had made him a contender for goat horns, delivered his game-winning kick after Browns quarterback Otto Graham had tossed his fourth TD pass of the day earlier in the fourth quarter (Cleveland trailed, 28-20, entering the last period).

HARDIN-SIMMONS, NEW MEXICO STATE

Opponents in the first Sun Bowl game, a postseason contest that predates one of the Big Four bowls—the Cotton Bowl—by one year. On January 1, 1936, in El Paso, Tex., Hardin-Simmons and New Mexico State played to a 14-14 tie.

REGGIE HARRISON

Pittsburgh overcame a 10-7 Dallas lead in Super Bowl X with 14 fourth-quarter points—and Harrison started the final-period thrust by blocking a Mitch Hoopes punt through the end zone for a safety. Roy Gerela then kicked field goals of 36 and 18 yards for the Steelers and Terry Bradshaw hit Lynn Swann on a 64-yard touchdown pass (the conversion kick failed) as Pittsburgh streaked to a 21-10 lead en route to a 21-17 triumph over the Cowboys in Miami.

Super Bowl X was the second straight National Football League championship game in which a safety was scored. In Super Bowl IX in New Orleans, the Steelers' Dwight White tackled Minnesota quarterback Fran Tarkenton in the end zone and Pittsburgh went on to a 16-6 victory over the Vikings.

HARVARD

Eastern power whose appearance in the 1920 Rose Bowl brought national stature to the Pasadena, Calif., game and perhaps ensured its future. The Crimson, Helms Athletic Foundation national champion, edged Oregon, 7-6, in the only postseason game in Harvard football history.

EDDIE HINTON, MEL RENFRO, JOHN MACKEY

Principals in a controversial play in Super Bowl V, which matched Baltimore against Dallas on January 17, 1971, in Miami. In the second quarter, Colts quarterback Johnny Unitas overthrew wide receiver Hinton, who managed to get a hand on the football. The ball then caromed off Dallas defensive back Renfro's fingertips and into the hands of Baltimore tight end Mackey, who went on to complete a 75-yard scoring play. Renfro insisted he had not touched the ball; if the officials had agreed with the Cowboys' defender, the touchdown would have been disallowed because existing rules stated that a pass could not be ruled complete if the ball caromed directly from one offensive player to another. The TD was upheld, however, and it proved crucial as the Colts posted a 16-13 victory over the Cowboys.

Versatile Paul Hornung (left), who scored 19 points while on leave from the Army to help the Green Bay Packers defeat the New York Giants in the 1961 National Football League championship game, was honored a month later as Green Bay Professional Player of the Year by the Washington Touchdown Club.

AL HOISCH

UCLA's 5-foot-7, 150-pounder who returned a kickoff a Rose Bowl-record 103 yards for a touchdown in the Bruins' January 1, 1947, game against Illinois. Hoisch was the smallest player on either Rose Bowl squad.

PAUL HORNUNG

On leave from the Army, Hornung scored 19 points in the 1961 National Football League championship game as the Green Bay Packers overwhelmed the New York Giants, 37-0. Hornung notched the first points of the game on a six-yard run, booted three field goals and kicked four extra points. Bart Starr tossed three touchdown passes for the Packers.

PERCY HOWARD

Dallas receiver who caught a touchdown pass in Super Bowl X against the Pittsburgh Steelers but never made a reception in a regular-season National Football League game. Howard hauled in a 34-yard TD pass from Roger Staubach in the Cowboys' 21-17 loss to Pittsburgh on January 18, 1976.

DIXIE HOWELL, DON HUTSON

On January 1, 1935, the day that the Orange Bowl and the Sugar Bowl made their debuts, Alabama's pass-catch combination of Howell and Hutson kept the collegiate postseason spotlight on the Rose Bowl by turning in dazzling performances in the Crimson Tide's 29-13 victory over Stanford. Howell completed nine of 12 passes for 160 yards, with five of the completions going to Hutson and netting 110 yards. Hutson had six receptions overall for 164 yards and scored on a 54-yard pass from Joe Riley and on a 59-yard toss from Howell. Alabama seized control of the game with a 22-point second quarter, a period in which Howell ran five and 67 yards for touchdowns (Dixie rushed for 107 yards overall and also excelled as a punter and punt returner).

CHUCK HOWLEY

The only member of a losing team, the first non-quarterback and the first defensive player to be named Most Valuable Player in the Super Bowl. Dallas linebacker Howley intercepted two Baltimore passes in Super Bowl V and was a Cowboys standout all day, but the Colts came out on top, 16-13.

AL HUDSON

With the score deadlocked at 6-6 in the 1946 Orange Bowl, Miami's Hudson intercepted a deflected Holy Cross pass on the final play of the game and returned the ball 89 yards for a touchdown as the Hurricanes pulled a 13-6 victory out of a hat.

HULA BOWL

A team of collegiate all-stars played a Hawaiian squad when this postseason game got off the ground in 1947 and that format continued until 1951, when the Hawaiian team was reinforced with players from the National Football League. Two Hula Bowl games were played one week apart each year until a one-game format was adopted in 1953. In 1960, the game became an all-collegiate clash (originally between East and West, then between North and South and then back to East vs. West).

ILLINOIS, UCLA

Participating teams in the 1947 Rose Bowl, the first Pasadena, Calif., classic to be played under the contract that bound Big Nine Conference and Pacific Coast Conference (today's Big Ten and Pacific-10) representatives to compete in the game. While Westerners were hoping to see Army, led by Glenn Davis and Doc Blanchard, in Pasadena on January 1, 1947, the Big Nine-Pacific Coast agreement dashed that idea. Illinois proved a worthy entrant, however, as evidenced by the Fighting Illini's 45-14 trouncing of UCLA. Illinois, representing a league that in June 1921 had adopted a no-bowls stance for member schools, scored 19 second-quarter points against the Bruins and then broke open the game with 20 points in the final period.

CHICK JAGADE

The Cleveland Browns scored a total of only two touchdowns in their 1952 and 1953 National Football League title-game losses to the Detroit Lions— and Jagade made both of them. Jagade ran seven yards for the Browns'

The Bears' Bill Hewitt (no helmet) laterals to Billy Karr on the winning touchdown play in the 1933 NFL championship game. Chicago beat the New York Giants, 23-21.

lone touchdown in their 17-7 setback to Detroit in 1952 and went nine yards for Cleveland's only TD in its 17-16 loss to the Lions in 1953 (Lou Groza booted three field goals for the Browns).

WILBUR JAMERSON

Kentucky player who caught a 23-yard touchdown pass from Babe Parilli and ran one yard for a second TD as Coach Paul (Bear) Bryant's Wildcats upset Oklahoma, 13-7, in the 1951 Sugar Bowl and ended the Sooners' 31-game winning streak.

DERRICK JENSEN, JACK SQUIREK

Los Angeles players whose first-half big plays against Washington in Super Bow XVIII sent the Raiders on their way to a 38-9 rout of the Redskins in a game played January 22, 1984, in Tampa, Fla. Jensen blocked a Jeff Hayes punt 4 minutes, 52 seconds into the game and recovered the ball in the Washington end zone for a touchdown. As the opening half was about to expire, Squirek intercepted Joe Theismann's risky pass at the Redskins' 5-yard line and ran the ball across the goal line as the Raiders mounted a 21-3 halftime lead.

BILLY KARR

Chicago player who took a lateral from helmetless Bill Hewitt and ran for the game-winning touchdown as the Bears defeated the New York Giants,

23-21, on December 17, 1933, in the National Football League's first championship game involving a matchup of divisional champions. The winning play went into the record books as a touchdown pass for Bronko Nagurski, who threw to Hewitt before Hewitt pitched the ball to Karr on a play that covered 32 yards overall. Nagurski passed for two TDs that day, also hitting on an eight-yard scoring strike to Karr.

BARRY KRAUSS

With his team leading top-ranked Penn State by seven points in the final 7 minutes of the 1979 Sugar Bowl, Alabama linebacker Krauss stopped Nittany Lions runner Mike Guman short on a fourth-down play at the Crimson Tide's 1-yard line. The No. 2 Tide continued to protect its lead, and the 14-7 triumph swept Alabama into the top spot in the Associated Press' final poll.

DARYLE LAMONICA

Oakland quarterback who burned Kansas City's defense for five touchdown passes in a 1968 American Football League playoff game that broke a Western Division tie and the man who threw for six TDs in the Raiders' 1969 AFL divisional playoff game against Houston. Oakland downed the Chiefs, 41-6, and overwhelmed the Oilers, 56-7.

HANK LAURICELLA

Tennessee All-America whose net gain of one yard on seven rushes typified the No. 1-ranked Volunteers' frustrations in a 28-13 loss to Maryland in the 1952 Sugar Bowl.

BOBBY LAYNE

He figured in all of Texas' scoring when the Longhorns defeated Missouri, 40-27, in the 1946 Cotton Bowl. Layne passed for two touchdowns, scored four TDs (three on runs and one on a reception) and kicked four extra points against the Tigers.

LIBERTY BOWL, PAUL (BEAR) BRYANT

The Liberty Bowl was the postseason game in which Bryant began and ended his streak of coaching Alabama teams to 24 consecutive bowl games. When Bryant's streak began in 1959, the Liberty Bowl was making its debut. Alabama lost to Penn State in that '59 game, played December 19 in Philadelphia, when the Nittany Lions scored on a fake field-goal play (Galen Hall passed to Roger Kochman for the touchdown) and notched a 7-0 victory. In the December 29, 1982, Liberty Bowl game that capped Bryant's coaching career, the Crimson Tide's Jeremiah Castille intercepted three passes and sparked Alabama to a 21-15 triumph over Tony Eason-led Illinois in Memphis, Tenn. Bryant's Tide won 12 of the 24 games—Alabama appeared in eight Sugar Bowls, five Orange Bowls, four Liberty Bowls, four Cotton Bowls, two Bluebonnet Bowls and one Gator Bowl—and played to two ties. And Alabama, which from 1967 through 1974 went 0-7-1 in postseason play under Bryant, won seven of its last eight bowl games under the Bear.

KEITH LINCOLN

San Diego player who rushed for 206 yards on 13 carries, gained 123 yards on seven receptions and scored two touchdowns as the Chargers walloped the Boston Patriots, 51-10, in the 1963 American Football League championship game.

CHUCK LONG

Iowa quarterback who passed for 461 yards and six touchdowns in the December 26, 1984, Freedom Bowl in Anaheim, Calif., leading the Hawkeyes to a 55-17 crushing of the Texas Longhorns.

SID LUCKMAN

Quarterback who threw five touchdown passes for the Chicago Bears in the 1943 National Football League championship game, leading his club to a 41-21 rout of the Washington Redskins at Wrigley Field. Four of Luckman's TD passes came in the second half as the Bears caught fire after building a 14-7 halftime lead.

ROB LYTLE

With his team leading Oakland, 7-3, in the third quarter of the 1977 American Conference title game, Denver running back Lytle tried to vault into the Raiders' end zone from two yards out but was met by defender Jack Tatum. The ball was jarred loose, and the Raiders' Mike McCoy came up with it. However, the officials ruled "no fumble"—they apparently were screened from the play—and the Broncos, despite Oakland's bitter protests, maintained possession. Jon Keyworth scored from the Raiders' 1-yard line on the next play, and the Broncos went on to a 20-17 triumph.

JOHNNY MAJORS

Tennessee All-America whose fourth-quarter fumble on a punt return set up Baylor at the Volunteers' 15-yard line in the 1957 Sugar Bowl, and the Bears went on to score the game-winning touchdown against the previously unbeaten and untied Vols on a one-yard run by Buddy Humphrey. The high-spirited game, won by Baylor, 13-7, was marred by a third-quarter incident in which the Bears' Larry Hickman kicked the Vols' Bruce Burnham in the face as the Tennessee player was getting off the ground. Tempers were cooled, Burnham recovered after an initial scare and Hickman apologized profusely.

The '57 Sugar Bowl outcome marked the fourth straight time that an undefeated and untied Tennessee team had its record sullied in a bowl game. The 1939 Volunteers, not only unbeaten and untied but unscored upon, lost to Southern California in the Rose Bowl; the '40 Vols fell to Boston College in the Sugar Bowl, and the '51 Tennessee team was beaten by Maryland in the Sugar Bowl.

DEXTER MANLEY

Washington Redskins defensive lineman who was double trouble for the

Dallas Cowboys in the 1982 National Conference championship game. First, Manley knocked Cowboys quarterback starter Danny White out of the game in the final half-minute of the opening half with a thunderous sack; then, with fewer than 7 minutes left in the game and the Redskins ahead by seven points, Manley tipped a Gary Hogeboom pass into the hands of tackle Darryl Grant, and Grant rumbled 10 yards for an insurance touchdown. Washington prevailed, 31-17.

GINO MARCHETTI

Baltimore defensive end who swung the momentum to the Colts' side in the 1959 National Football League championship game when, with his club trailing, 9-7, late in the third quarter, he stopped New York's Alex Webster short of a first down on a fourth-and-inches play at the Baltimore 28-yard line. The Colts then broke loose for 24 fourth-period points and drubbed the Giants, 31-16.

HARVEY MARTIN, RANDY WHITE

The only Co-Most Valuable Players in a Super Bowl, having shared the award as Dallas Cowboy teammates in Super Bowl XII for their defensive play against the Denver Broncos.

ROD MARTIN

Oakland linebacker whose three interceptions against Philadelphia on January 25, 1981, set a Super Bowl record. The Raiders stopped the Eagles, 27-10, in Super Bowl XV.

BO McMILLIN

Of the nine men who coached the College All-Stars more than once in Chicago's College All-Star Game, only one had a perfect record against the pro champions—McMillin. Head coach at Indiana, McMillin directed the College All-Stars to a 28-16 victory over the Washington Redskins in 1938 and coached the Stars to a 16-0 triumph over the Los Angeles Rams in 1946.

LYNNE McNUTT

Although trailing Georgia Tech, 20-14, in the final 2 minutes of the 1948 Orange Bowl, Kansas was on the edge of victory as it lined up for a play at the Ramblin' Wreck's 1-yard line—but Jayhawks quarterback McNutt proceeded to fumble. Georgia Tech's Rollo Phillips recovered the ball, preserving his team's six-point edge.

MERCY BOWL

The November 23, 1961, game that was played at the Los Angeles Memorial Coliseum to aid victims of the 1960 air crash that killed 16 members of the Cal Poly-San Luis Obispo football team, the team manager and five other persons and injured more than 20 passengers. Proceeds from the game—between Fresno State and Bowling Green (Fresno State won, 36-6)—were

Members of the victorious Michigan team participated in the Pasadena floral parade on January 1, 1902, before the first Rose Bowl game. The vital information, such as Michigan 49, Stanford 0, was added to the picture later by an industrious photographer.

used for funeral expenses and to help with hospital and related medical-care costs. The airplane carrying the Cal Poly team crashed at Toledo, Ohio, on October 29, 1960, after the Mustangs had played at Bowling Green that afternoon.

MIAMI DOLPHINS

The only team to be held without a touchdown in a Super Bowl game. All the Dolphins could muster against Dallas in Super Bowl VI was a 31-yard field goal by Garo Yepremian, with the Cowboys posting a 24-3 triumph.

MIAMI DOLPHINS

The only team to play in three consecutive Super Bowls. After losing to Dallas in Super Bowl VI, the Dolphins defeated Washington and Minnesota in Super Bowls VII and VIII.

MICHIGAN, STANFORD

Opponents in the first Rose Bowl game, played January 1, 1902, at Tournament Park in Pasadena, Calif. While freshman Willie Heston was the explo-

Horses, carriages and derby hats were the order of the day at the first Rose

sive player for Coach Fielding Yost's "point-a-minute" Wolverines, Michigan senior Neil Snow was the Player of the Game in the '02 Rose Bowl. Snow ran for five touchdowns as Michigan overwhelmed Stanford, 49-0. Far Western football obviously was no match for the Midwestern style of play, and West Coast teams were reluctant to renew the postseason game. Accordingly, it wasn't until 1916 that the second Rose Bowl game was played.

MICHIGAN

Forty-six years after embarrassing Stanford, 49-0, in the first Rose Bowl game, the Wolverines made their second appearance in the classic on January 1, 1948, and, led by Bob Chappuis' passing and running and a crunching defense, Michigan overwhelmed Southern California. The score was . . . 49-0.

MICHIGAN STATE, ARKANSAS, NEBRASKA

Teams that were unbeaten and ranked 1-2-3 in the Associated Press' last regular-season poll of 1965, the year in which AP first delayed its final rankings until after the bowl games had been completed. Michigan State had a Rose Bowl date against UCLA, Arkansas was to play Louisiana State in the Cotton Bowl and Nebraska was matched against Alabama in the second nighttime Orange Bowl. AP's post-bowls balloting experiment—in 1966, AP returned to its format of releasing its final poll at the end of the regular season—proved eventful as top-rated Michigan State fell to UCLA, 14-12; second-ranked Arkansas was upset by LSU, 14-7, and No. 3 Nebraska dropped a 39-28 decision to Alabama. The Crimson Tide, ranked No. 4 entering postseason play, leapfrogged the Spartans, Razorbacks and Cornhuskers and was rated No. 1 in AP's final poll, which was released on January 3, 1966. Michigan State was United Press International's national champion for 1965, with UPI's final poll having been issued a month earlier.

BILL MILLER

He scored both of Oakland's touchdowns in the Raiders' 33-14 loss to Green

Bowl game, played January 1, 1902, at Tournament Park in Pasadena, Calif.

Bay in Super Bowl II—and each TD came on a 23-yard pass from Daryle Lamonica. Miller, who played collegiately at Miami (Florida), had his big day, fittingly, in a Super Bowl played on January 14, 1968, at Miami's Orange Bowl. Overall, Miller had five receptions against the Packers for 84 yards.

WAYNE MILLNER

The intended receiver for Washington on a first-quarter pass play that proved critical in the Redskins' 1945 National Football League title game against the Cleveland Rams. With the Redskins positioned near their own goal line in a 0-0 game, quarterback Sammy Baugh retreated into the end zone and took aim on Millner. However, the wind at Cleveland Stadium slammed Baugh's pass into the goal post, giving the Rams a safety (an existing rule awarded a safety when a pass from behind the goal line hit the goal posts or the crossbar and struck the ground in the end zone). The Rams, playing their final NFL game in Cleveland before relocating in Los Angeles, parlayed the two points into a 15-14 triumph as rookie quarterback Bob Waterfield threw two touchdown passes and made one of two conversion kicks.

MINNESOTA

The first team to be honored with a wire-service national championship, having finished atop the Associated Press' final rankings of 1936. The Gophers also headed the first-ever poll in '36, released by AP on October 19, before losing the top spot to Northwestern two weeks later following a setback to the Wildcats. At season's end, the Gophers, Louisiana State and Pittsburgh were ranked 1-2-3 (while Northwestern, a loser to Notre Dame, had dropped to seventh place).

MISSOURI

From the 1962 season through the 1979 campaign, the Missouri Tigers went to eight bowl games—and they turned out to be eight *different* bowls. Mis-

Mr. Typical Fan (right), toting the goal post that was struck by Sammy Baugh's wind-swept pass in the Cleveland Rams' 1945 NFL championship game victory over Washington, was the honored guest at the Washington Touchdown Club's dinner after the season. Northwestern's Art Murakowski (below) fumbles at the California goal line in the 1949 Rose Bowl. Northwestern was given the controversial touchdown and went on to win, 20-14.

souri competed in the Bluebonnet Bowl after the '62 regular season, then participated in these bowls after the seasons indicated: Sugar (1965), Gator (1968), Orange (1969), Fiesta (1972), Sun (1973), Liberty (1978) and Hall of Fame (1979).

MISSOURI

Unable to complete a pass (zero for six with two interceptions) in the December 28, 1968, Gator Bowl, the Tigers nevertheless thrashed Alabama, 35-10, thanks to a rushing attack that ground out 402 yards.

JOE MONTANA

San Francisco 49ers quarterback who threw for a Super Bowl-record 331 yards against the Miami Dolphins on January 20, 1985. Montana's passing helped the 49ers to a 38-16 victory in Super Bowl XIX.

BRICK MULLER

California end whose 53-yards-in-the-air touchdown pass to Brodie Stephens on a feigned-injury play highlighted the Golden Bears' 28-0 mauling of Ohio State in the 1921 Rose Bowl. After a supposedly injured Cal player sprung to his feet and centered the ball into play (the Buckeyes' defense was caught off guard), Muller got the ball on a lateral and—stunning the opposition and the crowd alike with the strength of his arm—let fly with his pass to Stephens. The game capped a perfect season for the first of Coach Andy Smith's five Wonder Teams, teams that compiled a 48-game unbeaten record (44-0-4) from 1920 through 1924. (The 1925 Golden Bears extended Cal's undefeated streak to 50 games before losing.)

ART MURAKOWSKI, JAY BERWANGER

Northwestern runner who lost the ball at California's goal line in the 1949 Rose Bowl and the official who awarded him a touchdown on the controversial play. Northwestern, which went on to win, 20-14, on Ed Tunnicliff's late-game 43-yard touchdown run, was locked in a 7-7 tie in the second quarter when Murakowski took the ball at the Golden Bears' 2-yard line and headed goalward. Approaching, on or just inside the goal line—it depended upon your point of view—Murakowski fumbled the ball and a California player pounced on it in the end zone. But field judge Berwanger (of Heisman Trophy-winning fame) ruled that Murakowski had gotten the ball across the plane of the goal line and retained possession long enough for a touchdown. While Cal fans begged to differ, the Wildcats had their second TD of the day.

JOE NAMATH

While his top-ranked Alabama team was upset by Texas in the first nighttime Orange Bowl, played January 1, 1965, Namath turned in a stirring performance against the Longhorns. Not in the starting lineup because of an ailing knee, Namath was thrust into the game in the second quarter when the Crimson Tide fell behind, 14-0. Before the evening had ended,

Namath had thrown for 255 yards and two touchdowns and driven the Crimson Tide within inches of taking the lead in the fourth period. With Alabama behind, 21-17, and facing a fourth-and-one play from the Texas 1-yard line, Namath—gimpy knee and all—tried to dent the Longhorns' defense with a quarterback sneak. He was repulsed, barely, and Texas held on for the four-point victory.

NEBRASKA

Winner of United Press International's national title only once, in 1971. Preceding the Cornhuskers as one-time-only UPI national champions were Tennessee (1951), Maryland (1953), UCLA (1954), Louisiana State (1958), Syracuse (1959) and Minnesota (1960), while Pittsburgh (1976), Georgia (1980), Clemson (1981), Penn State (1982), Miami of Florida (1983) and Brigham Young (1984) have followed the Huskers as once-only UPI titlists.

NEBRASKA, OKLAHOMA, COLORADO

Big Eight Conference teams that ranked 1-2-3 in the Associated Press' final poll of the 1971 season, which was taken after the January 1, 1972, bowl games. Entering postseason play, AP listed Nebraska first, Oklahoma third and Colorado seventh (the same positions that United Press International had given those teams in its final poll of the season, announced in early December). The Cornhuskers, sparked by Johnny Rodgers' 77-yard punt return for a touchdown, rolled to a 28-0 halftime lead over No. 2 Alabama and walloped the Crimson Tide, 38-6, in the Orange Bowl; Oklahoma routed No. 5 Auburn, 40-22, in the Sugar Bowl, and Colorado downed Houston, 29-17, in the Astro-Bluebonnet Bowl (played New Year's Eve). Further helping to clear the way for Colorado's ascent in the final AP poll were No. 4 Michigan's 13-12 loss to Stanford in the Rose Bowl and No. 6 Georgia's shaky performance in a 7-3 triumph over North Carolina in the December 31 Gator Bowl. Nebraska finished with a perfect season, Oklahoma lost only once (to the Cornhuskers, 35-31, in their titanic Thanksgiving Day struggle) and Colorado dropped two games (to Nebraska and Oklahoma).

NEWCOMERS

From the 1980 collegiate football season through the 1984 campaign, the wire services' selections as the nation's top teams were schools that had never won a national championship previously. The Associated Press and United Press International, agreeing on the No. 1 team each season in the final polls, honored Georgia in 1980, Clemson in 1981, Penn State in 1982, Miami (Florida) in 1983 and Brigham Young in 1984.

ROBERT NEWHOUSE, LAWRENCE McCUTCHEON

Running backs who attempted one pass in Super Bowl competition—and each threw for a touchdown. Dallas' Newhouse fired a 29-yard scoring pass to Golden Richards in Super Bowl XII as the Cowboys downed Denver, 27-10, and McCutcheon completed a 24-yard TD pass to Ron Smith as the Los Angeles Rams slipped ahead of Pittsburgh in the third quarter of Super Bowl XIV before losing to the Steelers, 31-19.

NEW ORLEANS, MIAMI

Through Super Bowl XIX, the cities that have played host to the most Super Bowls—five. Super Bowls IV, VI and IX were played at Tulane Stadium in New Orleans and that city's Louisiana Superdome was the site of Super Bowls XII and XV. Super Bowls II, III, V, X and XIII were contested at Miami's Orange Bowl.

1951

The last year in which an Ivy League team finished in the Top 10 of the wire services' final polls, with Princeton ranking sixth that season in both the Associated Press and United Press International listings.

CHUCK NOLL

The winningest coach in Super Bowl history with four victories. Noll, unbeaten as a Super Bowl coach, directed the Pittsburgh Steelers to triumphs over the Minnesota Vikings (January 12, 1975), the Dallas Cowboys (January 18, 1976, and January 21, 1979) and the Los Angeles Rams (January 20, 1980). Second behind Noll in the Super Bowl victory column are Bill Walsh (2-0), Tom Flores (2-0), Vince Lombardi (2-0), Tom Landry (2-3) and Don Shula (2-4).

NOTRE DAME

Ranked fifth in both wire-service polls entering the major bowl games of January 2, 1978, the Fighting Irish intercepted three Texas passes and recovered three Longhorn fumbles on the way to a 38-10 dismantling of the No. 1-ranked Steers in the Cotton Bowl. The triumph boosted Notre Dame to the top of both news services' final ratings.

NOTRE DAME, ALABAMA, OKLAHOMA

Schools that have combined to win 17 of the Associated Press' 49 national championships, as reflected by AP's final polls from 1936 through 1984. Notre Dame has won the most AP national titles, seven, reigning in 1943, 1946, 1947, 1949, 1966, 1973 and 1977. Alabama and Oklahoma have five No. 1 AP rankings, with the Crimson Tide finishing on top in 1961, 1964, 1965, 1978 and 1979 and the Sooners rating No. 1 in 1950, 1955, 1956, 1974 and 1975.

Other multi-winners of AP national championships are Minnesota (four), Southern California (three), Ohio State (three), Army (two), Nebraska (two), Pittsburgh (two) and Texas (two). Minnesota was honored in 1936, 1940, 1941 and 1960; Southern Cal in 1962, 1967 and 1972; Ohio State in 1942, 1954 and 1968; Army in 1944 and 1945; Nebraska in 1970 and 1971; Pittsburgh in 1937 and 1976, and Texas in 1963 and 1969.

OAKLAND RAIDERS

The only wild-card team to have won a Super Bowl. The 1980 Raiders finished second to San Diego in the American Conference's Western Division race (both teams had 11-5 records, with the Chargers prevailing because of a better net-points record in division games), but Oakland won four straight postseason games to rule as National Football League champions. First, the Raiders defeated the Houston Oilers, 27-7, in the AFC wild-card playoff game in Oakland. Then the Raiders beat the Browns, 14-12, in a divisional playoff game in Cleveland and knocked off the Chargers, 34-27, in San Diego in the AFC title game. Oakland subsequently stopped Philadelphia, 27-10, in Super Bowl XV, played January 25, 1981, in New Orleans.

The 1975 Dallas Cowboys were the first wild-card team to reach the Super Bowl. Having finished one game behind St. Louis in the National Conference's Eastern Division with a 10-4 record, the Cowboys jolted the Minnesota Vikings, 17-14, in an NFC divisional playoff game in Bloomington, Minn., and then drubbed the Rams, 37-7, in the NFC title game in Los Angeles. In Super Bowl X, contested January 18, 1976, in Miami, the Cowboys fell to Pittsburgh, 21-17.

The Kansas City Chiefs, 11-3, finished second to Oakland, 12-1-1, in the Western Division of the American Football League in 1969, yet the Chiefs went on to win that season's Super Bowl. However, the Chiefs' success predated by one year the advent of the official "wild card" in pro football's playoffs. The AFL, in its final season, tried to stimulate postseason interest by adding a second tier to its playoff structure. The '69 plan called for first-round games matching the Eastern Division champion against the Western runner-up and the West titlist against the East's No. 2 team, with the winners to play for the AFL crown. The Chiefs, seemingly worthy of a wild-card designation regardless of playoff format or terminology, eliminated the defending Super Bowl-champion New York Jets, 13-6, in New York and then shut down the Raiders, 17-7, in Oakland. In Super Bowl IV in New Orleans on January 11, 1970, Kansas City upended NFL champion Minnesota, 23-7.

JIM O'BRIEN

Placekicker whose 32-yard field goal with 5 seconds remaining in Super Bowl V gave the Baltimore Colts a 16-13 victory over the Dallas Cowboys.

OHIO STATE

Stung by O.J. Simpson's 80-yard touchdown run and a 10-0 deficit, the top-ranked Buckeyes roared back and downed No. 2-rated Southern California, 27-16, in the 1969 Rose Bowl. Quarterback Rex Kern sparked the Buckeyes, tossing two touchdown passes.

OHIO STATE

Trailing 21-14 in the third quarter of the 1974 Rose Bowl, Ohio State blitzed Southern California, 28-0, the rest of the way and pounded the Trojans, 42-21. Sophomores Cornelius Greene and Archie Griffin and freshman Pete Johnson paced the Buckeyes' offense. Quarterback Greene guided the Ohio State attack masterfully, ran effectively and completed six of eight passes overall for 129 yards. Tailback Griffin finished with 149 yards rushing and scored the Buckeyes' final TD on a 47-yard scamper in the fourth quarter, while Johnson—used sparingly during the 1973 regular season—bulled his way to three touchdowns. Defensive back Neal Colzie's 56-yard punt return set up what proved to be Ohio State's winning TD, a one-yard run by Greene in the third period.

OKLAHOMA

The only school to win national championships in consecutive years in both the Associated Press and United Press International polls, scoring its sweep in 1955-1956.

While no team has ever won three straight No. 1 designations in either final wire-service poll, six schools have won consecutive AP national titles—and Alabama and Oklahoma have accomplished the feat twice. Alabama was AP's No. 1 team in 1964-1965 and 1978-1979, and Oklahoma ruled in 1974-1975, in addition to 1955-1956. Other teams to win two straight AP national championships have been Minnesota (1940-1941), Army (1944-1945), Notre Dame (1946-1947) and Nebraska (1970-1971).

Two schools, Oklahoma (1955-1956) and Texas (1969-1970), have captured consecutive UPI crowns.

ORANGE BOWL

Stadium that has been the site of the most Super Bowls, five. Super Bowls II, III, V, X and XIII were played at the Miami facility.

CHARLIE O'ROURKE

His 24-yard touchdown run off a fake pass snapped a 13-13 tie in the final 2 minutes of the 1941 Sugar Bowl and lifted Coach Frank Leahy's Boston College Eagles to a 19-13 victory over Tennessee. The game was the last at Boston College for Leahy, who was named coach at his alma mater, Notre Dame.

The '41 Sugar Bowl loss meant that Coach Robert Neyland's Volunteers had been outscored, 33-30, overall in bowl games that followed the 1938, 1939 and 1940 seasons—years in which the Vols had a cumulative 30-0 regular-season record and outscored their opponents, 807-42, while compiling that perfect mark. Tennessee won a penalty-filled, no-holds-barred 17-0 decision over Oklahoma in the 1939 Orange Bowl before falling to Southern California, 14-0, in the '40 Rose Bowl and then losing to Boston College in New Orleans.

BUDDY PARKER

The man who quit as the Detroit Lions' coach during training camp in 1957, saying he was pessimistic about his team's chances. About 4½ months later, the George Wilson-coached Lions captured the National Football League championship by smashing the Cleveland Browns, 59-14, as Tobin Rote fired four touchdown passes. (The outcome was a 91-point turnaround from the Cleveland-Detroit championship game of three years earlier, which the Browns won, 56-10.) Detroit earned its way into the '57 title game by overcoming a 27-7 deficit in its Western Conference playoff game against San Francisco and beating the 49ers, 31-27.

PRESTON PEARSON

The only man to play for three different teams in the Super Bowl. Pearson played for Baltimore in Super Bowl III, Pittsburgh in Super Bowl IX and Dallas in Super Bowls X, XII and XIII.

Pearson and six other players share the record for playing in the most Super Bowls, five. Larry Cole, Cliff Harris, D.D. Lewis, Charlie Waters and Rayfield Wright all played for Dallas in Super Bowls V, VI, X, XII and XIII, and Marv Fleming performed for Green Bay in Super Bowls I and II and for Miami in Super Bowls VI, VII and VIII.

VERNON PERRY

Houston defensive back who intercepted four passes against San Diego in a 1979 American Conference divisional playoff game and also blocked a Chargers field-goal attempt as the Oilers scored a 17-14 upset. Perry returned the blocked kick 57 yards, setting up Houston's first score (Toni Fritsch's 26-yard field goal).

PHILADELPHIA STARS

Down by a 38-17 score in the fourth quarter of their 1983 United States Football League semifinal playoff game against the Chicago Blitz, the Stars roared back on Chuck Fusina's three touchdown passes and netted a 38-38 tie at the end of regulation play. Seven minutes into overtime, Kelvin Bryant gave Philadelphia a 44-38 triumph by diving one yard for a touchdown.

PITTSBURGH, SOUTHERN CALIFORNIA

Coach Jock Sutherland's Pittsburgh Panthers were unbeaten entering their 1930 and 1933 Rose Bowl games against Southern California, but the Trojans blasted the Easterners by 47-14 and 35-0 scores. Pitt had a 9-0 record going into the '30 Rose Bowl and an 8-0-2 mark before the '33 classic in Pasadena, Calif. Coach Howard Jones' USC teams took 9-2 and 9-0 records into the games.

Sutherland's 1927 Pittsburgh team also was unbeaten (8-0-1) heading into the Rose Bowl, but the Panthers were handed a 7-6 loss by Stanford in the January 2, 1928, game. Sutherland and the Panthers finally scored a breakthrough in the 1937 Rose Bowl. While the '36 Panthers had suffered a regular-season loss and played to one tie, they swept past Washington, 21-0, in Pasadena.

PITTSBURGH STEELERS

The only team to have won more than two Super Bowls—and the Steelers have won four. Pittsburgh defeated the Minnesota Vikings, 16-6, in Super Bowl IX and then stopped Dallas in Super Bowls X and XIII, beating the Cowboys by scores of 21-17 and 35-31. Victory No. 4 came in Super Bowl XIV, with the Steelers downing the Los Angeles Rams, 31-19.

PLAYOFF BOWL

National Football League postseason game that matched the league's conference runners-up from 1960 through 1966. When the league went to four divisions in 1967, the Playoff Bowl became a battle of the two losers of the conference championship games (and retained that format following the 1968 and 1969 seasons). Detroit won the first Playoff Bowl, beating the Cleveland Browns, 17-16, on January 7, 1961, in Miami. The Lions, in fact, won the first three "runner-up" games. In the 10th and last Playoff Bowl, contested on January 3, 1970, at the Orange Bowl, the Los Angeles Rams walloped the Dallas Cowboys, 31-0.

POLO GROUNDS

New York stadium that was the site of the 1936 National Football League championship game between two non-New York teams—the Boston Redskins and the Green Bay Packers. The Redskins were in line for the home-field advantage, but Owner George Preston Marshall—upset over the lack of support from Boston fans—switched the game to the Polo Grounds. "They don't deserve to see this championship game," Marshall said of the Bostonians. "They don't deserve this team, either." Green Bay won, 21-6, over the Redskins, who moved to Washington in 1937.

PRO BOWL

The National Football League's all-star game, which made its debut on January 15, 1939, at Wrigley Field in Los Angeles when the NFL champion New York Giants played an all-star squad from the rest of the league (with independent Los Angeles professional teams also represented). The champions-vs.-Pro All-Stars format was used in the first five Pro Bowls (the 1938 season through the 1942 season). The Pro Bowl was not played following the next seven seasons, but the game was revived on January 14, 1951, at the Los Angeles Memorial Coliseum with a battle of all-star teams representing each NFL conference. The Coliseum played host to the contest for 22 consecutive seasons before the NFL began to move the game from city to city (Irving, Tex., Kansas City, Miami, New Orleans, Seattle, Tampa and back to Los Angeles). Following the 1979 season, the Pro Bowl was contested in Honolulu, which has been the game's site ever since.

BOB REYNOLDS, VOW BOYS

Stanford standout Reynolds made Rose Bowl history by playing all 60 minutes of three consecutive Pasadena, Calif., classics, the 1934, 1935 and 1936 games. Reynolds was a member of the Vow Boys, football players who as Stanford freshmen in 1932 vowed never to lose a varsity game against conference rival and national power Southern California. The Vow Boys were true to their word against Southern Cal (beating the Trojans, 13-7, 16-0 and 3-0), but success in the Rose Bowl was another thing. Despite Reynolds' yeoman work, Stanford lost the '34 and '35 Rose Bowls to Columbia and Alabama before defeating Southern Methodist in the '36 game.

RICE STADIUM

The first of four one-time-only Super Bowl sites, with the Houston facility having staged Super Bowl VIII. Additionally, the National Football League's championship game has been played once at the Pontiac Silverdome (Super Bowl XVI) in Pontiac, Mich., Tampa Stadium (XVIII) in Tampa and Stanford Stadium (XIX) in Stanford, Calif.

JACKIE ROBINSON

Standout player from UCLA (and future baseball great) who caught a 46-yard touchdown pass from Boston College's Charlie O'Rourke in the 1941 College All-Star Game in Chicago. Robinson's fourth-quarter TD catch and the ensuing extra point brought the collegians within three points of the Chicago Bears, but the Bears countered with a three-touchdown onslaught and scored a 37-13 victory.

JOHNNY RODGERS

Heisman Trophy winner who burned the Notre Dame defense in the 1973 Orange Bowl, scoring four touchdowns and passing for a fifth TD as Nebraska thumped the Fighting Irish, 40-6. Switched to I-back from his normal wingback position for the game, Rodgers had scoring runs covering eight, four and five yards and caught a 50-yard TD pass from David Humm. Rodgers also threw a 52-yard scoring pass to Frosty Anderson as Nebraska won its third straight Orange Bowl game.

SANTA CLARA

Winner of two straight Sugar Bowl games. The Broncos upended Louisiana State, 21-14, in 1937 and the Californians then beat LSU's Bayou Tigers, 6-0, in the 1938 game. The '38 setback marked LSU's third straight loss in the Sugar Bowl (on January 1, 1936, Sammy Baugh and Texas Christian slipped past the Tigers, 3-2).

ALEX SANTILLI

Fordham player whose first-period block of a Missouri punt resulted in a safety and produced all the points in a rain-swept 1942 Sugar Bowl as the Rams sloshed past the Tigers, 2-0.

BOB SCHLOREDT

Quarterback who led the Washington Huskies to 1960 and 1961 Rose Bowl victories over Wisconsin and Minnesota. Schloredt, virtually blind in one eye, shared Player of the Game honors with Huskies halfback-kicker George Fleming in the '60 game as Washington routed Wisconsin, 44-8, then won the outstanding-player honor outright in '61 when the Huskies upended No. 1-ranked Minnesota, 17-7. Until the Huskies' victories over the Badgers and Gophers, Big Ten Conference representatives had won 12 of 13 games against their Pacific Coast adversaries since the series contract had been signed. Washington's success, though, signaled the beginning of a shift in

Washington halfback George Fleming (25) and quarterback Bob Schloredt (15) were the centers of attention after leading the Huskies to a 44-8 victory over Wisconsin in the 1960 Rose Bowl.

power. Western representatives managed a 5-5 split in the Rose Bowls of the 1960s, and from January 1, 1970, through New Year's Day, 1985, Western teams won 14 of the 16 Pasadena, Calif., classics (with Southern California's victory over Ohio State on January 1, 1985, giving the Pacific Coast the series lead for the first time at 20-19).

GERHARD SCHWEDES, ERNIE DAVIS

Syracuse backfield standouts who got the 1959 national champion Orangemen rolling in their January 1, 1960, Cotton Bowl game against Texas. In the opening minute of play, Schwedes took a pitchout from quarterback Dave Sarette at the Syracuse 15-yard line and hit Davis with a pass near midfield. Davis, flashing his great speed, sprinted to the end zone on an 85-yard play and the Orangemen were never headed on the way to a 23-14 victory. The game was played amid an air of tenseness (some of which no doubt had racial overtones), with bickering, shoving and raised fists in evidence. And both teams were highly critical of the officiating.

JAKE SCOTT

The only defensive back to have been named the Most Valuable Player in a Super Bowl game. Miami's Scott won the honor in Super Bowl VII, a game in which he intercepted two Washington passes (picking off one throw in the

195

end zone and returning it 55 yards). The Dolphins defeated the Redskins, 14-7.

SENIOR BOWL

Collegiate seniors are introduced to play-for-pay football in this postseason game, which made its debut on January 7, 1950, in Jacksonville, Fla. In 1951, the clash of North and South all-star teams was moved to Mobile, Ala., which became the game's permanent site.

SEVEN

The number of times that United Press International and the Associated Press have differed on the nation's No. 1 team in their final rankings (since UPI joined AP in the polling business in 1950). In 1954, UPI chose UCLA and AP went for Ohio State; in 1957, UPI honored Ohio State and AP picked Auburn; in 1965, UPI selected Michigan State and AP, in an experimental post-bowls vote, tabbed Alabama; in 1970, UPI named Texas and AP, having now adopted a post-bowls final poll, picked Nebraska; in 1973, UPI chose Alabama and AP opted for Notre Dame; in 1974, UPI went to post-bowls balloting and selected Southern California and AP named Oklahoma (UPI refused to rank the unbeaten Sooners because of their NCAA-probation status), and in 1978, UPI favored Southern Cal and AP settled on Alabama.

LAWRENCE T. (BUCK) SHAW

The only man to own a coaching victory over a Vince Lombardi-directed team in either a National Football League championship game or a Super Bowl. Shaw's Philadelphia Eagles defeated Lombardi's Green Bay Packers in the 1960 NFL title game. Lombardi proceeded to win seven consecutive championship games, beginning with Green Bay's 1961 and 1962 conquests of Coach Allie Sherman's New York Giants in NFL title play. Lombardi's Packers then beat Blanton Collier's Cleveland Browns in the 1965 NFL championship contest and edged past Tom Landry's Dallas Cowboys in the 1966 and 1967 NFL title matches. And Lombardi's '66 and '67 teams notched Super Bowl crowns against Hank Stram's Kansas City Chiefs and John Rauch's Oakland Raiders.

DON SHULA

The only man to have coached two different franchises in the Super Bowl. Shula has taken the Baltimore Colts (once) and the Miami Dolphins (five times) to the National Football League's showcase game. Shula's Colts lost to the New York Jets in Super Bowl III, while his Dolphins defeated Washington and Minnesota in Super Bowls VII and VIII and lost to Dallas, Washington and San Francisco in Super Bowls VI, XVII and XIX.

Shula has coached in a record six Super Bowls—and he never has matched wits with the same coach twice. Shula's coaching adversaries in the Super Bowl have been Weeb Ewbank (Super Bowl III), Tom Landry (VI), George Allen (VII), Bud Grant (VIII), Joe Gibbs (XVII) and Bill Walsh (XIX).

FRANK SINKWICH

His three touchdown passes and one scoring run powered Georgia to a 40-26 triumph over Texas Christian in the 1942 Orange Bowl.

16-13, 38-9

Scores that have produced the closest game and the biggest rout in Super Bowl history. Baltimore slipped past Dallas by three points in Super Bowl V, and the Los Angeles Raiders were 29 points better than Washington in Super Bowl XVIII.

STEVE SLOAN, RAY PERKINS

Knowing that No. 1-ranked Michigan State and No. 2-rated Arkansas had lost earlier in the day, No. 4 Alabama took the field on the night of January 1, 1966, hoping that a victory over No. 3 Nebraska in the Orange Bowl would vault the Crimson Tide to the top of the final Associated Press poll (which, for the first time, was to be released after postseason play). And thanks in large part to the play of Sloan and Perkins, the Tide's objective was realized. Sloan passed for 296 yards and two touchdowns and Perkins, recipient of both of Sloan's scoring passes, made nine receptions overall as Alabama stung Nebraska, 39-28, and slipped into AP's No. 1 spot. Bob Churchich tossed three TD passes for the Cornhuskers.

JACKIE SMITH

After catching 480 passes in 15 seasons (1963-1977) with the St. Louis Cardinals, Smith came out of a short-lived retirement and joined the Dallas Cowboys in 1978—and he realized a career objective by playing in the Super Bowl that followed the '78 season. The dream-come-true had nightmarish overtones for Smith, though, when he dropped a third-quarter pass while wide open in the end zone against the Pittsburgh Steelers in Super Bowl XIII. Roger Staubach's pass to Smith came on a third-and-three play from the Steelers' 10-yard line, with Pittsburgh ahead, 21-14. Rafael Septien then kicked a 27-yard field goal for the Cowboys, who ended up 35-31 losers in a game that proved to be Smith's last as a pro.

SOONER SCHOONER

Oklahoma spirit group's horse-drawn covered wagon that drew a 15-yard penalty in the fourth quarter of the 1985 Orange Bowl for charging onto the field after the Sooners' Tim Lashar apparently had broken a 14-14 tie with Washington by booting a 22-yard field goal. Lashar's field goal was disallowed, however, because of an illegal-procedure penalty (five yards) against the Sooners—and Oklahoma was backed up 20 yards overall when an unsportsmanlike-conduct flag was dropped against the mini-wagon for its illegal presence on the field. When Lashar tried the kick from 42 yards out, the Huskies blocked the attempt. No. 2 Oklahoma, hoping to win handily and perhaps supplant top-ranked Brigham Young in the final polls, lost, 28-17, to Washington.

Veteran Jackie Smith came out of retirement in 1978 to join the Dallas Cowboys and soon realized his dream of playing in a Super Bowl. That dream turned to a nightmare, however, when Smith dropped a sure touchdown pass and suffered alone (right) in the end zone. The Oklahoma Sooners drew a key penalty (below) in their 1985 Orange Bowl loss to Washington when the Sooner Schooner charged onto the field after an apparent Oklahoma score.

SOUTHERN CALIFORNIA

Winner of the first Rose Bowl game played in the concrete stadium that has been the site of the New Year's Day attraction—earlier referred to as the Tournament of Roses game—since 1923. Southern Cal, making the first of a record 24 Rose Bowl appearances (through the 1985 game), defeated Penn State, 14-3, on January 1, 1923—a day on which the traffic-bound Nittany Lions arrived at the Pasadena, Calif., stadium 45 minutes after the scheduled kickoff time. The first eight Rose Bowl games (1902, 1916-1922) were played at Pasadena's Tournament Park.

SOUTHERN CALIFORNIA

After its first eight appearances in the Rose Bowl, Southern Cal boasted an 8-0 record in the Pasadena, Calif., classic. The Trojans' Rose Bowl winning streak came to an end on January 1, 1946, however, when the Harry Gilmer-led Alabama Crimson Tide walloped USC, 34-14.

SOUTHERN CALIFORNIA

The Trojans' 20-17 victory over Ohio State in the 1985 Rose Bowl gave Southern Cal a record 21 bowl victories overall and an unequalled 18 triumphs in Big Four (Rose, Orange, Sugar and Cotton) bowl games. USC leads Alabama by one victory in each category. All 18 of the Trojans' Big Four triumphs have come in the Rose Bowl (USC has never appeared in the Cotton, Sugar or Orange), and Southern Cal's other bowl victories have been scored in the Los Angeles Christmas Festival (December 25, 1924), the Liberty Bowl (December 22, 1975) and the Bluebonnet Bowl (December 31, 1977).

SOUTHERN CALIFORNIA

Winner of more United Press International national championships, five, than any other school since UPI began its football polls in 1950. Southern Cal was voted No. 1 in UPI's final rankings in 1962, 1967, 1972, 1974 and 1978.

UPI has named both Alabama and Oklahoma its national titlist four times, selecting the Crimson Tide in 1961, 1964, 1973 and 1979 and choosing the Sooners in 1950, 1955, 1956 and 1975. Texas has been a three-time winner (1963, 1969 and 1970), while Michigan State (1952 and 1965), Notre Dame (1966 and 1977) and Ohio State (1957 and 1968) have won UPI's top honor twice.

STEVE SPURRIER

With Florida trailing Missouri, 20-0, entering the fourth period of the 1966 Sugar Bowl, Spurrier led the Gators to three touchdowns—he passed for two scores and ran for another—but the furious rally proved in vain as the Gators came up empty on three two-point conversion attempts. Spurrier finished with 352 yards passing in the 20-18 setback.

KEN STABLER, RAY PERKINS

Stabler passed for 218 yards and Perkins totaled 178 yards on receptions as

Alabama's unbeaten and untied 1966 team, smarting from its third-place standing in both wire services' final polls (released four weeks earlier), smashed Big Eight Conference champion Nebraska, 34-7, in the 1967 Sugar Bowl. Notre Dame and Michigan State, which did not play in bowl games after the '66 season and finished with 9-0-1 records after playing to their momentous tie in mid-November, were 1-2 in the rankings.

KEN STABLER

His one-yard touchdown run in the final 10 seconds of the game lifted the Oakland Raiders to a 24-21 victory over the New England Patriots in a 1976 American Conference divisional playoff clash. The Raiders were helped goalward by a disputed roughing-the-passer call against New England's Ray Hamilton, who insisted he had tipped the ball and that his momentum had resulted in unintentional contact with Stabler. If the penalty had not been assessed, Oakland would have faced a fourth-and-17 situation; as it was, the Raiders got a first down at the Patriots' 13-yard line.

STANFORD

With Coach Clark Shaughnessy's innovative and deceptive T-formation dazzling opponents and spectators alike and the attack buoyed by the presence of such backfield operatives as Frankie Albert, Norm Standlee, Hugh Gallarneau and Pete Kmetovic, Stanford downed Nebraska, 21-13, in the 1941 Rose Bowl.

BART STARR, TERRY BRADSHAW, JOE MONTANA

The only two-time Most Valuable Players in the Super Bowl. Green Bay's Starr won the award in Super Bowls I and II, Pittsburgh's Bradshaw was honored in Super Bowls XIII and XIV and San Francisco's Montana was singled out in Super Bowls XVI and XIX.

ROGER STAUBACH

Limited to only 20 pass attempts during the 1972 regular season because of a shoulder injury, he came off the bench in the '72 National Conference divisional playoff game between Dallas and San Francisco and rallied the Cowboys from a 15-point deficit to a 30-28 triumph. Trailing 28-13 entering the final quarter, the Cowboys pulled out the victory on Toni Fritsch's 27-yard field goal, Staubach's touchdown passes to Billy Parks (20 yards) and Ron Sellers (10 yards) and Fritsch's two conversion kicks.

STEELERS, 49ERS, PACKERS, JETS

Teams that have a cumulative 9-0 record in the Super Bowl, with the Steelers leading the way with a 4-0 mark. San Francisco and Green Bay boast 2-0 records, and the New York Jets were victorious in their lone Super Bowl appearance. Ranking second to Pittsburgh in Super Bowl triumphs is the Raiders franchise, which has won three times overall (twice as an Oakland-based club and once as a Los Angeles team) and lost one game (representing Oakland).

BOB STILES

Defensive back who, with his UCLA team clinging to a 14-12 lead over No. 1-ranked Michigan State in the final half-minute of the 1966 Rose Bowl, stopped the Spartans' Bob Apisa short of the goal line on a two-point conversion attempt and enabled the Bruins to hang on for the victory. Stiles was knocked cold on the play. Gary Beban ran for both of UCLA's touchdowns in the second quarter (the second coming after the Bruins had gained possession on an onside kick), and UCLA maintained its 14-0 lead midway through the fourth period. A 38-yard TD run by Apisa and Steve Juday's one-yard scoring burst brought Michigan State close, but Stiles—with assists from Dallas Grider and Jim Colletto—foiled the Spartans' hopes for a tie when he flung himself into Apisa on the late two-point try.

SUPER BOWL TOURNAMENT

The 16-team playoff extravaganza that was the result of the 1982 National Football League players' strike, a walkout that began after the first two weeks of the season and lasted for 57 days. Following a settlement on November 16, the NFL announced that the regular season would be reduced from 16 games to nine and that postseason play would be expanded to include the top eight finishers in each conference (with divisional standings being tossed out). Conference playoff participants were seeded, based on regular-season records, with first-round play sending No. 1 against No. 8, No. 2 against No. 7, No. 3 against No. 6 and No. 4 against No. 5. Because of the format, two teams with losing records—Cleveland in the American Conference and Detroit in the National Conference, both 4-5—made the playoffs. Washington, the NFC's top seed with an 8-1 record, wound up as the tournament survivor, beating Detroit, Minnesota and Dallas in the NFC bracket and then defeating Miami in Super Bowl XVII.

SUPERDOME

New Orleans' superstructure that became home for the Sugar Bowl game on December 31, 1975. In the inaugural indoor Sugar classic, Alabama ended its eight-game winless streak in bowl competition by beating Penn State, 13-6. The move inside prompted Crimson Tide Coach Paul (Bear) Bryant to go without his houndstooth hat—"Mamma told me never to wear my hat inside a building," Bryant explained.

JERRY TAGGE

Breaking the plane of the goal line by stretching the ball over from inside the 1-yard line, Nebraska quarterback Tagge scored the game-winning touchdown in the fourth quarter of the 1971 Orange Bowl and lifted the Cornhuskers to a 17-12 triumph over Louisiana State and the No. 1 ranking in the Associated Press' final poll. Entering the January 1 bowl games, the Cornhuskers had ranked third behind top-rated Texas and Ohio State in both wire-service polls covering the 1970 season. Nebraska, though, zoomed to the top of the AP poll (United Press International had released its final rankings in early December) after Texas lost to Notre Dame in the Cotton Bowl, Ohio State was jolted by Jim Plunkett-led Stanford in the Rose Bowl and the Huskers overcame LSU in the nighttime Orange Bowl.

201

TENNESSEE

The last major-college team to go undefeated, untied and unscored upon during the regular season, accomplishing the feat in 1939—but the Volunteers' bubble, like Duke's the year before, was burst by Southern California in the Rose Bowl. While Southern Cal ruined Duke's unscored-upon record in the final 41 seconds of the January 2, 1939, Rose Bowl and beat the Blue Devils with that late score, the Trojans struck earlier on January 1, 1940. USC's Ambrose Schindler dented the Vols' goal line in the second period of the '40 Rose Bowl, running one yard for a touchdown. Then, in the fourth quarter, Schindler threw a one-yard touchdown pass to Al Krueger—the man whose TD catch a year earlier had foiled Duke—and USC posted a 14-0 triumph over Tennessee.

During the 1939 regular season, Tennessee went 10-0, defeating North Carolina State, 13-0; Sewanee, 40-0; Chattanooga, 28-0; Alabama, 21-0; Mercer, 17-0; Louisiana State, 20-0; The Citadel, 34-0; Vanderbilt, 13-0; Kentucky, 19-0, and Auburn, 7-0.

STEVE TENSI, FRED BILETNIKOFF

Florida State aerial combination that overwhelmed Oklahoma in the January 2, 1965, Gator Bowl. Tensi threw for 303 yards and five touchdowns against the Sooners—four of his scoring passes went to Biletnikoff—as the Seminoles romped, 36-19. Oklahoma played without consensus All-America tackle Ralph Neely and two other offensive stars, Jim Grisham and Lance Rentzel. The three were declared ineligible for having signed professional contracts.

TEXAS CHRISTIAN, MARQUETTE

When the first Cotton Bowl game was contested on January 1, 1937, in Dallas, Texas Christian and Marquette were the combatants—and the L.D. Meyer-led Horned Frogs prevailed, 16-6. Meyer, nephew of TCU Coach Dutch Meyer, scored all of his team's points on two TD receptions, an extra-point kick and a field goal.

TEXAS CHRISTIAN

The first of 14 one-time-only Associated Press national champions, having finished atop AP's final poll in 1938. Other teams singled out once as the nation's best in AP's final rankings of the year: Texas A&M (1939), Michigan (1948), Tennessee (1951), Michigan State (1952), Maryland (1953), Auburn (1957), Louisiana State (1958), Syracuse (1959), Georgia (1980), Clemson (1981), Penn State (1982), Miami of Florida (1983) and Brigham Young (1984).

JOE THEISMANN

Notre Dame quarterback who passed for one touchdown and ran for two TDs as the Fighting Irish upset No. 1-ranked Texas, 24-11, in the 1971 Cotton Bowl and ended the Longhorns' 30-game winning streak. While Texas' wish-

When football was dropped from the recreation fare after the first Rose Bowl game in 1902, chariot races became part of the holiday entertainment, held in conjunction with the annual parade, at Tournament Park in Pasadena, Calif. The next football game was played in 1916.

bone attack ground out more than 400 yards in total offense, the Longhorns fumbled nine times and lost possession on five of those bobbles.

38-37, 46-45, 38-36

The scores of three successive shootouts in the Holiday Bowl, with Brigham Young dropping the first of those games to Indiana (December 21, 1979) but defeating Southern Methodist (December 17, 1980) and Washington State (December 18, 1981) in the next two contests.

TOURNAMENT OF ROSES, 1903-1915

With football a part of the New Year's Day recreation fare in 1902 but not again until 1916, pageant officials in Pasadena, Calif., turned to polo, chariot races, bronco busting, pony races, track meets, ostrich races, tent-pegging and a race between an elephant and a camel for holiday entertainment that was held in conjunction with an annual parade.

TULANE, TEMPLE

Participants in the first Sugar Bowl game, contested at Tulane Stadium in New Orleans on January 1, 1935 (the same day that the Orange Bowl made its debut in Miami). Tulane defeated Temple, 20-14.

25

The total number of teams to have won either the Associated Press' national championship or United Press International's collegiate crown since AP introduced football polls in 1936 and UPI began its balloting in 1950. The following schools have been selected No. 1 in one final poll or the other (or both): Alabama, Army, Auburn, Brigham Young, Clemson, Georgia, Louisiana State, Maryland, Miami (Florida), Michigan, Michigan State, Minnesota, Nebraska, Notre Dame, Ohio State, Oklahoma, Penn State, Pittsburgh, Southern California, Syracuse, Tennessee, Texas, Texas A&M, Texas Christian and UCLA.

GENE UPSHAW

Raiders guard who competed in Super Bowls in three decades. Upshaw played for Oakland in Super Bowls II, XI and XV, which were contested on January 14, 1968, January 9, 1977, and January 25, 1981.

STEVE VAN BUREN

His running—first in the snow and then in the mud—helped the Philadelphia Eagles to victories over the Chicago Cardinals and the Los Angeles Rams in the 1948 and 1949 National Football League championship games. On a snow-covered field at Philadelphia's Shibe Park in '48, Van Buren rushed for 98 yards and the game's lone touchdown—which came on a five-yard run—as the Eagles downed the Cardinals, 7-0. And when a deluge turned the turf at the Los Angeles Memorial Coliseum into a mud bowl for the '49 NFL title game, Van Buren defied the elements and bulled his way for 196 yards as Philadelphia stopped the Rams, 14-0.

RON VANDERKELEN

Guarding a 13-10 lead against the Green Bay Packers in the fourth quarter of the 1963 College All-Star Game in Chicago, the College All-Stars stung the Packers on VanderKelen's 74-yard touchdown pass to fellow Wisconsin product Pat Richter and went on to a monumental 20-17 upset of the Pack. Green Bay, loser of only one game in 1962, had won the National Football League championship in both 1961 and '62. The victory proved the last in College All-Star Game history for the collegians, who dropped the final 12 games of the series to the pro champions.

VIKINGS, EAGLES, RAMS, BRONCOS, BENGALS

National Football League teams that have a combined 0-8 record in Super Bowl competition, with the Vikings at the bottom of the heap with four defeats and Philadelphia, the Los Angeles Rams, Denver and Cincinnati having lost in their lone Super Bowl appearances. While the Vikings lead the league in Super Bowl setbacks, Miami and Dallas are right behind as three-time losers (the Dolphins and Cowboys have both won the big game twice).

BILLY WADDY

With 2 minutes, 6 seconds left in a 1979 National Conference divisional playoff game, Waddy caught a 50-yard touchdown pass from Vince Ferragamo that boosted the Los Angeles Rams to a 21-19 victory over the Dallas Cowboys.

WAKE FOREST

The victor in the first Gator Bowl. On January 1, 1946, in Jacksonville, Fla., Wake Forest outscored South Carolina, 26-14.

FULTON WALKER

The only man in Super Bowl history to return a kickoff for a touchdown—and his 98-yard runback in Super Bowl XVII proved Miami's last big moment against the Washington Redskins. Walker's TD sprint, coupled with Uwe von Schamann's conversion kick, boosted the Dolphins into a 17-10 second-period lead over the Redskins in a game played in Pasadena, Calif. Washington then outscored Miami, 17-0, in the second half and posted a 27-17 victory.

WASHINGTON AND JEFFERSON

Little known in the West, Coach Greasy Neale's unbeaten Presidents from Washington, Pa., proved their mettle in the 1922 Rose Bowl by playing California to a scoreless tie. The Golden Bears had entered the game—the last Rose Bowl contested at Tournament Park in Pasadena, Calif.—with 18 consecutive victories.

WASHINGTON REDSKINS

The only pro champions to have a losing record in the 42-game College All-Star Game series in Chicago. The Redskins played the College All-Stars twice—in 1938 and 1943—and lost both times, falling by 28-16 and 27-7 scores.

WASHINGTON STATE, BROWN

Participants in the second Rose Bowl, played January 1, 1916. While Western teams wanted no part of Midwestern or Eastern teams in the 13 years that followed Michigan's thrashing of Stanford in the first Rose Bowl (1902), Washington State gave its section of the country a boost by beating Brown, 14-0.

WASHINGTON STATE

The Cougars were dressed to kill—or was it dressed to be killed?—for their 1931 Rose Bowl game against Alabama. Called the Red Devils by one writer because of their ferocious style of play, the Cougars tried to look the part and got themselves decked out in red helmets, red jerseys, red pants, red socks and red shoes for their appearance in Pasadena, Calif. They ended up red-faced. While the new uniforms proved attention-getters, Washington State fell to the Crimson Tide, 24-0.

J.C. WATTS

Oklahoma quarterback whose touchdown pass to Steve Rhodes and two-point conversion toss to Forrest Valora in the last minute of the 1981 Orange Bowl rallied the Sooners to an 18-17 victory over the Florida State Seminoles.

Colorado's Byron (Whizzer) White (left, light jersey), a future Supreme Court associate justice, fires a touchdown pass to Joe Antonio (26) during action in Rice's 28-14 victory in the 1938 Cotton Bowl.

BYRON (WHIZZER) WHITE

Colorado All-America and U.S. Supreme Court associate justice-to-be who threw an eight-yard scoring pass, returned an interception 47 yards for a touchdown and made two extra points as Colorado seized a 14-0 first-quarter lead over Rice in the second Cotton Bowl game, played January 1, 1938. But the Owls bounced back behind Ernie Lain, who passed for three TDs and ran for a fourth, and posted a 28-14 victory.

DANNY WHITE

With Atlanta ahead of Dallas, 24-10, entering the fourth quarter of their 1980 National Conference divisional playoff game, White drove the Cowboys to three final-period touchdowns and a 30-27 victory over the Falcons in Atlanta. Dallas netted its final two TDs on White-to-Drew Pearson passes of 14 and 23 yards, the latter coming with 42 seconds left to play and proving to be the game-winner.

WORLD BOWL

The title given to the World Football League's championship game. Only one World Bowl was played in the history of the ill-fated WFL, with the Birmingham Americans and Florida Blazers vying for the league crown on December 5, 1974, in Birmingham. The Americans built a 22-0 lead after three periods, then held off the Blazers for a 22-21 victory. Florida rallied on Bob Davis' two touchdown passes and Rod Foster's 76-yard punt return for a TD.

FOURTH QUARTER

TEAMS, LEAGUES AND OTHER THINGS

TONY ADAMS, JIM (KING) CORCORAN

The World Football League's No. 1 finishers in passing yardage and touchdown passes in the WFL's lone complete season, 1974. Adams, Southern California Sun quarterback, passed for 3,905 yards and the Philadelphia Bell's Corcoran threw for 31 TDs.

When the WFL collapsed in October of 1975, John Walton of the San Antonio Wings was the league's top passer for the '75 season (based on a newly adopted computer-rating system). Walton had passed for 2,405 yards and 19 TDs.

FRANKIE ALBERT

While passing for 3,137 fewer yards than Cleveland Browns quarterback Otto Graham in the four-year history of the All-America Football Conference, San Francisco 49ers standout Albert nevertheless was the AAFC's all-time leader in touchdown passes with 88. Graham threw for 86 TDs in the AAFC.

AMERICAN FOOTBALL LEAGUE, 1926

The first of four AFLs in pro football history, its formation was a result of the contract impasse between the Chicago Bears and Red Grange (or, at least, between the Bears and Grange's agent, C.C. Pyle). Grange had been a box-office sensation for the Bears late in the 1925 season (and on a postseason barnstorming tour) after joining the National Football League club upon completion of his eligibility at Illinois—and Pyle thus wanted his client to get a five-figure contract and one-third ownership in the Bears in 1926. The Bears balked. Pyle then did the improbable—he started a new league, with Grange the star attraction of Pyle's own team, the New York Yankees. Not even Grange's presence could pull the league through, though; after one season, the AFL died.

Besides the Yankees, other teams in the 1926 AFL were the Philadelphia Quakers, Cleveland Panthers, Chicago Bulls, Boston Bulldogs, Brooklyn Horsemen, Newark Bears, Rock Island Independents and Los Angeles Wildcats (a road team). Only the Yankees survived beyond '26, being taken in by the NFL in 1927.

AMERICAN PROFESSIONAL FOOTBALL ASSOC.

The original name of the National Football League. The APFA was born September 17, 1920, in Canton, O., when 11 pro football teams from four states (Ohio, Illinois, Indiana and New York), seeking some order out of what had become a chaotic situation of widespread player movement and structureless teams, decided to unify. While guidelines brought a sense of organization to the pro football world, APFA teams continued to play uneven schedules (featuring many non-league opponents) and there is no evidence that standings were kept in '20. Of the original 11 clubs that had met in Canton, 10 actually fielded teams in 1920—the Akron Pros, Canton Bulldogs, Cleveland Indians and Dayton Triangles, all of Ohio; the Decatur Staleys, Racine (Chicago) Cardinals and Rock Island Independents, all of Illinois; Indiana's Hammond Pros and Muncie Flyers, and the Rochester, N.Y., Jeffersons. Failing to field an APFA team after originally hoping to do so was Massillon, O. Added later in '20 were the Buffalo, N.Y., All-Americans, Detroit Heralds, Chicago Tigers and Columbus, O., Panhandles.

In 1921, with franchise changes and dropouts leaving the APFA's championship-contending membership at 13 teams, standings were kept—and the Staleys, now based in Chicago, won the title with a 10-1-1 record.

HEARTLEY (HUNK) ANDERSON

The man who succeeded Knute Rockne as Notre Dame football coach after

Rockne and seven other persons were killed in a March 31, 1931, plane crash. Rockne, whose 1929 and 1930 Fighting Irish teams had posted 9-0 and 10-0 records, was aboard a Kansas City-to-Los Angeles flight (he was going to California to make a football film and tend to personal business) when the plane went down near Bazaar, Kan. Anderson coached Notre Dame for three seasons, compiling a 16-9-2 mark.

ATLANTA FALCONS, NEW ORLEANS SAINTS

National Football League expansion teams that began play in 1966 and 1967. Norb Hecker coached the Falcons when the Atlanta club joined the NFL in '66, and Tom Fears guided the Saints when the New Orleans team was admitted into the NFL in '67.

ATLANTIC COAST CONFERENCE

League that was formed in May 1953, with Southern Conference withdrawals North Carolina, North Carolina State, Duke, Wake Forest, Clemson, Maryland and South Carolina being the seven charter members of the ACC. Virginia then joined the collegiate league in December of '53. Since Virginia's entry, the ACC has undergone only two membership changes—South Carolina's departure from the league in mid-1971 and Georgia Tech's admission in April 1978 (Tech first became eligible for the ACC football title in 1983).

BACHELORS III

The New York night spot that caused a major stir in the summer of 1969 when New York Jets quarterback Joe Namath, fresh from leading his team to a Super Bowl upset of the Baltimore Colts, retired from pro football rather than sell his interest in the establishment. National Football League Commissioner Pete Rozelle had ordered Namath to sever ties with Bachelors III because of its occasional "questionable" clientele (which, reportedly, included known gamblers). Six weeks after Namath's "retirement," Rozelle announced that Namath would comply with the commissioner's directive and that the Jets' star would return to his team.

BALTIMORE COLTS

A member of the All-America Football Conference in the league's last three seasons (1947, 1948 and 1949) and one of three AAFC franchises to be absorbed by the National Football League in 1950. These Colts lasted only one season in the NFL before folding.

In 1953, the Baltimore Colts returned to the NFL—only this entrant was a wholly different franchise than the one that went under after the '50 season. When the Dallas Texans failed to survive after playing in the NFL in 1952, the holdings of the defunct Texans were sold to Carroll Rosenbloom. And Rosenbloom started up a new NFL team in Baltimore, a club that also was called the Colts. The second-edition Colts played in Baltimore from '53 through 1983 before moving to Indianapolis in 1984.

SAMMY BAUGH

The National Football League's top-rated passer in a record six seasons. Baugh, playing for the Washington Redskins, led the NFL in passing in 1937, 1940, 1943, 1945, 1947 and 1949.

ALYN BEALS

San Francisco 49ers receiver who was the leading scorer in All-America Football Conference history, totaling 278 points. Beals caught 46 touchdown passes (also an AAFC career record) for the 49ers from 1946 through 1949 and also contributed two conversion points.

PHIL BENGTSON

The man who replaced Vince Lombardi as coach of the Green Bay Packers in 1968 after Lombardi had directed the team to five National Football League titles in his nine seasons at the helm. Bengtson coached the Packers for three years, posting a 20-21-1 record.

BILLS, HORNETS

Nickname changes involving two charter members of the All-America Football Conference. Known as the Bisons in the AAFC's first season, 1946, Buffalo switched to a Bills designation in 1947 and retained that nickname through 1949 (the league's final year). Chicago played its first three AAFC seasons as the Rockets, then became the Hornets in '49.

GEORGE BLANDA

The No. 1 scorer in National Football League history with 2,002 points. Blanda, who played a record 26 years in the NFL, scored 1,005 points on field goals (335), 943 points on conversion kicks and 54 points on touchdowns (nine). He played for the Chicago Bears, Baltimore Colts, Houston Oilers and Oakland Raiders in a pro career that began in 1949 and ended after the 1975 season (Blanda was inactive in 1959).

BOSTON BRAVES

A team that made its National Football League debut in 1932 and evolved into the Washington Redskins. George Preston Marshall changed the nickname of his franchise from Braves to Redskins in 1933 (after switching playing sites in Boston from Braves Field to Fenway Park) and then moved the club to Washington in 1937.

BOSTON SHAMROCKS, LOS ANGELES BULLDOGS

Champions of the second professional American Football League, which competed against the National Football League in 1936 and 1937 before folding. The Shamrocks won the '36 AFL crown with an 8-3 record, while the Bulldogs posted an 8-0 mark in winning the '37 title.

The Shamrocks, Rochester Tigers, Pittsburgh Americans and New York Yankees competed in the six-team AFL in both 1936 and 1937. The Cleveland Rams (a different franchise than the one by the same name that joined the NFL in 1937) and Brooklyn Tigers rounded out the AFL membership in '36, and the champion Bulldogs and Cincinnati Bengals were the league's other two teams in '37.

BROOKLYN DODGERS

A National Football League team from 1930 through 1943 and an All-America Football Conference club from 1946 through 1948.

Brooklyn's pro football history has not been confined to the Dodgers. The Brooklyn Lions competed in the NFL in 1926 and the Brooklyn Horsemen (featuring Harry Stuhldreher and Elmer Layden, former members of Notre Dame's Four Horsemen) were an American Football League club in the same season. The NFL franchise that called itself the Dodgers from '30 through '43 played as the Brooklyn Tigers in 1944, and another Tigers team —a 1936 squad—represented Brooklyn in the second AFL. And the AAFC Dodgers merged with the New York Yankees in '49 and played the AAFC's final season as the Brooklyn-New York Yankees.

AL BROSKY

Major-college football's all-time leading interceptor. Brosky, who played for Illinois from 1950 through 1952, made 29 career interceptions and also set a major-college record by picking off passes in 15 consecutive games.

JIM BROWN

Cleveland Browns standout who led the National Football League in rushing for a record five consecutive seasons, 1957 through 1961, and topped the NFL's ground-gaining chart an unprecedented eight times overall (also winning rushing crowns in 1963, 1964 and 1965).

JIM BROWN

The career leader in touchdowns scored in the National Football League. Brown made 126 TDs during his nine seasons (1957-1965) with the Cleveland Browns.

PAUL BROWN, LAWRENCE T. (BUCK) SHAW

Two of the eight original coaches in the All-America Football Conference— and they guided their teams through all four seasons (1946 through 1949) of the AAFC's history. Brown coached the Cleveland Browns, while Shaw directed the San Francisco 49ers.

When the AAFC began play in 1946, the league's other teams and coaches were: New York Yankees, Ray Flaherty; Brooklyn Dodgers, Mal Stevens; Miami Seahawks, Jack Meagher; Los Angeles Dons, Dudley DeGroot; Chicago Rockets, Dick Hanley; and Buffalo Bisons, Red Dawson (the replacement for Sam Cordovano, who resigned more than three months before the season opener after signing on as Buffalo's coach).

BROWNS, COLTS, STEELERS

The three old-line National Football League teams that joined the 10 American Football League teams in 1970 to form the American Football Conference. Full implementation of the merger between the 16-team NFL and the AFL in '70 called for rival conferences of 13 teams each and thus necessitated the switch-over of three senior-league clubs (which, after considerable haggling, turned out to be the Cleveland, Baltimore and Pittsburgh teams).

CANTON BULLDOGS

National Football League champions in 1922 and 1923—and the team for which Jim Thorpe excelled earlier. While Thorpe didn't play for the '22 or '23 Bulldogs (the famed athlete was with the Oorang Indians in those seasons), he was a superstar on Canton's pro teams of pre-NFL days. The Thorpe-led Bulldogs of 1916 were hailed as one of pro football's all-time great squads. Canton had Thorpe's services through 1920, then began structured league play (standings were first kept) without him in 1921. In '22 and '23, the Bulldogs, led by standout players Guy Chamberlin (also the team's coach), Wilbur (Pete) Henry and Link Lyman, went 21-0-3 overall while ruling the NFL. Needing more revenue, the Bulldogs moved to Cleveland in 1924—again winning the NFL crown—and Canton was without an NFL team that season. A new Canton Bulldogs franchise emerged in 1925 and Thorpe, giving it one last fling, rejoined the club in '26 (11 years after originally signing with Canton). But the Bulldogs won only one of 13 games in 1926, which proved the last NFL season for the storied team.

CAPITOL, CENTURY, COASTAL, CENTRAL

Names of the National Football League's divisions when the league played under a four-division alignment from 1967 through 1969. When the New Orleans Saints joined the NFL in '67 and gave the league its 16th franchise, the NFL formed two divisions within each of its two conferences (which formerly had stood alone). The Eastern Conference was made up of the Capitol Division and the Century Division, and the Western Conference consisted of the Coastal Division and the Central Division. In 1970, after its merger with the American Football League was fully implemented, the NFL went to six divisions.

GINO CAPPELLETTI

Having totaled 1,100 points in 10 seasons with the Boston Patriots, he was the No. 1 scorer in American Football League history (1960-1969). Cappelletti scored 42 touchdowns (all on receptions, for 252 points), kicked 170 field goals (510 points) and made 330 point-after-touchdown kicks and four two-point conversions (338 points overall on PATs).

CARD-PITT

The 1944 National Football League club that was the result of a Chicago Cardinals-Pittsburgh Steelers merger, a one-year union brought on by dwindling resources (both financially and player-wise, because of World War II).

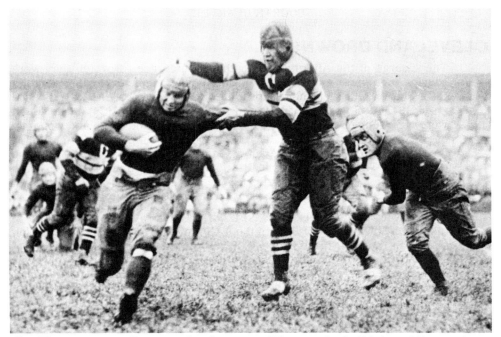

Jim Thorpe, generally recognized as one of the greatest athletes of the century, pulls down a ballcarrier during a 1926 game between the Canton Bulldogs and Frankford Yellowjackets.

Cardinals Coach Phil Handler and Steelers Coach Walt Kiesling shared coaching duties for the club, whose home games were divided between Chicago and Pittsburgh. Whether playing in the Windy City, the Steel City or on the road, Card-Pitt proved a hapless team. The squad finished 0-10.

CARLISLE INDIAN INDUSTRIAL SCHOOL

Opened in 1879 on the site of former cavalry barracks, this government-run institution in Carlisle, Pa., trained and educated Indian youths until its closing in 1918—and it fielded some of the nation's top football teams along the way. With Glenn (Pop) Warner as coach and Jim Thorpe its star player, Carlisle enjoyed its greatest acclaim in 1907, 1908, 1911 and 1912. The Indians went 43-5-2 in those seasons, with Thorpe scoring 53 touchdowns, kicking 17 field goals and making 70 extra points.

CHICAGO BEARS, GREEN BAY PACKERS

Their series, spanning 129 games through 1984, is the longest in the National Football League. The Bears lead the series (which includes a 1941 divisional playoff game won by Chicago), 68-55-6.

CINCINNATI BENGALS

Not only the name of a current National Football League franchise (which had its origin as a 1968 American Football League expansion team), but the name of a 1937 AFL club and the name of a 1940-1941 AFL entry.

CLEVELAND BROWNS

The scourge of the All-America Football Conference (of which they were charter members) and the National Football League from 1946 through 1955. The Browns were champions all four years of the AAFC's existence (1946, 1947, 1948 and 1949), captured NFL titles in 1950, 1954 and 1955 and were NFL runners-up in 1951, 1952 and 1953. And while Cleveland won only one NFL championship from 1956 through 1984 (ruling the league in 1964), the club enjoyed considerable success in that span—particularly into the early 1970s. The Browns went 9-2-1 in 1957, 9-3 in 1958 and 8-3-1 in 1960, and Cleveland won 10 or more games in a season six times from 1963 through 1972 (going 9-5 in three other seasons during that 10-year period).

The Browns, fierce rivals to the NFL during their AAFC domination, were taken in by the NFL in 1950 when the AAFC folded. In 1970, after a 20-season stretch in the NFL that included a 1960s war against—and an element of condescension toward—the new American Football League, the Browns became one of three NFL clubs to join the 10 AFL clubs in the formation of the NFL's American Conference (a product of the NFL-AFL merger).

CLEVELAND RAMS

National Football League club that entered the league in 1937, suspended operations in 1943 because of World War II, won the NFL crown in 1945 and, adrift in a sea of red ink, transferred to Los Angeles in 1946. The Los Angeles Rams played their home games at the Los Angeles Memorial Coliseum from '46 through 1979 and then moved to Anaheim Stadium in 1980.

COCOANUT GROVE

The Boston night spot where, on the evening of November 28, 1942, the No. 1-ranked Boston College Eagles had planned to celebrate a perfect season —provided they could handle a so-so Holy Cross team that afternoon. The Eagles entered the game with an 8-0 record; the Crusaders were 4-4-1. In a mind-boggling outcome, Holy Cross thrashed the Eagles, 55-12. Dejected Boston College officials canceled the party plans at the Cocoanut Grove . . . where 491 persons died in a fire that night.

COLGATE

School whose 1932 football team went unbeaten, untied, unscored upon and uninvited (to the Rose Bowl, in which it had hoped to participate). The Red Raiders compiled a 9-0 record and shut out their opponents, 264-0, but Pittsburgh—not Colgate—received the invitation to play Southern California in the Rose Bowl.

COLUMBUS BULLS

The Ohio team that captured the championship in both seasons, 1940 and 1941, of the third professional American Football League. Overall, the Bulls compiled a 13-2-3 mark in the AFL.

In '40, the AFL was made up of the Bulls, Buffalo Indians, Milwaukee Chiefs,

Cincinnati Bengals, New York Yankees and Boston Bears. The league went from six clubs to five in '41, with Boston dropping out (and the New York franchise changing its nickname to Americans).

DICK COURY

One of the 12 original coaches in both the World Football League and United States Football League. Coury was at the helm of the Portland Storm when the WFL began play in 1974, and he was the Boston Breakers' coach when the USFL—introducing a March-to-July schedule—got off the ground in 1983.

Coury's rival coaches when the WFL made its debut in '74 were Jack Gotta (Birmingham Americans), Jim Spavital (Chicago Fire), Dan Boisture (Detroit Wheels), Jack Pardee (Florida Blazers), Mike Giddings (the Hawaiians), Jim Garrett (Houston Texans), Bud Asher (Jacksonville Sharks), John McVay (Memphis Southmen), Babe Parilli (New York Stars), Ron Waller (Philadelphia Bell) and Tom Fears (Southern California Sun).

Besides Coury, the original USFL coaches in '83 were Doug Shively (Arizona Wranglers), Red Miller (Denver Gold), John Ralston (Oakland Invaders), Hugh Campbell (Los Angeles Express), Jim Stanley (Michigan Panthers), Rollie Dotsch (Birmingham Stallions), George Allen (Chicago Blitz), Steve Spurrier (Tampa Bay Bandits), Chuck Fairbanks (New Jersey Generals), Jim Mora (Philadelphia Stars) and Ray Jauch (Washington Federals).

'CRADLE OF COACHES'

Nickname applied to Miami University in Oxford, O., whose head football coaches have included Sid Gillman, Woody Hayes, Ara Parseghian, Bo Schembechler and John Pont. And among former Miami players who have prospered in the coaching ranks are Earl (Red) Blaik, Paul Brown, Weeb Ewbank, Paul Dietzel and Bill Arnsparger (Parseghian and Pont also played for the Redskins).

LARRY CSONKA, JIM KIICK, PAUL WARFIELD

Having played in the Miami Dolphins' second straight Super Bowl victory 2½ months earlier, Csonka, Kiick and Warfield shocked the pro football world on March 31, 1974, by signing contracts—which would take effect in the fall of 1975—with the Toronto Northmen of the World Football League. Before the WFL played its first league games in July 1974, the Toronto Northmen had become the Memphis Southmen. And by the time Csonka, Kiick and Warfield made their WFL debuts in 1975, the league was on increasingly shaky ground.

The WFL folded on October 22, 1975, at which time Kiick had played 11 games for Memphis, Warfield 10 and Csonka seven. Kiick rushed for 462 yards and scored 10 touchdowns overall in the WFL; Warfield caught 25 passes for 422 yards and three touchdowns for the Southmen (also known as the Grizzlies); and Csonka ran for 421 yards and scored two TDs overall.

DALLAS COWBOYS, MINNESOTA VIKINGS

Expansion teams that were added to the National Football League in 1960 and 1961. Tom Landry was Dallas' coach when the Cowboys made their NFL debut in the '60 season, and Norm Van Brocklin directed Minnesota when the Vikings entered the league in '61.

DALLAS COWBOYS, WASHINGTON REDSKINS

In a clash for the National Conference East title contested on the last weekend of the 1979 regular season, the Cowboys rebounded from a 13-point fourth-quarter deficit and stunned the Redskins, 35-34, in one of the most dramatic regular-season games ever played in the National Football League. Dallas, which had overcome a 17-point deficit earlier in the game, trailed by a 34-21 score with a little more than $3\frac{1}{2}$ minutes to play. However, the Cowboys rallied on two Roger Staubach touchdown passes, with the second—to Tony Hill—coming with 39 seconds remaining in the game. The loss was particularly painful for Washington, which entered the game with the divisional lead and then found itself out of the playoffs (because of the NFL's tiebreaker rules).

1952 DALLAS TEXANS

Texas' first National Football League team, a club that was transferred to Dallas in January 1952 as the NFL's former New York Yanks franchise. The Texans, coached by Jim Phelan, fared poorly on the field and at the gate in '52. And after seven games of a 12-game season—the Dallas club had gone 0-7—the franchise was turned over to the league. Commissioner Bert Bell then made a road team out of the Texans, who at that point already had played four of their six scheduled home games (at Dallas' Cotton Bowl). Bell based the team in Hershey, Pa., and the club's two remaining "home" games were moved to Akron, O., and Detroit. The Texans finished the '52 season with a 1-11 record, collecting their only triumph on Thanksgiving Day in Akron when they upset the Chicago Bears, 27-23. Dallas' NFL club folded at year's end, and the holdings of the defunct team were awarded to Baltimore interests in January 1953.

The Texans franchise had entered the NFL in 1944 as the Boston Yanks. After five seasons in New England, the Yanks became the NFL's New York Bulldogs in 1949. In 1950, the Bulldogs became the New York Yanks (and, in the process, divided players from the Brooklyn-New York Yankees franchise of the disbanded All-America Football Conference with the New York Giants). And in '52, the Yanks went to Dallas.

DALLAS TEXANS/KANSAS CITY CHIEFS

Franchise that won the most league championships, three, in the 10-year history of the fourth American Football League, which existed from 1960 through 1969. Dallas, a charter member of the AFL, used the same nickname as the city's 1952 National Football League club. The Texans captured the AFL title in 1962, then moved to Kansas City in 1963. The franchise continued to flourish, however, as the Chiefs won league crowns in 1966 and 1969. The Houston Oilers (1960, 1961) and Buffalo Bills (1964, 1965) were

Zollie Toth goes head over heels, courtesy of the Chicago Bears defense, in a 1952 game at Akron, O. Toth played for the ill-fated Dallas Texans, who were taken over by the league midway through their only NFL season. The Texans played their final two "home games" in Akron and Detroit.

two-time AFL titlists, and the San Diego Chargers (1963), Oakland Raiders (1967) and New York Jets (1968) were one-time champions.

CLEM DANIELS

The leading rusher in the 10-year history of the American Football League (1960-1969). Daniels, who played for the Dallas Texans in 1960 and for the Oakland Raiders from 1961 through 1967, rushed for 5,101 yards in his AFL career. He finished his pro career in 1968 as a member of the National Football League's San Francisco 49ers.

GLENN DAVIS, TONY DORSETT

They share the major-college record for career touchdowns with 59. Army's Davis notched touchdowns on 43 rushes, 14 receptions and two punt returns from 1943 through 1946, and Pittsburgh's Dorsett collected TDs on 55 running plays and four receptions from 1973 through 1976.

LEN DAWSON

The all-time leader in touchdown passes for the 1960-69 American Football

League. Dawson, who played for the Dallas Texans/Kansas City Chiefs franchise, tossed 182 scoring passes during his eight seasons in the AFL.

TIM DELANEY, ALFRED JENKINS

The World Football League's leaders in pass receptions and pass-reception yardage in the WFL's only complete season, 1974. Delaney, playing for the Hawaiians, caught 89 passes and the Birmingham Americans' Jenkins had 1,326 yards receiving.

DETROIT WHEELS, JACKSONVILLE SHARKS

World Football League franchises that ceased operations with six games remaining (out of a scheduled 20 games) in the WFL's first season, 1974.

TONY DORSETT

The leading career ground-gainer in major-college football. Dorsett, who played for Pittsburgh from 1973 through 1976, rushed for 6,082 yards.

JOHN FACENDA

The longtime narrator of National Football League highlight films whose distinctive voice provided an air of the dramatic to the events he was describing. Facenda died in 1984.

FEARSOME FOURSOME

The Los Angeles Rams' defensive front four that hounded the opposition in the 1960s. The original alignment consisted of ends Lamar Lundy and David (Deacon) Jones and tackles Roosevelt Grier and Merlin Olsen. When an injury forced Grier into retirement following the 1966 season, Roger Brown replaced him.

DOUG FLUTIE

The only player in major-college history to attain 10,000 yards passing in his career. Flutie threw for 10,579 yards while playing for Boston College from 1981 through 1984.

FRANKFORD YELLOWJACKETS

The metropolitan Philadelphia area team that joined the National Football League in 1924, won the NFL championship in 1926, went inactive in 1932 and was replaced in the NFL by the Philadelphia Eagles in 1933 when Bert Bell and Lud Wray were awarded a franchise for the Philadelphia territory.

BENNY FRIEDMAN

Detroit Wolverines passing sensation who was so coveted by New York Giants Owner Tim Mara that Mara, in effect, bought the Wolverines' dying one-year-old franchise to obtain him. Friedman, a collegiate standout at Michigan (where he teamed with receiver Benny Oosterbaan), began his National Football League career with the Cleveland Bulldogs in 1927 and joined the Wolverines in 1928. Then came Mara's maneuvering and Friedman's move to the Giants in 1929 (the New York club went 13-1-1 that year after finishing 4-7-2 the previous season). During his three seasons with the Giants and three more years with the Brooklyn Dodgers, Friedman helped the NFL to succeed in the New York area by thrilling fans and fooling defenses with his passing and running wizardry and inventive play.

Only Coach LeRoy Andrews and a handful of players accompanied Friedman from Detroit to New York. Mara obviously had no intention of reviving the Wolverine franchise; he wanted Friedman and, in the process, was able to acquire rights to other Wolverine players who interested him.

SID GILLMAN

Coach of the Los Angeles and San Diego Chargers for 135 of the 140 games that the franchise played in the American Football League from the league's beginning in 1960 to its entry into the National Football League after the 1969 season. Gillman resigned as the Chargers' coach after nine games of the '69 season because of ill health, turning the job over to assistant Charlie Waller.

OTTO GRAHAM

The all-time leader in All-America Football Conference passing yardage. In four seasons with the AAFC's Cleveland Browns, Graham threw for 10,085 yards.

ROY GREEN

The most recent of three National Football League players to return a kickoff 106 yards, which stands as the league record. Green, playing for the St. Louis Cardinals, made his sprint on October 21, 1979, against the Dallas Cowboys. Other 106-yard kickoff runbacks were accomplished by Al Carmichael of the Green Bay Packers in 1956 (against the Chicago Bears) and Noland Smith of the Kansas City Chiefs in 1967 (against the Denver Broncos).

GREEN BAY PACKERS

Wisconsin team that was added to the American Professional Football Association in 1921, two years after the Indian Packing Co. of Green Bay had provided equipment (and the nickname, obviously) for a football team started up by Curly Lambeau and George Calhoun. J.E. Clair of the Acme Packing Co., which had bought out the Indian Packing Co., was awarded the APFA franchise in August of '21 but turned the club back to the league five months later after the Packers had been disciplined for using college players under assumed names. Lambeau stepped in, however, and bought the team and the Packers carried on in 1922 (in the renamed National Football League). And by 1923, a community-owned, nonprofit corporation—which became the franchise's trademark—was in place to operate the club.

Lambeau, who had won a football letter at Notre Dame in 1918 before receiving an Indian Packing Co. job offer he couldn't pass up in his home

A panoramic view of Yale's football field in New Haven, Conn., during an early-

town of Green Bay, played for the Packers through the 1920s and coached the Pack from 1921 through 1949.

GREEN BAY PACKERS

The only team to win three consecutive National Football League titles—and the Packers accomplished the feat twice. Green Bay ruled the NFL in 1929, 1930 and 1931 and again in 1965, 1966 and 1967.

GREEN BAY PACKERS, CHICAGO BEARS

Teams that rank 1-2 in National Football League championships, with the Packers owning 11 NFL crowns and the Bears boasting eight league titles.

GREEN BAY PACKERS, PHILADELPHIA EAGLES

Teams that struggled to 1-10-1 (Packers) and 2-9-1 (Eagles) records in 1958 —and then met for the National Football League championship two years later.

GRIDIRON

When Walter Camp revolutionized U.S. football in 1880 by changing the game from its rugby style to a format that put 11 players on a side and introduced the scrimmage system (which necessitated a new position, quarterback), there was one flaw in his scheme: The scrimmage setup allowed unlimited possession of the ball unless it was fumbled or kicked away. The "problem" became painfully apparent in the 1881 Princeton-Yale game in which each team had the ball for an entire half without scoring. B-o-r-i-n-g. Camp, the "father of American football," had the answer in 1882, devising the rule that a team had to advance the ball five yards on three downs or lose possession. Thus came the emergence of the "gridiron." Chalk lines were put down to measure yardage gained, with the field being marked

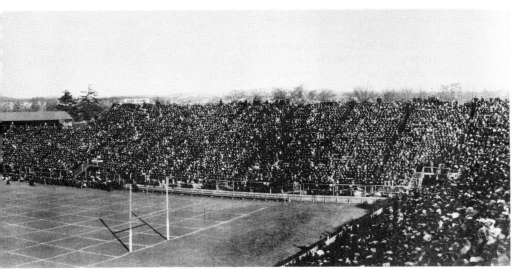

1900s Yale-Princeton game clearly shows how the term "gridiron" originated.

with lines parallel to the goal line every five yards. When passing was legalized in 1906 with the stipulation that the throw had to be five yards left or right of center, lines also were marked parallel to the sidelines at five-yard intervals (thereby making the "grid" appearance complete). By 1910, however, the lines parallel to the sidelines had disappeared, thanks to the dropping of the five-yard lateral restriction on passing.

By 1912, the system of four downs to make 10 yards was in effect.

RALPH HAY

Hupmobile dealer whose Canton, O., showroom was the site of a September 17, 1920, meeting of 11 team representatives from four states, a gathering out of which came the American Professional Football Association (the National Football League to be). Hay headed one of the ready-to-organize clubs—the Canton Bulldogs.

PAUL HORNUNG, ALEX KARRAS

National Football League stars who were suspended indefinitely by Commissioner Pete Rozelle in April 1963 for placing bets on their own teams and on other NFL games. After sitting out the '63 season, Green Bay halfback Hornung and Detroit defensive tackle Karras were reinstated by Rozelle in March 1964.

CHUCK HUGHES

Detroit's 28-year-old receiver who collapsed on the field late in the Lions' October 24, 1971, game against the Chicago Bears and was pronounced dead less than an hour later. Death was attributed to a heart attack.

DON HUTSON

The most frequent pass-receiving champion in National Football League history, having led the league in receptions eight times (1936, 1937, 1939 and 1941 through 1945) for the Green Bay Packers. Hutson also holds the NFL career record for touchdown catches with 99.

INTERCOLLEGIATE CONFERENCE OF FACULTY REPRESENTATIVES

The unwieldy but official name of what is known as the Big Ten Conference, whose seven charter members in 1896 were Wisconsin, Northwestern, Michigan, Minnesota, Chicago, Purdue and Illinois. Indiana and Iowa were admitted to the league in December 1899, and Ohio State joined the conference in April 1912 (the Buckeyes first competed for the league football title in 1913). Chicago formally withdrew from the league—also known as the Western Conference—in March 1946, having played its last football season in 1939. Michigan State was admitted to the league in May 1949 and became eligible for the Big Ten football championship in 1953.

IOWA

A university that from 1907 through 1910 played football in two leagues—the Missouri Valley Intercollegiate Athletic Association (which became the Big Eight Conference) and the Intercollegiate Conference of Faculty Representatives (the future Big Ten). The Hawkeyes went 1-0, 0-4, 1-3-1 and 3-1 during those seasons in the forerunner of the Big Eight and posted 1-1, 0-1, 0-1 and 1-1 records in "Big Ten" play. Iowa ended its Missouri Valley affiliation after the 1910 season.

ROBERT IRSAY, CARROLL ROSENBLOOM

Men who swapped National Football League franchises in July 1972. Irsay, an Illinois businessman who recently had purchased the Los Angeles Rams from the estate of the late Dan Reeves, traded the Rams to Rosenbloom for Rosenbloom's Baltimore Colts.

IVY LEAGUE

A non-organized collegiate football group existing in name only until 1956, when longtime athletic rivals Harvard, Yale, Princeton, Dartmouth, Cornell, Columbia, Brown and Pennsylvania played their first complete round-robin schedule and formally crowned their first football champion. In the Ivy's initial season as a bona fide football conference, Yale raced to the league crown with a 7-0 record.

RANDY JACKSON, TOM OWEN, MARV KELLUM

Jackson was a survivor of the 1970 airplane crash that killed his coach and 14 of his Wichita State teammates, while Owen and Kellum were among Wichita State's freshman-team members who were elevated to the varsity for the remaining six games of the Shockers' '70 season. All three players went on to the National Football League. Running back Jackson played for the Buffalo Bills, San Francisco 49ers and Philadelphia Eagles from 1972 through 1974. Owen was a quarterback for the 49ers in 1974 and 1975 and saw duty with the New England Patriots in 1976, 1978, 1979 and 1981. And Kellum was a reserve linebacker on the Pittsburgh Steelers' Super Bowl IX and X champions (he also played for the St. Louis Cardinals).

Another Tom Owen, a Floridian who was a junior running back for Wichita State, was killed in the crash. Quarterback Owen was from Kansas.

CHARLIE JOINER

The career leader in receptions in the National Football League, with 657 catches through the 1984 season. Joiner, who completed his 16th NFL season in '84, has played for the Houston Oilers, Cincinnati Bengals and San Diego Chargers.

JUNE 8, 1966

The day that a surprising merger accord was announced between the National Football League and the American Football League. The two leagues, which had been arch enemies and involved in a fierce signing war for player talent since the AFL's inception in 1960, agreed to meet in world championship games (the first of which would come after the 1966 season), begin a combined draft in 1967, engage in preseason competition in '67, play separate schedules through 1969 and become one entity, the NFL (with interlocking schedules), effective in 1970. Additionally, the AFL approved an $18 million indemnity payment to the NFL, and NFL Commissioner Pete Rozelle's authority was expanded to cover the two-leagues-in-one domain.

KANSAS, OKLAHOMA

Schools that have played the longest uninterrupted series in major-college football history. Through 1984, the Jayhawks and Sooners had met in 82 consecutive seasons (with Oklahoma winning 53 games, losing 23 and tying six).

JACK KEMP

He passed for more yards, 21,130, than any player in American Football League history (1960-1969). Kemp established his record while playing for the Los Angeles and San Diego Chargers and the Buffalo Bills.

PAUL KRAUSE

The leading interceptor in National Football League history. Krause, who played a total of 16 NFL years with the Washington Redskins and Minnesota Vikings in a pro career that ended after the 1979 season, collected 81 lifetime interceptions.

CURLY LAMBEAU, GEORGE HALAS

They share the record for having coached the most National Football League championship teams, each directing six clubs to NFL titles. Lambeau guided the Green Bay Packers to league crowns in 1929, 1930, 1931, 1936, 1939 and 1944; Halas coached the Chicago Staleys to the NFL championship in 1921, then led the Chicago Bears (the former Staleys) to titles in 1933, 1940, 1941, 1946 and 1963.

LITTLE BROWN JUG

The symbol of the Michigan-Minnesota rivalry. After the Wolverines and Gophers had clashed in Minneapolis in 1903, the Michigan team returned to Ann Arbor and discovered it was without its water jug. Coach Fielding Yost asked Minnesota to return the container and he was told to "come and get it." After a five-year lapse in the series (1904-1908), the teams began playing for the Little Brown Jug in 1909.

LOS ANGELES RAIDERS

After playing a total of 22 American Football League and National Football League seasons as an Oakland-based team, the Raiders took up residence in Los Angeles—at the Los Angeles Memorial Coliseum—beginning with the 1982 NFL season.

ED MARSHALL

Memphis Southmen receiver who topped the World Football League with 19 touchdown catches in 1974 and was leading the league with nine scoring receptions in 1975 when the WFL quit business on October 22.

MARSHALL UNIVERSITY

Having lost to East Carolina, 17-14, at Greenville, N.C., that afternoon, the Marshall University football team was returning to Huntington, W. Va., on November 14, 1970, when the plane carrying the 37-man squad and 75 persons overall crashed near the Huntington airport runway. There were no survivors.

Among the victims of the Marshall crash was assistant coach Frank Loria, a consensus All-America defensive back at Virginia Tech in 1967.

DON MAYNARD, LIONEL TAYLOR

The all-time leaders in pass-reception yardage and total receptions in the 10-season history, 1960-1969, of the American Football League. Maynard gained 10,289 yards as a New York Titans and Jets receiver, while Taylor caught 567 passes overall for Denver and Houston (543 with the Broncos and 24 with the Oilers).

Maynard also topped the AFL in career touchdown catches with 84.

DON MAYNARD

The No. 1 pass catcher in National Football League history in yardage gained. Maynard, who spent 13 seasons with the New York Titans/Jets and one year each with the New York Giants and St. Louis Cardinals, gained 11,834 yards (on 633 catches).

JIM McMAHON

Major-college football's record-holder for touchdown passes in a season (47) and in a career (84). McMahon, who played for Brigham Young in 1977, 1978, 1980 and 1981, established his single-season mark in '80.

DAVE MEGGYESY

A three-year letterman at Syracuse and a St. Louis Cardinals linebacker for seven seasons (1963 through 1969), he ruffled feathers with his late-1970 book, "Out of Their League," which focused on what Meggyesy called the "dehumanizing" aspects of football.

MIAMI DOLPHINS, CINCINNATI BENGALS

The two expansion teams that the 1960s American Football League took in during its 10-year history. The Dolphins joined the league in 1966, and the Bengals were admitted in 1968.

MIAMI SEAHAWKS

A charter member of the All-America Football Conference—but the Seahawks lasted only one season. Miami compiled a 3-11 record in 1946, then was replaced by the Baltimore Colts franchise in 1947 AAFC play.

MINNESOTA, WISCONSIN

Their series is the longest in major-college football. The Gophers and Badgers, who first met in 1890, had collided 94 times through the 1984 season (failing to get together only in 1906 since the series began). Minnesota leads the series, 50-36-8.

Through 1984, Missouri and Kansas had played 93 games in their series (missing only in 1918 after first squaring off in 1891). The Tigers own a 43-41-9 edge over the Jayhawks.

The longest NCAA football series (regardless of classification) is that involving Lafayette and Lehigh, who had met 120 times through 1984. Yale and Princeton had played 107 times, Yale and Harvard 101 times and Williams and Amherst 99 times.

ART MONK

Wide receiver who, playing for the Washington Redskins in 1984, established a single-season National Football League record with 106 receptions.

MARION MOTLEY

Having blasted his way to 3,024 yards in four All-America Football Conference seasons with the Cleveland Browns, he ranked as the career rushing leader in the AAFC.

NATIONAL FOOTBALL LEAGUE

The name that pro football's major league adopted in 1922 after playing its first two seasons (1920 and 1921) under the title of the American Professional Football Association.

NEBRASKA

The only team to defeat Notre Dame in the 30 games in which Harry Stuhldreher, Jim Crowley, Don Miller and Elmer Layden—the Four Horsemen—were members of the Fighting Irish varsity. And the Cornhuskers beat Notre Dame twice in that span, taking the 1922 season finale, 14-6, and downing the Irish, 14-7, in 1923. Notre Dame and the Four Horsemen exacted a measure of revenge in 1924, walloping Nebraska, 34-6.

NEW ENGLAND PATRIOTS

After playing 10 American Football League seasons and one National Football League campaign as the Boston Patriots, the Pats moved to their new stadium in Foxboro, Mass., in 1971 and became known as the New England Patriots.

THE NEW LEAGUE INC.

The corporate name of the 1975 World Football League which, legally, was a different entity than the 1974 WFL. While there was a major turnover in team ownerships, the league looked much the same in '75 as it did in '74. In fact, when the WFL began its '75 season, the league's 11-city field included 10 cities that had fielded WFL teams in '74. Six of the club nicknames were the same, and familiar personnel dotted the rosters. So, while the 1974 and 1975 WFLs were "separate and distinctive" legally, their existences (and records) are viewed as one by most football historians.

Joining the holdover names of the Memphis Southmen, Charlotte Hornets, Philadelphia Bell, Southern California Sun, Shreveport Steamer and the Hawaiians in the 1975 WFL alignment were the Birmingham Vulcans, Portland Thunder, Jacksonville Express, Chicago Winds and the San Antonio Wings (successors to the Florida Blazers franchise). The Winds lasted only five games in '75 before folding, and the other league members played a little more than half of their 20-game schedules before the league collapsed.

NEW YORK GIANTS

Owner Tim Mara's National Football League team that made its debut in 1925 and gave the league something it needed badly—a team in the nation's financial and media capital. The Giants franchise received a major boost on December 6, 1925, when the Red Grange-led Chicago Bears—the Illinois sensation had signed with the Bears only two weeks earlier—drew more than 70,000 fans to the Polo Grounds for a game with the Giants and brightened the economic picture for Mara and his crucial NFL franchise.

NEW YORK JETS

After playing the 1960, 1961 and 1962 American Football League seasons as the Titans, New York's AFL franchise changed its nickname to Jets in 1963

Beneath the pile of bodies is Notre Dame's Steve Miller, who had just plunged over the goal line for the first Irish touchdown in the fourth quarter of a 1935 game against Ohio State. The Irish allowed the Buckeyes a 13-0 lead before mounting a furious rally that produced an 18-13 victory.

(upon purchase of the club by Sonny Werblin's group) and at the same time switched its colors from navy blue and gold to kelly green and white.

NEW YORK STARS, HOUSTON TEXANS

The two World Football League teams that relocated during the WFL's first season, 1974. The New York Stars played 13 WFL games before moving to Charlotte, N.C., and playing their last seven games of '74 as the Hornets. The Houston Texans lasted 11 games before transferring to Shreveport, La., and playing the final nine games of the '74 season as the Steamer.

NEW YORK YANKEES

A name used by four professional football franchises in five leagues in a total of 10 seasons. The initial New York Yankees played in the first American Football League in 1926 and then, upon that AFL's demise after one season, competed in the National Football League in 1927 and 1928. The second New York Yankees team was a member of the second AFL, which existed in 1936 and 1937. The third New York Yankees club played in the third AFL in 1940, and the fourth New York Yankees were All-America Football Conference participants from 1946 through 1948 and carried a Brooklyn prefix in 1949 (Brooklyn-New York Yankees).

Not to be confused with the New York Yankees franchise was the New York Yanks entry, which played in the NFL in 1950 and 1951.

JERRY NORTON

The only player in National Football League history to have intercepted four passes in a game twice. Playing for the St. Louis Cardinals, Norton picked off four Washington passes on November 20, 1960, and stole four Pittsburgh passes on November 26, 1961.

NOTRE DAME, OHIO STATE

Through most of the first three quarters of the 1935 Notre Dame-Ohio State game, the action was spirited and intense. But it was hardly heartstopping. The Buckeyes had dominated play in this November 2 battle of unbeatens in Columbus and held a 13-0 lead. Then. . .Notre Dame's Andy Pilney ended the third period by returning an Ohio State punt to the Buckeyes' 13-yard line. Pilney then completed a 12-yard pass, and Steve Miller followed with a one-yard touchdown run (the conversion kick failed). Pilney was just getting warmed up. He sparked the Fighting Irish to their second touchdown late in the fourth period, the payoff coming on Pilney's 15-yard pitch to Mike Layden. The extra-point attempt was blocked. Buckeyes 13, Irish 12. Then, in the final minute of play, Notre Dame recovered an Ohio State fumble on the Irish 49. Repeatedly shaking off Ohio State defenders, Pilney made a clutch 32-yard run to the Buckeyes' 19—only to be injured on the play and carried from the field. Bill Shakespeare came in, though, and wrote the perfect ending for Notre Dame fans—a touchdown pass to Wayne Millner with 32 seconds remaining. The Irish, on the strength of a 15-minute thrill show capped by one of college football's most exciting finishes, were 18-13 winners.

OAKLAND RAIDERS

Team that set the American Football League record for the longest losing streak, dropping 19 consecutive games in a 1961-1962 stretch. The Raiders lost their last six games of the '61 season, then were beaten in their first 13 games of the '62 campaign. Oakland compiled 2-12 and 1-13 records in those years.

OKLAHOMA, OKLAHOMA A&M

Two of the original members of the Southwest Conference, which played its first football season in 1915. Other charter SWC institutions were Texas, Texas A&M, Arkansas, Baylor, Rice and Southwestern (Texas). Oklahoma spent five seasons in the league and Oklahoma A&M (now Oklahoma State) was a conference member for 10 years. Southwestern dropped out of the SWC after two seasons. Southern Methodist joined the league in 1918, Texas Christian was added in 1923, Texas Tech entered the SWC in 1956 (becoming eligible for conference football competition in 1960) and Houston brought the league membership to nine schools in 1971 (although the Cougars weren't eligible for the SWC football title until 1976).

Louisiana State had indicated an interest in joining the new league in 1914, but withdrew at a subsequent organizational meeting. Mississippi, another SWC contender at the outset, failed to pursue potential membership. Phillips (Oklahoma) was a conference member for one season, 1920.

OLD OAKEN BUCKET

The prize that goes to the winner of the Indiana-Purdue game. In the summer of 1925 in Chicago, alumni groups from both universities agreed that an award should be presented to the victor in the big game—and the bucket, described as a "typical Hoosier form of trophy," got the call.

OORANG INDIANS

A National Football League team (1922 and 1923) that was based in Marion, O. Jim Thorpe and Joe Guyon, who had played for Cleveland in 1921, helped to form the Oorang club, which was made up of Indian standouts (a number of whom, like Thorpe and Guyon, had competed for the Carlisle Indian Industrial School). The Oorang Indians found the going tough in the NFL, however, winning only three of 19 games in two seasons before disbanding.

"Oorang" was the name of the Ohio dog kennels owned by the football team's sponsor.

PACIFIC-10 CONFERENCE

Collegiate league whose origin dates to 1916, when the four-team Pacific Coast Conference began play. Charter members were Oregon, Oregon State, Washington and California. By 1928, the PCC had expanded to 10 teams with the addition of Washington State, Stanford, Southern California, Idaho, Montana and UCLA. Montana left the conference in 1950, and the PCC played as a nine-team league through 1958. The PCC gave way in 1959 to the Atlantic Association of Western Universities, which consisted of Southern Cal, UCLA, California, Stanford and Washington. In 1962, Washington State returned to the fold and in 1964 Oregon and Oregon State rejoined their old adversaries. The league was renamed the Pacific-8 Conference in 1968, and it became the Pacific-10 in 1978 with the addition of Arizona and Arizona State.

WALTER PAYTON

The National Football League's all-time leading rusher, having gained 13,309 yards through the 1984 season. Jim Brown had held the NFL career rushing record entering 1984, totaling 12,312 yards for the Cleveland Browns from 1957 through 1965. The Chicago Bears' Payton trailed Brown by 687 yards as the '84 campaign began, but he rolled to 621 yards in the Bears' first five games. Then, on October 7, 1984, Payton surpassed Brown's mark during a 154-yard rushing performance against the New Orleans Saints at Chicago's Soldier Field.

Payton, who entered the NFL in 1975, shattered another Brown record against the Saints, running for 100 yards in an NFL game for the 59th time. By the end of the '84 season, Payton had run his number of 100-yard games to 63 (five more than Brown).

PHILADELPHIA QUAKERS

American Football League champions in 1926 (this AFL folded after one season), the Quakers got a chance to exhibit their wares against a National Football League team in a postseason clash with the New York Giants. The Quakers didn't exactly strike a blow for equality between the leagues, losing to the Giants, 31-0—and the Giants had finished in seventh place in the NFL.

Brian Piccolo, former NCAA one-season rushing champion, was an effective runner for the Chicago Bears (left) in 1968. But, stricken by cancer, Piccolo died two years later. Pallbearers at his funeral (below) included former teammates Gale Sayers (striped suit) and Dick Butkus (center foreground).

PHIL-PITT

The 1943 National Football League team that was made up of players from the Philadelphia Eagles and the Pittsburgh Steelers. Because of the economic and manpower crunch caused by World War II, the NFL's two Pennsylvania clubs decided to merge forces for the '43 season and became known as Phil-Pitt. The so-called "Steagles," co-coached by Eagles Coach Greasy Neale and Steelers Coach Walt Kiesling, played home games in both Philadelphia and Pittsburgh and managed to post a 5-4-1 record despite the strange amalgam.

BRIAN PICCOLO

The 1964 NCAA rushing champion and four-year member of the Chicago Bears who died of cancer on June 16, 1970, at age 26. Piccolo ran for a nation-leading 1,044 yards as a Wake Forest senior, edging Illinois' Jim Grabowski by 40 yards. As a National Football League player from 1966 through 1969, he rushed for 927 yards on 258 carries, netted 537 yards on 58 receptions and scored five touchdowns overall.

When Piccolo stood out in the Wake Forest backfield in '64, the Demon Deacons' quarterback was John Mackovic (who in 1983 became coach of the NFL's Kansas City Chiefs).

PITTSBURGH PIRATES

Arthur J. Rooney's National Football League franchise that began play in 1933. Owning a pro football team proved discouraging for Rooney, who watched his clubs compile a 24-62-5 record from '33 through 1940. Rooney, in fact, sold his team—which had been renamed the Steelers in 1940—to Alexis Thompson after the '40 NFL season and bought into the Bert Bell-owned Philadelphia Eagles. But by springtime of 1941, Rooney was back on the scene in Pittsburgh as he and Bell swapped their Philadelphia franchise for Thompson's Pittsburgh club.

PORTSMOUTH SPARTANS

The 1930-1933 National Football League team that was moved from its southern-Ohio base to Detroit in 1934 and renamed the Lions. The club got off to a rousing start in '34, shutting out its first seven opponents and winning its first 10 games. However, the Lions lost their last three games (dropping the final two to the Chicago Bears, who finished 13-0 in the regular season).

POTTSVILLE MAROONS

Pennsylvania team that had a shot at the 1925 National Football League championship but threw away its title aspirations by arranging a big-money game against the Notre Dame All-Stars in Philadelphia—a scheduling decision that, considering the presence of the NFL's Frankford Yellowjackets in the Philadelphia metropolitan area, clearly was in violation of the league's territorial-rights provisions. While the Maroons defeated the squad of former Fighting Irish players, 9-7, in their December 12 meeting, Pottsville saw its franchise forfeited to the NFL with eight days remaining in the season (and the Chicago Cardinals won the league championship).

Fueling Pottsville's unhappiness was the fact that Maroon supporters insisted their team's 21-7 triumph over the Cardinals on December 6 came in a *postseason* game—a clash that Pottsville backers said decided the league championship since the victory gave the Maroons a better record (at the time) than Chicago. However, the NFL had a two-week extension to its firm schedule, a period lasting through December 20 in which financially sound teams could continue to play league games and thus improve their records. And Pottsville's game against the Cardinals fell into that portion of the "open-ended" schedule; thus it was merely a regular-season game that inched Pottsville ahead in the standings and not a postseason contest. The final NFL standings for 1925 (ties were thrown out) showed the Cardinals with an 11-2-1 record and Pottsville at 10-2. Perhaps offsetting the question of won-lost marks or how the Maroons might have fared in additional games is the fact that Pottsville—as a result of its defiance of the league's territorial rules—simply wasn't a league member at season's end.

PROVIDENCE STEAMROLLER

Coached by Jim Conzelman, the 1928 Providence team won the National Football League championship. The Steamroller franchise was a member of the NFL from 1925 through 1931.

In 1947, Conzelman coached the Chicago Cardinals to the NFL title.

PURPLE PEOPLE EATERS

Members of the Minnesota Vikings' outstanding defensive unit of the late 1960s and 1970s, a group anchored by ends Jim Marshall and Carl Eller and tackles Alan Page and Gary Larsen (and, later, Doug Sutherland).

TOMMY REAMON

The World Football League's leading rusher in the league's only full season, 1974. The Florida Blazers' Reamon ran for 1,576 yards in '74, edging J.J. Jennings of the Memphis Southmen by 52 yards.

Anthony Davis of the Southern California Sun was atop the 1975 WFL rushing list with 1,200 yards when the league folded on October 22 (just beyond the season's scheduled midway point).

EDDIE RICHARDSON

San Antonio Wings receiver who was leading the World Football League in pass receptions (46) and pass-reception yards (682) for the 1975 season when the WFL folded in October of that year.

ST. LOUIS CARDINALS

Professional football's oldest continuing operation. The Cardinals are an outgrowth of the Morgan Athletic Club, which was founded on Chicago's South Side in 1898. The Morgan team later became known as the Chicago

Normals and the Racine Cardinals (Racine being the name of a Chicago avenue) before taking on the name of Chicago Cardinals in 1922—the year a team from Racine, Wis., joined the National Football League. After the 1959 NFL season, the Cardinals franchise moved to St. Louis.

ST. LOUIS GUNNERS

A team whose National Football League history consisted of three games in 1934. The Gunners entered the NFL when the financially strapped Cincinnati Reds, a team that had gone 3-6-1 in its first NFL season, 1933, threw in the towel after dropping the first eight games of the '34 season. A handful of Reds players joined the Gunners, an independent professional team, and the St. Louis club played the final three games of Cincinnati's schedule. The Gunners defeated Pittsburgh, 6-0, in their NFL debut and then lost to Detroit, 40-7, and Green Bay, 21-14. Burdened with debts (many of which were incurred in Cincinnati), the Gunners franchise collapsed at season's end.

ORBAN (SPEC) SANDERS

Two-time rushing champion in the four-year history of the All-America Football Conference and the only AAFC player to run for 1,000 yards in a season. Playing for the New York Yankees, Sanders gained an AAFC-leading 709 yards in 1946 and then topped the league with a prodigious 1,432 yards in 1947.

SAN DIEGO CHARGERS

Based in Los Angeles when the American Football League began play in 1960, the Chargers franchise spent one season at the Los Angeles Memorial Coliseum before relocating in San Diego in 1961.

SAN FRANCISCO 49ERS

One of the eight original members of the All-America Football Conference in 1946, the 49ers were the AAFC's second-best team in terms of winning percentage in the league's four-year history, posting regular-season records of 9-5, 8-4-2, 12-2 and 9-3 (38-14-2, .722). The Cleveland Browns were 47-4-3, .898. In 1950, the 49ers—along with the Browns and the Baltimore Colts of the disbanded AAFC—began play in the National Football League.

SAN FRANCISCO 49ERS, CINCINNATI BENGALS

National Football League clubs that compiled 2-14 (49ers) and 4-12 (Bengals) records in 1979, yet met in Super Bowl XVI two seasons later.

SEATTLE SEAHAWKS, TAMPA BAY BUCCANEERS

National Football League expansion teams that began league competition in 1976. Jack Patera was the original coach of the Seahawks, who were aligned in the National Conference West in their first NFL season, while John McKay was at the helm of the Buccaneers when Tampa Bay started out as an American Conference West team in '76. In 1977, permanent divisional homes were set for the Seahawks and Bucs, with Seattle placed in the AFC West and Tampa Bay assigned to the NFC Central.

SEVEN BLOCKS OF GRANITE

The virtually impregnable line that led Fordham to 5-1-2 and 7-0-1 records in 1936 and 1937. The Rams' 1936 unit consisted of ends Leo Paquin and Johnny Druze, tackles Ed Franco and Al Babartsky, guards Nat Pierce and Vince Lombardi and center Alex Wojciechowicz. Despite its defensive prowess, the '36 Fordham squad saw its Rose Bowl hopes die in a 7-6 loss to New York University in the season finale. In '37, Druze, Franco, Babartsky and Wojciechowicz returned as "Blocks"; taking over for the graduated Lombardi were Jimmy Hayes and Joe Bernard (who split duty), replacing Pierce was Mike Kochel and succeeding Paquin was Harry Jacunski.

The "Seven Blocks" appellation was first used in reference to the 1930 Fordham line (and it also applied to the '29 forward wall).

SEVEN MULES

The 1924 Notre Dame line behind which the Four Horsemen operated. Ed Hunsinger and Chuck Collins were the ends, Edgar (Rip) Miller and Joe Bach handled the tackle positions, Noble Kizer and John Weibel filled the guard slots and Adam Walsh played center.

SLIPPERY ROCK

Western Pennsylvania university whose ear-catching name seems to delight football fans from coast to coast, particularly on Saturday afternoons when—at big-time stadiums—public-address announcers cap their list of collegiate scores with the Slippery Rock result. The college, which in 1983 changed its name from Slippery Rock State College to Slippery Rock University, is located in Slippery Rock, Pa., boasts a student enrollment of approximately 6,200, plays its football in NCAA Division II and has green and white as its school colors. The Rockets began playing football in 1900, 11 years after the school's founding, and went 7-0-1 in 1933 and 8-0 in 1939. Slippery Rock compiled a 9-1 record in 1962 and was 32-7-2 from 1971 through 1974. Perhaps best indicating the appeal of "The Rock" is that the university twice has been scheduled for games at Michigan Stadium, with more than 60,000 fans turning out for the Rockets' 1979 game in Ann Arbor against Shippensburg State.

Why "Slippery Rock"? Cavalrymen, the story goes, were able to escape a 1779 confrontation with Seneca Indians by crossing a rock-filled creek without incident—thanks to their heavy boots. However, the moccasin-clad Indians supposedly lost their footing on the large, smooth rocks and were unable to continue their pursuit of the soldiers (thus the origin of the names Slippery Rock Creek and Slippery Rock, the nearby settlement).

SOUTHEASTERN CONFERENCE

Collegiate league that had 13 members when it made its debut in 1933—Alabama, Auburn, Kentucky, Florida, Tennessee, Vanderbilt, Mississippi, Mis-

Slippery Rock University, located in western Pennsylvania, has a small-college football program with a big reputation.

sissippi State, Georgia, Georgia Tech, Sewanee, Louisiana State and Tulane. The conference currently has 10 teams, with dropouts Sewanee, Georgia Tech and Tulane having played their final SEC football seasons in 1940, 1963 and 1965.

During its eight years of SEC football competition, Sewanee (also known as University of the South, in Sewanee, Tenn.) compiled a league record of 0-37.

MAC SPEEDIE

Cleveland Browns receiver who established All-America Football Conference career records with 211 catches and 3,554 yards in receptions.

STALEY STARCH CO.

Decatur, Ill., firm whose company-sponsored football team evolved into the Chicago Bears of National Football League fame. In 1920, A.E. Staley, company owner, hired George Halas to work in his facility and form a Staleys Athletic Club football team. The Halas-guided Staleys proceeded to seek— and gain—a spot that year in the newly formed American Professional Football Association. Staley incurred financial setbacks in his business after the '20 season, though, and he ended his sponsorship of the team. Halas took over the club and moved it to Chicago, with a financial inducement prompting Halas to keep "Staleys" in the team name for the 1921 season. In 1922, with all ties to Staley and Decatur now history, Halas decided to call his club the Bears (he liked the idea of an association with baseball's Cubs, whose ballpark his football team was using). Having gone from the Decatur Staleys in '20 to the Chicago Staleys in '21 to the Chicago Bears in '22, the football team settled into success-laden stability. And from the day in 1920 when he founded the Staleys to his death on October 31, 1983, Halas was a constant part of that success as a player, coach (for 40 seasons) and owner.

STAPLETON STAPES

Staten Island-based team that competed in the National Football League from 1929 through 1932.

STEEL CURTAIN

The nickname given to the front four of the Pittsburgh Steelers' crunching defensive unit of the 1970s. Forming the "Curtain" were tackles Joe Greene and Ernie Holmes and ends L.C. Greenwood and Dwight White.

JAN STENERUD

The National Football League's all-time leader in field goals, having kicked 358 three-pointers through the 1984 season. Stenerud was the Kansas City Chiefs' placekicker from 1967 through 1979, handled the kicking duties for the Green Bay Packers from 1980 through 1983 and kicked for the Minnesota Vikings in '84.

HANK STRAM

One of the eight original coaches in the 1960-born American Football League, and he coached in the AFL—and for the same franchise—all 10 years of the league's existence. Stram directed the Dallas Texans from '60 through 1962, then coached the relocated AFL club from 1963 through 1969 when it was the Kansas City Chiefs. (Stram, in fact, guided the Chiefs through 1974, the club's fifth season in the National Football League.)

The seven other league coaches when the AFL began play in 1960 were Frank Filchock (Denver Broncos), Eddie Erdelatz (Oakland Raiders), Sid Gillman (Los Angeles Chargers), Lou Rymkus (Houston Oilers), Sammy Baugh (New York Titans), Lou Saban (Boston Patriots) and Buster Ramsey (Buffalo Bills).

FRAN TARKENTON

The National Football League's all-time leader in passing yardage and touchdown passes. Tarkenton, who began his pro career in 1961 and played a total of 18 NFL seasons with the Minnesota Vikings (two stints) and the New York Giants, threw for 47,003 yards and 342 TDs.

AUNDRA THOMPSON

He holds the distinction of having been traded—along with high draft selections—in deals a week apart that netted his former teams first John Jefferson and then Wes Chandler, two of the National Football League's premier wide receivers. On September 22, 1981, the Green Bay Packers swapped Thompson (also a wide receiver) and first-round picks in the 1982 and 1984 NFL drafts and second-round choices in 1983 and '84 to the San Diego Chargers for Jefferson and a first-round selection in '82. Then, on September 29, 1981, the Chargers dealt Thompson and first- and third-round picks in the '82 draft to the New Orleans Saints for Chandler.

JIM THORPE, JOE CARR

The first two presidents of what is now the National Football League. When the league was formed in September 1920 as the American Professional Football Association, Thorpe was awarded the presidency (mostly because of his high profile as a playing great). Within seven months, though, the APFA turned the presidency over to business-oriented Carr, manager of the Columbus Panhandles football club and a man with a strong background in sports-franchise operations.

TED TOLLNER

A survivor of the October 29, 1960, plane crash in Toledo, O., that killed 22 persons, including 16 players and the team manager of the Cal Poly-San Luis Obispo football team. The Mustangs had lost to Bowling Green, 50-6, that Saturday afternoon, and the plane that was to carry the team home crashed on takeoff.

Tollner, Cal Poly's starting quarterback in 1960 and 1961 (he passed for a total of 1,864 yards and 13 touchdowns in those seasons), became coach of the Southern California Trojans in 1983.

22, 8

The number of National Football League teams in 1926 and then in 1932 (when the nation was in the throes of the Depression). Eighteen teams that competed in the '26 NFL race had fallen by the wayside by the opening of the '32 season—the Kansas City Cowboys, Frankford Yellowjackets, Pottsville Maroons, Duluth Eskimos, Buffalo Rangers, Providence Steamroller, Hartford Blues, Detroit Panthers, Milwaukee Badgers, Brooklyn Lions, Akron Indians, Dayton Triangles, Hammond Pros, Canton Bulldogs, Columbus Tigers, Racine Legion and two road teams, the Louisville Colonels and Los Angeles Buccaneers. The Chicago Bears, Chicago Cardinals, Green Bay Packers and New York Giants were 1926 NFL entrants who were still in business six years later. Also in the 1932 NFL alignment were the Portsmouth Spartans, Brooklyn Dodgers, Stapleton Stapes and Boston Braves.

HOWARD TWILLEY, RON SELLERS, ELMO WRIGHT

Major-college football's career leaders in passes caught, receiving yardage and touchdown receptions. Twilley made 261 catches while playing for Tulsa from 1963 through 1965, Sellers amassed 3,598 yards in receptions as a Florida State receiver from 1966 through 1968 and Houston's Wright hauled in 34 touchdown passes from 1968 through 1970.

WASHINGTON (ST. LOUIS), IOWA

Two of the five original teams in the league that evolved into the Big Eight Conference. Joining the St. Louis school and the Hawkeyes when the Missouri Valley Intercollegiate Athletic Association opened play in 1907 were Kansas, Missouri and Nebraska. By the 1925 season, the league had grown to 10 schools, with Iowa dropping out early but Iowa State, Drake, Kansas State, Grinnell (Iowa), Oklahoma and Oklahoma A&M gaining admission. In May 1928, six of the state schools—Kansas, Missouri, Nebraska, Iowa State, Kansas State and Oklahoma—decided to go it alone, bringing about the Big Six Conference (although the league's original name was still its official title). Colorado was added to the conference in December 1947 and Oklahoma State (formerly Oklahoma A&M) rejoined the league in June 1957. The addition of Colorado, which began league football competition in 1948, changed the league into the Big Seven and Oklahoma State's entrance—the Cowboys first played for the conference football title in 1960—gave birth to the Big Eight.

It wasn't until 1964 that the name Big Eight Conference—while used almost exclusively—became official for the league (which through 1963 was, technically, still the Missouri Valley Intercollegiate Athletic Association).

WICHITA STATE

University whose football team was the victim of an October 2, 1970, airplane crash. One of two planes scheduled to transport the Shockers to Logan, Utah, for a game against Utah State crashed in the Colorado Rockies west of Denver, killing 31 persons. Among the fatalities were Coach Ben Wilson, Athletic Director Bert Katzenmeyer and 14 players.

Wichita State, which had played and lost three games in 1970 before the crash, did not call off the remainder of the season. Assistant Bob Seaman was named head coach, and the Shockers received NCAA permission to reinforce their squad with freshmen (who weren't eligible for varsity competition at that time). Wichita State began its so-called Second Season on October 24 in Little Rock against powerful Arkansas and was beaten, 62-0. At season's end, the Shockers were 0-9.

GEORGE WILSON, PAUL BROWN

Original coaches of the Miami Dolphins and the Cincinnati Bengals—the expansion teams that joined the American Football League in 1966 and 1968. Wilson, in fact, coached the Dolphins in all four of their AFL seasons (1966 through 1969); Brown guided the Bengals in both of their AFL campaigns (1968, 1969), plus six more years in the National Football League.

LUIS ZENDEJAS

Major-college football's all-time leading scorer, having made 368 points (78 field goals, 134 conversion kicks) from 1981 through 1984 as Arizona State's placekicker.

Among the oddities in football history are the careers of K. L. Berry and the brothers Nesser. Berry (right) lettered for Texas in 1912, 1914, 1915 and . . . 1924, at the unlikely age of 31. The Nesser brothers (below, left to right, Ted, John, Phil, Al, Frank and Fred) formed the nucleus of the Columbus Panhandles, an Ohio professional team in the first quarter of this century.

TWO-MINUTE WARNING

INNOVATIONS, ODDITIES, FIRSTS AND LASTS

RICK ABERNETHY

The Kansas linebacker who not only experienced a memorable final game as a collegian (apparently being the Jayhawks' "12th man" in the 1969 Orange Bowl), but saw his collegiate career get off to a strange start, too. Abernethy's first game in a Kansas uniform came on September 18, 1965, in Lubbock, Tex., against Texas Tech—and officials called the night contest early in the fourth quarter because of a tornado alert. Texas Tech, ahead 26-7 at the time, was declared the winner.

ACTION POINT

The World Football League's point-after-touchdown, which could be scored only on a pass or a run from 2½ yards out. In addition to disdaining football's conventional conversion kick, the WFL changed the worth of the touchdown from six points to seven.

HERB ADDERLEY, FORREST GREGG

Members of five National Football League championship teams while playing for the Green Bay Packers in the 1960s, they played their last pro games with the Dallas Cowboys. After spending nine seasons with the Packers, Adderley played his last three NFL years (1970 through 1972) for Dallas and appeared in two Super Bowls with the Cowboys. Gregg was a member of the Packers for 14 years, then finished his career in 1971 with Dallas.

Lance Alworth, like Adderley and Gregg a member of the Pro Football Hall of Fame, also finished his career with Dallas after winning acclaim elsewhere (with the San Diego Chargers). Alworth, a Charger for nine years, spent the 1971 and 1972 seasons with the Cowboys and played in Super Bowl VI with Dallas.

GEORGE ALLEN, DON CORYELL

Successive coaches for a California football team—and, no, it wasn't a National Football League club. Instead, it was the Whittier College squad. Allen, at age 33, took over as Whittier coach in 1951 and directed the Poets through 1956 before becoming an assistant coach with the NFL's Los Angeles Rams. Replacing Allen at Whittier in '57 was the 32-year-old Coryell, who spent three seasons as the Poets' coach before being named an assistant at Southern California.

LANCE ALWORTH

The first player from the American Football League of the 1960s to make the Pro Football Hall of Fame. Alworth, who played in the AFL for the San Diego Chargers from 1962 through 1969 and in the National Football League with the Chargers in 1970 and the Dallas Cowboys in 1971 and 1972, was inducted into the Canton, O., shrine in 1978.

ALAN AMECHE

Having arrived in Baltimore amid the fanfare of being a Heisman Trophy winner and a first-round draft choice, he ran 79 yards for a Colts touchdown on his first carry in the National Football League. Ameche's pro debut came on September 25, 1955, in Baltimore as the Colts knocked off the Chicago Bears, 23-17. Overall, Ameche gained 194 yards against the Bears on 21 rushing attempts.

JOE AUER

Miami player who returned the opening kickoff for a touchdown when the Dolphins played the first regular-season game in their history, September 2,

1966, against the Oakland Raiders. Despite Auer's dramatic 95-yard sprint at the Orange Bowl, the Raiders rebounded for a 23-14 American Football League triumph as Tom Flores rifled two touchdown passes for the winners.

BALBOA STADIUM

The first home of the San Diego Chargers. The Chargers played their American Football League home games at Balboa Stadium from 1961 through 1966.

LARRY BALL, MAULTY MOORE

Linebacker and defensive lineman who played for the 17-0 Miami Dolphins in 1972 and then saw action with the 0-14 Tampa Bay Buccaneers in 1976.

CLIFF BATTLES

Rushing for 215 yards on 16 carries for the Boston Redskins in an October 8, 1933, game against the New York Giants, he became the first National Football League player to run for 200 yards in a game (since the league started keeping statistics in 1932).

BEARS STADIUM

The name by which Mile High Stadium was known when the Denver Broncos first used the facility in 1960 as a member of the new American Football League. Originally a 16,000-seat minor league baseball park, Bears Stadium had a football capacity of more than 34,000 by the time the AFL began play in '60. The park, renamed Mile High Stadium in December 1968, has undergone periodic expansion, with capacity reaching 75,100.

K.L. BERRY

Texas lineman who earned letters in 1912, 1914, 1915 and . . . 1924. Berry entered military service in 1916 and didn't return to college life until '24, when he proceeded to win All-Southwest Conference honors for the Longhorns at age 31.

HUGO BEZDEK

The man who coached the Cleveland Rams in their first National Football League season, 1937. Bezdek's club staggered to a 1-10 record in '37.

GEORGE BLANDA

Longtime quarterback/placekicker who scored the final four points of his National Football League-record 2,002 career points in a December 21, 1975, game in Oakland against the Kansas City Chiefs. Blanda made four conversion kicks—the last coming after Pete Banaszak's one-yard touchdown run in the fourth quarter—as the Raiders downed the Chiefs, 28-20.

MARLIN BRISCOE

The first black player to start at quarterback in as many as five games in

243

one season in National Football League-American Football League history. Briscoe started for the Denver Broncos in game four of the 1968 AFL season, then drew game-opening assignments in the final four contests of the year. Overall, he appeared in 11 games for the '68 Broncos, throwing 14 touchdown passes and gaining 7.5 yards per carry on 41 rushing attempts.

BROWN, GRAY AND GREEN

The colorfully named pass-reception leaders in the National Football Conference in 1983. Topping the NFC with 78 catches each were Charlie Brown of the Washington Redskins, Earnest Gray of the New York Giants and Roy Green of the St. Louis Cardinals.

JIM BROWN

Cleveland Browns great who scored the first of his National Football League-record 126 touchdowns on a five-yard pass from Tom O'Connell in the Browns' 24-7 triumph over the Philadelphia Eagles on October 13, 1957, in Cleveland. The TD came in Brown's third game as a pro.

ADRIAN BURK

The back judge in the September 28, 1969, game in Bloomington, Minn., in which Joe Kapp of the Minnesota Vikings threw seven touchdown passes against the Baltimore Colts. Burk was no stranger to such performances, having passed for seven TDs himself while quarterbacking the Philadelphia Eagles against the Washington Redskins in a 1954 National Football League game. Burk and Kapp are two of only five players in NFL history to hit on seven scoring passes in one contest.

BUSCH STADIUM

The longtime St. Louis ballpark (formerly called Sportsman's Park) in which Cleveland's Jim Brown scored his 126th and last touchdown in National Football League play. Brown, the NFL's all-time leader in touchdowns scored, collected the TD on a three-yard run as the Browns defeated the St. Louis Cardinals, 27-24, on December 19, 1965.

CHICAGO CARDINALS

The team against whom George Blanda scored the first three points of his 26-season professional football career. Blanda, the National Football League's all-time top scorer with 2,002 points, first got on the scoreboard with a 36-yard field goal for the Chicago Bears in an October 2, 1949, NFL game against the Cardinals at Comiskey Park. The first-period kick helped the Bears to a 17-7 triumph.

'CHINESE BANDITS'

The name that Paul Dietzel gave to his gung-ho defensive units at Louisiana State and Army in the late 1950s and early 1960s. The coach said he borrowed a line from the "Terry and the Pirates" comic strip—"There is nothing tougher than a Chinese bandit"—in naming his defensive stalwarts, whose scrap, hustle and swarming style of play helped LSU to the national title in 1958. Dietzel said the 1959 "Bandits" were more than a plucky group, calling them truly gifted athletes (who played a major role in the Bayou Tigers' No. 3 national ranking that year). Dietzel continued to field a "Bandits" unit when he became coach at West Point in 1962.

Dietzel devised a three-platoon system at LSU in 1958, deftly deploying the units within the substitution rules in effect at the time (the return of platoon football was still seven years away, but substitution was becoming more liberalized all the time). He had a "White" unit that consisted of the Tigers' top 11 all-around players and played offensively and defensively, a "Go" or attack team made up of LSU's best offensive players from the remainder of the squad and the defense-minded "Bandits."

GEORGE (POTSY) CLARK

The first coach in the history of the Detroit Lions, directing the club from 1934 through 1936. Clark, who coached Portsmouth in its four seasons in the National Football League before the Spartans moved to Detroit and became the Lions, was succeeded as Lions coach by another Clark—Earl (Dutch) Clark.

CLEVELAND BROWNS, NEW YORK JETS

Opponents in the first game of ABC-TV's Monday Night Football series, squaring off on September 21, 1970, in Cleveland. With play-by-play man Keith Jackson and colleagues Howard Cosell and Don Meredith describing the action, the Browns prevailed, 31-21, in a National Football League game that featured a 94-yard kickoff return by the Browns' Homer Jones to start the second half.

Cleveland's Gary Collins was the first man to score in the history of the Monday telecasts, taking an eight-yard touchdown pass from Bill Nelsen in the first quarter of the '70 Browns-Jets game.

CLEVELAND BROWNS, NEW YORK YANKEES

Opponents in the All-America Football Conference's first championship game, played December 22, 1946, in Cleveland. The Browns won, 14-9, with Otto Graham's 16-yard touchdown pass to Dante Lavelli in the fourth quarter proving decisive.

COLUMBUS PANHANDLES, BROTHERS NESSER

The Ohio professional team of the first quarter of this century and the football-playing brothers—six in all—who dominated the squad. Since most team members were employed by the Panhandle Division of the Pennsylvania Railroad, the nickname "Panhandles" obviously fit the rough-and-tumble squad, which featured the play of Ted, John, Phil, Fred, Frank and Al Nesser. Ted coached the team.

Another Nesser, Ted's son Charles, was added to the Columbus Panhandles cast in the early 1920s.

OGDEN COMPTON, DICK (NIGHT TRAIN) LANE

Chicago Cardinals players who hooked up on a 98-yard touchdown pass against the Green Bay Packers on November 13, 1955—and the spectacular strike proved to be the only scoring pass of Compton's National Football League career and the lone TD reception for Lane in the NFL.

COTTON BOWL

Home stadium for the Dallas Cowboys from their first season in the National Football League, 1960, through mid-October of 1971. On October 24, 1971, the Cowboys played their first game at Texas Stadium in Irving, Tex., beating the New England Patriots, 44-21.

JIM CROWLEY, ELMER LAYDEN

When Crowley was named commissioner of the All-America Football Conference on November 22, 1944 (the AAFC didn't begin play until 1946), it meant that U.S. pro football's two major leagues were under the rule of former members of Notre Dame's Four Horsemen. Elmer Layden had been selected National Football League commissioner in 1941. Layden served as head of the NFL until January 1946, while Crowley was AAFC commissioner until January 1947.

DAYTON-COLUMBUS, ROCK ISLAND-MUNCIE

The matchups in the first games in the history of the American Professional Football Association (later renamed the National Football League). On October 3, 1920, the Dayton Triangles downed the Columbus Panhandles, 14-0, in Dayton, O., and the Rock Island Independents—led by Arnold Wyman's three touchdowns—walloped the Muncie Flyers, 45-0, in Rock Island, Ill.

Some football historians claim that the 1920 APFA, which did not keep standings, made no distinction between games involving two league members and contests between one league club and an outside team. They also contend that early-season "outsiders" probably were considered league members once they agreed to follow APFA rules (which curbed player raids) and met APFA teams. However, the Football Trivia Book is basing APFA historical data on games involving two "established" APFA clubs (teams that were among those represented during the league's founding at a September 17, 1920, meeting in Canton, O., plus the four clubs that joined the APFA soon thereafter).

LORIN F. DELAND

The chess expert and military strategist who devised football's flying wedge, the devastating team-wide charge downfield that concealed the ball-carrier. First employed by Harvard in 1892, the mass-momentum play was outlawed in 1894 because of its risks to life and limb.

DENVER BRONCOS

The first American Football League team to defeat a National Football

League club—and although the Broncos' victory came in an exhibition game, the triumph was special for the respect-hungry AFL. In the second meeting of any kind between the leagues—the first was Green Bay's 35-10 thumping of Kansas City in Super Bowl I almost seven months earlier—the Broncos upset the Detroit Lions, 13-7, on August 5, 1967, in Denver.

Lance Alworth, one of the AFL's all-time greats, remembers the night well. "We (the San Diego Chargers) were playing the Raiders and were in the huddle when the score was announced," said Alworth, recalling an exhibition game in Oakland that was contested the same evening. "I was so interested in the score I didn't pay any attention to (quarterback) John Hadl's call. I wound up going to the wrong side to line up."

DENVER BRONCOS, BOSTON PATRIOTS

Meeting in Boston on the night of September 9, 1960, they played the first game in the history of the 1960-69 American Football League—and the Broncos won, 13-10. The Patriots' Gino Cappelletti scored the league's first points, kicking a 34-yard field goal in the opening quarter; Denver's Al Carmichael notched the AFL's first touchdown, scoring on a 59-yard pass from Frank Tripucka in the second period.

DENVER BRONCOS 35, PITTSBURGH STEELERS 35

The final score in the first regular-season overtime game in National Football League history. With the NFL having adopted the sudden-death system of breaking ties (with a maximum of one 15-minute period) in the off-season, the Broncos and Steelers were deadlocked at 35-35 in week two of the 1974 season when Pittsburgh's Roy Gerela attempted a 25-yard field goal with 5 seconds remaining in regulation play. The Broncos blocked the kick, however, sending the September 22 game at Mile High Stadium into an overtime session. In the only scoring threat of the extra 15 minutes, Denver's Jim Turner tried a 41-yard field goal—but was wide (barely).

Pittsburgh quarterback Joe Gilliam was the day's outstanding player, completing 31 of 50 pass attempts for 348 yards and one touchdown and also running one yard for a TD.

DETROIT LIONS, NEW YORK GIANTS

Teams that played the last 0-0 game in National Football League history, battling to the deadlock in rain and mud on November 7, 1943, in Detroit. Neither club moved inside its opponent's 15-yard line (New York advanced into Detroit territory only once) during a game in which the Lions' Augie Lio missed on three field-goal tries and the Giants' Ward Cuff was off target on one attempt.

DAN DEVINE

Longtime college coach who suffered a leg fracture while making his National Football League coaching debut on September 19, 1971. Devine, directing the Packers against the New York Giants in a '71 NFL season opener in Green Bay, went down in a pileup near the Pack's bench in the fourth quarter. Green Bay's Doug Hart had intercepted a Fran Tarkenton pass seconds earlier, and players from both teams went sprawling out of bounds on Hart's return. The Giants' Bob Hyland, a former first-round draft choice of the Packers, couldn't slow his momentum and plowed into Devine, who was carried from the field on a stretcher. New York further ruined Devine's day by beating the Packers, 42-40.

DOME-ICILE

Quarterback Archie Manning played for a total of three teams in the 1982 and 1983 National Football League seasons—and never got outdoors for a home game. Manning saw duty with the New Orleans Saints, Houston Oilers and Minnesota Vikings, all of whom have covered stadiums (Louisiana Superdome, Astrodome and Hubert H. Humphrey Metrodome).

BUFF DONELLI

He coached the Duquesne University Dukes football team and the Pittsburgh Steelers at the same time for a one-month stretch of the 1941 season. While the Dukes continued toward an unbeaten season during Donelli's dual reign (Duquesne finished 8-0 in '41), the Steelers went 0-5 under his tutelage. Donelli, who replaced Bert Bell as Pittsburgh coach after two games of the 1941 National Football League season, was ordered to relinquish his job as the Steelers' coach by NFL Commissioner Elmer Layden (who said Donelli's double coaching role was not in the league's best interests).

FORREST DOUDS

The first coach in the history of the Pittsburgh Steelers franchise. When Douds coached Pittsburgh's National Football League team in 1933, it was known as the Pirates.

PADDY DRISCOLL

The Chicago Cardinals player who put a damper on Red Grange's debut with the Chicago Bears by repeatedly punting away from the former Illinois sensation during a 0-0 National Football League game played before 36,000 fans at Wrigley Field on November 26, 1925. Driscoll's tactics in the Thanksgiving Day game incurred the wrath of Chicago fans (on both sides), who had hoped to see Grange ramble on runbacks.

Grange, who played his last collegiate game five days before the scoreless deadlock, had agreed to join the Bears for the remainder of the '25 season and for a lucrative and far-flung postseason tour (which greatly enhanced pro football's appeal nationwide).

FAKING IT

The tactics Notre Dame was accused of using in salvaging a 14-14 tie with Iowa on November 21, 1953, as the Fighting Irish scored their touchdowns after "injuries" stopped the clock in the dying seconds of each half. The Irish, unbeaten in seven games entering the contest and eyeing the national championship (Notre Dame would finish second to Maryland), were poised

Charles Follis (left center) is regarded as the first black professional football player. Follis was a member of the Shelby (Ohio) club when this picture was taken in 1904.

at Iowa's 11-yard line in the closing moments of the first half but had no way to stop the clock—or so it appeared. However, Notre Dame tackle Frank Varrichione was spotted stretched out on the field, and a timeout was called with 2 seconds left in the first half to tend to the "injured." Quarterback Ralph Guglielmi proceeded to hit Dan Shannon with a touchdown pass, and the extra-point kick netted Notre Dame a 7-7 deadlock. Trailing 14-7 with fewer than 30 seconds remaining in the game, the Irish were positioned at the Hawkeyes' 9 but had no way to stop the clock—ah, guess again. This time, tackle Art Hunter and end Don Penza went down for the Irish, necessitating another "injury" timeout. Guglielmi, after firing two incompletions, teamed with Shannon on another scoring pass as the clock showed 6 seconds to play in the game. The conversion kick was good, enabling the Irish to tie Iowa.

In 1954, collegiate rules-makers condemned the faking of injuries to stop the clock, calling the action "dishonest, unsportsmanlike and contrary to rules."

DON FAUROT

The coach who created the split-T offense, having introduced the formation in 1941 at Missouri. The '41 Tigers went 8-1 in the regular season, then lost to Fordham in the Sugar Bowl. Faurot posted a 101-79-10 record in 19 seasons (1935 through 1942, 1946 through 1956) as Missouri's coach.

BEATTIE FEATHERS

The first 1,000-yard rusher in National Football League play (since the league began keeping statistics in 1932), running for 1,004 yards in 1934 as a Chicago Bear rookie. It was 13 years before another NFL player attained 1,000 yards on the ground, with Steve Van Buren of the Philadelphia Eagles gaining 1,008 in 1947.

RAY FLAHERTY

The coach of the Redskins in their first season in Washington, 1937—and he directed the 'Skins to the National Football League championship that year. Flaherty had coached the Boston Redskins to a divisional title in 1936.

CHARLES FOLLIS

The man regarded as professional football's first black player, with documented evidence showing that he played for pay as early as 1904 with the Shelby Athletic Club of Shelby, O. A halfback who was called the "Black Cyclone From Wooster" (he grew up in Wooster, O.), Follis played for the Shelby team from 1902 through 1906.

ROBERT FOLWELL

After five seasons as Navy's football coach, he became the first coach of the National Football League's New York Giants in 1925. In his lone season at the Giants' helm, Folwell guided New York to an 8-4 record.

FORDHAM, PITTSBURGH

Collegiate teams that fought to 0-0 ties in three successive seasons—1935, 1936 and 1937.

FRED GEHRKE

Los Angeles Rams halfback who changed the look of National Football League headgear in 1948. Tired of the plain leather helmets that were prevalent in the league at the time, Gehrke—an art major at the University of Utah—decided to do something about the "dull" look. Before the '48 NFL season, Gehrke hand-painted 70 leather helmets blue and then made a free rendering of a ram's horns in gold on each headgear. Gehrke's work not

Fred Gehrke, the Los Angeles Rams halfback who changed the look of National Football League headgear, models his new-look helmet as he shakes hands with Glenn Davis in 1948. Davis, the former Army great, was on leave from the service at the time.

only was a hit within the Rams' organization, it proved a leaguewide attention-getter and led to the introduction of colorful, emblem-oriented helmets by other professional teams.

JOHN GILLIAM

Rookie who got the New Orleans Saints off to a rousing start in their first regular-season National Football League game, returning the opening kickoff 94 yards for a touchdown in a September 17, 1967, contest against the Los Angeles Rams. The Rams ruined the Saints' NFL debut, though, by coming back for a 27-13 victory at Tulane Stadium.

PETE GOGOLAK

The first of the soccer-style kickers in U.S. pro football, breaking in with the Buffalo Bills of the American Football League in 1964. Gogolak spent two years with the Bills and then played nine seasons for the New York Giants of the National Football League.

Charlie Gogolak, Pete's brother, kicked in the NFL for the Washington Redskins from 1966 through 1968 and for the Boston and New England Patriots from 1970 through 1972. Charlie also used the soccer style.

GREY CUP GAME, 1962

The Canadian Football League championship game, played in Toronto, that took two days to complete. The December 1, 1962, title game between the Winnipeg Blue Bombers and the Hamilton Tiger-Cats was called because of dense fog with 9 minutes, 29 seconds remaining in the fourth quarter. The contest was finished December 2, with Coach Bud Grant's Winnipeg team emerging as a 28-27 victor.

DAVE HAMPTON'S 1,000, ER, 995

Atlanta's Hampton achieved a running back's season goal in the fourth quarter of the Falcons' December 17, 1972, regular-season finale against Kansas City, gaining his 70th yard of the day and thus increasing his year's rushing total to exactly 1,000 yards. The game was stopped when fourth-year pro Hampton—who had made a total of only 787 yards with Green Bay in the three previous seasons—joined the 1,000 club, and he was awarded the game ball. Later in the contest, though, Hampton was nailed for a six-yard loss. He carried the ball only once more, picking up one yard and thereby closing with a season total of 995 yards, as the Falcons went down to a 17-14 defeat in Atlanta.

There was more agony for Hampton in 1973. Needing 87 yards against New Orleans in the Falcons' final game to reach 1,000, Hampton was given the ball 27 times. Despite the furious attempt to hit the select figure, Hampton rushed for only 84 yards and ended the '73 National Football League season with 997 yards.

Hampton finally made it to 1,000—barely—in 1975, finishing with 1,002 yards for the Falcons after netting 61 yards in the season finale against Green Bay.

William (Pudge) Heffelfinger (left) became the first known professional football player in 1892 when he received $500 to play in a game for the Pittsburgh-based Allegheny Athletic Association team.

JIM HART, BOBBY MOORE

They teamed on a 98-yard pass completion for St. Louis in a December 10, 1972, National Football League game against the Los Angeles Rams—but the Cardinals failed to score on the play. With the Cards at their 1-yard line in the second quarter after Los Angeles had been stopped for no gain on a fourth-down rushing attempt, quarterback Hart threw to Moore, who made a leaping catch at the St. Louis 40 and sped goalward. Los Angeles defensive back Al Clark collared Moore at the Rams' 10 and rode the Cardinals' receiver to the ground at the 1. The Cardinals, getting a TD burst from Donny Anderson after the 98-yard play, went on to a 24-14 triumph in the game played in St. Louis.

In 1973, Moore took the name Ahmad Rashad.

WILLIAM (PUDGE) HEFFELFINGER

The first known professional football player in the United States, with an expense account showing a $500 payment to the former Yale star for play-

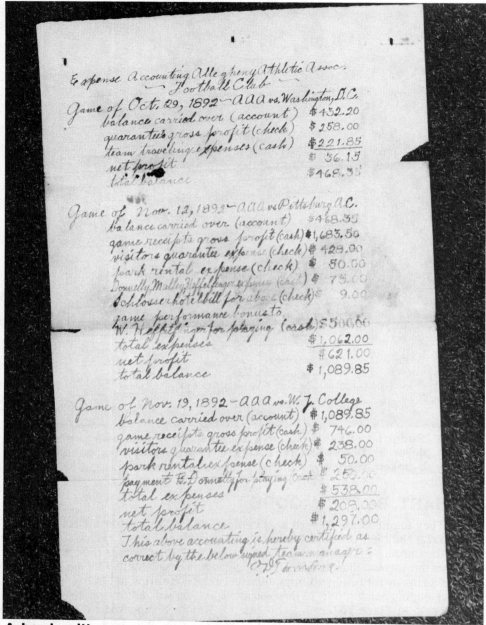

A hand-written expense account for the Allegheny Athletic Association team in 1892 documents the $500 payment to William (Pudge) Heffelfinger, making him the first known professional football player.

ing with the Pittsburgh-based Allegheny Athletic Association team in a November 12, 1892, game against the Pittsburgh Athletic Club. Lineman Heffelfinger, a member of the first All-America team in 1889, scored the lone touchdown of the game (worth four points in those days) as the Allegheny squad stopped the Pittsburgh AC, 4-0.

MARK HENDERSON

A member of the maintenance crew at the New England Patriots' stadium in Foxboro, Mass., on December 12, 1982, and the man who drove a snow sweeper onto the field that day and cleared a path for the Pats' John Smith as Smith prepared to try a fourth-quarter field goal in a 0-0 game with Miami. Henderson, who was on a work-release program from a correctional facility, was waved onto the snow-blanketed turf by Patriots Coach Ron Meyer—much to the consternation of Dolphin players. Smith, who after the game said that Henderson (who cleared yard-line stripes regularly during the game) actually made his job tougher by pushing snow onto the spot from which he preferred to kick, was on target with his 33-yard boot and New England held on for a 3-0 National Football League victory.

"The game's over, so what can you say?" said Miami Coach Don Shula, who had been told by officials that the Dolphins would have been afforded the same "service" had the opportunity presented itself.

HOWARD (RED) HICKEY

The coach who installed the shotgun formation in the San Francisco 49ers' offense in late November of 1960 as the 49ers prepared to play the Baltimore Colts, National Football League champions in 1958 and 1959. Wanting quarterback John Brodie to have a fighting chance November 27 against the Colts' rush, Hickey, pulling out of the closet a formation that had not been used in many years, positioned Brodie seven yards behind center and hoped the alignment would force Baltimore to change its defense. The 49ers upended the Colts, 30-22, as reserve quarterback Bobby Waters—pressed into service because of injuries to Brodie and Y.A. Tittle—rallied his team from a 22-20 fourth-quarter deficit. San Francisco won three of its final four games of the '60 season while using the shotgun after splitting its first eight games.

The 49ers rode the shotgun to a 4-1 start in 1961, a mark that included successive 49-0 and 35-0 victories over the Detroit Lions and Los Angeles Rams. However, in the October 22 Chicago-San Francisco game, Bears middle linebacker Bill George helped turn the shotgun into a popgun by playing on the line of scrimmage and harassing the 49ers' center and quarterback. The Bears coasted, 31-0. San Francisco's shotgun attack—and its season— came undone, with the 49ers finishing with a 7-6-1 record.

ELROY (CRAZY LEGS) HIRSCH

Best known for his pass-receiving feats with the Los Angeles Rams of the National Football League (53 touchdown receptions in nine years, 17 coming in one season), Hirsch played his first three pro seasons—1946, 1947 and 1948—with the Chicago Rockets of the All-America Football Conference.

ROLAND HOOKS

Buffalo running back who carried the ball only four times in the second half of the Bills' September 9, 1979, National Football League game against the Cincinnati Bengals—but scored on each carry. Hooks, who rushed once in the first half for three yards (a non-scoring play), went 3, 32, 4 and 28 yards for his touchdowns as Buffalo broke away from a 10-10 halftime tie and overwhelmed the Bengals, 51-24, in Orchard Park, N.Y.

DON HUTSON

Green Bay receiver whose first catch in the National Football League resulted in an 83-yard scoring play. Hutson, playing his second league game with the Packers, teamed with passer Arnie Herber on the long-distance connection, which came on the first play after the opening kickoff of the September 22, 1935, Packers-Chicago Bears game. Hutson's TD proved enough for Green Bay as the Packers scored a 7-0 victory.

Hutson, the NFL's career leader in touchdown catches with 99, made his final TD reception (Irv Comp was the passer) on November 18, 1945, against the Boston Yanks.

DON HUTSON

The first National Football League player to attain 1,000 yards in receptions in one season (since the league began keeping statistical records in 1932), totaling 1,211 yards for the Green Bay Packers in 1942. Hutson made 74 catches that season, with 17 going for touchdowns.

FRANK (POP) IVY

The last coach in Chicago Cardinals history. Ivy coached the Cardinals in their final two National Football League seasons in Chicago, 1958 and 1959, directing the club to 2-9-1 and 2-10 records. He continued as the Cards' coach when the franchise moved to St. Louis in 1960 and guided the team through 1961.

JEPPESEN STADIUM

The high school facility that served as home for the Houston Oilers in the club's first five seasons (1960 through 1964) as an American Football League franchise.

KENNY JOHNSON

Atlanta defensive back whose 26-yard interception return for a touchdown with 1 minute, 57 seconds left in a November 27, 1983, game against Green Bay broke a 34-34 tie and seemingly won the contest for the Falcons. However, the Packers deadlocked the game at 41-41 in the final 3 seconds of regulation play and denied Johnson his moment of glory. Or so it seemed. With 2:13 having elapsed in overtime, Johnson picked off another Lynn Dickey pass and returned this one 31 yards for a TD. Atlanta 47, Green Bay 41.

JOE KUHARICH

The only coach in Notre Dame history to have compiled a losing career record while guiding the Fighting Irish. In fact, Kuharich is the lone Irish coach—there have been 24 coaches at Notre Dame since the school began playing football in 1887—never to have had a winning season. Kuharich coached Notre Dame from 1959 through 1962, posting a 17-23 record overall (with the Irish going 5-5, 2-8, 5-5 and 5-5).

FRANK KUSH

The last man to coach the 1953-1983 Baltimore Colts of the National Football League. Kush coached the NFL club in 1982 and 1983, then accompanied the team to Indianapolis when the franchise relocated in that city in 1984 and coached the Indianapolis Colts for one season.

JACKY LEE

The quarterback whom the Denver Broncos "leased" from the Houston Oilers for 1964 and 1965. Coming off a 2-11-1 American Football League season and badly in need of quarterback help, the Broncos swung a deal with Houston in August 1964 in which they sent defensive lineman Bud McFadin, a first-round draft choice and cash to the Oilers for the services of Lee for two seasons. At the time of the trade, Denver stressed the possibility of obtaining Lee (who had been George Blanda's backup at Houston) on a permanent basis once the lease expired, but the Broncos never made such an acquisition. While playing for Denver in 1964 and 1965 (seasons in which the Broncos went 6-21-1), Lee completed 177 of 345 passes for 2,303 yards and 16 touchdowns (he was intercepted 23 times). In 1966, Lee was returned to the Oilers.

WILLIAM LEWIS

The first black player to win All-America honors. Lewis, Harvard center, was named an All-America in 1892 (and again in 1893).

LIGHT FAILURE

A fate that befell the World Football League's first nationally televised game. The lights at the Gator Bowl went out during halftime of the July 11, 1974, game between the Jacksonville Sharks and the New York Stars, with the outage delaying the start of the second half for approximately 10 minutes and thus giving the fledgling WFL just the kind of public-relations start it didn't need. Once the darkness ended, the Sharks went on to a 14-7 victory.

'LONELY END'

The name given to Army receiver Bill Carpenter in 1958 when he lined up 20 to 25 yards away from his Cadet teammates and returned to his position immediately after each play instead of going to the huddle. "I wanted to chase all the teams out of their compact defenses," Army Coach Earl (Red) Blaik explained, "and the 'Lonely End' did that." The no-huddle concept for the far flanker served three purposes, Blaik contended: It kept Carpenter relatively fresh, enabled Army to run more plays and forced the defense to commit itself early. Carpenter, who primarily got the signals from the positioning of quarterback Joe Caldwell's feet, caught 22 passes for 453 yards and two touchdowns in '58 as Army—featuring the play of the "Lonely End," Caldwell, Heisman Trophy-winning halfback Pete Dawkins, standout runner Bob Anderson and a tough defense—rolled to an 8-0-1 record.

In 1959, Carpenter totaled 43 receptions for 591 yards and three TDs.

CLINT LONGLEY

Playing in his first National Football League game, Dallas' Longley fired a 50-yard touchdown pass in the final 28 seconds that—coupled with Efren Herrera's extra-point kick—enabled the Cowboys to overcome the Washington Redskins, 24-23, on November 28, 1974, in Irving, Tex. Longley, who replaced the injured Roger Staubach in the third quarter, completed 11 of 20 passes overall for 203 yards and two TDs in his pro debut.

LOS ANGELES RAMS

The team with whom Joe Namath ended his National Football League career in 1977. Namath, after passing for 170 touchdowns in 12 seasons with the New York Jets, fired three scoring passes for the Rams in '77.

LOUISIANA SUPERDOME

Site of the Tampa Bay Buccaneers' first National Football League victory. The Bucs' breakthrough triumph, which ended an NFL-record 26-game losing streak, was recorded on December 11, 1977, as Tampa Bay turned three interceptions into touchdowns and walloped the New Orleans Saints, 33-14. Coach John McKay's Bucs had gone 0-14 in their first NFL season, 1976, and dropped the first 12 games of the '77 campaign.

A week after defeating the Saints, the Buccaneers finished the '77 season by upsetting the St. Louis Cardinals, 17-7, in Tampa.

GINO MARCHETTI

Renowned for his defensive-line play in 13 years with the Baltimore Colts, he played his first National Football League season in 1952 for the Dallas Texans.

CHESTER MARCOL

The Green Bay placekicker who saw his overtime field-goal attempt blocked against Chicago on September 7, 1980, but turned the agony into ecstasy by running 25 yards for a touchdown after the deflected ball bounced into his arms. "That's a new way to get beat," Bears Coach Neill Armstrong moaned after the 12-6 National Football League loss to the Packers.

ROBERT (RUBE) MARSHALL

End who was the first black to play in the American Professional Football Association (which later took the name of National Football League), performing for the Rock Island Independents in an October 3, 1920, game against the Muncie Flyers.

Fritz Pollard, a gifted black halfback, made his APFA debut for the Akron Pros on October 10, 1920, against the Columbus Panhandles. And end Paul Robeson, another black, also competed in the APFA in '20, playing for Hammond and Akron.

JAMES MAYBERRY

Atlanta player whose six-yard interception return for a touchdown in his first National Football League game gave the Falcons a 40-34 overtime triumph over the New Orleans Saints on September 2, 1979. Mayberry, a running back, was on special-teams duty in the extra session when Saints punter Russell Erxleben—also appearing in his first NFL contest—tried a desperation pass near New Orleans' goal line after running down an errant snap from center. Mayberry picked off Erxleben's shovel pass and dashed in for the TD, breaking a 34-34 tie that had been forged on Erxleben's 38-yard field goal in the final 44 seconds of regulation play.

MIAMI DOLPHINS, NEW YORK JETS

National Football League teams whose December 20, 1980, game was telecast nationally by NBC without the usual play-by-play audio or color commentary. While there were no television announcers for the game played in the Orange Bowl, viewers could hear the public-address system (and thus follow play in that manner), crowd noise and the quarterbacks' barking of signals. NBC periodically played taped comments of players, and the network cut in from time to time with summaries of the game action. Facts and figures also were superimposed on the screen during the experiment in coverage. The Jets defeated the Dolphins, 24-17.

MICHIGAN PANTHERS

The United States Football League's first championship team. Paced by Bobby Hebert's 314 yards passing and Anthony Carter's 179 yards in receptions (on nine catches), the Panthers fought off the Philadelphia Stars, 24-22, in the 1983 USFL title game, which was played on July 17 at Denver's Mile High Stadium.

RALF MOJSIEJENKO

Michigan State placekicker whose first collegiate field-goal attempt was good—and it came from 61 yards out. Mojsiejenko's long-distance boot was in vain as the Spartans fell to Illinois, 23-16, on September 11, 1982, in Champaign, Ill.

KEITH MOLESWORTH

The first coach in the history of the National Football League's Colts franchise that was based in Baltimore from 1953 through 1983. Molesworth's '53 Colts compiled a 3-9 record.

MERCURY MORRIS

Miami running back who was credited with 991 yards rushing when the 1972

National Football League season ended—but four days later had 1,000 yards. NFL Commissioner Pete Rozelle, after reviewing films, ruled that Miami quarterback Earl Morrall—and not Morris, as was recorded—should have been charged with the fumble that resulted in a nine-yard loss for the Dolphins in an October 22 game against Buffalo. Not only did Rozelle's ruling enable Morris to attain the "magic" 1,000 figure, it made the Dolphins the first team in NFL history to have two 1,000-yard rushers in one season (Larry Csonka gained 1,117 yards in '72 for Miami).

MARION MOTLEY

Cleveland fullback whose 63-yard touchdown run highlighted the last championship game in All-America Football Conference history. Motley's big play came in the third quarter, and the Browns went on to defeat the San Francisco 49ers, 21-7, on December 11, 1949, in Cleveland.

GEORGE MUSSO

He played football against two future Presidents of the United States. In 1929, Musso competed for Millikin against Eureka in a battle of Illinois colleges—and Eureka had a player named Ronald Reagan. In the 1935 College All-Star Game in Chicago, lineman Musso and his Chicago Bears teammates went against a College All-Star squad that included a center from Michigan named Gerald Ford.

NAVY 24, ARMY 0

The outcome of the first Army-Navy game, played November 29, 1890, at the U.S. Military Academy in West Point, N.Y.

NEW ORLEANS SAINTS

Through the 1984 season, the only current National Football League team never to have appeared in the playoffs. The Saints, in fact, had not even enjoyed a winning season through '84, with 8-8 records in 1979 and 1983 being New Orleans' best efforts since entering the NFL in 1967.

NEW YORK JETS, NEW YORK GIANTS

Opponents in the National Football League's first regular-season overtime game played to a decision. In a November 10, 1974, game in New Haven, Conn., the Jets edged the Giants, 26-20, on Joe Namath's five-yard touchdown pass to Emerson Boozer that came approximately 7 minutes into the sudden-death period.

NIPPERT STADIUM

The University of Cincinnati facility that the Cincinnati Bengals used as their home park in 1968 and 1969, the first two years of the American Football League expansion team's existence.

19, 7

The total of team nicknames in World Football League history and the

San Francisco rookie R. C. Owens, with the help of quarterback Y. A. Tittle, made the "Alley Oop" pass a part of NFL playbooks in 1957.

number of singular nicknames therein (more than one-third). WFL entrants in 1974 and/or 1975 with singular nicknames were the Philadelphia Bell, Chicago Fire, Portland Storm, Southern California Sun, Shreveport Steamer, Jacksonville Express and Portland Thunder.

1965

The season in which National Football League officials switched from white to gold flags.

R.C. OWENS

The man credited with originating the "Alley Oop" play while a rookie receiver with the San Francisco 49ers in 1957. The 6-foot-3 Owens perfected the method of springing into the air and outjumping defenders for passes, and 49ers quarterback Y.A. Tittle proved a master at getting the ball to him.

BUDDY PARKER

Having quit as Detroit's coach in the summer of 1957 only to see the Lions win the National Football League title that year, Parker resigned as Pittsburgh's coach during the 1965 exhibition season. Anticipating a potentially distressing season for his team each time, Parker—while wrong in '57—was a prophet in '65 as the Steelers, with former assistant coach Mike Nixon at the helm, experienced a 2-12 campaign.

PHILADELPHIA

Site of the only regular-season Canadian Football League game ever played in the United States. The Hamilton Tiger-Cats, in the process of negotiating their stadium contract, moved their September 14, 1958, game against the Ottawa Rough Riders to Franklin Field in Philadelphia and the CFL contest drew 15,110 fans. Hamilton won, 24-18.

JOE PISARCIK

New York Giants quarterback who followed the play-calling orders from the sidelines in the final minute of a November 19, 1978, game against Philadelphia and tried to hand off the ball to Larry Csonka. The Giants were leading, 17-12, at the time and the clock was running (the Eagles had used their final timeout). While virtually everyone at Giants Stadium in East Rutherford, N.J., thought Pisarcik would simply fall on the ball at New York's 29-yard line on the third-and-two play, the signal-caller did as instructed—or at least he attempted to do so. However, Pisarcik never got a firm grip on the football during the exchange from center. The ball glanced off Csonka's hip, hit the ground and bounced into the hands of Philadelphia's Herman Edwards, who sped 26 yards for a touchdown on the fumble recovery as the scoreboard clock ticked down to the game's last 20 seconds. "I've never seen so horrifying a finish to a game," Giants Coach John McVay said after the Eagles' 19-17 National Football League triumph.

DICK PLASMAN

The last man known to have played without a helmet on a major level of football competition (major-college or professional ranks), having seen helmetless duty for the Chicago Bears in the 1940 National Football League championship game. Plasman, an end, played eight seasons in the NFL.

Helmets became mandatory football equipment for college players in 1939 and for NFL players in 1943.

FRITZ POLLARD

The only black head coach in National Football League history, having served as a player-coach for the NFL's Milwaukee Badgers in 1922 and for the Hammond Pros in 1923, 1924 and 1925. Pollard, a standout halfback whose football expertise was recognized throughout the league, apparently also guided the league's Akron team for at least half of the 1921 season.

AHMAD RASHAD

Recipient of Fran Tarkenton's 342nd and last regular-season touchdown pass in National Football League play. Tarkenton, the NFL's all-time leader in scoring passes, hit Rashad with a 24-yard TD strike in the fourth quarter

Chicago's Dick Plasman became pro football's last known helmetless performer when he played in the 1940 NFL championship game sans headgear.

of the Minnesota Vikings' December 17, 1978, game in Oakland against the Raiders. While Tarkenton threw three touchdown passes that day, he was intercepted five times as the Raiders took a 27-20 victory.

JOHN REAVES

Six weeks after throwing five touchdown passes in his varsity debut (an unprecedented first-game feat in major-college history), Florida's Reaves rewrote the national record book again—this time by being intercepted nine times (a major-college mark). Auburn's Tigers rode the piracy to a 38-12 victory over the Gators on November 1, 1969.

RUTGERS, PRINCETON

Universities whose teams competed in the first game of U.S. intercollegiate football, played November 6, 1869, in New Brunswick, N.J. In what basically was a soccer-style contest with 25 players to a side, Rutgers defeated the visiting Princeton squad, 6-4.

Harvard, opting for a style of game in which the ball could be picked up and a player could be tackled, played host to McGill University of Montreal in

1874 in the first intercollegiate rugby game ever played in the United States. While the clash ended, 0-0, the spirited action thrilled spectators and prompted Harvard's adoption of the carry-and-tackle game. Enthusiasm for the sport spread quickly and widely, setting into motion the evolution of rugby—and not soccer—into American football.

SAN DIEGO CHARGERS

The team for whom Johnny Unitas played in his final National Football League season, 1973. After having tossed 287 touchdown passes in 17 years with the Baltimore Colts, Unitas concluded his NFL career by throwing for three TDs in '73 as a member of the Chargers.

BOB SCHNELKER

The man who caught Fran Tarkenton's first National Football League touchdown pass, a 14-yard pitch that came in the second quarter of the Minnesota Vikings' September 17, 1961, game against the Chicago Bears. The contest was the first regular-season NFL game in Vikings' history and also marked the pro debut of Tarkenton (who went on to throw an NFL-record 342 touchdown passes in his career). With Tarkenton throwing four TD passes that day and also running for a score, Minnesota jolted the Bears, 37-13, in Bloomington, Minn.

LAWRENCE T. (BUCK) SHAW

The coach of the San Francisco 49ers when the club played its first National Football League season, 1950. Shaw coached the 49ers for five NFL seasons overall, posting a 33-25-2 record.

SKULL AND CROSSBONES

While Paul Dietzel, in his first season at West Point, was busy firing up his Army squad for the Cadets' 1962 game against Navy, Midshipmen Coach Wayne Hardin and friends weren't resting on the laurels of three straight victories in the service-academy classic. Trying to counteract a Dietzel-inspired surge of enthusiasm at West Point, sparked in part by the hoopla over the Cadets' "Chinese Bandits" defensive unit, the Midshipmen had the words "Beat Army" inscribed in Chinese on the side of their helmets for the December 1 game in Philadelphia. Additionally, a skull and crossbones—representing "Jolly Roger," a ship that never lost a battle—adorned the front of the Middies' helmets. Another "Jolly Roger," Navy sophomore quarterback Roger Staubach, provided more than psychological fireworks that day. He passed for two touchdowns and ran for two others as the Midshipmen drubbed the Cadets, 34-14.

DAVE SMITH

Pittsburgh Steelers receiver who started celebrating a "touchdown" nearly five yards too soon in an October 18, 1971, National Football League game against the Chiefs in Kansas City. Thinking he had crossed the goal line after catching a fourth-quarter pass from Terry Bradshaw on a play that

Navy Coach Wayne Hardin used some symbolic psychology to fire up his troops for the 1962 game against arch-rival Army. A skull and crossbones, representing "Jolly Roger," a ship that never lost a battle, was added to the front of the Midshipmen helmets and sophomore quarterback Roger Staubach (above) proceeded to lead Navy to a 34-14 victory.

began at midfield, Smith let loose of the football just inside the Chiefs' 5-yard line and the ball bounced through the end zone for a touchback. Kansas City won the Monday night game, 38-16.

MARSHALL SMITH

The coach of the Racine (Chicago) Cardinals in 1920 when the Cards began play in the American Professional Football Association.

FRED STEINFORT

The man who succeeded George Blanda, the National Football League's all-time leading scorer, as the Oakland Raiders' placekicker in 1976 and then displaced Jim Turner as the Denver Broncos' kicker in 1980 when Turner ranked No. 2 on the NFL career scoring list. (Jan Stenerud supplanted Turner as the runner-up to Blanda in 1983.)

Steinfort, troubled by a leg injury, held the Raiders' kicking job for only half of the '76 season before giving way to Errol Mann, and he served as Denver's kicker for two years before Rich Karlis replaced him.

WOODY STRODE, KENNY WASHINGTON

They became the National Football League's first black players in 13 years when they saw service with the Los Angeles Rams in 1946. While blacks had appeared in the NFL from the league's inception in 1920 through 1933 (a total of only 13 blacks competed in those 14 seasons, however), none appeared in a league game from 1934 through 1945. End Strode and halfback Washington, onetime standouts for UCLA, then joined the Rams.

Lineman Bill Willis and fullback Marion Motley, both black, actually beat Strode and Washington into the pro football wars in '46 as members of the Cleveland Browns of the new All-America Football Conference, which began league play three weeks earlier than the NFL.

LIONEL TAYLOR

The first player in either the American Football League or the National Football League to catch 100 passes in a season, totaling exactly 100 receptions for the AFL's Denver Broncos in 1961.

WILLIE THROWER

The man credited with being the first black quarterback in National Football League history, having appeared in a relief role (three completions in eight pass attempts for 27 yards, with one interception) as a T-formation signal-caller for the Chicago Bears in an October 18, 1953, game against the San Francisco 49ers. The game was Thrower's only appearance in the NFL.

George Taliaferro, who as a tailback in single-wing formation play had attempted 124 passes in quarterback-like duty for the All-America Football Conference's Los Angeles Dons (1949) and also had done some passing for the NFL's New York Yanks (1950, 1951) and Dallas Texans (1952), made his NFL debut as a T-formation quarterback for the Baltimore Colts on No-

Vertically striped socks were a distinctive, if not eye-pleasing, part of the Denver Broncos' 1960 and 1961 American Football League uniforms.

vember 22, 1953, against the Los Angeles Rams. As the first black to start at quarterback in an NFL game, Taliaferro reeled off a 44-yard touchdown run against the Rams.

GAYNELL TINSLEY

Through 1984, there had been five 99-yard pass completions in National Football League history, six 98-yard hookups and three 97-yarders, and only one player was a principal figure in two of those plays—Chicago Cardinals receiver Tinsley. He combined with Pat Coffee on a 97-yard touchdown strike against the Chicago Bears on December 5, 1937, and teamed with Doug Russell on a 98-yard scoring pass against the Cleveland Rams on November 27, 1938.

BURL TOLER

The first black official in National Football League history. Toler, a head linesman, began officiating in the NFL in 1965.

EMLEN TUNNELL

The first black player to be named to the Pro Football Hall of Fame in Canton, O., gaining election in 1967. Defensive back Tunnell, who played 11 seasons with the New York Giants and three years with the Green Bay Packers, recorded 79 career interceptions in the National Football League.

VERTICALLY STRIPED SOCKS

The distinctive—and hideous—part of the brown and gold uniforms that the Denver Broncos wore during their first two seasons in the American Football League, 1960 and 1961. The Broncos played almost as poorly as they looked, winning only seven of 28 games in those years. Seeking a new image, Denver burned the vertically striped socks in 1962 and changed its team colors to orange and blue. And the Broncos proceeded to post a 7-7 record in '62, which proved Denver's only non-losing mark until 1973 (when the team went 7-5-2 in the National Football League).

One pair of the Broncos' infamous socks did escape the torch—and those socks are on display at the Pro Football Hall of Fame.

ADAM WALSH

The last coach for the National Football League's Cleveland Rams and the first coach of the NFL's Los Angeles Rams. Walsh led the Cleveland Rams to a 9-1 record and the league championship in 1945 and directed the Rams to a 6-4-1 mark in 1946 when they played their first season in Los Angeles.

ARCH WARD

The Chicago Tribune sports editor who founded the Chicago College All-Star Game (first played in 1934) and the All-America Football Conference (which played its first season in 1946).

Ward also was the originator of major league baseball's All-Star Game.

PAUL WARFIELD

The only member of the Pro Football Hall of Fame who played in the World Football League. Warfield was a member of the WFL's Memphis club in 1975.

WAR MEMORIAL STADIUM

Home stadium for the Buffalo Bills franchise throughout the 10-year life (1960-1969) of the fourth professional American Football League.

BYRON (WHIZZER) WHITE

Major-college football's top rusher and leading scorer in 1937, the year that official individual statistics were first kept for collegians. White ran for 1,121 yards and totaled 122 points (16 touchdowns, one field goal and 23 extra points) for the Colorado Buffaloes.

WILFORD WHITE

The "other" Whizzer White of collegiate football fame. Wilford (Whizzer) White was the leading ballcarrier in the major-college ranks in 1950, rushing for 1,502 yards as an Arizona State senior. He then played for the National Football League's Chicago Bears in 1951 and 1952.

Danny White, a quarterback standout at Arizona State before entering pro football in 1974, is the son of Wilford White.

WILLIE WOOD

He became pro football's first black coach in 50 years—since Fritz Pollard directed Hammond of the National Football League in 1925—upon being named coach of the World Football League's Philadelphia Bell on July 29, 1975.

In 1980, Wood became the first black coach in Canadian Football League history when he was selected coach of the Toronto Argonauts.

LUD WRAY

The first coach of two National Football League teams—the Boston franchise that evolved into the Washington Redskins and the Philadelphia Eagles. Wray coached the Boston Braves to a 4-4-2 record in 1932 and his Eagles compiled a 9-21-1 mark from 1933 through 1935.

TIM WRIGHTMAN

UCLA tight end who became the first player to sign with a United States Football League team. Wrightman, a third-round draft choice of the National Football League's Chicago Bears in 1982, signed with the USFL's Chicago Blitz on August 5 of '82. (The USFL did not conduct its first draft until January 1983.)

WRIGLEY FIELD

Site of five National Football League championship games (1933, 1937, 1941, 1943, 1963) involving the Chicago Bears, it last served as the Bears' home field in 1970.

YALE BOWL

Home stadium for the National Football League's New York Giants for the last five games of the 1973 season and all of 1974. The Giants switched to the New Haven, Conn., facility after playing their first two home games of '73 at Yankee Stadium, the NFL club's home park since 1956. Yankee Stadium underwent massive remodeling from late 1973 through 1975.

The Giants used Shea Stadium as their home field in 1975 before moving into Giants Stadium in East Rutherford, N.J., in 1976.

FRANK YOUELL FIELD

The first Oakland-based home park of pro football's Raiders franchise. After playing their first two American Football League seasons, 1960 and 1961, as tenants of San Francisco stadiums (Kezar Stadium and Candlestick Park), the Oakland Raiders moved to Frank Youell Field in 1962 and played their home games there through 1965.

The lucky number for Syracuse University coaches and fans is 44. That's the number worn by three of the top running backs in college football history—Ernie Davis (below left), Jim Brown (below right) and Floyd Little.

NUMBERS

0

The number of times that Joe Namath led the American Football League, American Football Conference or National Football League in passing.

0

The number of field goals that the Dallas Texans made in the 1952 National Football League season. The Texans, who attempted four three-pointers in '52, are the last of 14 NFL clubs to go an entire season without collecting a field goal.

0

The number of home games that Notre Dame played in its perfect season of 1929. With Notre Dame Stadium under construction, the Fighting Irish fashioned a 9-0 record away from South Bend, Ind.

0

The number of losing seasons that George Allen had while coaching 12 years in the National Football League and two seasons in the United States Football League. Allen compiled a 118-54-5 record as coach of the NFL's Los Angeles Rams and Washington Redskins from 1966 through 1977, and went 24-16 as coach of the USFL's Chicago Blitz in 1983 and Arizona Wranglers in 1984.

John Madden never had a losing season during his 10 years as coach of the Oakland Raiders, fashioning a 112-39-7 mark from 1969 through 1978.

0

The number of games that the San Diego Chargers won within their own division—the American Conference West—while compiling a 7-9 record in National Football League play in 1984. The Chargers went 0-8 against divisional rivals Denver, Kansas City, Seattle and Los Angeles (Raiders), but built a 7-1 mark against outside competition.

0

Since the National Football League began keeping individual statistics in 1932, the number of 1,000-yard rushers in the NFL in '32, 1933, 1935, 1936, 1937, 1938, 1939, 1940, 1941, 1942, 1943, 1944, 1945, 1946, 1948, 1950, 1951, 1952, 1955, 1957 and strike-shortened 1982.

0-11-1

The record of Coach Tom Landry's Dallas Cowboys in the team's first season (1960) in the National Football League.

1

The number of seasons that Knute Rockne-coached Notre Dame teams played in Notre Dame Stadium. The Fighting Irish held their home games at Cartier Field through 1928, faced an all-away schedule in 1929 and then opened Notre Dame Stadium in 1930.

1

The number of losing seasons that the Cleveland Browns experienced in their first 28 years (1946 through 1973) of pro football competition. The Browns enjoyed 26 winning seasons in that span, went 5-7 in 1956 and finished 7-7 in 1970.

2

The number of National Football League teams that have had two 1,000-

272

yard rushers in one season. After Miami's Larry Csonka and Mercury Morris both hit the select figure in 1972, Pittsburgh's Franco Harris and Rocky Bleier became the NFL's second 1,000-yard tandem in 1976 (Harris ran for 1,128 yards and Bleier gained 1,036).

2

The number of coaches that the University of Chicago had during the 48 years (1892 through 1939) that the school played major-college football—and those coaches were Amos Alonzo Stagg, 41 years, and Clark Shaughnessy, seven years.

2

Beginning in 1958, the number of points awarded in NCAA football for a successful run or pass from the 3-yard line on a conversion play. An option to the one-point conversion kick, the two-point play marked the first change in football scoring since 1912 (when the worth of a touchdown was increased from five points to six).

2, 4, 5

The points credited for a touchdown in collegiate play in 1883, from 1884 through 1897 and from 1898 through 1911. Earlier, all "goals" counted one point.

2-0

The score by which Amos Alonzo Stagg's University of Chicago team defeated Fielding Yost's Michigan squad in the final game of the 1905 season, ending the Wolverines' 56-game unbeaten streak.

3

The number of downs in which a Canadian Football League team must gain 10 yards or lose possession of the ball.

3

The number of National Football League ballcarriers who have rushed for exactly 1,000 yards in a season. Willie Ellison of the Los Angeles Rams hit that magic figure on the button in 1971, Mercury Morris of the Miami Dolphins did so in 1972 and Greg Pruitt of the Cleveland Browns performed the feat in 1976.

3

The number of different teams that Chuck Knox has coached into the National Football League playoffs—and the figure represents an NFL record. Knox has directed the Los Angeles Rams (1973 through 1977), Buffalo Bills (1980, 1981) and Seattle Seahawks (1983, 1984) into postseason play.

3

The record number of safeties that the Los Angeles Rams recorded in one

National Football League game in 1984. The Rams collected all three of the safeties in one quarter—the third period of a September 30 game—en route to a 33-12 drubbing of the New York Giants.

3-11

The first-year records of five expansion teams in pro football—the Minnesota Vikings (1961), Atlanta Falcons (1966), Miami Dolphins (1966), New Orleans Saints (1967) and Cincinnati Bengals (1968).

4

The number of tie games that Temple played in its nine-game season of 1937. All four of the Owls' deadlocked contests—against Mississippi, Boston College, Holy Cross and Bucknell—ended 0-0. Temple's season record was 3-2-4.

4

The number of pass interceptions that the Seattle Seahawks returned for touchdowns in a November 4, 1984, game against the Kansas City Chiefs—and none of the runbacks covered fewer than 58 yards. Seattle romped, 45-0, in the National Football League game.

5

The number of running backs who have achieved 1,000-yard seasons for two teams in National Football League-American Football League history. Accomplishing the feat: Mike Garrett (1967 Kansas City Chiefs, 1972 San Diego Chargers), John Riggins (1975 New York Jets, 1978-1979-1983-1984 Washington Redskins), Delvin Williams (1976 San Francisco 49ers, 1978 Miami Dolphins), Chuck Muncie (1979 New Orleans Saints, 1981 Chargers) and Wendell Tyler (1979-1981 Los Angeles Rams, 1984 49ers).

5

The number of yards that Chicago Bears quarterback Bobby Douglass had to traverse to score four touchdowns in a November 4, 1973, National Football League game against the Green Bay Packers. Douglass, accounting for all of the Bears' TDs with his three one-yard runs and a two-yard burst, sparked Chicago to a 31-17 triumph.

5

The number of times since 1932 (when official statistics-keeping began) that National Football League and American Football League teams have played entire games without making a first down—and three of the no-first-down clubs won their games. Failing to notch a first down but winning nevertheless were the New York Giants, 10-7 victors over the Green Bay Packers on October 1, 1933, and 14-7 winners over the Washington Redskins on September 27, 1942, and the Pittsburgh Pirates, who defeated the Boston Redskins, 16-14, on October 29, 1933. Philadelphia went without a first down in the Eagles' 35-0 loss to the Detroit Lions on September 20, 1935, and the

Denver Broncos failed to collect a first down in their 45-7 loss to the Houston Oilers on September 3, 1966.

5

The number of downs that Cornell, trailing 3-0, was given from the Dartmouth 6-yard line late in the 1940 Big Red-Big Green game—and Cornell scored on the fifth down in the game's final 3 seconds. The mixup seemingly enabled Cornell to extend its unbeaten streak to 19 games with a 7-3 triumph. However, when film sequences later confirmed that an official had miscounted the downs, Cornell yielded its claim to victory and proclaimed Dartmouth a 3-0 winner.

6

The number of victories UCLA scored in its undefeated, 10-game season of 1939. In addition to beating Texas Christian, Washington, Montana, Oregon, California and Washington State, the Bruins tied Stanford, Santa Clara, Oregon State and Southern California.

7

The number of years that end Barney Poole lettered in major-college football, thanks to liberal eligibility rules in effect because of World War II. Poole lettered for Mississippi in 1942, North Carolina in 1943, Army in 1944, 1945 and 1946 and for Ole Miss again in 1947 and 1948.

7

The record number of consecutive divisional championships won in the National Football League. The Los Angeles Rams set the mark, reigning as National Conference West titlists from 1973 through 1979.

7

The major-college record for most field goals in one game, established by Western Michigan's Mike Prindle on September 29, 1984, against Marshall.

8

The number of equally spaced lacings on footballs used in NCAA play.

8

The most seasons that a National Football League player has rushed for 1,000 yards. Walter Payton and Franco Harris share the record.

8, 7

The number of passes that Chicago Bears rushing star Walter Payton had completed in his regular-season National Football League career through 1984 and the number of those completions that had gone for touchdowns. Payton had attempted 24 passes overall.

In NFL postseason play through '84, Payton had thrown two passes and hit on one—the completion going for a touchdown.

9

The total number of players—veterans and draft choices—that the Los Angeles Rams dealt to the Chicago Cardinals in 1959 for standout National Football League running back Ollie Matson.

9.9

The yards-per-attempt rushing average—a National Football League record over one season—that Beattie Feathers of the Chicago Bears attained in 1934. Feathers amassed 1,004 yards on only 101 carries.

10

The height, in feet, above the ground for the top of the goal post's horizontal crossbar in NCAA football and the National Football League.

11

The number of players that the Los Angeles Rams traded to the Dallas Texans in 1952 for linebacker Les Richter. Richter had been the Texans' No. 1 choice in the '52 National Football League draft.

12

The number of players on a side in a Canadian Football League game.

12

The uniform number worn by the winning quarterback in nine consecutive Super Bowls. Dallas' Roger Staubach started the streak in Super Bowl VI and was followed by Miami's Bob Griese in Super Bowls VII and VIII, Pittsburgh's Terry Bradshaw in Super Bowls IX and X, Oakland's Ken Stabler in Super Bowl XI, the Cowboys' Staubach in Super Bowl XII and the Steelers' Bradshaw in Super Bowls XIII and XIV.

12½ to 13½

The air pressure, in pounds, of an inflated football in NCAA and National Football League play.

13

Through Super Bowl XIX (played on January 20, 1985), the number of current National Football League teams that had not appeared in a Super Bowl game. Yet to play in pro football's showcase contest were the National Football Conference's Falcons, Saints, Bears, Lions, Buccaneers, Cardinals and Giants and the American Football Conference's Chargers, Seahawks, Browns, Oilers, Bills and Patriots. (The AFC's Colts, now based in Indianapolis, played in the Super Bowl twice when the franchise was located in Baltimore.)

The Los Angeles Rams made Les Richter feel wanted in 1952 when they acquired him from the Dallas Texans for 11 players.

14

The record number of interceptions in one National Football League season by one player—and a rookie defensive back, Dick (Night Train) Lane, established the mark in 1952 while playing for the Los Angeles Rams.

14 to 15

The weight, in ounces, of an inflated football in NCAA and National Football League play.

16

The number of 1,000-yard rushers in the National Football League in 1983, the most in one NFL season.

17

The number of consecutive regular-season shutouts that the Tennessee Volunteers posted from the seventh game of the 1938 campaign through the third game of the 1940 season.

18, 0

The number of passes that West Virginia attempted in an October 18, 1946, game against Temple and the number that the Mountaineers completed against the Owls. Despite the dreadful aerial performance, the Mountaineers made a game of it before losing, 6-0.

18 FEET, 6 INCHES; 23 FEET, 4 INCHES

The distance between the goal post's uprights in the National Football League and the distance between the uprights in NCAA football.

19

The most seasons any National Football League player has spent with one club. Jim Marshall played for the Minnesota Vikings from 1961 through 1979.

21

The number of seconds of overtime play that the Chicago Bears needed to defeat the Detroit Lions on November 27, 1980, in Pontiac, Mich. The Bears, who had trailed, 17-3, entering the fourth quarter before tying the score on an extra-point kick that came after time had expired in regulation play, won the shortest overtime game in National Football League history by a 23-17 score when Dave Williams returned the overtime-opening kickoff 95 yards for a touchdown.

22-3-1

Through the 1984 National Football League season, the record of the Oakland/Los Angeles Raiders in games televised by ABC on the network's Monday Night Football series.

23-17

The score of not only the National Football League's first overtime game that "counted" (Baltimore's triumph over the New York Giants in the 1958 NFL title game), but the outcome of the league's first overtime game of any kind—and the Giants lost that one, too. New York's first 23-17 overtime setback came in an August 28, 1955, exhibition game against the Los Angeles Rams in Portland, Ore.

25

The number of pounds that the Heisman Trophy weighs. The solid-bronze trophy is 14 inches long, 13½ inches high and 6½ inches wide.

28

The most points overcome by a victorious National Football League team. The San Francisco 49ers trailed the New Orleans Saints, 35-7, at halftime of their December 7, 1980, game, but rallied for 28 second-half points to tie the score and then won the game, 38-35, on Ray Wersching's 36-yard field goal in overtime.

29

The most consecutive years served as coach of one National Football League club. Curly Lambeau coached the Green Bay Packers from 1921 through 1949.

31

The number of points by which Denver trailed Buffalo with 4 minutes, 39 seconds remaining in the third quarter of their November 27, 1960, American Football League game—but the Broncos were able to salvage a tie. Three Frank Tripucka-to-Lionel Taylor touchdown passes helped the Broncos rebound from a 38-7 deficit and earn a 38-38 deadlock.

31

The largest point deficit ever overcome by a winning team in major-college football history. Maryland trailed Miami (Florida), 31-0, at halftime of their November 10, 1984, game in the Orange Bowl, but the Terrapins struck for 21 points in each of the last two quarters and scored a 42-40 victory.

32

Starting in 1937, the number of consecutive times that Oklahoma defeated Kansas State—and the uninterrupted domination ranks as the longest for one team over another in major-college football history. The Wildcats, shut out 19 times during the streak, ended their futility against Oklahoma with a vengeance in 1969, smashing the Sooners, 59-21.

33

The most consecutive years of coaching in the National Football League. After guiding the Green Bay Packers for 29 straight seasons (through 1949), Curly Lambeau coached the Chicago Cardinals in 1950 and 1951 and the Washington Redskins in 1952 and 1953.

34

The most consecutive losses by a major-college football team, with Northwestern establishing the record from September 22, 1979, through September 18, 1982.

40

The most seasons coached in the National Football League. George Halas holds the record, having guided the Chicago Bears for four 10-year periods —1920-1929, 1933-1942, 1946-1955 and 1958-1967. (Halas did not complete the '42 season, departing for U.S. Navy service in November.)

44

The number worn at Syracuse by three of the top ballcarriers in collegiate football history—Jim Brown, Ernie Davis and Floyd Little. Brown excelled for the Orangemen from 1954 through 1956, Davis stood out for Syracuse from 1959 through 1961 and Little starred for the Orange from 1964 through 1966.

46

The number of consecutive non-losing seasons that Penn State had recorded through 1984, a major-college record. The Nittany Lions enjoyed 26 straight winning years (another national mark) from 1939 through 1964, had 5-5 seasons in 1965 and 1966 and put together 18 consecutive winning campaigns from 1967 through '84.

48

The age at which George Blanda played his last National Football League season (1975, for the Oakland Raiders).

48-48

The highest-scoring tie game in major-college history, played between Utah State and San Jose State on September 8, 1979, in San Jose, Calif.

49-0

The score by which Portland State led Delaware State after the first quarter of their November 8, 1980, NCAA Division I-AA game. Portland State went on to win, 105-0, as quarterback Neil Lomax threw eight touchdown passes.

51.4

The highest season punting average in National Football League history, achieved by Sammy Baugh of the Washington Redskins in 1940. Baugh also holds the NFL career mark, averaging 45.1 yards per punt over 16 seasons.

52.1

The average margin of victory for the 1944 Army Cadets. Blasting its way to a 9-0 record, Army scored 504 points overall (an average of 56 per game) and held the opposition to 35 points (an average of 3.9). The Cadets' victims, in order, were: North Carolina, 46-0; Brown, 59-7; Pittsburgh, 69-7; Coast Guard, 76-0; Duke, 27-7; Villanova, 83-0; Notre Dame, 59-0; Pennsylvania, 62-7, and Navy, 23-7.

'53'

The Miami Dolphins' defense that was created in 1972 and named for Dolphins linebacker Bob Matheson, who wore uniform number 53 and was an integral part of the alignment. Matheson was used as a fourth linebacker in passing situations, and he was given the option of blitzing the quarterback or retreating into pass coverage.

56

The number of receptions that end Bud Grant had in his National Football League career—and all of the catches came in one season, 1952 (when Grant, playing for the Philadelphia Eagles, ranked second in the league in receiving). Grant played his next four seasons in the Canadian Football League, averaging 54 receptions per year with Winnipeg. In 1957, Grant—at age 30—began his coaching career in the CFL.

57

The number of years that Amos Alonzo Stagg was a head coach in collegiate football.

59

The number of different teams that have finished in United Press International's final Top 10 rankings of the season since UPI began its polls in 1950. A team-by-team breakdown of UPI Top 10 finishes, with the year and final-poll position indicated:

TEAM	RANKING									
	#1	#2	#3	#4	#5	#6	#7	#8	#9	#10
Air Force								'58		
Alabama	'61,'64 '73,'79	'71,'74 '77,'78	'66,'75	'65,'72	'62	'80,'81	'67		'52,'63,'76	'60
Arizona St.		'75				'71,'82		'70		'73
Arkansas		'64,'65	'69,'77			'62,'75	'60	'54,'61,'82	'59,'68,'79	'78
Army			'58		'50		'54			
Auburn		'57	'83	'58	'71	'63,'74	'72		'70	'55
Baylor									'51	
Boston College				'84						
Brigham Young	'84							'83		
California				'50						
Clemson	'81					'78				
Colorado							'61,'71			
Florida						'83	'84			
Florida St.					'80			'79		'82
Georgia	'80			'66,'68 '82,'83	'59,'81			'71		'76
Georgia Tech		'52		'56	'51		'55	'66	'53	
Houston				'76	'79					
Illinois			'51	'63			'53			'83
Indiana						'67				
Iowa		'58,'60	'56		'57					'53
Kansas						'68			'60	
Kentucky							'50			
Louisiana St.	'58		'59,'61			'70	'64,'69	'62		'71,'72

TEAM	RANKING									
	#1	#2	#3	#4	#5	#6	#7	#8	#9	#10
Maryland	'53		'55	'51						
Miami (Fla.)	'83					'56			'54	'66
Miami (Ohio)										'74
Michigan			'76	'64,'71,'80	'74,'78	'50,'72,'73	'56,'70	'69,'75,'77	'83	'81
Michigan St.	'52,'65	'51,'55,'66	'53,'57						'50,'61	'56,'63
Minnesota	'60					'61			'56	'62
Mississippi		'59	'60,'62		'61	'54	'52,'63	'57	'55	
Missouri				'60		'65,'69				
Navy		'63			'54	'57,'60				
Nebraska	'71	'83	'65,'70 '82,'84		'63	'64	'66,'76 '79,'80	'74,'78	'72,'75,'81	'77
North Carolina									'81	'80
N. Carolina St.										'74
Notre Dame	'66,'77	'53	'52,'64	'54,'67 '73,'74	'70	'78		'55,'65,'68	'57,'69	'80
Ohio St.	'57,'68	'54,'61,'70	'72,'73,'74	'75,'79	'69,'76	'55	'58	'60,'83	'64	'50
Oklahoma	'50,'55 '56,'75	'72,'73	'54,'67,'71 '78,'79,'80	'52,'57	'53,'58	'76,'77,'84	'62	'63		'68
Oklahoma St.					'84					
Oregon St.								'64,'67		
Penn St.	'82	'69	'68,'81	'77,'78	'73		'74	'72,'80	'62	'59,'75
Pittsburgh	'76	'80,'81	'63			'79	'77		'82	
Princeton						'51		'50		
Purdue						'66			'67	'79
Rice						'53	'57			
Southern Cal	'62,'67,'72 '74,'78	'68,'76,'79		'69	'52		'73		'65,'84	'64
SMU		'82						'84	'66	
Stanford							'51			'70
Syracuse	'59							'56		'58
Tennessee	'51	'56,'67	'50	'70			'65,'68	'52	'71	
Texas	'63,'69,'70	'50		'59,'61 '62,'81	'64,'68,'72 '77,'83		'75	'53,'73	'78	
Texas A&M					'56			'76		'57
TCU					'55			'59	'58	'51
Texas Tech										'65
UCLA	'54			'53,'55	'65,'66 '75,'82	'52			'73	'67,'69,'84
Utah St.										'61
Washington		'84			'60		'59,'81,'82		'77	
Wisconsin		'62				'58,'59		'51		'52,'54
Wyoming					'67					

60

The number of games that New England wide receiver Darryl Stingley had played in the National Football League before he suffered a disabling injury in a 1978 exhibition game against the Oakland Raiders. When his NFL career ended at age 26, Stingley—a first-round draft choice of the Patriots in 1973—had caught 110 passes and scored 16 touchdowns overall in his five years in the league.

60, 62, 76, 77, 98

Uniform numbers worn, at one time or another, by backfield stars of earlier

The McKeever twins, Mike (left) and Marlin, spelled double trouble for Southern Cal opponents in 1958, 1959 and 1960.

collegiate and professional eras—numbers that backs couldn't wear today because of standardized numbering systems. Otto Graham (60), Charley Trippi (62), Marion Motley (76), Red Grange (77) and Tom Harmon (98) weren't alone, of course, in wearing high numbers as pro football didn't adopt a compulsory numbering system until 1952 and college football didn't introduce number guidelines until 1956.

63

Of the 85 Army-Navy games contested through 1984, the number that had been played in Philadelphia. Eleven games had been played in New York, three in West Point, N.Y., three in Annapolis, Md., two in Baltimore, one in Chicago, one in Princeton, N.J., and one in Pasadena, Calif.

66-24

The score by which the American Football League's Kansas City Chiefs defeated the National Football League's Chicago Bears in an August 23, 1967, exhibition game. The game was the first for the Chiefs against an NFL club after their 35-10 loss to the Green Bay Packers in Super Bowl I.

68, 86

The uniform numbers worn by Southern California's Mike and Marlin McKeever, twin brothers and standout football players who competed for the Trojans in 1958, 1959 and 1960. Mike McKeever, a guard, won all-league honors for USC in '59 but was forced to end his football career during the '60 season because of a head injury. Marlin McKeever, an end, gained all-conference recognition three times for Southern Cal and went on to play 13 years in the National Football League. (Mike McKeever died in August 1967 of injuries he had suffered 20 months earlier in an automobile accident.)

71, 45

The number of passes that Northwestern quarterback Sandy Schwab attempted and completed in an October 23, 1982, game against Michigan—and both figures are major-college records for one game. Despite Schwab's aerial show, Northwestern fell, 49-14.

74

The number of consecutive games that Oklahoma won in conference play from November 16, 1946, through October 24, 1959. The Big Eight juggernaut saw its streak end on October 31, 1959, in Lincoln, Neb., as the Nebraska Cornhuskers upset the Sooners, 25-21. The defeat was the first league loss for Sooners Coach Bud Wilkinson, who was in his 13th season at Oklahoma.

78

Since official statistics-keeping began in the National Football League, the number of different players who have rushed for 1,000 yards in one season in the NFL (1932-1984) and American Football League (1960-1969).

82

The number of different teams that have finished in the Associated Press' final Top 10 rankings since AP introduced its polls in 1936. A team-by-team breakdown of AP Top 10 finishes, with the year and final-poll position indicated:

TEAM	RANKING									
	#1	#2	#3	#4	#5	#6	#7	#8	#9	#10
Air Force						'58				
Alabama	'61,'64,'65 '78,'79	'45,'77	'66,'75	'36,'37 '71,'73	'62,'74	'47,'80	'72,'81	'63,'67	'52,'60	'42,'59
Arizona St		'75				'70,'82		'71	'73	
Arkansas		'64	'65,'77			'62,'68	'60,'69,'75	'79	'59,'61,'82	'54
Army	'44,'45	'46,'50	'58	'49		'48	'54			
Auburn	'57		'83	'58	'63,'72			'55,'74		'70
Bainbridge					'44					
Baylor									'51	
Boston College					'40,'84			'42		
Brigham Young	'84						'83			
California		'37	'49	'48	'50					
Carnegie Tech						'38				
Clemson	'81					'78		'82		'50
Colorado			'71				'61			
Cornell				'39						
Dartmouth							'37			
Del Monte P								'43		
Duke		'41	'38				'43	'39		'60
Duquesne								'41		'39
Florida			'84			'83				
Florida St					'80	'79				
Fordham			'37			'41				
4th AAF										'44
Georgia	'80	'42	'46	'66,'82,'83	'59	'81	'71	'48,'68		'76
Georgia Tech		'52		'56	'42,'51		'55	'53,'66		'47
Great Lakes						'43				
Holy Cross									'38	
Houston				'76	'79					'73,'78
Illinois			'63	'51	'46		'53			'83
Indiana				'45,'67						
Iowa		'58	'56,'60			'57			'39,'53	
Iowa Pre-Flight		'43				'44				
Kansas							'68			
Kentucky						'77	'50			
Louisiana St	'58	'36	'59	'61			'62,'64,'70	'37,'46,'65	'49	'69
March Field										'43
Maryland	'53		'51,'55					'54,'76		
Miami (Fla.)	'83					'56		'81	'66	
Miami (Ohio)										'74
Michigan	'48	'47	'40,'43 '74,'76	'64,'80	'41,'78	'45,'46,'71 '72,'73	'49,'56	'44,'75,'83	'42,'50,'69 '70,'77	
Michigan St	'52	'51,'55 '65,'66	'53,'57					'50,'61	'56,'63	
Minnesota	'36,'40 '41,'60				'37	'61		'49		'38,'62
Mississippi		'59,'60	'62		'61	'54	'52,'57,'63	'69		'55
Mississippi St									'40	
Missouri					'60	'39,'65,'69	'41		'68	

TEAM	#1	#2	#3	#4	#5	#6	#7	#8	#9	#10
Navy		'63	'45	'43,'44,'60	'54,'57					'41
Nebraska	'70,'71	'83	'82	'72,'84	'65	'63,'64,'66	'73,'80	'40,'78	'36,'74,'75 '76,'79	
North Carolina			'48						'46,'47,'81	'80
Northwestern							'36,'40,'48		'43	
Notre Dame	'43,'46,'47 '49,'66 '73,'77	'48,'53,'70	'41,'52,'64	'54	'38,'67 '68,'69	'42,'74	'78	'36	'37,'44,'45 '55,'65,'80	'57
Ohio St	'42,'54,'68	'44,'57 '61,'73		'69,'74 '75,'79	'55,'70	'49,'76		'58,'60	'64,'72,'83	
Oklahoma	'50,'55,'56 '74,'75	'49,'71,'72	'54,'67,'73 '78,'79,'80	'38,'52 '53,'57	'48,'58,'76	'84	'77	'62		'51,'63
Oklahoma St.					'45		'84			
Oregon									'48	
Oregon St.							'67	'64		'56
Pacific										'49
Pennsylvania							'47	'45		'36
Penn St.	'82	'68,'69	'81	'47,'78	'71,'73,'77		'74	'80	'62	'67,'72,'75
Pittsburgh	'37,'76	'80	'36	'63,'81		'50,'51	'79	'38,'77		'82
Princeton						'50,'51				
Purdue					'43		'66		'67	'68,'79
Randolph Field			'44							
Rice					'49	'53		'57		'46
St. Mary's							'45			
Santa Clara						'36				'37
Southern Cal	'62,'67,'72	'74,'76 '78,'79	'39,'69	'68	'52		'38,'44	'47,'73		'64,'65,'84
SMU		'82	'47		'81			'84		'48,'66
Stanford		'40					'51	'70		'71
Syracuse	'59							'56	'58	
Tennessee	'51	'38,'39 '56,'67		'40,'50,'70			'42,'46,'65	'52,'72	'71	
Texas	'63,'69	'81	'50,'61,'68 '70,'72	'41,'59 '62,'77	'47,'64,'83	'75			'78	'45,'52
Texas A&M	'39				'56	'40	'76		'41,'57	
TCU	'38					'55	'59			'58
Tulane					'39					
Tulsa				'42						
UCLA		'54		'46,'55,'65	'53,'66 '75,'82	'52	'39		'84	
Utah St.										'61
Villanova						'37				
Washington		'84			'36	'60		'82	'59	'40,'77,'81 '53
West Virginia					'36					
Wisconsin		'62	'42			'59	'58	'51	'54	
Wyoming						'67				

83.34, 71.43, 62.50

The gradually decreasing yards-per-game rushing averages needed in the National Football League to reach a 1,000-yard total for one season. The 83.34 figure was for a 12-game schedule (which the NFL last played in 1960), and the 71.43 was for a 14-game season (in effect from 1961 through 1977). The 62.50 represents the yards needed per contest to hit 1,000 under the current 16-game schedule.

286

New York Jets rookie Steve O'Neal follows through on the 1969 punt that netted 98 yards.

96, 97

The yards covered on Denver pass plays in successive American Football League games in 1962. In a September 15 game at Buffalo, the Broncos' Frank Tripucka and Al Frazier combined on a 96-yard touchdown pass. Six nights later in Boston, Denver's George Shaw teamed with Jerry Tarr on a 97-yard scoring pass.

97

The number of career touchdowns that Glenn Davis (59) and Felix (Doc) Blanchard (38) scored for Army.

98

The number of yards that a punt by New York Jets rookie Steve O'Neal netted in a September 21, 1969, American Football League game against the Broncos in Denver. With the Jets positioned at their 1-yard line, O'Neal boomed a punt (out of his end zone) that sailed beyond Denver return man Billy Thompson and bounced to a stop at the Broncos' 1.

99

The number of yards that a punt by Nevada-Reno's Pat Brady covered in an October 28, 1950, game against Loyola of Los Angeles.

100

Through 1984, the number of regular-season overtime games played in the National Football League since the NFL adopted the sudden-death method of breaking ties in 1974. Ninety-two of the games were played to a decision.

103

Since 1937, when official collegiate statistics were first kept, the most points scored in one game by a major-college team. On November 5, 1949, Wyoming overwhelmed Colorado State College (now Northern Colorado), 103-0.

Houston's 100-point spree against Tulsa in 1968 ranks as the highest point total attained by a major-college team against a major-college opponent since the introduction of statistics-keeping.

109

The turnaround in points of National Football League shutouts that were recorded two seasons apart at Baltimore's Memorial Stadium. In 1962, the Chicago Bears embarrassed the hometown Colts, 57-0; in 1964, Baltimore blitzed the Bears, 52-0.

110

The length, in yards, from goal line to goal line on a Canadian Football League field.

160

In college football and the National Football League, the width of the field, in feet, from sideline to sideline.

172

The number of 1,000-yard individual rushing performances in the National Football League (from the first year of statistics-keeping, 1932, through 1984) and in the American Football League (1960 through 1969). The breakdown, by teams, with each team's total number of 1,000-yard performances and the number of individuals accounting for that total:

NFL/AFL Club	Tot.	No.
ATLANTA FALCONS	6	3

1975—Dave Hampton (1,002), 1979—William Andrews (1,023), 1980—Andrews (1,308), 1981—Andrews (1,301), 1983—Andrews (1,567), 1984—Gerald Riggs (1,486).

| **BALTIMORE COLTS** | 4 | 2 |

1975—Lydell Mitchell (1,193), 1976—Mitchell (1,200), 1977—Mitchell (1,159), 1983—Curtis Dickey (1,122).

| **BUFFALO BILLS** | 11 | 5 |

1962—Cookie Gilchrist (1,096), 1972—O.J. Simpson (1,251), 1973—Simpson (2,003), 1974—Simpson (1,125), 1975—Simpson (1,817), 1976—Simpson (1,503), 1978—Terry Miller (1,060), 1980—Joe Cribbs (1,185), 1981—Cribbs (1,097), 1983—Cribbs (1,131), 1984—Greg Bell (1,100).

CHICAGO BEARS   12   4

1934—Beattie Feathers (1,004), 1956—Rick Casares (1,126), 1966—Gale Sayers (1,231), 1969—Sayers (1,032), 1976—Walter Payton (1,390), 1977—Payton (1,852), 1978—Payton (1,395), 1979—Payton (1,610), 1980 —Payton (1,460), 1981—Payton (1,222), 1983—Payton (1,421), 1984— Payton (1,684).

CHICAGO CARDINALS   0   0

CINCINNATI BENGALS   2   2

1968—Paul Robinson (1,023), 1981—Pete Johnson (1,077).

CLEVELAND BROWNS   17   4

1958—Jim Brown (1,527), 1959—Brown (1,329), 1960—Brown (1,257), 1961—Brown (1,408), 1963—Brown (1,863), 1964—Brown (1,446), 1965— Brown (1,544), 1966—Leroy Kelly (1,141), 1967—Kelly (1,205), 1968— Kelly (1,239), 1975—Greg Pruitt (1,067), 1976—G. Pruitt (1,000), 1977— G. Pruitt (1,086), 1979—Mike Pruitt (1,294), 1980—M. Pruitt (1,034), 1981—M. Pruitt (1,103), 1983—M. Pruitt (1,184).

DALLAS COWBOYS   9   2

1972—Calvin Hill (1,036), 1973—Hill (1,142), 1977—Tony Dorsett (1,007), 1978—Dorsett (1,325), 1979—Dorsett (1,107), 1980—Dorsett (1,185), 1981—Dorsett (1,646), 1983—Dorsett (1,321), 1984—Dorsett (1,189).

DALLAS TEXANS, NFL Club   0   0

DALLAS TEXANS, AFL Club   1   1

1962—Abner Haynes (1,049).

DENVER BRONCOS   4   3

1971—Floyd Little (1,133), 1974—Otis Armstrong (1,407), 1976—Armstrong (1,008), 1984—Sammy Winder (1,153).

DETROIT LIONS   4   2

1971—Steve Owens (1,035), 1980—Billy Sims (1,303), 1981—Sims (1,437), 1983—Sims (1,040).

GREEN BAY PACKERS   10   4

1949—Tony Canadeo (1,052), 1960—Jim Taylor (1,101), 1961—Taylor (1,307), 1962—Taylor (1,474), 1963—Taylor (1,018), 1964—Taylor (1,169), 1971—John Brockington (1,105), 1972—Brockington (1,027), 1973—Brockington (1,144), 1978—Terdell Middleton (1,116).

HOUSTON OILERS   7   3

1962—Charlie Tolar (1,012), 1967—Hoyle Granger (1,194), 1978—Earl Campbell (1,450), 1979—Campbell (1,697), 1980—Campbell (1,934), 1981—Campbell (1,376), 1983—Campbell (1,301).

INDIANAPOLIS COLTS   0   0

KANSAS CITY CHIEFS   3   3

1967—Mike Garrett (1,087), 1978—Tony Reed (1,053), 1981—Joe Delaney (1,121).

LOS ANGELES CHARGERS   0   0

LOS ANGELES RAIDERS   2   1

1983—Marcus Allen (1,014), 1984—Allen (1,168).

LOS ANGELES RAMS   11   5

1962—Dick Bass (1,033), 1966—Bass (1,090), 1971—Willie Ellison (1,000), 1973—Lawrence McCutcheon (1,097), 1974—McCutcheon

(1,109), 1976—McCutcheon (1,168), 1977—McCutcheon (1,238), 1979—Wendell Tyler (1,109), 1981—Tyler (1,074), 1983—Eric Dickerson (1,808), 1984—Dickerson (2,105).

MIAMI DOLPHINS   5   3
1971—Larry Csonka (1,051), 1972—Csonka (1,117), 1972—Mercury Morris (1,000), 1973—Csonka (1,003), 1978—Delvin Williams (1,258).

MINNESOTA VIKINGS   4   2
1975—Chuck Foreman (1,070), 1976—Foreman (1,155), 1977—Foreman (1,112), 1981—Ted Brown (1,063).

NEW ENGLAND PATRIOTS   4   3
1966—Jim Nance (1,458), 1967—Nance (1,216), 1977—Sam Cunningham (1,015), 1983—Tony Collins (1,049).

NEW ORLEANS SAINTS   3   2
1979—Chuck Muncie (1,198), 1981—George Rogers (1,674), 1983—Rogers (1,144).

NEW YORK GIANTS   2   1
1970—Ron Johnson (1,027), 1972—Johnson (1,182).

NEW YORK JETS   2   2
1975—John Riggins (1,005), 1984—Freeman McNeil (1,070).

OAKLAND RAIDERS   5   3
1963—Clem Daniels (1,099), 1972—Marv Hubbard (1,100), 1976—Mark van Eeghen (1,012), 1977—van Eeghen (1,273), 1978—van Eeghen (1,080).

PHILADELPHIA EAGLES   5   2
1947—Steve Van Buren (1,008), 1949—Van Buren (1,146), 1978—Wilbert Montgomery (1,220), 1979—Montgomery (1,512), 1981—Montgomery (1,402).

PITTSBURGH STEELERS   11   3
1962—John Henry Johnson (1,141), 1964—Johnson (1,048), 1972—Franco Harris (1,055), 1974—Harris (1,006), 1975—Harris (1,246), 1976—Harris (1,128), 1976—Rocky Bleier (1,036), 1977—Harris (1,162), 1978—Harris (1,082), 1979—Harris (1,186), 1983—Harris (1,007).

ST. LOUIS CARDINALS   7   3
1960—John David Crow (1,071), 1975—Jim Otis (1,076), 1979—Ottis Anderson (1,605), 1980—Anderson (1,352), 1981—Anderson (1,376), 1983—Anderson (1,270), 1984—Anderson (1,174).

SAN DIEGO CHARGERS   6   5
1963—Paul Lowe (1,010), 1965—Lowe (1,121), 1972—Mike Garrett (1,031), 1974—Don Woods (1,162), 1981—Chuck Muncie (1,144), 1984—Earnest Jackson (1,179).

SAN FRANCISCO 49ERS   5   4
1953—Joe Perry (1,018), 1954—Perry (1,049), 1959—J. D. Smith (1,036), 1976—Delvin Williams (1,203), 1984—Wendell Tyler (1,262).

SEATTLE SEAHAWKS   1   1
1983—Curt Warner (1,449).

TAMPA BAY BUCCANEERS   2   2
1979—Ricky Bell (1,263), 1984—James Wilder (1,544).

Paul (Bear) Bryant was the center of attention (left) on November 28, 1981, when he notched career coaching victory No. 315 against Auburn. That win made Bryant No. 1 on the all-time major-college list, one victory ahead of Amos Alonzo Stagg (below right) and two ahead of Glenn (Pop) Warner (below left).

WASHINGTON REDSKINS 7 3

1970—Larry Brown (1,125), 1972—Brown (1,216), 1976—Mike Thomas (1,101), 1978—John Riggins (1,014), 1979—Riggins (1,153), 1983—Riggins (1,347), 1984—Riggins (1,239).

174.6

The number of rushing yards that Ed Marinaro averaged per game while playing for Cornell from 1969 through 1971—a major-college career record. Marinaro ran for 4,715 yards in 27 games.

313

The number of games that Glenn (Pop) Warner won in 44 seasons (1895 through 1938) as coach at Georgia, Cornell (two stints), Carlisle (two stints), Pittsburgh, Stanford and Temple. The victory total is the third highest in major-college history.

314

The number of collegiate coaching victories posted by Amos Alonzo Stagg, a figure that now ranks second on the all-time major-college list. Stagg coached at Springfield (Massachusetts) in 1890 and 1891, the University of Chicago from 1892 through 1932 and the College of the Pacific from 1933 through 1946.

Stagg's victory total ranked No. 1 until 1981, when Paul (Bear) Bryant surpassed it. Bryant notched his 314th career coaching triumph on November 14, 1981, when his Alabama team defeated Penn State, 31-16, and then collected No. 315 on November 28, 1981, as the Crimson Tide downed Auburn, 28-17.

323

The record number of major-college coaching victories compiled by Paul (Bear) Bryant. In his 38 years as a coach, Bryant won six games in one season at Maryland (1945), 60 games in eight seasons at Kentucky (1946 through 1953), 25 games in four seasons at Texas A&M (1954 through 1957) and 232 games in 25 seasons at Alabama (1958 through 1982). Bryant's final triumph came in the December 29, 1982, Liberty Bowl as Alabama defeated Illinois, 21-15.

Grambling Coach Eddie Robinson had 320 victories on the NCAA Division I-AA level through the 1984 season.

325

The record number of National Football League coaching victories rung up by George Halas. Through the 1984 season, runner-up Tom Landry had 243 victories and Don Shula had 242. Curly Lambeau is the only other 200-game winner in NFL coaching history, having won 234 games.

338-293-7

The regular-season series record from 1970 through 1984 in games between American Football Conference and National Football Conference teams, with AFC clubs holding the 45-game lead. The AFC's Miami Dolphins have been particularly rough on NFC opposition, posting a 40-8 National Football League record in interconference play.

349

The number of yards in receptions that Chuck Hughes of Texas Western (now Texas-El Paso) totaled in a September 18, 1965, game against North Texas State. The yardage figure—achieved on only 10 catches—ranks as the major-college receiving record for one game.

360

The length, in feet, of the complete playing area (including both end zones) in college football and the National Football League.

501, 0

The point totals for Michigan and for the Wolverines' 10 opponents in the 1901 regular season. Michigan then trampled Stanford, 49-0, in the Rose Bowl.

576

The number of yards that made Cliff Battles of the Boston Braves the National Football League's first rushing champion in 1932.

677

The number of rushing yards that the Air Force defense yielded to two running backs in consecutive games of the 1978 season. After surrendering 356 yards on the ground to Georgia Tech's Eddie Lee Ivery on November 11, 1978, the Falcons were victims of a 321-yard rushing performance by Vanderbilt's Frank Mordica on November 18, 1978.

693

The number of yards Stanford gained overall (581 passing, 112 rushing) in an October 24, 1981, game against Arizona State that the Cardinal team *lost*—by 26 points. Arizona State, collecting 743 yards in total offense, outscored Stanford, 62-36.

697

The number of yards that O.J. Simpson, Heisman Trophy-winning running back from Southern California, gained rushing in his first pro season (1969, with the American Football League's Buffalo Bills).

697

The number of yards that Marcus Allen, Heisman Trophy-winning running back from Southern California, gained rushing in his first pro season (1982, with the National Football League's Los Angeles Raiders).

.762

Notre Dame's all-time winning percentage, the best in major-college football. Through 1984, the Fighting Irish had won 641 games, lost 186 and tied 40.

.881

The best winning percentage ever fashioned by a coach with 10 years or more of major-college experience—and that figure belongs to Knute Rockne. In 13 seasons at Notre Dame (1918 through 1930), Rockne compiled a 105-12-5 record.

Ranking second on the college winning-percentage list with an .864 mark is Frank Leahy, whose Boston College and Notre Dame squads went 107-13-9. Leahy coached at Boston College in 1939 and 1940, then directed the Fighting Irish from 1941 through 1943 and from 1946 through 1953.

883

The yards of total offense—a major-college record—that Nebraska amassed while crushing New Mexico State, 68-0, on September 18, 1982. The Huskers also set a national mark with 43 first downs and they rushed for 677 yards.

2,522

The number of yards that the 1975 California Golden Bears football team gained rushing in 11 games.

2,522

The number of yards that the 1975 California Golden Bears football team gained passing in 11 games.

61,946

The number of fans on hand at the Los Angeles Memorial Coliseum on January 15, 1967, for Super Bowl I between the Green Bay Packers and Kansas City Chiefs—the smallest crowd in Super Bowl history.

73,885, 74,313

The Denver Broncos' total home attendance (seven games) for the 1961 American Football League season and the Broncos' average per-game home attendance from 1977 through 1984 in the National Football League.

110,000

The number of fans who attended the 1926 Army-Navy game at Chicago's newly expanded Soldier Field and thereby accounted for the first crowd of 100,000 or more to see a football game—whatever the level—in the United States. The Cadets and Midshipmen played to a stirring 21-21 tie.

CELEBRITY FOOTBALLERS

CLIFF ABERSON

A member of football's Green Bay Packers in 1946 (he made three interceptions) and then a member of baseball's Chicago Cubs in 1947 (he batted .279, with four home runs, in 47 games). Aberson, an outfielder, also played briefly for the Cubs in 1948 and 1949.

HARRY AGGANIS, TOM GASTALL

Football standouts who had a lot in common, including athletic renown at the same university, major league skills in another sport (baseball)—and tragedy. Agganis led Boston University in passing in 1949, 1951 and 1952, and Gastall topped BU in that department in 1953 and 1954. As Terrier teammates in an October 18, 1952, game, they combined on two touchdown passes (including the game-winner)—Agganis did the throwing, Gastall the catching—as Boston University overcame William & Mary, 33-28. Agganis, a New England athletic hero, signed with the Boston Red Sox organization in late 1952 and was the Red Sox's regular first baseman in 1954. Gastall, a catcher, signed a bonus contract with the Baltimore Orioles on June 20, 1955. Seven days after Gastall signed, Agganis died of a "massive pulmonary embolism" at age 25 (he had been hospitalized because of pneumonia). Then, on September 20, 1956, the 23-year-old Gastall was killed when the plane he was piloting crashed into Chesapeake Bay.

Agganis batted .251 with 11 home runs and 57 runs batted in for the Red Sox in '54 and was hitting .313 at the time of his death in '55. Gastall played a total of 52 games for the Orioles in '55 and '56, batting .181.

LYLE ALZADO

A talented amateur boxer in his boyhood days in New York and a tenacious defensive end since entering the National Football League with the Denver Broncos in 1971, he returned to the ring in 1979 when he fought an eight-round exhibition bout in Denver against retired heavyweight boxing champion Muhammad Ali.

MORRIS (RED) BADGRO

After playing in the National Football League in 1927 and 1928, he left the NFL and focused on baseball. As a part-time outfielder for the St. Louis Browns in 1929 and 1930, Badgro appeared in 143 games overall and batted .257. He returned to the NFL in the fall of '30 and was a standout end on powerful New York Giants teams during the early part of the decade.

SAMMY BAUGH

One of the top passers in National Football League history, he pursued a baseball career in 1938. Baugh impressed observers with his third-base play at the St. Louis Cardinals' spring camp in '38, and he was assigned to Columbus of the American Association. After playing 16 games at shortstop for Columbus and hitting .220, Baugh was moved to Rochester of the International League. He batted only .183 in 37 games for the Red Wings and never played professional baseball again.

JIM BAUSCH, PETE MEHRINGER

Gold medalists in the 1932 Olympic Games, they saw action in the National Football League. Bausch, the decathlon champion in the '32 Los Angeles Games, played for the NFL's Cincinnati Reds and Chicago Cardinals in 1933. Mehringer, the freestyle light-heavyweight wrestling champion in '32, was a member of the Cardinals from 1934 through 1936 and then played for the American Football League's Los Angeles Bulldogs in 1937. Both athletes attended Kansas.

Hale Irwin (above left), who went on to fame and fortune as a professional golfer, was an all-Big Eight defensive back in the mid-1960s. Sammy Baugh (above right), one of the top passers in pro football history, had a brief fling as a shortstop-third baseman in the Cardinals organization in 1938. Ron Luciano (left), a three-year letterman at Syracuse, made his mark in professional baseball as an American League umpire.

CHARLIE BERRY

A standout football player at Lafayette and as a member of the 1925 and 1926 Pottsville Maroons of the National Football League, he later coached and officiated college ball, was a longtime NFL official, played 709 games in baseball's big leagues in the 1920s and 1930s (he was a catcher for the Philadelphia Athletics, Boston Red Sox and Chicago White Sox), coached in the majors, managed in the minor leagues and umpired in the American League from late in the 1942 season through 1962.

HUGO BEZDEK

Known primarily as a football coach (at Arkansas, Oregon and Penn State on the collegiate level and with the Cleveland Rams in the pros), he also served as a big-league baseball manager. Bezdek, who had been working for the Pittsburgh Pirates as a scout, was thrust into the Pirates' managerial position during the 1917 season and guided Pittsburgh through the 1919 National League campaign.

WARD BOND

An actor who probably was best known for his portrayal of Maj. Seth Adams, wagon master on the hit television series "Wagon Train," Bond played for the Southern California Trojans in the 1930 Rose Bowl. Bond, a lineman, lettered in 1928, 1929 and 1930 for Southern Cal.

PHIL BRADLEY

Missouri quarterback who was the Big Eight Conference's passing and total-offense leader in 1978, 1979 and 1980, he began a professional baseball career in 1981. By the final month of the 1983 season, Bradley had reached the major leagues as an outfielder with the Seattle Mariners.

JIM BROWN

Having retired from pro football at age 29—after turning in a 1,544-yard rushing season for the Cleveland Browns in 1965—Brown took his rugged physique to Hollywood and soon appeared in such motion pictures as "Rio Conchos," "The Dirty Dozen," "Ice Station Zebra" and "100 Rifles."

JOHNNY MACK BROWN

A standout player in the 1926 Rose Bowl, Alabama's Brown remained a Saturday afternoon hero after his football-playing days ended. He proved a matinee film favorite for his roles in such Westerns as "Billy the Kid," "Riding the Apache Trail," "Wells Fargo," "Bad Man From Red Butte" and "Ride 'Em Cowboy"—and countless others.

TOM BROWN

A starter at safety for the Green Bay Packers in Super Bowls I and II, he first reached the athletic "big time" in 1963 with Washington—the Washington Senators, that is. In 61 games as an outfielder-first baseman and pinch-

Gerald Ford (below left) was an outstanding player for Michigan in 1934, 40 years before becoming President of the United States. Little did Chub Peabody (below right) know during his Harvard playing days in 1941 that he would one day serve as governor of Massachusetts. And Jack Kemp (left) was a successful pro quarterback long before he decided to run for the U.S. House of Representatives.

hitter, Brown batted .147 with one home run for the American League baseball club. He played six seasons in the National Football League, ending his pro football career with the Washington Redskins in 1969.

MILT CAMPBELL

The decathlon champion in the 1956 Olympic Games in Melbourne, Australia, he appeared in nine National Football League games for the Cleveland Browns in 1957. The former Indiana athlete carried the ball seven times for 23 yards and returned 11 kickoffs for 263 yards as a Browns halfback. He had one pass reception—and it was good for 25 yards and his lone NFL TD. Campbell also played in the Canadian Football League.

MICHAEL CARTER

Five months after winning the silver medal in the shot put in the 1984 Olympic Games in Los Angeles, former Southern Methodist athlete Carter played in Super Bowl XIX as a reserve defensive lineman for the San Francisco 49ers.

SAM CHAPMAN

A consensus All-America back for California in 1937 and a participant in the Golden Bears' 1938 Rose Bowl triumph over Alabama, he went directly from the Berkeley campus to baseball's major leagues. Chapman, an outfielder, played 1,368 games in the majors—1,274 of them with the Philadelphia Athletics—and slugged 20 home runs or more in five seasons. He played in the 1946 All-Star Game at Boston's Fenway Park.

GALEN CISCO

A senior co-captain of the 1957 Ohio State team that ranked as United Press International's national champion and won the Rose Bowl over Oregon, fullback Cisco averaged five yards per rushing attempt in the Buckeyes' big season. As a junior, he had gained 6.8 yards per crack for Coach Woody Hayes' team. Cisco became a big-league pitcher in the 1960s, posting a 25-56 record for the Boston Red Sox, New York Mets (for whom he tossed three shutouts) and Kansas City Royals, and then took on pitching-coach duties in the majors.

BILL COSBY

A man known for weaving football stories into his comic routines, actor Cosby can—and does—draw on his own reminiscences. And with good reason. Cosby did indeed play collegiate football in the early 1960s, seeing action in the Temple Owls' backfield. In 1961, Cosby averaged 3.5 yards per carry on 36 rushing attempts for the Owls, who posted a 2-5-2 record against Kings Point, Bucknell, Muhlenberg, Lafayette, Buffalo, Hofstra, Delaware, Gettysburg and Toledo.

ALVIN DARK

An infielder who played in 1,828 big-league baseball games and later a

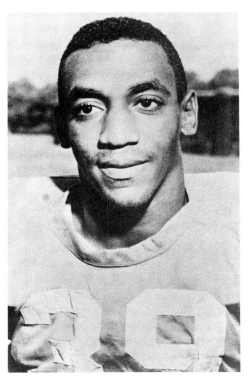

Television and movie buffs should not have any trouble identifying these three faces. Comedian Bill Cosby (above left) saw playing time for Temple in the early 1960s, about the same time that Harvey Lee Yeary, better known these days as actor Lee Majors (above right), was playing at Eastern Kentucky. Alex Karras (left) was a young lineman for Iowa in the mid-1950s before going on to fame in pro football and the silver screen.

manager in the majors, Dark led the Louisiana State football team in passing and rushing in 1942. Dark's backfield talents forced Steve Van Buren, future National Football League running great, into blocking-back duty for the '42 Bayou Tigers.

GLENN DAVIS

The gold-medal winner in the 400-meter hurdles in both the 1956 Olympic Games in Melbourne, Australia, and the 1960 Olympics in Rome, he was a receiver for the Detroit Lions in '60 and 1961. Davis, who attended Ohio State, caught 10 passes in his National Football League career.

CHARLIE DRESSEN

A former major league baseball player who probably was best known for his managerial stints with the Brooklyn Dodgers, Cincinnati Reds, Washington Senators, Milwaukee Braves and Detroit Tigers, he played quarterback on George Halas' first professional football team, the 1920 Decatur Staleys.

PADDY DRISCOLL

Not only did Driscoll play for the Chicago Cardinals and the Chicago Bears, he saw brief service with the Chicago Cubs. A gifted runner, passer and kicker in the National Football League, Driscoll was an infielder who appeared in 13 games with the 1917 Cubs. He had three hits in 28 at-bats (.107) for the National League team.

DWIGHT D. EISENHOWER

A starting halfback for Army in the Cadets' November 9, 1912, game against Carlisle and Jim Thorpe, a contest that Carlisle dominated, 27-6. Eisenhower, a sophomore and future great military commander, saw his collegiate football career end abruptly on November 16, 1912, when he suffered a major knee injury in the Army-Tufts game. Responsible for coordinating and directing the Allied invasion of Europe in June 1944, Eisenhower later became president of Columbia University and then served as the 34th President of the United States (1953-1961).

CHUCK ESSEGIAN

He led Stanford's linebackers in minutes played in the 1951 season (intercepting three passes in those 235 minutes) and competed against Illinois in the 1952 Rose Bowl. Essegian also was a key Stanford performer in the '52 season before turning his attention to professional baseball. Playing for the Los Angeles Dodgers against the Chicago White Sox in 1959, he became the first player to hit two pinch home runs in one World Series.

STEVE FILIPOWICZ

He batted .205 with two home runs in 35 games for the National League's New York Giants in the summer of 1945 and then scored two touchdowns for the National Football League's New York Giants in the fall of '45. As a major league outfielder, Filipowicz also played for the baseball Giants in

1944 and for the Cincinnati Reds in 1948; as an NFL fullback and linebacker, the former Fordham star also played for the football Giants in 1946 (and made a TD for New York in that season's NFL title game).

GERALD FORD

Chosen the outstanding player on the 1934 Michigan squad and named to the College All-Stars team that played the Chicago Bears in the 1935 College All-Star Game, he served in the U.S. House of Representatives for 24 years before becoming vice president of the United States in 1973 and then President of the United States in 1974.

STEVE GARVEY

The National League record holder for consecutive games played (1,207 with the Los Angeles Dodgers and San Diego Padres, 1975-1983), he was second among Michigan State defensive backs in minutes played during the 1967 season. Sophomore Garvey, who saw 184 minutes of action, had 22 unassisted tackles for the Spartans, who posted a 3-7 record in '67 (after going 9-0-1 in the previous season).

LARRY GATLIN

He saw only 12 minutes of action in the entire 1968 season for the Houston Cougars, but that was enough time to make a contribution in one of college football's most memorable games. With Houston leading Tulsa, 86-6, in a November 23, 1968, game, Gatlin boosted the Cougars' point total to 92 by catching a 26-yard touchdown pass. Houston went on to win, 100-6, while Gatlin went on to stardom as a country-and-western performer.

JAKE GIBBS

After winning consensus All-America honors at quarterback in 1960 and playing on Mississippi teams that fashioned a 29-3-1 record (including three consecutive bowl triumphs) during his varsity career, Gibbs saw duty with the New York Yankees from 1962 through 1971. The catcher had a lifetime major league batting average of .233.

PAUL GIEL

A consensus All-America back at Minnesota in 1953, Giel compiled an 11-9 lifetime record while pitching for four big-league franchises in six seasons. Primarily a reliever, he had his best all-around year in the majors in 1955 when he went 4-4 for the New York Giants with a 3.39 earned-run average in 34 games and allowed 70 hits in 82 innings.

JACK GING

A starting halfback for Oklahoma in the 1954 Orange Bowl, Ging scored five career touchdowns for the Sooners and made eight interceptions while playing three seasons for Coach Bud Wilkinson. As a senior, he averaged 5.4 yards on 32 rushing attempts. In the early 1960s, Ging was a co-star on "The

Eleventh Hour" television series, portraying Dr. Paul Graham, a clinical psychologist.

OTTO GRAHAM

Famed college and pro quarterback whose first taste of professional athletic competition came in the National Basketball League. Graham, a consensus All-America basketball player at Northwestern in 1943-44 (but never a consensus All-America in football), appeared in 32 games for the NBL's Rochester Royals in 1945-46 and averaged 5.2 points per game.

BUD GRANT

Before turning his attention to pro football, the versatile Grant played two seasons in the National Basketball Association with the Minneapolis Lakers. In the first of those seasons, 1949-50, the Lakers won the league championship. Grant, who had been a standout athlete at Minnesota, played in 96 NBA games overall and averaged 2.6 points per contest.

ANDY GRIFFITH

A football player he was not. At least not on the college or pro level. But there's little doubt that football helped rocket the entertainer into America's consciousness. At age 27, singer-guitarist-actor-humorist Griffith was four years out of the University of North Carolina and performing in front of Southern clubs and convention groups when one of his monologues—"What It Was, Was Football"—caught on. The drawled monologue, recounting a hillbilly's impressions of his first football game, was recorded late in 1953 and soon proved a hit nationwide. Discussing what he had come upon at a "pretty little green cow pasture," Griffith told of seeing "five or six convicts a-runnin' up and down and a-blowin' whistles. They was. And friends, Ah seen that evenin' the awfullest fight that Ah have ever seen in mah life. Ah did. They would run at one another and kick one another and th'ow one another down and stomp on one another . . . and Ah don't know what-all." And on it went. And on Griffith went—to eventual stage, film and television fame.

GEORGE HALAS

More than 16 months before he attended the 1920 meeting in Canton, Ohio, that spawned the National Football League, Halas suited up for a game in Philadelphia. The game was baseball, Halas' team was the New York Yankees and the date was May 6, 1919. Halas, 24, made his major league debut that day, leading off for the Yankees and playing right field. He went 1 for 4 against Athletics pitching. After another 1-for-4 performance in his second game, Halas went 0 for 14 and left the big leagues with a .091 lifetime average over 12 games. By the time the 1920 season rolled around, the Yankees had come up with a solid right fielder—Babe Ruth.

CARROLL HARDY

A man who made touchdowns on four of the 12 receptions he had for the San Francisco 49ers in 1955 (his lone National Football League season after starring at Colorado), Hardy went on to play the outfield for four big-league baseball clubs. In 1960, he had the distinction of pinch-hitting for Ted Williams after the Boston Red Sox slugger fouled a pitch off his ankle and was unable to continue. (Hardy lined into a double play in his memorable pinch role.)

BOB HAYES, HENRY CARR

U.S. gold medalists in the 100- and 200-meter runs in the 1964 Olympic Games in Tokyo, they went on to play in the National Football League—and Hayes did so with scintillating results. Wide receiver Hayes, from Florida A&M, had 371 career receptions and 456 lifetime points (76 touchdowns) in the NFL while playing for the Dallas Cowboys from 1965 through 1974 and for the San Francisco 49ers in 1975. Defensive back Carr, from Arizona State, intercepted a total of seven passes while a member of the New York Giants in 1965, 1966 and 1967.

JIM HINES, TOMMIE SMITH

Olympic gold medalists in 1968 who went on to brief U.S. professional football careers. Hines, winner of the 100-meter run, and Smith, victor in the 200 meters, were wide receivers in the American Football League in 1969 and combined for three catches. Hines, from Texas Southern, had two receptions for 23 yards for the Miami Dolphins. San Jose State's Smith, remembered for his black-power salute on the victory stand at the '68 Mexico City Games, had one catch—a 41-yarder—for the Cincinnati Bengals.

HERBERT HOOVER

The 18-year-old team manager of Stanford's first football squad, he helped arrange the first intercollegiate football game on the West Coast (between Stanford and California, in 1892). Hoover, who played a role in the hiring of Walter Camp as Stanford's first coach, demonstrated keen management skills at Stanford—abilities that apparently would take him a long way in life. A long way, indeed. Hoover served as the 31st President of the United States, with his term running from 1929 to 1933.

HALE IRWIN

An All-Big Eight Conference defensive back in 1965 and 1966 for the Colorado Buffaloes (he had a total of eight interceptions in those two seasons), Irwin now rates as one of the top performers worldwide in his sport—golf. Irwin, whose first PGA Tour victory came in the 1971 Heritage Classic, has surpassed $200,000 in yearly winnings five times on the pro golf tour. Through 1984, he had won two U.S. Open championships—in 1974 at Winged Foot in Mamaroneck, N.Y., and in 1979 at Inverness in Toledo.

RANDY JACKSON

He played for Texas Christian in the 1945 Cotton Bowl, competed for Texas in the 1946 Cotton Bowl and saw service for the Brooklyn Dodgers in the 1956 World Series. "Handsome Ransom" enjoyed his best big-league baseball seasons from 1951 through 1955 as the Chicago Cubs' regular third baseman.

VIC JANOWICZ

Having abandoned his baseball career after batting .151 in 41 games for the 1954 Pittsburgh Pirates, the former Ohio State athlete emerged as a top-flight National Football League player in 1955. He led the Washington Redskins in rushing in '55, scored on three of his 11 pass receptions, made seven touchdowns overall and contributed 46 points via kicking (28 conversions, six field goals). Janowicz suffered career-ending injuries in an automobile accident in 1956.

JACKIE JENSEN

After rushing for 1,010 yards in 1948 for California and scoring on a 67-yard run for the Golden Bears in the 1949 Rose Bowl, Jensen went on to stardom in major league baseball. He drove in 100 runs or more five times in the American League and also had a 97-RBI year. Jensen played seven of his 11 big-league seasons for the Boston Red Sox, winning A.L. Most Valuable Player honors with Boston in 1958 when he slugged 35 home runs, knocked in 122 runs and batted .286. Twenty-one months after playng in the Rose Bowl, Jensen made a pinch-running appearance for the New York Yankees in the 1950 World Series.

ED (TOO TALL) JONES

Dallas Cowboys defensive end who, after playing five years in the National Football League, retired from pro football in 1979 to embark on a professional boxing career. Jones won all six of his bouts, but gave up the ring and returned to the Cowboys in 1980 (after a one-season absence).

ALEX KARRAS, MERLIN OLSEN

Usually cast as funny or kindly characters in their acting roles, these behemoths weren't so lovable—just ask their adversaries—while excelling from their defensive-tackle positions in the National Football League. Karras, a star at Iowa, wreaked havoc on opposing offenses during his 12 seasons with the Detroit Lions (1958 through 1962, 1964 through 1970), and Olsen, a standout at Utah State, displayed little of a "Father Murphy" disposition while playing for the Los Angeles Rams for 15 years (1962 through 1976).

JACK KEMP

The man who quarterbacked the Los Angeles and San Diego Chargers to American Football League divisional titles in 1960 and 1961 and then sparked the Buffalo Bills to AFL championships in 1964 and 1965, he has been a member of the U.S. House of Representatives since 1971. Kemp serves New York's 31st Congressional District.

EDWARD M. (TED) KENNEDY

He appeared in a total of 14 games for Harvard in his junior and senior

Haywood Sullivan (above left) and Jackie Jensen (above right) were both successful college football players who went on to good careers in major league baseball. Sullivan, a quarterback at Florida, became a big-league catcher and now serves as Chief Executive Officer of the Boston Red Sox. Jensen, a 1,000-yard rusher for California in 1948, starred for seven seasons with the Red Sox. Bob Mathias (below), a Stanford fullback in 1951 and 1952, is best known as a two-time Olympic decathlon champion.

seasons of 1954 and 1955 and caught two touchdown passes for the Crimson in '55. Playing against Columbia in an October 15, 1955, game in New York, end Kennedy latched on to a deflected pass in the end zone—Harvard passer Jim Joslin was attempting to hit John Simourian from 20 yards out—and the TD helped the Crimson to a 21-7 triumph. On November 19, 1955, Kennedy scored Harvard's lone touchdown of the day on a seven-yard pass from Walt Stahura as the Crimson fell to Yale, 21-7, in New Haven, Conn. Massachusetts voters first elected Kennedy to the U.S. Senate in 1962, and they have re-elected him four times.

EDWARD J. KING

A member of the All-America Football Conference's Buffalo Bills in 1948 and 1949 and a lineman for the National Football League's Baltimore Colts in 1950, this former Boston College player served as governor of Massachusetts from 1979 to 1983.

TED KLUSZEWSKI

A man who slugged 279 home runs in a major league career that began in 1947 and ended in 1961 (he played for the Cincinnati Reds, Pittsburgh Pirates, Chicago White Sox and Los Angeles Angels), Kluszewski also was a menacing figure on the football field. He was a standout player on the Indiana Hoosiers' 1945 team, catching three touchdown passes as the Hoosiers rolled to a 9-0-1 record.

KRIS KRISTOFFERSON

Listed as a 5-foot-11, 170-pound end for the Pomona-Claremont Sagehens in a 1957 college football program, future singer-actor Kristofferson was further identified in the program as a "defensive standout and a senior returning letterman" on the Claremont, Calif., squad. Pomona-Claremont competed in the Southern California Conference, along with Redlands, Whittier, Occidental and California Institute of Technology. (Pomona-Claremont is now under the title of Pomona-Pitzer Colleges.)

RON LUCIANO

A lineman who lettered in 1956, 1957 and 1958 at Syracuse and played for the Orangemen in the 1959 Orange Bowl against Oklahoma, he gained considerably more attention in baseball as an animated American League umpire from 1968 through 1979.

DON LUND

A talented halfback for Michigan in 1944, he made three pinch-hitting appearances for the Brooklyn Dodgers in 1945. By the time his big-league baseball career had ended in 1954, outfielder Lund had played for three teams in the majors (Dodgers, St. Louis Browns and Detroit Tigers) and batted .240 in 281 games.

ED MARINARO

The runner-up to Auburn's Pat Sullivan in the 1971 Heisman Trophy voting,

A successful political career was but a distant dream in 1954 and 1955 for Ted Kennedy (right, left photo), a young Harvard end. Even more remote was the chance that Herbert Hoover (below, standing, in suit), team manager of Stanford's first football team in 1892, would become the 31st President of the United States.

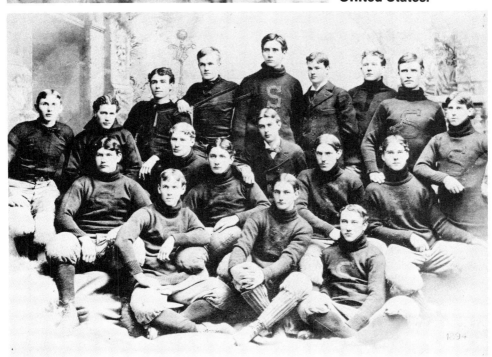

he last wore a football uniform in 1977 as a short-term member of the National Football League's Seattle Seahawks (after playing four seasons with the Minnesota Vikings and one year with the New York Jets). Nowadays, the former Cornell star is most familiar in a police officer's uniform because of his Joe Coffey role in television's "Hill Street Blues" show.

CHRISTY MATHEWSON

Before going on to big-league pitching fame (373 victories from 1900 through 1916), Mathewson was a football star at Bucknell. He was particularly adept at drop-kicking.

BOB MATHIAS

The Olympic Games decathlon champion in 1948 at London and in 1952 at Helsinki (he was 17 years old when he first won the gold medal), Mathias was a football letterman in 1951 and 1952 as a Stanford fullback. He returned a kickoff 96 yards for a touchdown against Southern California in '51 and played against Illinois in the '52 Rose Bowl. Mathias eventually turned to politics, and California voters elected him to the U.S. House of Representatives in the mid-1960s.

OLLIE MATSON

Before beginning a 15-year National Football League career in the fall of 1952, Matson won two medals in the '52 Olympic Games in Helsinki. The former University of San Francisco athlete won a bronze medal in the 400-meter run and a silver medal in the 1,600-meter relay.

LLOYD MERRIMAN

Having rushed for 672 yards and 10 touchdowns for Stanford in 1946, he became a major league outfielder in 1949. In a big-league career consisting of 455 games with the Cincinnati Reds, Chicago White Sox and Chicago Cubs, Merriman batted .242.

MARION MORRISON

A football player for the Southern California Trojans in 1925 and 1926, Morrison found fame in front of the movie camera and not on the gridiron. A name change was deemed necessary to boost the fledgling actor's marquee appeal, so Marion Morrison became John Wayne.

BRICK MULLER

The silver medalist in the high-jump competition in the 1920 Olympic Games in Antwerp, Muller went on to football acclaim at California and played one season in the National Football League (1926, with the Los Angeles Buccaneers).

GREASY NEALE

An innovative and successful coach on the collegiate level and in the Na-

In 1925 and 1926, young Marion Morrison (left), better known later as John Wayne, was fighting his battles on the football field for Southern Cal. Paul Robeson (below left) was a standout player for Rutgers and later in the NFL before becoming a successful singer-actor. Singer-actor Kris Kristofferson (below right) played football for Pomona-Claremont in 1957.

tional Football League (he directed the Philadelphia Eagles to league titles in 1948 and 1949), Neale played 768 big-league baseball games and batted .357 in the 1919 World Series as the Cincinnati Reds' right fielder.

ERNIE NEVERS

A pro football sensation with the Duluth Eskimos and Chicago Cardinals after completing an outstanding career at Stanford, Nevers found time to pitch for the St. Louis Browns in 1926, 1927 and 1928 and posted a 6-12 record in the major leagues. In '27, he yielded two of the 60 home runs that Babe Ruth hit for the New York Yankees.

RICHARD M. NIXON

"Although sometimes taking a lacing in scrimmage, he always came back for more." That's how Wallace (Chief) Newman, longtime Whittier College coach, once described one of his former reserve players, a 155-pounder named Nixon. Twenty years after his last season (1933) as a college football player in California, Nixon was vice president of the United States; 35 years after that final bench-warming season, he was President-elect of the United States.

CLARENCE (ACE) PARKER

A standout back for the National Football League's Brooklyn Dodgers and one of the top all-around players in league history, he also played major league baseball—as the record books duly note. Infielder Parker earned a place on baseball's list of achievements by slugging a home run in his first plate appearance in the big leagues. Batting against Wes Ferrell of the Boston Red Sox on April 30, 1937, Parker hit a pinch two-run homer in the ninth inning for the Philadelphia A's. He played a total of 94 games for the '37 and 1938 A's, batting .179.

ENDICOTT (CHUB) PEABODY

Harvard's last consensus All-America (on the major-college level) as a guard for the 1941 Crimson, Peabody went on to serve as governor of Massachusetts from 1963 to 1965.

RONALD REAGAN

A 1932 graduate of Eureka College and a former football player for the Illinois school, he became a broadcaster in Des Moines, a motion-picture actor (once portraying Notre Dame's George Gipp), a television-show host, governor of California and the 40th President of the United States.

RICK REICHARDT

After appearing for Wisconsin in the 1963 Rose Bowl and then leading the Big Ten Conference in pass receptions the next fall, he went on to play 997 games in baseball's American League. Outfielder Reichardt, playing for the California Angels, Washington Senators, Chicago White Sox and Kansas City

Little did teammates of players at Whittier and Eureka colleges realize that they were playing football with future Presidents of the United States. Young Richard Nixon (No. 23 above) was a reserve for Whittier in the early 1930s, while Ronald Reagan (below left) saw action for Eureka in the late 1920s and early '30s.

Royals in a big-league career that began in 1964 and ended in 1974, posted a .261 lifetime average and hit 116 home runs.

MIKE REID

A consensus All-America defensive tackle at Penn State in 1969, he played five years with the Cincinnati Bengals before quitting the National Football League club at age 27 and focusing on a music career. Reid, an accomplished pianist who had performed with symphony orchestras, formed a band after his retirement from football and went touring. And he tried his hand at writing music. In 1984, versatile musician Reid became a Grammy-winning songwriter (thanks to the country hit "Stranger in My House").

BURT REYNOLDS

Known as Buddy Reynolds during his collegiate days, the actor-to-be posted impressive statistics for the 1954 Florida State freshman team. Reynolds carried the ball 16 times for 134 yards, an average of 8.4 yards per crack, and scored two touchdowns. He also had four receptions for 76 yards and intercepted a pass. Although posting only modest figures with the varsity (three rushes for 12 yards in 1957, for example), Reynolds is credited with having earned letters for the Seminoles in 1955 and '57.

BO ROBERSON

Runner-up to Ralph Boston in the long jump in the 1960 Olympics in Rome, former Cornell athlete Roberson played six seasons in the American Football League and saw duty with the San Diego Chargers, Oakland Raiders, Buffalo Bills and Miami Dolphins. The fleet flanker had his best AFL years in 1964 and 1965, totaling 90 receptions in those seasons.

PAUL ROBESON

A consensus All-America at Rutgers in 1917 and 1918 and one of the first standout players in National Football League history, he became a noted singer and actor and a highly influential black activist.

JACKIE ROBINSON

Before breaking major league baseball's modern racial barrier in 1947, Robinson was a standout football player for UCLA. He rushed 40 times for 456 yards, an average of 11.4 yards per carry, and intercepted four passes in 1939 as the Bruins fashioned a 6-0-4 record. During UCLA's 1-9 season in 1940, Robinson was limited to 3.2 yards per rushing attempt but scored five touchdowns and passed for two other scores.

STEVE SABOL

"If there's one thing I can't stand," said Steve Sabol, now the executive vice president of NFL Films Inc. and a multi-Emmy winner, "it's not being noticed." Sabol uttered those words 20 years ago, as a collegian. While his camera talents (coupled with those of father Ed, president of NFL Films) keep him in the spotlight today, Sabol took other steps to ensure proper

Buddy Reynolds, known now to his movie fans as Burt, was a running back at Florida State in 1957. Reynolds, who average 8.4 yards per carry as a freshman, went on to earn varsity letters in 1955 and 1957.

fanfare while attending Colorado College. Upon enrolling at the Colorado Springs school in 1961, aspiring football player Sabol of Villanova, Pa., claimed he was from a Pennsylvania community called Coaltown Township —a place that didn't exist but had a gritty, macho sound to it. After an undistinguished freshman season, the 170-pound fullback announced he actually hailed from Possum Trot, Miss. Calling himself the "Fearless Tot From Possum Trot" (a fictitious locale) and "one of the most mysterious, awesome living beings" around and eventually "the most dynamic athlete of modern times," Sabol paid for newspaper advertisements, publicity releases, T-shirts, color postcards, lapel buttons and more—all of which proclaimed the sophomore's gridiron greatness. He also adopted the nickname "Sudden Death." Sabol, though, was actually an average small-college player until adding 40 pounds before his junior year. He then won all-conference honors, becoming talented enough, perhaps, to have been worthy of an ad that once appeared in a Colorado College program. "Coach Jerry Carle congratulates Sudden Death Sabol on a fantastic season," the ad read. Of course, Carle wasn't responsible for that message. Sabol—who else?—was.

OTTO SCHNELLBACHER

The National Football League's leading interceptor in 1951 with 11 pass thefts for the New York Giants, he had played pro basketball in 1948-49 with the Providence Steamrollers and St. Louis Bombers of the Basketball Association of America. Schnellbacher, from Kansas, averaged 6.4 points per game in his lone pro basketball season.

CLYDE SCOTT

A silver medalist in the 110-meter hurdles in the 1948 Olympic Games in London, Scott (a football letterman at Navy and Arkansas) was a halfback for the National Football League's Philadelphia Eagles from 1949 through 1951 and then played for both the Eagles and the Detroit Lions in 1952.

HANK SOAR

He played a total of 10 seasons of professional football in the 1930s and 1940s (one year with the American Football League's Boston Shamrocks and nine seasons with the National Football League's New York Giants), coached pro basketball's Providence Steamrollers for 19 games of the 1947-48 season and umpired in baseball's American League from 1950 through 1971.

JOHN STEARNS

The self-proclaimed "Bad Dude" of Colorado football in the early 1970s, he set the Buffaloes' career record for pass interceptions with 16 before beginning a professional baseball career. Through 1984, Stearns had played in 810 major league games, fashioned a .260 lifetime batting average and, representing the New York Mets, caught in three All-Star Games.

GEORGE (SNUFFY) STIRNWEISS

A versatile football player at North Carolina in the late 1930s and a man

Ed Marinaro (44), better known to many television fans as Joe Coffey of "Hill Street Blues" fame, finished second in the Heisman Trophy voting in 1971 after a fine collegiate career as a running back for Cornell.

who once rushed 86 yards for a Tar Heel touchdown, Stirnweiss won the American League batting championship in 1945 while playing second base for the New York Yankees. He also performed for the St. Louis Browns and Cleveland Indians in a 1,028-game major league career.

WOODY STRODE

UCLA's leading receiver in 1938 and 1939 and a member of the National Football League's Los Angeles Rams in 1946, he became one of Hollywood's first steadily used black actors, appearing in numerous character roles and "muscle man" parts in Western and epic films beginning in the early 1940s. Strode was cast in his first major role in 1960, portraying a cavalry officer on trial for rape and murder in "Sergeant Rutledge."

HAYWOOD SULLIVAN

A passer for the Florida Gators in 1950 and 1951 (he threw for a total of 13 touchdowns in those seasons), Sullivan primarily was a catcher for the Boston Red Sox and the Kansas City Athletics in a big-league baseball playing career that began in 1955 and ended in 1963. Sullivan, who batted .226 in 312 major league games, went on to manage the A's for most of the 1965 season.

JIM THORPE

Early-day football superstar who also appeared in 289 big-league baseball games for the New York Giants, Cincinnati Reds and Boston Braves. It was outfielder Thorpe who drove in the only run of the game on May 2, 1917, after Cincinnati's Fred Toney and Chicago's Jim Vaughn had pitched no-hit ball through nine innings. The Reds broke through against Vaughn in the

10th, with Thorpe's infield single (Cincinnati's second hit of the inning) scoring Larry Kopf. Toney then completed his no-hitter as the Reds beat the Cubs, 1-0.

Thorpe's athletic skills weren't confined to football and baseball. In 1912, he won decathlon and pentathlon gold medals in the Olympic Games in Stockholm, Sweden. The championships later were taken away from Thorpe because of a breach in amateur rules in effect at the time, but the medal honors eventually were restored.

GERALD TINKER, JOHNNY JONES, RON BROWN

Members of gold medal-winning 400-meter relay teams in Olympic competition—and all three athletes later competed in the National Football League. After winning his Olympic Games gold in 1972 in Munich, Tinker, who attended Kent State, played wide receiver for the Atlanta Falcons in 1974 and 1975 and also was a member of the Green Bay Packers in '75. Jones earned his gold in 1976 in Montreal, then became a standout wide receiver at Texas (where he was nicknamed "Lam") and for the New York Jets. And Brown, from Arizona State, claimed his gold in 1984 in Los Angeles before playing his rookie NFL season that fall as a wide receiver with the Los Angeles Rams.

CHARLEY TRIPPI

He played minor-league baseball in 1947 before playing his rookie year in the National Football League that fall. Trippi showed his baseball prowess, batting a robust .334 as an outfielder-first baseman for the Atlanta Crackers of the Southern Association. He then displayed his football talents, helping the Chicago Cardinals to the '47 NFL championship. Trippi concentrated on football for the next five years, then toyed with the notion of returning to baseball in 1953 with the Jacksonville club of the South Atlantic League (a team that would include a 19-year-old second baseman named Henry Aaron). However, the NFL Cardinals persuaded Trippi to give up any lingering baseball ambitions.

PETE VARNEY

Five years after catching the game-tying conversion pass for Harvard in the Crimson's classic 29-29 tie with Yale in 1968, he was catching major league pitchers. Varney played a total of 69 big-league games for the Chicago White Sox and Atlanta Braves from 1973 through 1976, batting .247.

COTTON WARBURTON

A consensus All-America back for Southern California in 1933, he turned his attention toward Hollywood. In 1964, Warburton won an Oscar for his film editing of "Mary Poppins."

CARL WEATHERS

An obscure linebacker for the Oakland Raiders in 1970 and 1971, he later was thrust into prominence because of his Apollo Creed film role opposite Sylvester Stallone's "Rocky."

BYRON (WHIZZER) WHITE

The National Football League's leading rusher while playing for the Pittsburgh Pirates in 1938 and the Detroit Lions in 1940, White sat out the 1939 NFL season because of his Rhodes scholar studies and played only three years of pro football overall as military service and a law career beckoned. He eventually became law clerk to Chief Justice Fred Vinson of the U.S. Supreme Court, a Denver-based lawyer and deputy attorney general of the United States before being named an associate justice of the Supreme Court by President John F. Kennedy in 1962. White succeeded Charles Evans Whittaker on the high-court bench.

RON WIDBY

The Dallas Cowboys' punter in Super Bowls V and VI, he played pro basketball in 1967-68 with the New Orleans Buccaneers. Widby, a former Tennessee athlete, appeared in 20 games for the American Basketball Association's Bucs and averaged 2.9 points per game.

ROBERT (RED) WILSON

Wisconsin football player who was named the Big Ten Conference's Most Valuable Player in 1949 and then became a major league catcher for the Chicago White Sox, Detroit Tigers and Cleveland Indians in a big-league baseball career that began in 1951 and ended in 1960.

LONNIE WRIGHT

After intercepting four passes for the Denver Broncos in the 1967 American Football League season, Wright traded his cleats for sneakers and averaged 9.8 points per game for the American Basketball Association's Denver Rockets in 1967-68. While his pro football career consisted of only two seasons (1966 and '67, both with the Broncos), Wright wound up playing five years in the ABA. The former Colorado State Rams basketball star enjoyed his best ABA season in 1968-69, when he averaged 16.4 points per game with Denver.

HARVEY LEE YEARY

A "Six Million Dollar Man"-type of body would have enabled injury-troubled Lee Majors to prolong his football career at Eastern Kentucky in the early 1960s, but the actor-to-be was no Steve Austin in those days—in fact, he wasn't even Lee Majors. The man who eventually would portray Austin, "The Six Million Dollar Man" of television series fame, was known as Harvey Lee Yeary during his undergraduate days. Yeary, a 1963 graduate of Eastern Kentucky, played offensive and defensive end for Eastern before a back injury shortened his career. He served one season as a graduate assistant at the Richmond, Ky., school.